THE  **TIMES**

GREAT WAR
LETTERS

CORRESPONDENCE FROM
THE FIRST WORLD WAR

EDITED BY JAMES OWEN
AND SAMANTHA WYNDHAM

Published by Times Books

An imprint of HarperCollins Publishers
Westerhill Road
Bishopbriggs
Glasgow G64 2QT
www.harpercollins.co.uk
times.books@harpercollins.co.uk

First edition 2018

© This compilation Times Newspapers
Ltd 2018

The Times® is a registered trademark of
Times Newspapers Ltd

The contents of this publication are
believed correct at the time of printing.
Nevertheless the publisher can accept no
responsibility for errors or omissions,
changes in the detail given or for any
expense or loss thereby caused.

A catalogue record for this book is
available from the British Library.

ISBN 978-0-00-831845-1

10 9 8 7 6 5 4 3 2 1

Printed and bound in Great Britain by
CPI Group (UK) Ltd, Croydon, CR0 4YY

Cover image © MSSA / Shutterstock

Our thanks and acknowledgements
go to Lily Cox and Robin Ashton at
News Syndication and, in particular,
at The Times, Ian Brunskill and, at
HarperCollins, Gerry Breslin, Jethro
Lennox, Karen Midgley, Kerry Ferguson,
Sarah Woods and Evelyn Sword.

CONTENTS

In memory of the dead of the Great War, among them
John Anstruther (1888-1914), Reggie Wyndham (1876-1914)
and Ian Chrystal (1888-1917).

INTRODUCTION

"The correspondence column of *The Times* may be regarded as the Forum of our modern world," wrote the evangelist Frederick Meyer to the newspaper in 1915, "in which the individual may deliver his soul."

The paper has published letters since its establishment in 1785, but in the nineteenth century these had often been lengthy political tracts rather than brief observations on current events. As Meyer noted, however, by the time what became known as the Great War began, the Letters Page had started to assume a form we would recognise today.

This was partly because they were, for the first time, at least on occasion, being grouped together rather than distributed throughout the paper. This greater focus arguably increased their impact, cementing in turn the page's status as Meyer's contemporary Roman forum – a meeting place-cum-soap box, albeit principally for the ruling class.

These developments were to be accelerated by the war that dominated everyone's thoughts between 1914 and 1918. The letters in this selection track its progress, albeit with the proviso that strict government censorship meant that the public was unaware for much of the conflict about the true state of events, and the conflict's real horrors.

Even so, these letters offer the most direct of routes back into the mentality of a society that was on the cusp of changing forever. And, besides delivering their soul and having their say, in a perhaps surprising way correspondents bare it, too. Set among letters from familiar names – David Lloyd George on the danger of drink, Edith Cavell on nursing before she was executed by the Germans – and ones from the pseudonyms then permitted, there are those from grieving parents still (within the conventions of the day) raw from their loss.

Many of the letters speak for themselves but it may be of help to have an outline of their increasingly distant context. The war did not come as a surprise. Conflict between the great European powers had been long feared, and expected, particularly given Germany's desire in the preceding decades to challenge Britain's naval, and hence imperial, supremacy.

Nonetheless, it was with some reluctance that the prime minister, Herbert Asquith, whose party had strong pacifist traditions, committed his Liberal government to war at the start of August 1914. This was technically in response to Germany's violation of Belgium's neutrality in entering its territory to get around France's defences; but in reality, it was the inevitable outcome of a complex system of international alliances and dynastic ambitions.

The assassination of the heir to the Austro-Hungarian throne at Sarajevo by Serbian-backed terrorists had given the Austrians a pretext to declare war on Serbia, egged on by their German cousins under Kaiser Wilhelm II. This in turn brought to the fray Russia, ruled by Tsar Nicholas II, as Serbia's pan-Slavic protector. Germany, which had built up a huge army and navy, had long planned to fight at the same time Russia and France, who were both allied with Britain.

Other nations eventually became involved. Bulgaria and the Ottoman Empire sided with the Central Powers, while Japan and Italy came in with the Allies, the latter in 1915 after being promised historically Austrian territory on its then frontiers. The war spread through European colonies across much of the globe, although the United States remained neutral at first.

The British public hoped for a short conflict, but the secretary of state for war, Lord Kitchener, foresaw that it would last for years and that Britain's small standing army would need massive expansion. Initial German successes in Belgium and France were stemmed in part by the British Expeditionary Force and the two sides settled into a slow, grim slog for territory, characterised as trench warfare.

For much of the war the British population had little detailed or accurate information about what was happening on the various fronts. The press played its part in concealing the truth, publishing rumours of German atrocities and spinning defeats as successes. Even so, the mounting toll of casualties could not be hidden, eventually approaching three-quarters of a million British dead (although this was far less than suffered by the French, Russian and German armies). The upper and middle classes, which supplied most of the junior officers who led attacks, were especially hard hit. Eton, for instance, lost 1,157 former pupils out of 5,619 who served.

After much debate, conscription was introduced in Britain for men between the ages of 18 and 41 in 1916; the age limit was raised to 50 two years later. Before then, recruitment had been supplied by volunteers – "Your Country Needs You", as the famous poster had it. There had been political hesitation particularly over imposing armed service on working class men, who often did not have the vote since they were not property owners.

The continued strain of the war exposed many fracture lines. Suffragists kept up the pressure to give the vote to women, although some of the main campaigners focused their efforts on encouraging women to do war work to show their worth. Long-standing tensions within Ireland, then part of the United Kingdom, as to whether it should take its orders from London led in 1916 to the Easter Rising in Dublin (and eventually to an independent Republic). In Russia, catastrophe in battle ultimately led to the overthrow of the Tsar in 1917.

Many efforts were made to break the deadlock in the trenches. British efforts to outflank their enemies by forcing the Dardanelles and seizing Constantinople were thwarted by the Turks at Gallipoli, notwithstanding much gallantry and suffering by Australian and New Zealand troops, among many others. The failure led in time to the resignation from the cabinet of Winston Churchill, seen as the architect of the plan at the Admiralty.

By then, revelations in *The Times* about a shortage of artillery shells held responsible for recent setbacks on the Western Front led to Asquith being forced in mid-1915 to reconstitute his government as a coalition with the Conservatives and the first Labour cabinet minister. Lloyd George was placed in charge of a nationalised munitions policy and his successful implementation of it, together with the backing of *The Times's* owner Lord Northcliffe, enabled him to unseat Asquith as prime minister at the end of 1916.

This was only shortly after the end of the prolonged Battle of the Somme, which came to symbolise the apparent futility of the conflict and its mass carnage. Civilians on the home front had also felt the effects of war as never before, with Zeppelins carrying out the first air raids over Britain and the depredations of submarines leading by 1918 to extensive rationing.

U-boat attacks on shipping bound for Britain, most notoriously the sinking of the liner *Lusitania* in 1915, with American passengers aboard, helped prompt President Woodrow Wilson to bring his nation to the Allied cause in 1917. The tide of the war did not turn decisively, however, until the summer of 1918, when breakthroughs on the Western Front and widespread discontent with the Kaiser in Germany led to his abdication and the signing of armistices in November.

The reverberations of the war would be felt for decades to come. The old order had been decisively shattered. Not only would the map of Europe, and indeed of the world, have to be redrawn as empires were dismembered and new nations created, but society's assumptions had been shaken by the conflict, not least that as to which class was the only one fit to govern. And millions of those who had been affected by the war would have to live for the rest of their lives with the effects of wounds, shellshock, poison gas, grief and trauma. These letters were to prove to be the last snapshots of a vanishing age.

Notwithstanding that the letters in this anthology were written at a time when views that might give offence today were tolerated, the original language, style and format of them as they appeared in the newspaper has not been amended. The date on the letter is that on which it first appeared in the newspaper, and an index of the letter-writers can be found at the end of the book. Explanatory footnotes have been added where some clarification of the subject matter of a letter may be of use.

JAMES OWEN AND SAMANTHA WYNDHAM

GREAT WAR LETTERS

1914

THE MENACE OF WAR

DOMINANCE OF RUSSIA OR GERMANY

1 August 1914

SIR,—A NATION'S FIRST duty is to its own people. We are asked to intervene in the Continental war because unless we do so we shall be "isolated." The isolation which will result for us if we keep out of this war is that, while other nations are torn and weakened by war, we shall not be, and by that fact might conceivably for a long time be the strongest Power in Europe, and, by virtue of our strength and isolation, its arbiter, perhaps, to useful ends.

We are told that if we allow Germany to become victorious she would be so powerful as to threaten our existence by the occupation of Belgium, Holland, and possibly the North of France. But, as your article of to-day's date so well points out, it was the difficulty which Germany found in Alsace-Lorraine which prevented her from acting against us during the South African War. If one province, so largely German in its origin and history, could create this embarrassment, what trouble will not Germany pile up for herself if she should attempt the absorption of a Belgium, a Holland, and a Normandy? She would have created for herself embarrassments compared with which Alsace and Poland would be a trifle; and Russia, with her 160,000,000, would in a year or two be as great a menace to her as ever.

The object and effect of our entering into this war would be to ensure the victory of Russia and her Slavonic allies. Will a dominant Slavonic federation of, say, 200,000,000 autocratically governed people, with a very rudimentary civilization, but heavily equipped for military aggression, be a less dangerous factor in Europe than a dominant Germany of 65,000,000 highly civilized and mainly given to the arts of trade and commerce?

The last war we fought on the Continent was for the purpose of preventing the growth of Russia. We are now asked to fight one for the purpose of promoting it. It is now universally admitted that our last Continental war—the Crimean War—was a monstrous error and miscalculation. Would this intervention be any wiser or likely to be better in its results?

On several occasions Sir Edward Grey has solemnly declared that we are not bound by any agreement to support France, and there is certainly no moral obligation on the part of the English people so to do. We can best serve civilization, Europe—including France—and ourselves by remaining the one Power in Europe that has not yielded to the war madness.

This, I believe, will be found to be the firm conviction of the overwhelming majority of the English people.

Yours faithfully,
NORMAN ANGELL

TRAVELLING FROM GERMANY

6 August 1914

SIR,—IN TO-DAY'S ISSUE of *The Times* you publish a letter by John Jay Chapman to which I and, I am sure, many others must take serious exception.

Your correspondent describes in lurid terms the sufferings experienced by travellers in Germany the last few days. "The hand of ruthless force which regarded neither God nor man was laid on them. Every decency of existing society had vanished. No appeal to any principle or power in the universe remained," and so on *ad nauseam*.

I should like to chronicle my personal experience, which was of a vastly different character. Accompanied by another woman I travelled from Baden-Baden to Berlin on Friday last on a crowded train and we were, I believe, the only English people on board. The majority of the travellers were Germans and Russians. The stations *en route* were packed with people vainly desiring places, this state of things getting worse as we neared the capital. Everywhere we met with much more than the ordinary courtesy extended to women travelling. I was very much impressed by the real kindness and chivalry shown to us on three different occasions by German men, who voluntarily gave up their places to save us from sitting on our bags in a crowded corridor, and who put themselves to much trouble to obtain food for us at the stations.

We returned from Berlin last Saturday at 1 o'clock, and on arriving at Osnabruck at 5.30 heard that mobilization had begun. The train was held up several times to allow others to pass, all crowded with soldiers, and we knew that it might be our fate to be left stranded, should the authorities have required our train to convey troops in. Happily for us we reached England via Flushing without more inconvenience than would happen on any overcrowded train or boat.

I should like to put on record that during all those hours of intense excitement, with a nation newly called to arms, we did not meet with a single instance of rudeness in Germany. What is more, we never saw so much as a glance of enmity directed towards us. Even in Berlin itself last Saturday, where the whole town was in the throes of a deep national emotion, walking and driving among the huge crowd we never experienced anything but kindness.

Whatever our feelings may be as to the causes and nature of this war, it is devoutly to be hoped that English people will not be led astray by the irresponsible statements of travellers. We are at war with a great nation, and it behoves us to be true to ourselves and our English traditions of fair play.

FLORENCE PHILLIPS

OUR LATENT FORCES

8 August 1914

SIR,—THE FUTURE IS dark and we do not know that we will not need our last ounce of strength before we are through. We can afford to neglect nothing.

Will you allow me to point out how a reserve force can be formed which will be numerically large and which if it does nothing else can relieve more mobile and trained troops for the fighting line? In a word, the suggestion is to form civilian companies of the National Reserve. There are tens and hundreds of thousands of men in this country from 35 to 55 who are often harder and fitter than their juniors, but for whom no place is found in our scheme of defence. Many of them are good shots, they are longing to help in any possible way, and they would fall into line instantly if they could only see how to do it. They would speedily become capable of guarding railways or buildings, helping to garrison fortresses or performing many other military duties.

If I may quote the example of this little town, we held our first meeting to discuss this on Tuesday, by Wednesday night we had enrolled 120 men, and to-day we start drill and practice at the butts. Many of the men are fine shots and all are exceedingly anxious to be serviceable. It is not possible for them to take on long engagements or to live out in permanent camps, but they could do much useful work and in case of a raid they would do anything. They would from our "Land-sturm." But at present there is no organization into which such men can be fitted. Local effort would rapidly form the various companies, but some method of common action has to be devised.

The obvious danger of such organization is lest it should divert men from the Territorials or any other more useful branch of the Service. But to recognize the danger is to avoid it. The Reserve company would not go the length of refusing to enlist young men who cannot or will not become Territorials, but it has the constant end before it of encouraging them to go further and of preparing them so that if they do join the more active Services they are already partly instructed. I am convinced that if they are properly run these civilian National Reserve companies would be not only of value in themselves but would be a stepping-stone for the younger men to take them into the fighting line.

The official organizations have so much upon them for the moment that the work can only be done by independent local effort. But when the men are there, as in the case of the existing National Reserve, they will command attention and find some means of arming themselves. We have our own record of organization, and I should be happy to send copies of our method to anyone who may desire to form other centres.

Yours faithfully,
ARTHUR CONAN DOYLE

THE USE OF THE UNTRAINED

8 August 1914

Sir,—There is now no thought in the mind of any reasonable Englishman but to bring this war to a speedy and successful conclusion. Every man with any military training will be already in touch with his proper centre for utilization, and with that sort of man I, who am altogether untrained, have no concern. But I wish to point out that there is in the country a great mass of useful untrained material available and that it may be very readily called upon at the present time by the establishment of local committees. I suggest the formation at once of corps of local volunteers for use in local services, keeping order, transport, guerilla work in case of a raid, and so forth. I have in mind particularly the boy of 15, the man of 47, the mass of the untrained, the Boy Scouts and ex-Boy Scouts who have not gone on to any military training. There is no reason why all the surplus material should not be enrolled now. With it would be a considerable quantity of bicycles, small cars, and other material. This last line need not be drilled; it should not be expected to use either bayonet or spade; but upon the east and south coast at any rate it should have bandoliers, rifles, and Brownings (for close fighting) available, and by way of uniform it should have a badge. Perhaps it would not be a very effective fighting force, but it would permit of the release of a considerable number of men now keeping order, controlling transport, or doing the like work. Nobody wants to be a non-combatant in a war of this sort.

Very sincerely yours,
H. G. WELLS

CUTTING DOWN ON TEA-CAKES

11 August 1914

Sir,—We housewives of England might assist the country somewhat during the coming time of stress by cutting off or cutting down the supply of cakes which are consumed at the tea-table both in the drawing-room and servants' hall. In that way we could economize flour for the bread which is a necessity.

MRS. STANLEY BALDWIN

ENGLISH NURSING IN BRUSSELS

15 August 1914

Sir,—I notice that there is a big movement on for the establishment of Red Cross hospitals in England. In the natural course of things these will get almost exclusively naval men, whereas the Army wounded will have to be dealt with on the Continent, and as far as can be seen at present mainly at Brussels.

Our institution, comprising a large staff of English nurses, is prepared to deal with several hundreds and the number is being increased day by day.

May I beg on behalf of my institution for subscriptions from the British public which may be forwarded with mention of the special purpose to H.B.M.'s Consul at Brussels.

Thanking you in anticipation, I am, Sir, yours obediently,
E. CAVELL, Director of the Berkendael Medical Institute, Brussels

British nurse Edith Cavell would be executed by the Germans in 1915 for aiding Allied soldiers hiding in Occupied Belgium.

MOURNING CLOTHES

17 August 1914

SIR,—IF THE COUNTRY should decide to dispense with such mourning the economic effect will be to save a disturbance of cash expenditure. Mourning will still be bought for those who die natural deaths. But we should have a huge additional and artificial expenditure, temporarily inflated by the heavy death-toll of the next few weeks; and the money so saved will be available for the support of ordinary trade.

MRS. EDWARD LYTTELTON

The war's heavy death toll ended the expensive Victorian ritual of mourning expressed through gradual changes of clothing.

———◆———

EMPLOYMENT OR RELIEF

18 August 1914

SIR,—WILL YOU ALLOW me to raise my voice on behalf of the many women workers who are being rapidly thrown out of employment by this tremendous inrush of well-meant but short-sighted voluntary work?

The matter is one which has already received her Majesty's serious attention, and also that of the council of Queen Mary's Needlework Guild. It has also been the subject of a few broad hints on the part of our leading newspapers. But still the inrush continues, the tide of voluntary work still rises, and is already beginning to swamp the vast hosts of needy women who depend on their skill or their handiwork for bread for themselves and their little ones.

There are three points which I would like to place before all those who at the present moment are throwing themselves so whole-heartedly and so injudiciously into this veritable vortex of voluntary assistance.

1. Have they thought out the fact that by all that voluntary work—typing, secretarial, nursing, as well as needlework, they are creating the very evil which they are preparing to relieve later on—namely, unemployment?
2. Have they thought out the fact that every garment sewn or knitted by an amateur is so much bread taken out of the mouth of a poor seamstress?
3. Have they thought that it would be a far finer and more patriotic thing to deny themselves the pleasure of working and sewing parties and to use their

local funds for purchasing made garments from their local outfitters or giving out the work to their needy sisters?

The purchase of certain descriptions of ready-made garments has almost entirely ceased in some small country towns. The small drapery dealers will very soon have to shut up their establishments or in any case greatly reduce them, and thus one of the many channels through which the poor seamstress, the shop assistant, the clerk earns her precarious livelihood will be closed to her, and presently she will have to be relieved out of the local fund or left to starve if she is too proud to ask for relief.

She would be far happier in earning her bread to-day than in accepting relief from any fund later on.

I am, Sir, yours faithfully,
EMMUSKA ORCZY

A PROTEST AGAINST SECRECY

5 September 1914

SIR,—YOUR CORRESPONDENT MR. Charles Whibley is obviously not interested in the lives of sons and husbands at the front. As one who comes from a fighting family of many generations and who has three sons in France to-day, I cannot too strongly express the dislike of the present secret methods felt by all whose dear ones are opposing the German hordes. We want no revelation of military secrets, but we would like to know the kind of life being led by our kith and kin, and we strongly object to the abandonment of the British tradition of the publication of generals' dispatches. At the time of writing we have received practically nothing from Sir John French, except through Lord Kitchener's statement of last Sunday.

Your obedient servant,
A FATHER

LADY FRENCH'S APPEAL

11 September 1914

SIR,—WILL YOU ALLOW me, through the medium of your columns, to convey my gratitude to those who have responded so generously to my appeal for socks and other comforts for the troops? I have received many contributions of money, which I am spending on wool, flannel, &c., and also on employing some women (who are out of employment in consequence of the war) to knit and to make garments. Some ladies who are very kindly helping me have collected a small fund for providing a substantial mid-day dinner and tea for these workers, which in many cases is their chief or only meal; and Messrs. Harrods have most kindly placed a room at my disposal for the women to work in. I shall still be most grateful for any further help.

Yours faithfully,
ELEONORA FRENCH

◆

GREATCOATS FOR SOLDIERS

19 September 1914

SIR,—I HAVE BEEN told on most excellent authority that 200,000 of our newly-raised Army are without greatcoats. It will take some time to make them, and cold weather is coming on.

May I suggest a temporary substitute? In the Civil War in America in 1861-65 thousands of the Confederate soldiers wore blankets altered as follows:—A slit was cut in the centre just large enough to put the head through. The slit was then hemstitched to prevent its getting larger. A flat button was then sewn on one side at the centre of the slit, and a tab with a buttonhole on the other side, so as to close the hole when not in use. Some of the Southerners added a small slit or a piece of tape in which they carried a toothbrush instead of a flower.

Previous to the Civil War I had seen this plan adopted by some of my shipmates when forming part of naval brigades landed on active service.

Yours faithfully,
ELLENBOROUGH, Commander, R.N., (Retired)

ALIEN ENEMIES

19 September 1914

SIR,—MAY I CONGRATULATE the police on having arrested and secured conviction for Mr. Rufus Royal?

The arrest of this man in the Central Hall of the House of Commons shows how easily aliens of a thoroughly mischievous type may be in our midst unknown to these around them.

I have known this man for months as the secretary of some labour organization. He often spoke to me in the lobby and corresponded with me, and only 10 days ago a big stationery firm rang me up stating that he had given my name as a reference, I need hardly say without the slightest authority; but the point is that all this time, so perfect was his English and his appearance, that I never had the slightest suspicion that he was an alien. My correspondence has shown for weeks past the well-grounded suspicion that there are a number of these dangerous people in our midst, particularly all round our coasts, and this arrest and conviction shows, I think clearly, the need for increased vigilance on the part of our police, and perhaps, stricter conditions in regard to aliens in our midst.

Yours, &c.,
W. JOYNSON-HICKS

Popular authors had stoked fears of spies even before the war; there were said to be 60,000 Germans and Austrians living in Britain when the war started.

———◆———

HINTS TO RECRUITS

22 September 1914

SIR,—AS ONE WHO volunteered and went through part of the South African War as a Tommy, I hope the following tips may prove useful. They may be obvious or controversial, but I give them for what they are worth, and because I know that to some at least they will prove useful.

First of all I strongly recommend all now enlisting to possess themselves of a good strong pair of leather gloves—such as the old omnibus drivers used to wear. The nights will soon be getting cold, windy, and frosty, and I know that when in South Africa I would have given anything when on sentry-go for a pair of such, for the barrel of one's rifle was ofttimes icy, and one's hands got too cold to hold it properly. Many now becoming soldiers, too, are not used to manual labour. Put a company of these to dig a "one hour's shelter trench"—*i.e.*, to work hard for one hour with pick and spade, and then count the blistered hands. The spade, we all know now, is almost as important as the rifle, and gloves will help here. Further, in the rough and tumble of war hands will get cut and torn, and sometimes fester. Gloves then again useful. And finally, with much crawling to do over possibly gorse and thorn, strong gloves certainly save the hands, and so make for efficiency. But, to save myself from an obvious reply, kid is certainly not the leather such gloves should now be made of. Another point. Campaigning, a fork is a luxury, but what you do want is a spoon, a good strong clasp-knife, and a tin-opener. I was in Switzerland last week, and when there bought one of the knives that every Swiss soldier is supplied with. It is extremely practical, and contains a good strong blade, a tin-opener, a screw-driver, and a piercer or marline-spike, all strong and well made and not too heavy. A very useful gift, too, is a well-made pair of folding pocket scissors.

In South Africa those of us were lucky who had the chance of buying a strong, fairly large enamelled iron mug, which we hung on to the strap of our water-bottle by the handle. It was handy as an extra article of mess equipment, for filling one's bottle when streams were too shallow, and also for getting in a hurry a dollop of anything that was going—even a drink from a stream or a lucky pull from a water-cart. The regulation mess tin—and what a practical and handy article this is—cannot be got at without taking off one's kit, and besides, in our case, used often to contain our day's ration of meat.

Bootlaces, bachelor's buttons, safety pins, a large hook and eye or two, and a few split copper rivets may, of course, obviously be useful, and a good tip is to sew two brace buttons side by side in place of one on the trousers, and to start off with only the very best braces.

The loss of a button or the breaking of a brace may temporarily put a man quite out of action. For papers, wrap them in a large square of green oiled silk. This "kind of" gets stuck together in the pocket, and my papers, after many months in the field, were quite legible and not much the worse at the end from the damp coming from both within and without. One sentence more. Chocolate is good—very, very good—but to many one thing is better. Good hot, strong peppermint drops; not bull's-eyes—they are too sticky—but the hard white sort. They are grateful and comforting if you like when one's hungry and cold. But some may prefer chocolate—so let's send both.

Yours faithfully,
RIGBY WASON, late O.R.Sgt., Inns of Court O.T.C.

THE VALUE OF COCA LEAVES

28 September 1914

Sir,—In your issue of to-day's date you have a letter recommending coca leaves. It is well that the public should be warned that cocaine is a most dangerous drug. The cocaine vice has only recently been introduced into India, but it is now in many places recognized that the cocaine habit is a much more serious vice than either opium or hemp. It is therefore most seriously to be hoped that no individual hearing of the marvellous effects of this drug will unwittingly allow himself to become a victim to the vice.

Yours faithfully,
C. STREATFEILD, late District Magistrate, Benares, India

SHILLINGSTONE'S RECORD

30 September 1914

Sir,—The little village of Shillingstone in Dorsetshire, with a total population of 575, has sent 66 men to the Colours. It would be interesting to know whether any other village of the same size has beaten this record.

Yours faithfully,
BASIL THOMSON

TEMPERANCE AMONG WOMEN

6 October 1914

SIR,—IN YOUR ISSUE of to-day (October 3) your correspondent Margaret Taylor pleads for pressure to be put on Government for earlier closing of publichouses, a plea that cannot be too strongly endorsed by the women of England. When we see the increasing numbers of our poorer sisters in and out of gin palaces, we realize the immediate possibility of the degeneration of the homes our men "have left behind them."

When the first war panic burst the dread of supply stoppage caused hundreds of homes to be broken up, the women living in lodgings instead. They are now in receipt of more money than they have ever had in their lives. This, with no man at home to see to, gives them hours of the day to get through. Can we blame them if they forgather in the only social place that opens its welcoming arms to them? To save the "home-life" for our men to find on their return, can we not take rooms in the most congested parts of our great cities, encourage our women to meet there, supply them with papers, the latest war news hung on the walls, paper, pen, and ink, free of charge, coffee, cocoa, and tea to be had at cost price? With cheery fires and simple amusements at night we shall soon find our women ceasing to care for the doubtful joys of the gin palaces. This plan has been carried out most successfully along our coasts, for the concentration camps, and been much appreciated by the men. These men are under discipline; our women are not; therefore their need is greater. The whole scheme can be carried through at very little expense—each local centre managed by a local committee. As we are starting immediately in Hammersmith, I shall be glad to give all details to anyone who is willing to inquire.

Yours, &c.,
EMILY JUSON KERR

THE DEATH OF MARK HAGGARD

10 October 1914

Sir,—In various papers throughout England has appeared a letter, or part of a letter, written by Private C. Derry, of the 2nd Battalion, Welsh Regiment. It concerns the fall of my much-loved nephew, Captain Mark Haggard, of the same regiment, on September 13 in the battle of the Aisne.

Since this letter has been published and, vivid, pathetic, and pride-inspiring as it is, does not tell all the tale. I have been requested, on behalf of Mark's mother, young widow, and other members of our family, to give the rest of it as it was collected by them from the lips of Lieutenant Somerset, who lay wounded by him when he died. Therefore I send this supplementary account to you in the hope that the other journals which have printed the first part of the story will copy it from your columns.

It seems that after he had given the order to fix bayonets, as told by Private Derry, my nephew charged the German Maxims at the head of his company, he and his soldier servant outrunning the other men. Arrived at the Maxim in front of him, with the rifle which he was using as Derry describes, he shot and killed the three soldiers who were serving it, and then was seen "fighting and laying out" the Germans with the butt end of his empty gun, "laughing" as he did so, until he fell mortally wounded in the body and was carried away by his servant.

His patient and heroic end is told by Private Derry, and I imagine that the exhortation to "Stick it, Welsh!" which from time to time he uttered in his agony, will not soon be forgotten in his regiment. Of that end we who mourn him can only say in the simple words of Derry's letter, that he "died as he had lived—an officer and a gentleman."

Perhaps it would not be inappropriate to add as a thought of consolation to those throughout the land who day by day see their loved ones thus devoured by the waste of war, that of a truth these do not vainly die. Not only are they crowned with fame, but by the noble manner of their end they give the lie to Bernhardi and his school, who tell us that we English are an effete and worn-out people, befogged with mean ideals; lost in selfishness and the lust of wealth and comfort. Moreover, the history of these deeds of theirs will surely be as a beacon to those destined to carry on the traditions of our race in that new England which shall arise when the cause of freedom for which we must fight and die has prevailed— to fall no more.

I am, Sir, your obedient servant,
H. RIDER HAGGARD

PROFESSIONAL FOOTBALLERS
AND THE WAR

14 October 1914

Sir,—I AM WRITING to suggest that the professional footballers of the hundreds of clubs throughout the country should be allowed to enlist under certain conditions which might be arranged between the War Office and the Football Association. The men might be allowed to take part in the Saturday fixtures both at home and away, arrangements being made that men of the London clubs should be trained in and near the metropolis, those of the Lancashire clubs in and near Manchester and Liverpool, &c. Possibly a professional football brigade could be formed, and as their training will take a long time their services will not be required out of the country until the football season is practically over. Hundreds of amateur footballers, and other sportsmen have already joined the ranks, and surely the professional will not be less patriotic than his fellows, and will be proud to help to keep the flag flying and the ball rolling at the same time.

Yours faithfully,
WILLIAM A. BECKETT

———◆———

INVASION BY AIR

16 October 1914

Sir,—ONE DOES NOT want to raise an unnecessary scare, but in the case of invasion by Zeppelins the total or partial obscuration of the lights of London will be of little avail if an airship is able to pick up a guide on the coast to direct it on its way. Is there at present anything to prevent some of the well-to-do aliens who show such an affection for the east coast from guiding the invader by driving a motor with a bright headlight along the road to London? The hour and place of the airship's arrival might very well be arranged beforehand, and the car could easily be identified from above by preconcerted distinguishing marks.

Yours truly,
MAKE SURE

GERMAN SPIES

19 October 1914

Sir,—I was glad to read your article to-day in *The Times* on German espionage and preparation for this war. Here is an instance. About three years ago I was staying in Norfolk, and I asked a friend of mine if the Germans had ever found out a place called Weybourne, on the coast, where Nelson said was the place to land an invading force for England. My friend answered: "Found it out; the Germans have bought land there and built a hotel." About 10 days ago I was motoring along the coast there and was stopped several times by the cycle corps guarding the coast. I happened to ask one of the men how much coast they looked after, and he told me from Hunstanton to Weybourne. I said, "There is a hotel at Weybourne which belongs to the Germans." And he replied, "I don't know about that; but a short time ago we made a raid on the hotel and found several Germans in it." I send you this in case it may be of interest to know preparations have been made in this country just as in France and Belgium.

Yours faithfully,
J. B. STRACEY-CLITHEROW

———◆———

WAITERS AND MILLIONAIRES

22 October 1914

Sir,—As I talked this morning with a distinguished German, long resident in this country, he observed:—"From our point of view it is inconceivable that your Government should permit Germans and Austrians to reside freely in your midst, knowing that in the event of a successful raid upon England they will at once rush to the help of the invaders."

On the important question of German and Austrian waiters and managers at English hotels he said:—"It is equally inconceivable that the German people would for one moment tolerate English waiters in German hotels at any time. Hotel managers and waiters have particular opportunities for spying on visitors to hotels. They have master keys in their possession opening all the bed-rooms, and can therefore search correspondence in the absence of the visitor; they have opportunities of listening, and it should be noted," he remarked, "that there is hardly a naval or military town, hardly any resort of British military and naval officers, hardly any strategic point of Great Britain, that is not provided with its German hotel waiters.

"As to the hardship caused by the expulsion of such as are married," he added, "surely some of the wealthy naturalized German financiers who have so long thriven in this country might look after the wives and children of such of their compatriots as may suffer from a necessary measure of protection. I observe," he added, "that their names, as a rule, are noticeably absent from the charitable and other funds now appearing in the newspapers, despite their recent lavish expenditure on town and country houses, racing stables, yachts, and Scottish and other shootings."

I enclose my card and the name of my German informant.

Yours faithfully,
VIGILANT

———◆———

THE NAME OF "THOMAS ATKINS"

27 October 1914

SIR,—WITH REGARD TO a letter in your issue of 24th inst., signed "Arthur Mercer," I am afraid your correspondent's account of why the British soldiers are called "Tommies" is incorrect; the true reason is that in all the old War Office forms of soldiers' accounts the method company officers were to pursue in keeping them was illustrated by one finished example, and the name taken was "Thomas Atkins," hence the name.

I am,
THE EDITOR OF "HISTORY OF 32ND LIGHT INFANTRY"

———◆———

THE INDIAN WOUNDED

5 November 1914

SIR,—AS WOUNDED INDIAN soldiers are being received at Netley, the need for Indian volunteer orderlies is greater than ever. Nearly 70 members of the local Indian corps are already serving as nurses there. Leaving aside the medical members of the corps there are now very few left to answer the further call when it comes. May I therefore trespass upon the hospitality of your columns to appeal to the Indian young men residing in the United Kingdom to enlist without delay? In my humble opinion it ought to be our proud privilege to nurse the Indian soldiers back to health. Colonel Baker's cry is for more orderlies. And in order to make up the requisite number, and also to encourage our young men, several elderly Indians occupying a high position have gone or are going to Netley as orderlies. One of them is a barrister, having a Privy Council practice, another is an educationist ex-Vice-Principal of a celebrated college for Indian Princes, and a third is a retired member of the Indian Medical Service, having served in five campaigns.

I hope that the example set by these gentlemen will infect other, with a like zeal, and that many Indians who can at all afford to do so will be equal to the emergency that has arisen. Those who desire to enlist can do so at the Indian Volunteers' Committee's rooms at 10, Trebovir-road near Earl's-court, at any time during working hours.

I am, &c.,
M. K. GANDHI

In 1906, while living in South Africa, Gandhi had been a volunteer stretcher-bearer in a war against the Zulus and had become politicised by witnessing the attitudes of British troops to non-whites.

---◆---

MORE HELP FOR THE WOUNDED

5 November 1914

SIR,—WE READ IN your columns and we also learn from private friends how urgently additional, and especially speedy, surgical aid is needed for the wounded in France and Belgium. A few hospital units officered entirely by women are already there and are doing splendid work. Will your readers help us to send more? The Scottish Federation of the National Union of Women's Suffrage Societies, under the leadership of Dr. Elsie Inglis, have specialized in this form of national service. They have money enough to dispatch one complete unit, which is on the point of starting. They are keen to send at least three if the necessary funds can be obtained. They ought not to start with less that £1,000 per unit. Please help us to raise the money quickly.

Yours obediently,
MILLICENT GARRETT FAWCETT, President, N.U.W.S.S.

Fawcett was the leader of the main organisation campaigning for the right of women to vote. Her sister, Elizabeth Garrett Anderson, was the first British woman to qualify as a doctor.

THE NATION AND THE WAR

A FALSE PERSPECTIVE

9 November 1914

Sir,—Is it not time that the Government took the country into its confidence and told us what, in its opinion, we have got to face? Unless they do, the country is in danger of being misled. Owing perhaps largely to the censorship arrangements, the mass of the people are gaining a false perspective, which is obviously having its effect on recruiting. They read in the official news—as is natural—mainly of the successes and heroism of the Allied troops, and for the rest they are fed for the most part on imaginative and incredible stories of the utter demoralization of their enemies. The determination and vigour with which the Germans are pressing their attacks and the critical nature of the struggle is thus hidden, and the great mass of the public is lulled into the belief that the war is as good as over, and that it is only a question of holding on till the Germans give way.

To anybody who understands the true position this complacent optimism is without foundation. We have got to beat, not hold, the Germans, and the task of driving them out of Belgium alone from line after line of trenches, yard by yard, mile by mile, is bound to be tremendously difficult and costly. We shall do it, it is true, but only if we spare no effort to bring every ounce of the fighting strength of the nation to bear, and that means pouring into Belgium men, more men, and ever more men, as fast as they can be trained, until a decisive superiority is established and all hope of success to the German arms disappears. An equal battle is a bloodyand a fruitless battle. Decisive superiority in numbers is the surest, the shortest, and in money and life alike the cheapest road to victory. This course, too, is the only one consistent with our pledged word to Belgium and to France.

Can we get the men voluntarily? Let the Government tell Parliament what is required, and we can then give our answer. If we cannot get them, then let us have done with fervid appeals and unfair pressure on individuals, and let us shoulder manfully as a nation our common burdens, just as at the crisis of her fate that other great Anglo-Saxon democracy did 50 years ago during the Civil War. Nothing will do more to bring about an early peace, or more to hearten our Allies and depress our enemies, than a declaration by Parliament that it intends to invoke its ancient common law right and if need be to call upon every citizen to serve the country in arms until the war is over and the battle for freedom is won.

Yours faithfully,
ARATUS

DEEDS AND NAMES

9 November 1914

SIR,—MAY I, AS AN Englishwoman and the widow of a soldier and mother of a soldier, enter my protest, through your columns, against the silence in official quarters regarding the county names of our Regular regiments which are so gloriously upholding England's honour at the front?

Up to the time the London Scottish were officially mentioned by name for their splendid action we all submitted to this silence as being possibly a wise line to take, but now it is unbearable to know our Surreys, Hampshires, Kents, &c., are performing quite as heroic deeds as the Scots and only to come at the fact through seeing their county names in the casualty lists and through reading an occasional uncensored private letter.

I remain yours truly,
ELIZTH. BUTLER

TEMPTATIONS TO SOLDIERS

9 November 1914

SIR,— WILL YOU KINDLY allow me, through the medium of your paper, to make an appeal to my country men and women upon a most vital subject which is causing me very great uneasiness? All classes in the United Kingdom are showing a keen interest in our Forces engaged in the struggle now going on for our country's existence as a nation, and they are being munificent in their efforts to supply the wants of our gallant soldiers and sailors fighting abroad. But I feel it my duty to point out to the civil population that putting temptation in the way of our soldiers by injudiciously treating them to drink is injurious to them and prejudicial to our chances of victory. Thousands of young recruits are now collected together in various places, and are having their work interfered with and their constitutions undermined by being tempted to drink by a friendly but thoughtless public, and also by the fact that publichouses are kept open to a late hour of the night. I cannot believe that the owners of such houses are less patriotic and more self-seeking than their fellow-subjects, or that they would deliberately, for the sake of gain, prevent our soldiers being sufficiently trained in body and nerve to enable them to undergo the strain of the arduous service which is before them—a strain which only the strongest physically and morally can be trusted to endure. I therefore beg most earnestly that publicans in particular and the public generally will do their best to prevent our young soldiers being tempted to drink. My appeal applies equally for the members of the Oversea Contingents, who have so generously and unselfishly come over here to help us in our hour of need. I hear that 300 of the Canadian Contingent are to take part in the Lord Mayor's Show next Monday, and my sincere hope is that, while extending to them a hearty British welcome, no temptation to excess may be put in the way of these soldiers of the King, men whom the nation delights to honour, which will tend to lower them in the eyes of the world.

ROBERTS, F.M.

Field Marshal Earl Roberts was a former Commander-in-Chief of the forces. He died shortly after writing this letter, while visiting troops in France.

———◆———

THE LEAGUE OF THE KHAKI BUTTON

13 November 1914

Sir,—May I through your paper ask your readers to join the League of the Khaki Button? There is no subscription and no expense other than to buy and wear a small khaki button. Every one wearing the button pledges himself not to stand anyone a drink or to be stood a drink until after the war is over and peace has been declared. If every one would pay for their own drinks we should save our soldiers from a great deal of temptation. The pledge of the Khaki Button is not intended to interfere in any way with hospitality in our own homes.

I am, &c.,
E. F. CROSSE, Archdeacon of Chesterfield, Founder of the League

A LAST TALK WITH LORD ROBERTS

16 November 1914

Sir,—As I was probably one of the last persons who saw Lord Roberts, outside of his family, on Tuesday night, the day before he left for the Continent, I think it might interest the public to know what were almost the last words be spoke in England in a public capacity. He had granted me an interview for the *Echo de Paris*, and, before giving me his views on the situation and on the work done by the French Army, he spoke of his visit to France on the morrow and of the reasons for which he was going over to see Sir John French. I have not, in my interview, reported everything he said there, for one at least of his utterances seemed to me to interest solely England. But to you it will certainly be very interesting.

Lord Roberts said that, while the primary reason of his visit was to see his dear Indian troops (of which he was Colonel-in-Chief), he intended to speak to General French about the too great secrecy which was, to his mind, kept by the military authorities at the front and at home concerning the work and the brave deeds of the English soldiers.

"I naturally approve," said Lord Roberts, "that all the military movements, whatever they be, should be kept absolutely secret from all war correspondents; but it seems to me that they should be allowed to receive at least a fair modicum of information. Why not allow them to write, for instance, in detail of the glorious actions fought by our troops, several days, it goes without saying, after these actions have taken place? I am referring naturally to the English lines. You in France are in a position different from us. You have conscription. Every man is called to the Colours, and you do not rely on the public enthusiasm to recruit your Army, which can very well afford to be 'la grande silencieuse.' In England we want men, many more men, and if we do not let our people at home know in detail of the life of our soldiers at the front, of their brave fights and gallant deeds, how shall we awake in the soul of our young men the high sentiment of emulation which will strongly contribute to lead them to the recruiting office? They are brave, no doubt, willing to offer their lives to their country if necessary. But they often do not know that it is absolutely necessary, and that every minute they lose now is a priceless minute, maybe a battle jeopardized in the future. They do not know enough that our men are always fighting against tremendous odds, that we want more men and still more men to equalize matters. They are not sufficiently able to follow day by day—as much, at any rate, as the military necessities would allow it—the life and the fighting of their friends who have enlisted. What has been done for the London Scottish might to my mind be done with great good result for many of the other units, and I will talk to French about it."

I thought, Sir, that these views would certainly interest you. Lord Roberts spoke strongly and felt, I have no doubt of it, the urgent need of more "advertisement" for the Army, although he did not utter the word, if England was going to get all the men she wants.

It does, perhaps, not become me as a foreigner to broach upon these matters. We value, in France, too highly the value of the English alliance to think of—I would not say criticizing—but even scrutinizing too closely the methods, through which England has got together and increases every day her valiant Army. It is England's sole business, and nobody in my country would presume to intrude upon these matters. But, knowing the deep interest which is felt in the matter here, I thought it was almost my duty to let you know what he said about it. I have therefore—let me say it once more—only expressed Lord Roberts's views on a subject on which I personally have none, would have none, and on which I heard no Frenchman ever venture an opinion.

May I add that Lord Roberts expressed that which gave me infinite pleasure— the highest opinion of the French Army, of the French generals, and of General Joffre in particular. He spoke highly, too, of the French gun—"as a gunner," said he—of the wonderful power of our 75. He added that he knew very well that France had had up to now to hold the longest line of battle, that all her men able to carry arms had been drafted into the Army, that part of France had suffered terrible devastation. But he added that we should shortly feel the effects of the great support which England was preparing to give us.

I am, Sir, your obedient servant,
GASTON DRU

———◆———

"FOLLOW YOUR PRINCE"

19 November 1914

SIR,—THE APPEALS FOR recruits are too long and not simple enough. I suggest the following, printed in bold type:—"The Prince of Wales is at the front. Men are badly wanted to save the country. Enlist and follow your Prince."

Yours faithfully,
HENRY F. DICKENS

SIR OLIVER LODGE ON THE SOUL'S SURVIVAL

24 November 1914

SIR,—IN VIEW OF THE eminent position of Sir Oliver Lodge and the prominence you have given in *The Times* of to-day to the report of his statement that he has obtained definite scientific proofs of the continued existence of some of his dead friends, I ask for permission to request him not to delay longer the publication of his promised information regarding the nature of the proofs on which he bases this announcement.

Sir Oliver's belief that he has talked with the dead has been published before this; and this is not the first time he has been challenged to produce his proofs to the scientific world. But hitherto he has confined himself to the mere reiteration of his conviction of the reality of his discovery.

That a serious statement of this kind, on such a grave subject, solemnly given forth *ex cathedra* by a professor of science, must surely have harmful results on the minds of many needs no argument. Numerous mental wrecks have been occasioned by so-called "spiritualistic" studies among the large class of persons who are ready to believe most of what they hear. It is not too much to say that, unless Sir Oliver Lodge is prepared to submit his evidence to competent judges, the reiteration of his claim to have talked with the dead is unjustifiable and even inexcusable.

Your obedient servant,
H. BRYAN DONKIN

Lodge was an eminent physicist who came to believe that the spirit lived on after death in an invisible substance that he thought filled the universe: ether.

ST. ANDREW'S DAY AT ETON

24 November 1914

SIR,—IT HAS BEEN decided to transfer the usual fixtures on St. Andrew's Day at Eton to Saturday, November 28. This has been done for the benefit of the very large number of Old Etonians serving in the forces, for whom Saturday is a much more convenient day for getting leave.

The Wall match will begin at the usual time; and there will be an Old Etonian match in the afternoon.

Yours faithfully,
ANTHONY BEVIR, Captain of the School

IN CASE OF A RAID

3 December 1914

SIR,—THERE IS CONSIDERABLE talk in East Anglia and Essex of the martial spirit of the civilian inhabitants and of the deeds they mean to perform against invading Germans if they get the chance. This martial spirit is creditable, but it cannot be too clearly stated that at the present time a civilian's martial spirit can only be properly shown in one way.

That way is to enlist in the Regular Forces.

The Germans have not fought according to the rules of civilized warfare as laid down at The Hague. But in this regrettable fact we can find no excuse for imitating them. It is against the rules of civilized warfare for civilians to attempt to kill soldiers. Single snipers would expose their villages to reprisals whose nature we know; and, further, no bands of snipers formed suddenly in an emergency would have the slightest chance of being recognized by the enemy as combatants.

Moreover, the majority of potential snipers could only be armed with a shot-gun, a weapon hopelessly outranged by, and practically useless against, the military rifle.

But there is a stronger reason against civilian fighting. As the military representative on the Emergency Committee which has charge of a large district as dangerously situated as any, I have received a personal positive instruction from the General Officer commanding the South Midland Division that the military authorities absolutely discountenance, and strongly object to, any form of civilian fighting. The arrangements to repel a raid are in their hands;

the responsibility is theirs; and any man who acts contrary to their wishes must thereby confuse their plans, impede their operations, and endanger their success.

Any civilian who wants to help against a raid should go to the chairman of his parish council, and through him offer his services to the Emergency Committee of his district. The details of the very exhaustive and elaborate arrangements are now being completed, and there is, or will be, should the moment come, sufficient work to employ all male civilians with wit enough to understand the high value of hearty and obedient cooperation. It would perhaps be impolitic to publish particulars, but the chairman of every parish council has full information and is in a position to allocate duties.

Any civilian, whatever his motive, who tries to repel a raid on his own initiative and by his own devices will be guilty of an act essentially unpatriotic.

ARNOLD BENNETT, Military Representative on the Emergency
Committee of the Tendring Division (Essex)

WOMEN DOCTORS AND THE WAR

5 December 1914

SIR,—AMONG THE MOST urgent national necessities of the moment is an ample supply of experienced, and well-trained doctors—and there is a very marked shortage. Many of our best physicians and surgeons have already gone to the front and as their ranks are thinned by the inevitable wastage of war many more are prepared to follow.

To some extent medical women are already filling the vacancies thus caused at hospitals and other institutions, and are proving themselves equal to their professional and administrative duties. Partly in consequence of the present emergency it has become apparent that the demand for the services of medical women is greatly in excess of the supply. In addition to this the principal missionary societies are suffering from the impossibility of obtaining sufficient medical women to staff their hospitals and dispensaries, and a similar difficulty exists at home in the case of various departments of the public service.

May we not hope that when this urgent demand for women doctors is realized by the public many women of good birth, education, and ability will be desirous of entering the medical profession? It is certain that all such women cannot, and do not, expect to marry, and that in default of this most natural and desirable condition of life some women must seek other spheres of usefulness. From an experience of medical life now verging on 40 years, I venture to think that no career could offer greater happiness and satisfaction to a woman, nor greater opportunities of practical usefulness, than medicine. I should like to point out that women medical students need not of necessity be very young. The more mature woman has certain great qualifications for the task; her verbal memory may not be so strong as that of her juniors, but her trained mind, experience of life, and general *savoir faire* are of considerable service to her as a student and still more as a practitioner.

That women are capable of rendering efficient professional aid is proved by the fact that at the present time several hospitals officered entirely by women are at work in the theatre of war, and that the services of these medical women are much appreciated by their professional brethren and by their patients.

I am, Sir, faithfully yours,
MARY SCHARLIEB

THE TREATMENT OF THE GERMAN WOUNDED

8 December 1914

SIR,—I HAVE JUST returned from an official visit to the military and private hospitals organized for the care of British and French wounded at Paris and Versailles.

In many of these hospitals are German wounded. I spoke to every German wounded man that I saw and learnt from them that not only had they no complaints but were more than satisfied with the way they are tended and treated. As far as I could learn there is no difference of condition between a German wounded soldier and a British or French. I understand that in Germany there is a widespread erroneous impression that their wounded are being harshly treated by us. So strong is this belief that I hear that my brother, a colonel of the Guards, who is lying very grievously wounded in the military hospital at Frankfurt a/M, although now admirably cared for, is not allowed to be visited by German friends in retaliation for the supposed ill-treatment of their wounded by us. The German wounded in British and neutral hospitals in France are allowed to be visited by the many kind ladies who bring gifts and comforts for the wounded, and receive their share.

In view of the wide circulation of *The Times*, which I understand still continues in Germany, I shall be glad if you can publish this letter.

I am, Sir, your obedient servant,
LIONEL EARLE

SWISS RESORTS FOR THE WOUNDED

9 December 1914

SIR,—WILL YOU KINDLY permit me to contradict the rumours more or less prevalent to the effect that St. Moritz and the other resorts in the Engadine will not be open to visitors this winter owing to the war? St. Moritz already has a fair number of its old patrons, and although it is not expected that the season will be a full one, still the conditions now prevailing ought to encourage those who wish to enjoy their usual holiday in the High Alps to do so under favourable circumstances. Perhaps the following facts might help to dispel all hesitation:—(1) The journey out by Paris, Lyons, Culoz, and Geneva with sleeping cars is short and comfortable. Passengers may take as much luggage with them as they please. (2) There need be no fear whatever with regard to the supply of provisions; food of all sorts is abundant in Switzerland; the same may be said with regard to fuel, and there will be no lack of servants. (3) An English chaplain is already in residence at St. Moritz. (4) There are no difficulties about money; English cheques are cashed at the current rate of exchange. (5) The skating and curling rinks will be efficiently maintained as in previous years.

The hotels at St. Moritz are throwing open their doors in a very hospitable fashion to our wounded and invalid officers. A certain number of these will be received gratis, the others at merely nominal charges, and the local medical men are generously offering their professional services free. There will be no subscriptions demanded from officers for the use of rinks, or any outdoor or indoor amusements. I may here mention that the Swiss Government offers a warm welcome to our soldiers, provided they do not appear in our own uniform, and the War Office offers no objection whatever to their going.

Any officers wishing, therefore, to avail themselves of the opportunity presented to them of recruiting health and strength in the splendid climate of the Engadine are requested to apply to Georgina Countess of Dudley, British Red Cross Society, 83, Pall-mall.

I am, Sir, yours truly,
J. FRANK HOLLAND, M.D., H.B.M. Consul

GRUMBLING—AND MORE SWEATERS

11 December 1914

SIR,—THE WEATHER IS very cold, and the troops are very wet, and the mud is very bad, and the embarcation officer at Southampton sends our parcels to the German by mistake, and Mr. Penoyre proves to be an elderly alien female enemy making enormous profits out of sweaters in Mile End-road, and everything is wrong and it's all the fault of the Government.

Thus my correspondents. Otherwise I should have thought that the Government of this country is engaged at its proper task of carrying on war advantageously with the enemy. To this end it has called for brave hearts, and is now engaged in equipping the brave bodies that contain them. But this will take till the day after to-morrow or longer, and meantime voluntary help, such as your readers have lavished through me, must do its best and keep its temper. I am very sorry, Madam, that one of your mits got into the Gloucester's sack and the other into the Worcester's. But would ladies please stich these most useful things together? And, yes, Madam, it is quite true that I did give your nice golf coat (the very small one of rose du Barry silk with the lace insertions) to a Belgian lady— and much comforted she was, poor thing. But would some of my kind senders mingle more discretion with their kindness?

I submit that the knell of Empire will not sound for these blunders of mine. But I do foresee grave ill if once the great civil population of these islands begins to count as a thing of any merit the little they can give and do for those who, through wet and cold and worry and waiting, give and do all for us. It is laid on us all, as never before, to do our utmost and keep, though it be a very mask for tears, a cheerful countenance.

I had almost forgotten. I want, please, a great many more sweaters to dye khaki, and a great many more ladies' golf coats—long or short, but not the very small ones. The response to my asking for these has been prodigious, I know, but I want a great many more.

Yours faithfully,
JOHN PENOYRE

FRIGHTENED EWE FLOCKS

28 December 1914

Sir,—At an audit dinner held here yesterday the farmers present stated that on the previous Friday night the ewe flocks for a distance of 20 miles round had been scared, had smashed through their pens, and were found scattered about the country. One farmer stated that his ewes had been penned in by iron hurdles strong enough to contain bullocks, but the sheep in their mad rush had broken them down.

The general opinion was that an aeroplane must have passed over the district and frightened the ewes, and I was asked to write to the War Office about it. The evidence of this, however—to the effect that some one in a neighbouring town was reported to have heard an aeroplane that night—is too slender to justify me in troubling the War Office at this moment. Moreover, the same thing happened three years ago, and one of the farmers present recalled a similar occurrence 20 years back, long before aeroplanes were invented.

The matter is of some importance, because an injury to our ewe flocks at this period of the year may prejudicially affect the lambing season. It is possible that the cause may be traced to some atmospheric disturbance, and it is in the hope that some one may be able to suggest the true factor in the case that I have ventured to trouble you with this letter.

Your obedient servant,
HOLCOMBE INGLEBY

1915

THE SWORDS OF FALLEN OFFICERS

2 January 1915

SIR,—MANY SWORDS SENT home from the front by the regimental authorities have been so badly labelled that it has been impossible to identify them, and they lie derelict. Some also are said to have disappeared *en route*. The pain caused to relatives by the non-receipt of a lost one's sword is great. Every care should be taken in the transmission of so precious a relic.

Yours,
THE FATHER OF AN OFFICER KILLED IN ACTION

"GOING WEST"

4 January 1915

SIR,—IN REFERENCE TO the question in one of your "Letters from the Front" in to-day's issue, as to the origin of the soldiers' expression for death—"going west"—it may be of interest to your readers to know that the idea that the souls of the departed have to journey westwards is a very ancient one. It was the belief of the ancient Egyptians and Babylonians. The sun was supposed to descend through a hole in the ground and to travel all night eastwards through the realms of the dead. Souls had thus to travel west to reach the entrance to this happy underworld. The belief is still held by many pagan peoples all over the world—Brazilians, Australians, and Fijians, among others. Dr. F. B. Jevons ("Introduction to History of Religion," p. 310) says:—

"The funeral dirges of the Dayaks describe how the spirits of the departed have to run westwards at full speed through brake and briar over rough ground and cutting coral to keep up with the sun and slip through the crashing gates by attaching themselves to him. The ghost who could not keep up with the sun and arrive at the entrance simultaneously with him had to recommence the journey next day."

Yours, &c.,
ETHEL M. WALLACE

THE GOVERNMENT AND THE
OPPOSITION

11 January 1915

SIR,—I HAVE READ WITH the greatest surprise the following statement made by Lord Crewe in a letter in your issue of to-day:—

"My object was rather to remind the House that in the suspension of free Parliamentary attack the Opposition Party in the country might partly console themselves by the reflection that the exceptional action taken in the crisis by the Executive has in most subjects of importance been within the preliminary knowledge of one or more of their leaders, and has been taken after hearing their opinions."

I acknowledge with thanks the courtesy of the Government in permitting Lord Lansdowne and myself to see dispatches from General French, as well as from our representatives abroad.

I have, however, received no information from the Government, which has not been given publicly, as to the steps which they have hitherto taken or the steps which they propose to take for the prosecution of the war, and I am authorized by Lord Lansdowne to state that he is in the same position.

Yours truly,
A. BONAR LAW

As Conservative Party leader, Bonar Law was the leader of the opposition. Lansdowne was the Tories' leader in the Lords and Crewe his Liberal counterpart.

"THE GREAT WAR"

15 January 1915

SIR,—I WONDER WHETHER you or any of your readers could give me any certain information as to what is or is going to be the official name for the present war. Those of us who have to record matters are in a difficulty with regard to it. The general opinion rather seems to point to the use of the term "European War," but this, of course, ignores a very important part of the fighting in which this country is concerned in China, South Africa, Asiatic Turkey, and elsewhere.

I am, Sir, your obedient servant,
A. C. FOX-DAVIES, Editor of "Burke's Landed Gentry"

FROSTBITE IN THE TRENCHES

25 January 1915

SIR,—REFERRING TO A letter headed "Frostbite" in your issue of yesterday, it may interest your correspondent to know that we were served out with grease before going up to the trenches on Christmas Eve. I rubbed my legs and feet thoroughly with this and was careful to leave my boots and puttees loose—but I arrived home on January 1 with frostbite in both feet, and am still laid up.

As to comparing us with men who explore the Poles, I do not know much about Polar expeditions, but I imagine that the men contrive to keep their legs and feet fairly dry, and have plenty of opportunities of taking exercise and keeping the circulation going. Whereas, in my particular case, I was for 36 hours in a trench which was so badly knocked about and fallen in, and had such an ineffective parapet, that it was simply "asking for trouble" to stand in anything like an upright position. The main trench was over knee deep in liquid mud (frozen over on Christmas morning), and the consistency of the ground in my particular traverse was such that if I kept my feet in the same place for a few minutes on end it was quite an effort to pull them out. You will readily see, then, that stamping or "marking time" was quite impossible, and we were reduced to knocking our feet together or hammering them with an entrenching-tool handle. I spent most of Christmas Eve and the following morning in such cheerful pastimes, but by lunch-time my feet and ankles were quite numbed. Our cubby-hole, by the way, had fallen in, and we had no hot shower-baths, stoves, drawing-room carpets, or other luxuries which abound in these Aladdin's-Cave-cum-Ritz-Hotel trenches I have read about in the papers.

If your correspondent will excuse me saying so—when speaking, as he does in the last sentence of his letter, about "proper precautions" and so on, he does not realize the difficulties with which the authorities have to contend, especially when the trenches are only some 80 yards away from the Germans, as ours were. And I can assure him that when I left any amount of things were being done to improve the condition, and make things more comfortable for the men. But mud and frost are difficult things to deal with at any time, and how much more so when one or two crack shots are waiting to put a bullet through the first head or arm that appears.

Yours truly,
ONE WHO'S TRIED IT

PRIVATE LETTERS AND THE CENSORSHIP

27 January 1915

SIR,—MAY I APPEAL TO you on a matter which interests a large number of persons, who, like myself, must be at a loss to know how to act?

Before Christmas I wrote a letter to my friend Mr. Compton Mackenzie, the novelist, who lives in Capri. It was delivered, after a very long delay (of which we make no complaint), but it was accompanied by a curtly-worded communication from the English censorship, desiring Mr. Mackenzie to tell his correspondent that, in future, if the latter wished his letters to be delivered he must write "shortly and clearly." As far as "clearness" is concerned, my handwriting, whatever its demerits, is as clear as print. As far as "shortness" is concerned, my letter was not longer than one is accustomed to write to a friend abroad. I wrote exclusively about a literary matter interesting to Mr. Compton Mackenzie and myself. Political questions, even the war itself, were not mentioned or approached. Mr. Mackenzie's reply, which was as long as my letter, and dealt with precisely the same subject, came to me without delay, and without having been opened.

As I desire nothing less than to incommode a busy public department, I wrote privately to the Censor, stating what I have mentioned above, and asking for definite instructions. I have had a civil reply, but not the least explanation or information. Can you, Sir, therefore inform me what number of words the Censor permits a friend in England to address to a friend in a neutral country?

I am, Sir, your obedient servant,
EDMUND GOSSE

LEECHES

28 January 1915

SIR,—OUR COUNTRY HAS been for many months suffering from a serious shortage of leeches. As long ago as last November there were only a few dozen left in London, and *they* were secondhand.

Whilst General Joffre, General von Kluck, General von Hindenburg, and the Grand Duke Nicholas persist in fighting over some of the best leech-areas in Europe, possibly unwittingly, this shortage will continue, for even in Wordsworth's time the native supply was diminishing, and since then we have for many years largely depended on importations from France and Central Europe. In November I made some efforts to alleviate the situation by applying to America and Canada, but without success. I then applied to India, and last week, owing to the kindness of Dr. Annandale, Director of the Indian Museum at Calcutta, and to the officers of the P. and O. Company and to Colonel Alcock, M.D., of the London School of Tropical Medicine, I have succeeded in landing a fine consignment of a leech which is used for blood-letting in India. It is true that the leech is not the *Hirudo medicinalis* of our pharmacopœias, but a different genus and species, *Limnatis granulosa*. Judging by its size, always a varying quantity in a leech, we may have to readjust our ideas as to a leech's cubic capacity, yet I believe, from seeing them a day or two ago, they are willing and even anxious to do their duty. They have stood the voyage from Bombay and the changed climatic conditions very satisfactorily, and are in a state of great activity and apparent hunger at 50, Wigmore-street, London, W.

It is true that leeches are not used to anything like the extent they were 80 years ago—Paris alone, about 1830, made use of some 52 millions a year—but still they are used, though in much smaller numbers.

It may be of some consolation to my fellow-countrymen to know that our deficiency in leeches is more than compensated by the appalling shortage of sausage-skins in Middle Europe. With true German thoroughness they are trying to make artificial ones!

I am yours faithfully,
A. E. SHIPLEY

WELSH GUARDS

2 February 1915

SIR,—IN THE MAGNIFICENT response made by all the nations to the Empire's call Wales has nobly borne its share. Even before the appeal of Mr. Lloyd George for the formation of two Welsh Army Corps it had already sent some 40,000 men to the Regular Army. The 23rd Royal Welsh Fusiliers, the 24th South Wales Borderers, and the 41st, the Welsh Regiment, occupy a position of high honour. Between August 4 and January 9 the number of men recruited in Wales exceeded 70,000, and it was estimated that districts from which returns were at that time incomplete would bring the total over 85,000. Since then the response of Welshmen to the call to join the new Army has been prompt and steady.

This being so, by way of recognition of the magnificent behaviour of the men of Wales of age to join the colours, having regard, too, to their "excellent character" as soldiers, and to further rouse the martial spirit of their nation in support of this just war, would it not be a graceful compliment, which no Welshman would be ever likely to forget, to form a Regiment of Welsh Guards? The sister nations of England and Scotland have for a long time past had their Guards Regiments, and only a few years ago the formation of the Irish Guards afforded ample evidence of how much gratification and pride that most tactful idea of the late Queen Victoria created in the national sentiment of Ireland.

No suggestion would be more popularly acclaimed in Wales. No idea would more vividly stir the imagination of the people. A battalion could be raised in very quick time, especially, as might, perhaps, be necessary, if the standard of height usual in Guards Regiments were slightly reduced. Then, with Wales's own young Prince as Colonel-in-Chief, there would exist a new regiment of Guards of which both Wales and the British Army would have every justification in feeling proud. A highly-emotional and always loyal people, the Welsh even now let none of the Empire's races outvie them in valour or in loyalty, and I confidently submit it would be sound policy for Lord Kitchener to carry out the proposition set forth.

I am, Sir, yours faithfully,
J. AUBREY REES

Four days after the publication of this letter, King George V commanded that a battalion of Welsh Guards be raised.

INTRUSION ON BEREAVEMENT

9 *February 1915*

SIR,—MAY I, AS ONE whose sad privilege it has been to announce the death of one of his sons in action in your paper, venture to make an appeal on behalf of those who in the future may have to follow in my footsteps?

I appeal first to those who in the interests of their business watch your obituary columns, and think they afford an opportunity of pushing the sale of their wares in the form of sculptured urn or Iona cross, forgetful, perhaps, that our boy lies "within some lonely glen," the very site of whose grave may have passed already from human memory, or may perhaps be identified by some faithful French peasant in whose cottage he died when we go on our way weeping to find it when the war is over. I would ask these tradesmen to respect our mourning and to remember that few of us, be we father, mother, husband, wife, have not already had recourse some time or other to their services, and when the time appropriate occurs may seek it again.

Then, again, there are the photograph enlargers, miniature painters, &c., and finally I would appeal to those who, with a singular lack of delicacy and failure to understand the ethics of Christianity, take the opportunity of plunging our stricken souls into vexed questions of eschatology, and ask us to ponder the probability of our dear one's "soul being saved" by means of circulars dwelling on this solemn subject. It is not only impertinent but fatuous, and would seem almost incredible that people should have such bad taste; but it is the case, and only last week such a pamphlet found its way into my fire.

Then, again, there are other societies of a philanthropic character who take the opportunity of a chance appearance of one's name in the paper to urge the insistence of their claims at a moment when personal sorrow does not make even the most benevolent the most approachable.

I suppose these worthy tradesmen and societies can have no knowledge of the pain and annoyance they give in systematically opening wounds that God's comfort is quietly healing, but if they have not, I would ask them to put themselves in our place, and not to exploit our grief for their advantage, and whilst we mourn our fallen soldier, leave us alone in our glory.

Yours faithfully,
PATER MÆRENS

THE ZEPPELIN RAID ON THE EAST COAST

11 February 1915

Sir,—I REGRET I WAS not in the House of Commons when the Home Secretary, in answer to a question put by Sir William Bull, unexpectedly made a statement regarding the motor-cars alleged to have accompanied the Zeppelins in their raid on the East Coast. Perhaps, under these circumstances, you will kindly allow me the hospitality of your columns in order to submit a counter-statement, for I am anxious that the public should be placed in possession of the real facts of the case.

Let me first test the value of the Home Secretary's statement that there were eight cars traced by the Norfolk Constabulary about the time of the raid and satisfactorily accounted for. The Constabulary were singularly blind that night. There were no less than six cars in different parts of Snettisham at the time mentioned, three of which were open to the gravest suspicion. Of these three the constable saw nothing. Similarly, the constable stationed at Heacham, where two bombs fell, informed me that after 6.30 p.m. no car passed through that place. As a matter of fact two cars visited the lower part of the village, one immediately before and one immediately after the raid, and both excited suspicion. Again, within 20 minutes of each other three cars dashed through Brancaster Staith, which is 10 miles distant from Heacham, the last one closely followed by the Zeppelin. The audacity of the occupants of that car passes belief, but in order that the statement of the witness I am about to quote may not be brushed aside too lightly, I ought to explain that the Zeppelin, whilst over Brancaster Staith, was flying very low, scarcely higher, as another witness states, than the telegraph wires. And I may as well here say that all my statements are based upon the evidence of what I believe to be perfectly credible witnesses. Here is the statement referred to:—

"On that particular night I was in my home in Brancaster Staith. About 10 p.m. I heard a Zeppelin passing over the house. It remained some minutes above the field adjoining, as if uncertain about something. A motor-car with the most brilliant headlights imaginable then rushed along the road from Deepdale towards Brancaster, and when by the side of the field mentioned above the occupants in the car all shouted very loudly, and two small lights were flashed as a reply from the Zeppelin. Then the latter travelled off after the motor-car. I saw the headlights and heard the shouting, but did not see the two lights from the Zeppelin, as I was in the front of the house; but the lights were seen by other occupants of the house... My observations were those of many people in Brancaster Staith."

When it is remembered that the night was very still and that the Zeppelin (as remarked to me by witnesses in other parts of the county) occasionally shut off her engines, I submit there is nothing incredible in this statement.

I have a number of letters before me giving evidence of the presence of motor-cars that night in various parts of the county, but it is unnecessary to belabour that portion of the evidence. Correspondents from all parts of the county speak of seeing a motor-car with extraordinarily powerful lights in different places followed by an airship and sometimes throwing up flashes. A well-known and much-respected farmer living on the land high above Snettisham Church speaks to seeing flashes of light sent up from six different parts in the neighbourhood, and he has forwarded me a diagram giving the approximate position of the Zeppelin as judged by the noise of her engines and the spots whence the flashes proceeded. Another farmer, also perfectly trustworthy, gives evidence of a powerful light on the other side of Snettisham being directed on the church a moment before the dropping of the bomb. There are eight credible witnesses who can speak to the flashes that proceeded from "Sixpenny Hole" and attracted the Zeppelin to the church. The car that threw these flashes went off by a narrow side lane, which no one who could avoid it would take by night. This car reappeared at the turning into Dersingham and there threw up what appeared to be a definite signal—two upward flashes and one cross flash. At the turning by the church, which leads directly to Sandringham, it threw up more flashes. Similar evidence is forthcoming from the other districts from west to east, right up to the suburbs of Norwich. What a strange series of coincidences are required to explain the circumstance that a powerfully lighted motor-car constantly preceded the Zeppelin in its journeyings through Norfolk that night! And can anyone suggest a reason why the sober inhabitants of Norfolk should be found rushing about the county at a particular moment bombarding the heavens with flashes?

Many of us have a great admiration for our Norfolk Constabulary, who are a fine set of men, and do their duty to the best of their ability. They are usually, however, planted at night in the main streets of our villages, and there is no need for anyone on devilry bent to trespass on their beat. They saw nothing of motor-cars on the night of the raid, and they are not willing to accept evidence that they cannot personally verify. I was so afraid that the Under-Secretary of State for War, relying on their evidence, might give a wrong answer to the question I put to him in the House on Monday last, that I called at the War Office on the previous Saturday and produced certain evidence for his guidance, if necessary. Indeed, a suggestion, which I accepted, was made to me that an officer should call and examine the evidence in my possession. In the meanwhile the Home Secretary has rushed in with a statement which ought not to have been made until that evidence was tested. Had such been the case, I feel sure his answer to Sir William Bull's question would have been on entirely different lines.

I am, Sir, your obedient servant,
HOLCOMBE INGLEBY

———◆———

OVAL OR INTELLIGENT?

17 February 1915

SIR,—A LITTLE LIGHT might be shed, with advantage, upon the high-handed methods of the Passports Department at the Foreign Office. On the form provided for the purpose I described my face as "intelligent." Instead of finding this characterization entered, I have received a passport on which some official, utterly unknown to me, has taken it upon himself to call my face "oval."

Yours very truly,
BASSETT DIGBY

HELP FOR ARTISTS

23 February 1915

SIR,—IN WEDNESDAY's issue of *The Times* there was printed a report of a public meeting held to consider means for assisting distress in the artistic professions. That art is one of the luxuries of life which cannot at this time expect public support is a view held by most people. But surely if art be in truth the noble and inspiring thing our foremost statesmen annually assure us it is, it should be of service in time of war as well as in time of peace. Your leader writer to-day writes warmly commending the spirit shown by those painters who are giving their works for the benefit of the Red Cross Fund. It must be remembered that only painters whose names are generally known can well offer their services on such an occasion. There are other ways of serving, and throughout the country there are numbers of men and women, not painters only, but followers of every kind of craft, eager to devote their skill and energy to the service of the Empire. In order that their services be employed it is not charity which is needed, but a wider understanding of the fruitful use to which their talents may be put. In past ages the practical value of the artist's vision has been shrewdly appreciated. To-day we have schools and public buildings of every kind which might bear witness to the constant beauty of men's vision, hospitals which may be so decorated as to bring renewed hope to the sick and wounded. The war, which brings suffering and distress to so many, also brings added prosperity to many industries. May not some of our industrial leaders be persuaded to employ local craftsmen to decorate workshops and factories, shops and city offices, both outside and within? A few thousand pounds spent in London and our great provincial cities would provide rich opportunities for a great number of eager craftsmen, so many of whom are now unemployed, and would serve to convince people more eloquently than even the passionate appeals of Ruskin and William Morris what skill and beauty live in the hands and hearts of men.

Many of our provincial galleries have funds for the purchase of contemporary paintings, and a part of these, increased by the generosity of public-spirited citizens, might well be used for the decoration of local public buildings. Will not the Trustees of the National Gallery, of the British and Victoria and Albert Museums, set an example to the country by devoting some small portion of their funds, usually dedicated to the purchase of ancient works of art, to some such purpose?

We are already so rich in works of the past, so poor in public expression of our own vision. I believe able and inspiring men could be found who would gladly give their time and experience to such a cause, under whom younger men and women would be proud and willing to work for modest remuneration.

Faithfully yours,
W. ROTHENSTEIN

RACING AND FOOTBALL

4 March 1915

Sɪʀ,—Lᴏʀᴅ Rᴏʙᴇʀᴛ Cᴇᴄɪʟ, speaking in the House of Commons, asserts that football and horse-racing are on exactly the same footing. I am curious to know how he arrives at this conclusion. Football is played with a ball and 22 strong and sturdy young men. Racing is played with horses, ridden by small men, the majority under 8st., and never more than 9st. A football when its day is over is useless. Racehorses when they can no longer race, if they have proved themselves on a race-course to be sound and good, retire to the stud, where, as stallions or brood mares, they continue the stock of the English thoroughbred, which forms the foundation of horse-breeding in this country, and from which have come those horses that, in the earlier stages of war, rendered such invaluable service. To be a good football player you must be big, strong, courageous, active, and alert, all the qualities you look for in a soldier. To be a good jockey, you require these qualities, except that instead of being big, you must be small—no one can be a jockey who weighs over 9st., and a large majority weigh very much less. Consequently they are not fit to be soldiers.

If there was no racing a great many people who are unfitted for other employment would be thrown out of work; can anyone say that the same result would arise if those professional football matches did not take place? If professional football matches were not allowed, it would not stop football; and there can be no one who wants to stop it when played as a game—but if race-meetings are stopped, the whole machinery comes to a standstill, and needless loss is caused to every one connected with it. The arguments for the continuance of racing are many, there are also arguments against it, and for which we most of us have sympathy, but the former outweigh the latter considerably, and I can say from my own personal knowledge that many owners of racehorses, had they simply studied their own inclinations and convenience, would have shut up their racing establishments at the beginning of the war.

Yours, &c.,
GEORGE LAMBTON

The Football League was shortly to suspend competitive matches. Horse-racing continued for another two years.

FOOLISH OPTIMISM

6 March 1915

Sir,—I have been asked to repeat in the form of a letter to you some of the remarks that I made in the City yesterday.

I was dealing with actual and impending strikes, and I said that such action, taken by men so patriotic, could only be explained by the fact that those concerned did not in the least appreciate the extreme gravity of the crisis in which our country still finds itself. They think, or many of them think, that the crisis is past, that all is going well with the Allies, and that the war will very soon be over. How can we wonder that such a deplorable impression should exist? The Press Bureau consistently slurs over bad news and exaggerates good news. The Press lays every emphasis by poster, headline, and paragraph on all that side of the war which is flattering to our pride or soothing to our excited feelings. It keeps further in the background the news which is disagreeable to us, and the result is that our sense of proportion is being destroyed, and that perspective is ceasing to exist. I could multiply instances of what I mean. Frequently lately we have seen a roll of casualties of some battalion in Flanders amounting to 200, 300, 400 men, or even to half a battalion. These casualties took place in February, January, or December, but who can recollect that at the time he received any impression of such a loss by the news published? The fact is that these casualties have usually occurred when we have lost a trench or a line of trenches, and the men holding them have been killed or made prisoners. A day or two after this had happened we were probably told that a trench which had been lost had been brilliantly recaptured, but we had never been told previously that we had lost the trench, and we were never told at the time what the loss of the trench or its recapture had cost us.

When the Prime Minister spoke in the House of Commons the other day he spoke with quiet confidence as to the issue of the war. He was quite right, and we all share that confidence; but I do wish that he had laid more stress on the extreme difficulty and gravity of the task which still lies before us before a successful issue can be reached. The naked facts of the situation are that, notwithstanding the magnificent courage of the soldiers of the Allied Armies, the Germans are holding very nearly the same ground in France and Belgium as they held four months ago, and that the Germans and the Austrians together have been able to hold their own in the Eastern field of war against the splendid endurance of the Russian Army. The silent pressure of the Fleet has no doubt caused much inconvenience to the German Government and some hardship to the German people, but there is no more likelihood of Germany than of the Allies being starved into an early submission.

My own belief is that at the very best there are many months of cruel war before us and that we have need of every effort which every civilian in the United Kingdom can make, as well as of every effort of the seamen in the Fleet and of the soldiers in the trenches; and that far the greatest danger which now confronts us is lest slackness in the United Kingdom, from whatever cause arising, should protract the war many months beyond the time at which it could otherwise be finished. As a people we cannot be frightened or depressed into panic by bad news; we can very easily be made too confident by good news. If those who control the Press Bureau understood the temperament of their fellow-countrymen they would not only never conceal any bad news from them, they would lay all the stress upon it which it could honestly bear, and they would be very careful not to give any good news a prominence at all disproportionate to its importance in the vast scale of the war. I have said that we all agree with the Prime Minister in quiet confidence as to the issue of the war, but that confidence must be conditional on the belief that the people of the United Kingdom will fight the war through in the United Kingdom in the same spirit in which they began it.

I am, Sir, your obedient servant,
SELBORNE

SUBMARINES: AN OFFER

9 March 1915

SIR,—THE PATRIOTIC OFFER of Mr. Hoult in *The Times* of to-day of £500 to the captain and crew of each of the first four vessels of the British mercantile fleet who destroy a German submarine—followed by the excellent letter from Sir Oliver Lodge saying that £1000 would not be a penny too much for the nation to pay to men who risk their lives in such a service, induces me to say that I shall be prepared to add £100 to each of Mr. Hoult's £500 patriotic donations. I do this also in the further hope that four of my old friends who have the means will follow suit and add four times the £100 to make the donations up to £1000 to each gallant captain and crew. Truly their lives are worth more than that to us all. Of course, if those lives are sacrificed in the service, the amount will go to their dependents.

Submarine is at best a sneaking kind of warfare, and the sooner it is extinguished among "Kultur"ed nations the better.

I am, Sir, yours faithfully,
HENRY KIMBER, Bt.

WOMEN'S DRESS IN WAR

11 March 1915

SIR,—MAY I, WRITER ON fashion, plead its cause so ruthlessly snubbed by "A Husband" in your Tuesday columns? I need not advance the "good for trade" argument; the emergency work rooms conclusively point to its essential value. I would urge as an unanswerable excuse for new clothes their exhilarating effect upon nine-tenths of womankind. Women want some panacea these times, some distraction from sorrow and suffering. It is on record that a teagown has proved an incentive to the bed-bound to seek the sofa, and that a becoming hat is a tonic strong enough to make a persistent invalid go for a walk. Also I can assure "A Husband" that no great expenditure is required to conform the costumes of yester-year to the rules of this. The addition of a kilt to the walking dress and a tulle tunic to the evening dress will do the trick, and not a few dressmakers whose names I will reveal on demand gladly undertake these renovating jobs on reasonable terms. All grief and no joy makes Jill a dull creature; and even "A Husband" may benefit by the improved spirits of a cheery victim to the dress habit.

Yours faithfully,
(MRS.) E. ARIA

THE CASE FOR AMUSEMENTS

13 March 1915

SIR,—MAY I IN THE midst of profound grief be allowed to express a humble opinion as to what I conceive to be one's duty in the colossal task that we have before us? The outcry of certain people against all forms of entertainment and recreation during this crisis seems to me a false cry. To "entertain" means to engage the attention and to occupy it agreeably, and to "recreate" means to refresh. Many of us earn our livelihood in ways that appear not vital to national existence. But what is vital? At the present moment all that is vital to our existence as a nation is the wherewithal to carry on the war to a successful issue. It is our duty to provide this first and foremost. Equally with this it is surely our duty to provide those who are dependent on us with the necessities of life. There are hundreds of thousands of men and women unfit and unqualified to help their country in a direct way at the present moment, but for whom paid employment is as individually vital as our national existence. Is it not better for such as cannot fight for their country to earn a living even in racing stables, in theatres, and music-halls, or as novelists, artists, musicians—in fact in a hundred other ways—rather than starve or live upon the charity of the already overburdened ratepayer? Looking at it from an economic point of view the question presents an aspect that is vital, not only to those who are directly concerned, but to the millions who are only indirectly affected. The manufacture and consumption of the superfluities of life outweigh the necessities to an extent impossible to calculate. To stop racing, to close theatres and music-halls, to put an end for the time to literature, art, music and—if we are to be logical—to cease the consumption of wines, the manufacture of spirits, beer, tobacco, jewelry, or even the cultivation of flowers, must inevitably result in a reduced circulation of money and a corresponding increase of taxation, which would prove the ultimate ruin of those few industries vital to the existence of a great nation.

Yours faithfully,
GERALD DU MAURIER

Du Maurier's brother and his nephew, one of the children who inspired the writing of *Peter Pan*, had recently been killed.

THE STATE AND WOMEN'S LABOUR

19 March 1915

Sir,—The announcement by the President of the Board of Trade that a register of women for war service is to be opened at the labour exchanges throughout the country will no doubt evoke the same patriotic response to national service which has characterized the attitude of women towards the emergency created by the war. This organized effort on the part of the State to register and employ "the reserve force of women's labour, trained or untrained" will be welcomed by the many women's societies already engaged in this work of classification as an earnest of future co-ordination.

In the official statement setting out the Government scheme we find the following paragraph, "Any woman who by working helps to release a man, or to equip a man, for fighting does national war service. Every woman should register who is able and willing to take employment."

This is in fact an appeal to every able-bodied woman, not bound by family ties, to enlist in industrial war service. That women have forestalled this appeal is shown by the fact that one society alone, the Women's Emergency Corps, received 10,000 offers of personal service during the first two weeks of the war. Women doctors, interpreters, chauffeurs, motorcyclists, gardeners, omnibus conductors, omnibus and taxi-cab drivers, lift women, &c., were ready to qualify for men's posts during the war, so as to release men for military service. That this service has not been largely utilized up to the present is attributed to the attitude of men workers, and not to the lack of response among women.

Lord Kitchener recently said, "I feel strongly that the men working long hours in the shops by day and by night, week in and week out, are doing their duty for their King and country in a like manner with those who have joined the Army for active service in the field, and I am glad to be able to state that his Majesty has approved that where service in this great work of supplying the munitions of war has been thoroughly, loyally, and continuously rendered, the award of a medal will be granted on the successful termination of the war."

To women workers engaged in war service at home, the cessation of hostilities will bring a grave dislocation of employment, and the sacrifice of their ordinary duties, for work which will necessarily only be temporary, should meet with some public recognition. It would be a cause for satisfaction among women to know that official recognition will not be denied to those women who, in the words of the Board of Trade, "by working, help to release a man, or to equip a man, for fighting." The present emergency and the Government's appeal to women form a propitious occasion for creating a precedent in the bestowal of honours in which other countries have already set us an example. In Russia all honours and decorations are conferred on women doing men's work, even the war medal is conferred on women, and King Albert of Belgium has recently bestowed the Order of Leopold on the women members of one of our field ambulances. In these circumstances it would amount to an invidious distinction were women rendered ineligible for the Industrial War Medal and an announcement as to the Government's intentions would be welcomed by women in general.

Yours faithfully,
CONSUELO MARLBOROUGH

———◆———

GERMANY AND ENGLAND AT WAR: AN AMERICAN COMPARISON

20 March 1915

SIR,—ON A PREVIOUS occasion you permitted me, an American and fervent supporter of the Allies, to have the honour of addressing the readers of *The Times*. I trust that you will now allow me to compare a few impressions received during the past few weeks in Germany and Austria with those I have since received in London.

I possess the average American's loathing of the military government of Germany; but, none the less, I must confess to admiration for the marvellous manner in which that government, often by specious methods I have no doubt, has united the German people and its Austrian and Hungarian allies. To arrive in England and find your upper class discussing horse-racing and some of your workpeople on strike comes as a cold douche to an enthusiast for your cause like myself.

The Germans are singularly well informed as to what is happening in England. It seems to me that their newspapers are more frank about the whole war than yours, while among the upper and official class it is fairly obvious that private communications reach Germany from England with great speed, whether by letter or by word of mouth I am unable to say. The universal impression in Germany is that there is no enthusiasm for the war in England. Fellow-citizens who were here at the period of your Boer War tell me that the enthusiasm of that time was splendid and contagious. Germans are under the impression that the English are afraid of this war. That is obviously quite untrue. On the other hand, there is, unquestionably, much complacency here. It does not seem to an outside observer that your men and women are doing their utmost to bring this conflict to a successful issue. The Germans, as you are probably aware, are under the belief that the British Empire is practically at their mercy. Nevertheless, they are straining every nerve, by land, by sea, by uniting their people, by active diplomacy in neutral countries, to win decisive victory. Among the official class in Germany such optimism does not reign, though your labour troubles are without doubt reviving hopes that were extinguished by the unsuccessful march on Paris.

Is it not possible for some of your great public orators to awaken the middle class—the "commuters" as we call them—and the democracy? Within the past 48 hours I have met one man of business who told me that he "never read the war news," and another who obviously took very little interest in the war. He admitted it was a serious matter, but believed that the Germans were on the eve of collapse from a shortage of food, copper, and cash.

It would be absolutely impossible to find people of this kind in Germany. You may laugh at their hate campaigns and cunning tricks to arouse the world's sympathies by pretending that they are being starved by Great Britain, but you must confess that their strenuous and enthusiastic unity and the sober preparation of the nation for a long, long struggle is an example to the world. We went through something like the same thing at home in 1861. We prepared even more slowly than you, but before the end of the war, which had been expected to last three weeks, but which did not terminate until 1865, we had in the field practically the whole of our manhood down to the age of 17, aye, and even younger than that. That is the case with Germany. There lads of 15 and 16 are drilling and preparing, and, outside the horrible newly-rich class in Berlin, the German women are all engaged in immense preparations for the comfort of the troops and the reception of the vast army of wounded they are expecting.

I trust these observations from an American of purely British descent on both sides will not be taken amiss.

Yours faithfully,
D. T. C.

EXEANT SWEATERS

24 March 1915

SIR,—MAY I INVADE YOUR columns, for the last time, to say that as I now have enough sweaters on hand to fulfil all promises made, and as we are within measurable distance of warmer weather, I propose to close my work? Your readers should on no account take this as any kind of *ex cathedra* statement that no more warm clothing is needed. I only state the fact that I have enough to carry on my small venture till the warmer weather comes. There are, however, some things which are wanted throughout the year—*e.g.*, socks, shirts, and all cheerful little things like cigarettes, packets of tobacco and sweets, writing-paper, other personalia, and small medicaments. Any of the above I am willing to continue sending weekly throughout the summer. I venture further to suggest that it is a pity for ladies to let the "knitting habit" die down. Should we not do well to begin forming laagers of warm things for the autumn and winter? It is neither difficult nor pessimistic to prophesy a revival of the need for comforts towards the close of the year. When peace is signed, Israel cannot return to his tents in an afternoon.

I render account of my sweaters:—10,443 is the number to-day, the miscellanea kindly sent to make filling for the sacks bringing the figures close up to 20,000. We are told that this supplement of sweaters, &c., has been of some sort of use and comfort to you, soldier and sailor too, while you have been training, watching, fighting, and dying for us, the long wet winter through. *E superabundantia cordis os loquitur*—we are honored indeed that this should have been so. I thank my helpers for much unlooked-for kindness. They send me the sweaters and pay for the dyeing. I merely win the wager and get the credit. So no more of sweaters—till the autumn.

Yours faithfully,
JOHN PENOYRE

DR. LYTTELTON AND GERMANY
AN UNNECESSARY SERMON

30 March 1915

SIR,—HAS NOT A LITTLE too much been made of the address of the Headmaster of Eton? It seems a well-meant effort to do what is not necessary—viz., to stir in Englishmen feelings of moderation as regards Germany. As a matter of fact, throughout the whole of the war, we have been remarkable for the calmness with which we have taken the actions of our enemies and for the extremely reasonable attitude of speakers and of the Press on the subjects at issue.

Dr. Lyttelton has not lived as many years in Germany as I have done, and he cannot remember Prussia at the time of the Franco-Prussian War. He seems under the impression that only in recent years has there been feeling against England on the part of Germany. I can remember July, 1870, when it was not easy for an English boy even to walk along the streets of some German towns without being hooted and having distinctly unpleasant statements hurled at one. For one or two days in that month we were popular, because an idea prevailed that we were going to join Germany; then for a day or two we were unpopular, because it was said we were going to join France. After that time we were thoroughly disliked, because we decided to remain neutral. The dislike for England dates back certainly to that period and has never been lost. Dr. Lyttelton assumes that we are to take the German view of ourselves as being correct, and that because they have a particular view we are to take up an attitude of weakness in order that we may "save 60,000,000 people from the ruin of a poisoned mind." One thing is certain—we shall never do that by showing any weakness. Only the other day we were told that our kindly treatment of German prisoners meant that we were afraid of what would happen at the end of the war. Germany is not at the present time able to see with unprejudiced eyes anything like generosity of action. I am perfectly satisfied that the one thing we must do now is to bring Germany to her knees, and to show her that the ideals which have been hers ever since Prussia became the dominant power in Germany are unworthy and lead to disaster.

Of course, I would go further myself, and I would say this—that England, having been placed in a position in which she can, through her naval power, to a very large extent lay down the principles in international life, should now accept the responsibility, ensure for the future that her wishes shall be carried out, and secure for her great Allies and herself relief from the constant strain of knowing that there is a Power accumulating every conceivable strength in order to foist upon nations principles alien entirely to the spirit of Christ. There seems to be in some people nowadays the idea that Christianity means a weak application of what is called the principle of Christian charity, but there is a forgetfulness that Christ advised strict dealing with, and strict punishment for, national unworthiness.

Frankly, I think our duty at the present time is not so much to consider how to behave when peace comes as how we are to gain the victory which will bring peace. At any rate, one would beg public men to whom the curious twists in the German mind are not well known to refrain from rather dangerous suggestions at the present time. Dr. Lyttelton's address was meant well, but when read in Germany will only form the text in a great many places for suggestions that we are beginning to weaken and are prepared to give Germany very good terms.

Yours faithfully,
H. R. BIRMINGHAM

———◆———

TO GOLFERS

6 April 1915

SIR,—MAY I TRESPASS upon your kindness to allow me to call the attention of those who take their cars to golf to take wounded soldiers from one of the hospitals with them and give them luncheon and tea? They will be more than repaid by the gratefulness of our wounded heroes.

Yours truly,
ONE WHO HAS TRIED IT

MR. LLOYD GEORGE ON DRINK

9 April 1915

Sir,—I observe from a report in the papers that Mr. Keir Hardie, addressing an Independent Labour meeting at Norwich, stated that workers who were putting in 84 hours a week had been "maligned and insulted and the lying word—on the authority of Mr. Lloyd George—had gone round the world that the British working classes were a set of drunken wasters."

I need hardly say that there is not a word of truth in this wild accusation. I have only made two references to the effect of drinking upon the output of munitions of war. Speaking at Bangor on February 28, I said:—

"Most of our workmen are putting every ounce of strength into this urgent work for their country, loyally and patriotically. But that is not true of all. There are some, I am sorry to say, who shirk their duty in this great emergency. I hear of workmen in armaments works who refuse to work a full week's work for the nation's need. What is the reason? They are a minority. *The vast majority belong to a class we can depend upon. The others are a minority.* But you must remember a small minority of workmen can throw a whole works out of gear. What is the reason? Sometimes it is one thing, sometimes it is another; but let us be perfectly candid. It is mostly the lure of the drink. They refuse to work full time, and when they return their strength and efficiency are impaired by the way in which they have spent their leisure. Drink is doing us more damage in the war than all the German submarines put together."

I call special attention to the italicized passages. I went out of my way to make it clear that in my judgment drink only affected a minority, even a small minority, of the workmen, and that the vast majority were doing their duty loyally. So that as far as the first speech I delivered on the subject is concerned there is not a syllable to justify Mr. Keir Hardie's reckless assertion, but quite the reverse.

Now I come to my second reference to this topic. It was on the occasion of the deputation received by me from the Shipbuilding Employers' Federation. The shipbuilders made it clear repeatedly that their complaints were confined to a section of the men. As one of them put it:—"There are many men doing good work, probably as good work as the men in the trenches." In my speech in reply I said that the excessive drinking took place "among a section, may be a small section, but a very important section of workmen." Neither in one speech nor the other was any reflection cast upon the men who, according to Mr. Keir Hardie, are working 84 hours a week. On the contrary, the complaint was against the men who failed at this critical time to put in anything approaching even 53 hours a week. On both occasions the work of those who were doing their best to help their country in this time of urgent need was fully recognized not only by me but by the employers, and I made it clear that my criticism was confined entirely to a minority and may be a small minority of the workmen.

I hope that after this explanation Mr. Keir Hardie will think it right to withdraw a statement which he must know must be very mischievous in its effect at a time when we are considering the best remedy for the serious limitation in output which is, at any rate, partly attributable to excessive drinking amongst a section of the workmen. He was, I believe, a supporter of temperance legislation for Scotland. His support was not due to any conviction that his fellow-countrymen were a nation of "drunken wasters," but to his knowledge that a minority were so completely subdued by the drink habit that nothing but strong legislative action would enable the community either to protect them or protect itself against injury done to the state by them.

The difficulties are great enough without adding to them by exciting prejudices so easily excited when there is a suspicion of an attack being made upon a whole class of workmen. No such attack was intended—no such attack was made. On the contrary, the vast majority of the workmen engaged in the production of munitions of war were specifically excluded from any suggestion of excessive drinking that was made. The trouble is, however, that the drinking habits of the minority have the effect of diminishing—and seriously diminishing—the output of war material at a time when the success of the Allies depends entirely on that material being largely increased. The evidence upon which the Government has been reluctantly forced to come to this conclusion does not depend on statements made by employers, but upon independent inquires made on behalf of the Government. The result of these investigations will soon be published.

Yours, &c.,
D. LLOYD GEORGE

As chancellor of the exchequer, Lloyd George was to bring in new licensing laws which curbed all-day drinking for the next 80 years.

"KILLED"

9 April 1915

SIR,—THERE HAVE BEEN handed in here two returned letters which more than
a few weeks ago the fair friend of a soldier, an English corporal, had written,
addressing them to his regiment at different places in the wish to discover his
whereabouts, and in the hope that he would be alive to receive them. Outside
the envelopes appears the one word, "Killed." The intelligence is conclusive,
nor is any further information vouchsafed; but if this be the regulation made
of breaking the news in such cases, it is a curt and cheap one and had need to
be improved upon by more consideration being shown for the feelings of the
friend writing the soldier and whose letters will, of course, have been opened
in the post.

Yours truly,
JOHN KEATING

ARMED MERCHANTMEN

10 April 1915

SIR,—SURELY IT WOULD be no innovation if vessels in the merchant navy to-day
were armed to repel attack. When I first went to sea in '59 it was a period when
the work of the old "John Company's" ships was being taken up by what were
known as "East Indiamen," the fine ships of "Green's" and "Money Wigram's,"
and other shipowners. These ships all carried in the waist on the maindeck two
guns of the calibre of the man-o'-war gun of that day, and on the taffrail they
carried two brass swivel long-carronades to repel chasers. They also carried an
arm chest with muskets and cutlasses sufficient to arm the crew, also a number
of long boarding pikes, these last being kept around the mizzen-mast on the
poop deck, ready for instant use, and I as midshipman was responsible for
them. The Straits of Sunda and the China Seas were then infested with pirates,
and ships had to protect themselves. Enemy submarines would, I think, fare
badly if merchant ships to-day were similarly armed.

Your obedient servant,
C. E. MOGRIDGE HUDSON

THE TREATMENT OF PRISONERS

13 April 1915

SIR,—IT IS DIFFICULT TO know how to act in the case of these European Red Indians who torture their prisoners. It is clear that we cannot retaliate by spitting on, kicking, beating, starving, or freezing the Germans who are in our power. All appeals to good feeling are unavailing, for the average German has no more understanding of chivalry than a cow has of mathematics. He is honestly unable to understand our attitude when we speak kindly of Von Muller, Weddigen, or any of our opponents who have shown some approach to decency. His papers ascribe it partly to sentimentality and partly to hypocrisy. I have no doubt that when German aeroplanes drove away our boats while we were endeavouring to pick up the survivors of the Blücher they were really unable to conceive what it was that we were trying to do.

It is worth noting, since they endeavour to excuse their barbarity by saying that it is a retaliation for our naval blockade, that they acted in exactly the same fashion to our prisoners before this maritime policy had been declared. The narrative of the British Red Cross doctors who were taken in Belgium shows that they endured a similar inhuman persecution. If there is no retaliation which we as a nation can employ there is at least one line of action which might be taken. That is to print Major Vandeleur's account with the American official reports, and such documents as the narrative in the Dutch paper *Tyd* of the torture of three wounded British prisoners in a frontier station in October. This paper should be officially sent, not only to all neutral countries, but it should be circulated among our soldiers in France. No man fights the worse for having his soul aflame with righteous anger, so we should use the weapon which the enemy has put into our hands. It will teach our men, also, if any of them still need the lesson, that it is far better to die upon the field than to trust to the humanity of a German victor. If our enemy is unchivalrous he is at least intensely practical, and if he realizes that we are gaining any military advantage from his misdeeds he may, perhaps, reconsider, not their morality, but their wisdom.

Yours faithfully,
ARTHUR CONAN DOYLE

THE RECRUITING CIRCULAR TO
HOUSEHOLDERS

21 April 1915

Sir,—Will you give me the opportunity to ask a question, which I think you will agree is important? When the Circular to Householders was issued, many heads of families gave in their names on the assumption that they would be called up only in the last resort, and under circumstances in which no patriotic man could refuse his help. Married men with large families are now being called up apparently without the slightest regard to their home circumstances. Many of the best of them are surprised and uneasy at leaving their families, but feel bound in honour to keep their word, some even thinking they have no choice. The separation allowances for these families will be an immense burden on the State, and, if the breadwinner falls, a permanent burden. Is the need for men still so serious and urgent as to justify this? If it is, then I for one, who have up to now hoped that the war might be put through without compulsion, feel that the time has come to "fetch" the unmarried shirkers, and I believe there is a widespread and growing feeling to that effect.

I am, Sir, &c.,
CHARLES G. E. WELBY

———◆———

A NEW SOCIAL QUESTION

24 April 1915

Sir,—It is time that a little common sense was brought to bear upon what is getting to be known as the war baby question. I speak from the standpoint of a middle-aged married woman who has all her life been interested and often a helper in social work among young girls. The town in which I have lived for the last 20 years has 30,000 inhabitants, including about 5,000 female factory workers, and since the war began we have had many thousands of soldiers, chiefly Territorials, billeted among us. The town took kindly to its astonishingly new state of things and has treated the men very well indeed. No sooner, however, had the first excitement died down, and the fear of invasion passed, than rumours began to be heard about the bad behaviour of our girls with the men. Nothing was done, as our only large girls' club building had been taken for a billet. However, eventually it was suggested that we should follow the example of other towns and appoint women patrols to look after the streets. I was told on all sides that the state of things was terrible, that the number of "expectants" ran into hundreds, some even specified 900. This, coupled with a moving address from a lady from another town to a meeting of ladies in our town, was a little too much for some of us to believe. (I may here say that the stranger lady averred in her speech that a "level-headed" friend of her own had told her that in her particular village there was not one girl of suitable age who was not an expectant.) We therefore undertook to make inquires of every one having the knowledge and authority to answer that we could think or hear of, and two ladies went a systematic round of the doctor, Poor Law authorities, inspectors, insurance, and police, among other sources of information. I am thankful to say that the report was most satisfactory in every way. The doctor, who knows the most about the illegitimate births, said there were very few expected, under half a dozen, not more than generally occur, unhappily, in the town in the time, and nothing to do with the military.

Now I believe that if people would look these scandals in the face, and insist upon authentication before they believed and passed them on, sometimes in the form of letters to the Press, that a great injustice would be removed from our soldier friends and our working girls.

I have no doubt whatever that other towns would be found the same if things were looked into, as, no doubt, they have been in many places. It is nothing short of wicked even to believe without strict authentication the bad stories that are circulated. At the meeting I have referred to it seemed to me that exactly the right note was struck by a factory worker who quietly said, "I am willing to do anything I can to help girls, but I will not be a patrol because I am a factory worker myself, and it is not for me to sit in judgment upon my fellow workers"; and she added, "There are several hundred in the factory where I work, but there are no cases among them such as have been mentioned."

I could multiply instances that prove things are not so bad as many seem willing to believe, but I have already taken up too much space.

I remain, Sir, &c.
E. M. Y.

LOSS OF KIT

6 May 1915

Sir,—I am writing to ask you to help all wounded and sick officers and men, by bringing to notice the loss to which they are put on returning from the front. Nearly every wounded officer I met while on the journey to England made the complaint that they had lost all their personal belongings, haversack field glasses, revolver, belt, &c. The loss to which I refer takes place in the "field ambulances" and in the "clearing hospitals," not in the field. I give you my own experience. I reached the "field ambulance" one afternoon with all my belongings strapped on my person; they were taken off me and laid at my side on the straw; that evening, when I was removed on a stretcher, I asked that these things might be placed under my head on the stretcher, but was told that it was against the order. I refused to be moved until the medical officer in charge of the "field ambulance" allowed me to have my things; permission was then given and my things reached the "clearing hospital" with me. I lay on the floor of a room that night with my equipment beside me. The following morning, on being removed on a stretcher to the train, I asked to take the equipment with me, but was again informed that I could not have it, and that it would be sent after me. As most wounded officers of my regiment have written afterwards to say they have lost all their belongings in hospitals on the way to the base, I would not agree to this, and had an extremely heated argument with the R.A.M.C. captain on the subject; he eventually let me have the things. As I had all the cash I possessed in my haversack, I naturally wished to keep it with me. In the train all the wounded near me were complaining that they had lost everything. The officer next me in the ambulance train, in France, said he had been wounded at Ypres in November and had lost literally everything he had; he was again wounded last month after having been at the front only a week, and lost all his things for the second time. With his previous experience he tried to keep his things, and insist on taking them with him, but was not allowed to; he said he was so weak from the loss of blood that he could not argue the point. Field glasses, revolvers, &c., cost a certain amount to replace, and it is a scandal that we should be put to the unnecessary expense of buying them again.

No doubt, an order has been issued that nothing heavy is to be carried on the stretcher, but the above-mentioned articles are a part of one's personal equipment, and as they must in all cases have been carried on the stretcher (sometimes for long distances) in the field before they reach the field ambulance at all, it is absurd that this procedure cannot be continued on leaving the hospital, where the stretcher is usually only carried a few paces.

I am informed that in the town where the "clearing hospital" is to which I was taken there is a shop where second-hand field glasses can be bought, supposed to be the property of wounded officers! In view of the appeal made by Lady Roberts for field glasses to be lent to the troops, it is an abuse that they should be purloined in this fashion. I do not presume to say who disposes of these things to the shop, I do not entirely blame the orderlies, the chief fault lies in the order which prevents the personal equipment being carried on the stretcher. Perhaps if this state of affairs is brought to the notice of the public something may be done to rectify it.

This is my personal experience as an officer; the men may also have money or other effects that they are loth to part with; they are exposed to the same treatment.

The "field ambulance" is not a vehicle, as might be supposed, but a place, usually a house, that is being used as a temporary hospital.

AN OFFICER

LOST KIT

28 May 1915

SIR,—MORE THAN ONCE you have drawn attention to the robberies committed on wounded officers by the orderlies who have dealt with the wounded. Usually these cases are connected with the transit of the wounded from the field of action. There has come to my knowledge the case of an officer in a Highland regiment, severely wounded at Ypres, and who arrived lately at Charing Cross, and now lies in a London hospital. Through all his journey he managed to retain his revolver and a flask given him by a relative. It was a stretcher case, and the officer became slightly unconscious on reaching Charing Cross. In that interval he found he had been robbed at the station of these two articles of his equipment which he had managed to retain till close to the hospital, where he will have to lie for many months. The fact that the orderlies commit these robberies again and again, and that the shops of certain towns in France are full of "secondhand" glasses and other effects taken from officers, is a matter of common notoriety. Is there no possibility of some discipline being exercised in this matter, or if it is part of a system to permit this form of perquisite, that the War Office should amply, and above all rapidly, compensate the officer, who is probably not so rich as not to feel the loss in a pecuniary as well as a personal manner?

Yours faithfully,
FRANCES BALFOUR

SIR,—IN *THE TIMES* OF May 28 you published a letter signed by Lady Frances Balfour, charging the orderlies who were responsible for removing "an officer" in a "Highland Regiment, severely wounded at Ypres, and who arrived lately at Charing-cross and now lies in a London hospital," with having stolen his revolver and flask. The charge is a disgraceful one, wantonly made. It is untrue. The officer in question, Second Lieutenant C. Warr, of the Argyll and Sutherland Highlanders (T.F.), was removed from Charing-cross on Monday, May 17, by the ambulance column attached to the London district to St. Thomas's Hospital. The revolver and flask referred to were, in accordance with practice, handed to the orderlies in charge of the luggage van, and a voucher therefor was properly made out in the delivery book. The revolver and flask were delivered at St. Thomas's Hospital within a few hours and the receipt therefor duly signed by the hospital authorities. The revolver and flask were then placed with Second Lieutenant Warr's Burberry coat, all tied, together, in the hospital kit room, duly labelled. They were quite safe there as late as June 3. The wicked accusation so lightly made and so unfounded has caused the greatest pain to those concerned. I desire to add that this organization is a voluntary one, recognized by the War Office, and has removed upwards of 22,000 cases from the stations to the hospitals.

Yours faithfully,
L. W. DENT, in Charge of the Ambulance Column attached to the
London District

SIR,—ON MAY 28 LAST you published a letter of mine referring to the losses sustained by wounded officers on removal from the field of action, and giving details of an instance where a similar loss had, apparently, been sustained by an officer between Charing Cross and the hospital in London to which he was being removed. The removal of the wounded is, I understand, entrusted to the Ambulance Column attached to the London District, a voluntary association. Colonel Giles, the Commandant of the Corps, at once gave me every facility to investigate the case, with the result, I am glad to say, that it has been conclusively established that the officer in question had not sustained any loss and that his kit had been safely delivered at the hospital shortly after he arrived there, and has ever since remained there. I am told that the Ambulance Column for the London District is composed of gentlemen of position and standing, who since the war have voluntarily given their services to the care of our wounded, and

I regret very much the pain that my accusation must have caused, and as in all fairness your readers should know that the charge made against the Corps was mistaken, and that there was no foundation for any imputation upon it, I hope that you will see your way to allow this letter of withdrawal and apology the same publicity in your paper as you were good enough to accord to my original letter.

Yours faithfully,
FRANCES BALFOUR

———◆———

WHAT GAS MEANS

A VISIT TO A FRENCH HOSPITAL

7 May 1915

We have received from a correspondent, whose authority is beyond question, the following grim account of a visit to the victims of "gassing."

Our correspondent complains that the whole truth about this diabolical form of torture is not sufficiently realized by the world. The publication of his letter should remove any doubts on the subject.

Yesterday and the day before I went with — to see some of the men in hospital at — who were "gassed" yesterday and the day before on Hill 60. The whole of England and the civilized world ought to have the truth fully brought before them in vivid detail, and not wrapped up as at present.

When we got to the hospital we had no difficulty in finding out in which ward the men were, as the noise of the poor devils trying to get breath was sufficient to direct us. We were met by a doctor belonging to our division, who took us into the ward. There were about 20 of the worst cases in the ward, on mattresses, all more or less in a sitting position, propped up against the walls.

Their faces, arms, hands were of a shiny grey-black colour, with mouths open and lead-glazed eyes, all swaying slightly backwards and forwards trying to get breath. It was a most appalling sight, all these poor black faces, struggling, struggling for life, what with the groaning and noise of the effort for breath. Colonel — who, as every one knows, has had as wide an experience as anyone all over the savage parts of Africa, told me to-day that he never felt so sick as he did after the scene in these cases.

There is practically nothing to be done for them, except to give them salt and water to try to make them sick.

The effect the gas has is to fill the lungs with a watery, frothy matter, which gradually increases and rises till it fills up the whole lungs and comes up to the mouth; then they die; it is suffocation; slow drowning, taking in some cases one or two days.

We have lost hundreds of men who died in the trenches, and over half the men who reached hospital have died. Eight died last night out of the 20 I saw, and most of the others I saw *will* die; while those who get over the gas invariably develop acute pneumonia. It is without doubt the most awful form of scientific torture. Not one of the men I saw in hospital had a scratch or wound.

The nurses and doctors were all working their utmost against this terror; but one could see from the tension of their nerves that it was like fighting a hidden danger which was over-taking every one.

A German prisoner was caught with a respirator in his pocket; the pad was analysed and found to contain hypo-sulphite of soda with 1 per cent. of some other substance.

The gas is in a cylinder, from which when they send it out it is propelled a distance of 100 yards; it there spreads.

Please make a point of publishing this in every paper in England. English people, men and women, ought to know exactly what is going on, also members of both Houses. The people of England can't know. The Germans have given out that it is a rapid, painless death. The liars! No torture could be worse than to give them a dose of their own gas. The gas, I am told, is chlorine, and probably some other gas in the shells they burst. They think ammonia kills it.

The Germans had used banned chlorine gas for the first time on April 22 (against French and Canadian troops). The Allies soon followed suit.

POISON GAS

WHY RETALIATION IS NECESSARY

11 May 1915

SIR,—I HAVE JUST returned from the war zone in France, where I have had the opportunity of talking to those in high command, to medical officers, and to others at the front. I have also seen men brought down to the clearing station suffering from excruciating tortures and distress caused by the devilish gas launched against our forces by the barbarous and inhuman German scientists, the precise nature of which is not at present known for certain, the various exhalations apparently differing somewhat in character, though chlorine gas undoubtedly enters largely into its composition. People safely at home in England have so far both failed to realize the deadly nature of this gas and its soul-destroying properties, and our soldiers have no means of defence and are utterly powerless against it; but, notwithstanding the apathy of ignorance apparent in this country, those at the front are talking of little else than this mode of warfare inaugurated by the Germans, probably the most devilish ever invented by human ingenuity. No troops have proved themselves braver than the Canadians, the tale of whose prowess will be handed down among the deeds that saved the Empire for generations to come, though they would be the first to acknowledge that their bravery and patriotism was equally shared by the British regiments who stood by them shoulder to shoulder; but I know that the feeling of these brave men is that, while they are ready to make any sacrifice and take any personal risk for the good of the Empire, they cannot uselessly stand still to be overwhelmed and tortured by this poisonous gas, against which they have no efficient weapon of offence or defence. Up to the date of their using this gas the British Army looked upon the Germans with a good-natured tolerance; but their latest methods of warfare have converted this feeling into one of intense hatred, and I would not give much for the life of a German who comes within reach of a British or Canadian bayonet.

In this intensely critical situation it is up to the people of this country to use their utmost endeavour to immediately put means of protection and weapons of offence into the hands of our brave soldiers. I note with satisfaction that steps are being taken to provide a means of defence which has so far met with some measure of success; but we must hope that, difficult as the problem is, our scientists may be able to very shortly provide a complete means of protection from the poisonous miasma. Next, it is up against us in loyalty to our brave defenders, in spite of Hague Conventions, which the Germans entirely ignore, to place at the earliest possible moment in their hands a "counter-gas" that may teach the Germans a lesson. In the preparation of such a weapon, however, there is no call to imitate the barbarous cruelty of the Germans, for a gas might be prepared that would produce temporary unconsciousness without pain, and at the same time cause no ultimately injurious effect. No humanitarian could object to this, and everybody would be grateful except those pro-Germans of whom there are still for too many at large in this country.

It is most distasteful to me to appear to write in a spirit of exaggeration or of an alarmist, but I have seen sights that arouse one's deepest indignation, and I cannot help thinking of 400 brave Canadians brought to a terrible death, before their comrades' eyes, without being able to retaliate, and I cannot forget the purple flush that I saw on the faces of dying heroes, many of them splendid-looking men and unwounded, but to whom the Angel of Death was appearing in most dreadful form. The time has come when we must stifle sentiment, and be prepared in every case to meet force by force, and strategy by strategy, if we hope to eventually come out victors in the colossal struggle on which depends our very existence as a nation.

I am, Sir, your obedient servant,
ARMSTRONG

WHERE PROTEST IS DUE

11 May 1915

SIR,—THE SINKING OF the Lusitania, involving the cruel murder of hundreds of helpless and innocent non-combatants, affords those Germans who are naturalized British citizens holding prominent positions in this country an opportunity of performing an act which, even in the opinion of many who bear them no particular ill-will, is long overdue. We are in the tenth month of a war which has from the beginning been carried on by Germany with almost unspeakable treachery and vileness; but up to the present time not a single one of the distinguished Germans in our midst has thought fit to make a public avowal of his disagreement with the deliberate policy of barbarism pursued by the German Powers or to utter a word of indignation and disclaimer. Surely the moment has arrived when these gentlemen, in their own interests, if for no higher reason, should break silence and individually or collectively raise their voices against the infamous deeds which are being perpetrated by Germany. I venture to suggest that they might with propriety band together and present a loyal address to the King embracing an expression of their detestation of Germany's methods of warfare; but perhaps this may be better left to their own discretion and good feeling. What I would emphasize, however, is that continued silence on their part lays them open to the supposition that, thinking that the fate of England is hanging in the balance, they are—to use the common phrase—sitting on the gate. A word of warning, therefore, is neither gratuitous nor unfriendly. The temper of this country, slow to rouse, is becoming an ugly one. The gate may fall from its hinges.

Your obedient servant,
ARTHUR PINERO

The British liner *Lusitania* had been sunk on May 7 off the coast of Ireland by a U-boat. Among the 1,200 who died were 128 neutral Americans. Despite official denials, the vessel had been carrying munitions.

MOBILIZE THE NATION

25 May 1915

HOW TO GET MEN AND SHELLS

SIR,—I HAVE JUST returned from the front, where I have spent the last month in giving what help I could to our chaplains and troops in Northern France and Flanders. It was the most glorious month I have ever spent, and I want, if I can, to pass on to others a few of the impressions which were burnt into my soul during that time—for the days are critical.

I had never doubted that the spirit of our troops was as fine as men told us it was, but I never realized how fine it was until I had lived in it and with it. It beggars description; it is amazing. It is all the more so when you realize, as you do when you are up at the front, that this spirit is there in spite of the fact that the men who show it feel it in their bones that somehow the nation is not backing them as the nation could and should. That, I am convinced, is the feeling right through the Army in France and Flanders; and the reason for it is not far to seek.

AT THE FRONT

After fighting desperately day and night for days and weeks, with frightful losses, the men who are left are dog tired and need a rest. When they are "pulled out" to get this rest, and after three days are sent back into the firing line again, the only conclusion they can draw is that there are not enough troops available to take their places. When battalion after battalion of infantry—and, as was recently the case in the Ypres salient, regiment after regiment of cavalry, too—have to sit in trenches day after day and night after night, being pounded by high explosives from enemy guns, with no guns behind them capable of keeping down the enemy's fire, then the conclusion they draw is obvious—namely, that the nation has failed to provide sufficient guns of ammunition to meet those of the enemy. When night after night and day after day, the men in the trenches know that for every one hand grenade or rifle grenade or trench mortar bomb which they throw at the enemy they will get back in answer anything from five to 10, then the conclusion they draw is also obvious—namely, that the nation does not somehow realize the situation, or, if it does, has not made it its business to supply what is necessary. Man for man they know that they have nothing to fear either from German infantry or cavalry; they have proved it again and again. But they know also that it is little short of murder for a nation to ask men, however full of the right spirit, to face an enemy amply equipped with big guns and the right kind of ammunition, unless they are at last equipped with equally effective munitions of war.

There can be only one impression left on the minds of men in such a case, and that is, that somehow or other the nation does not know the truth, does not understand, and is not backing them, for, knowing the old country as they do, they have no doubt that if Germany can produce these things we can, if we will. And yet, in spite of it all, they carry on, they keep cheery, they do their best, they die gaily. The fact is that as a nation we are just gambling on this spirit. We know it to be there; we recognize it as the finest thing in the world; we believe it is unconquerable, whatever happens. So it is; but it will not win the war alone. It is this spirit, backed by guns and high explosives—legitimate munitions of war—which is going to smash this enemy of ours, and nothing else. Let no one think that we are going to do it by descending to the level of the German Imperial Staff and using any sort of gas. This talk of reprisals by gas (perhaps next we shall near of reprisals by poisoning water supplies!) is simply another method of chloroforming the nation and blinding its eyes to the real issue— the adequate supply of big guns and high explosive shells and other legitimate munitions of war.

THE SOLDIER'S QUESTION

And these munitions of war have to be made, not by the men at the front who are doing the fighting, but here in the British Isles. The men at the front know this; they know that the making of munitions of war, the making of clothes and equipment, the provision of food and of the thousand and one other things necessary to an army in the field—all these are just as much an integral part of the business as theirs is. And then they ask (I have heard them myself— wounded men in hospitals and whole men on the field), "Why should I, who enlisted under a voluntary system, because my part of the job is to loose of the ammunition my next-door neighbour at home has made, be compelled to do so under the extreme penalty of death for disobedience to orders or desertion from my job, while my neighbour at home is allowed to chuck his job with impunity whenever he wants to? Why should I be punished for refusing to go into the trenches because my pay is not raised a penny an hour, and the other fellow be allowed to strike and then be cajoled into going back to work by the special visit of a Cabinet Minister and the promise of extra pay? Why should I have to stick it out, night after night and day after day, in water and mud up to my knees, when the other fellow (who is only doing another part of the same job) can make his own conditions as to hours of work?"

Why, indeed? Why should any one of us who claims citizenship in the Empire, when the Empire is fighting for its very existence, be free to do what we like at such a time? That is the question I asked myself as I came away one evening from visiting a private soldier who had fought through the first three or four months of the war and had then deserted (his excuse was drink) and was to be shot, and was shot, and rightly too, at 5.30 the next morning. Why, indeed? That is what the men at the front are asking.

The news which they will have read these last few days will have put fresh heart into them all. For nine solid months they have been wondering why on earth the nation has not done what it has at last been decided to do—viz., to form a National Government. And now what? Is this National Government going to be the real thing or not? Is it going to be merely a combination of representatives of existing political parties on some sort of basis of numbers in the House of Commons? Is the cloven hoof of party politics still going to be found in it, or is it going to be a Government composed of the very best men whom the nation can produce, irrespective altogether of politics and parties? Is it still going to keep half an eye on votes, or is it going to get on with the one and only thing which matters now—the smashing of the enemy in the shortest time possible, for that is the object of war? Is this new Government going to tackle this business on the same ridiculous principles of voluntary service as heretofore, or in the only way in which it can be tackled with any certain hope of ultimate success? Is it going to tell the nation at once that we can't win this war, and shall uselessly sacrifice thousands of lives, unless the Government has the power given to it to call upon the services of every single man, woman, and child, if need be, for whatever each individual is most capable of doing directly or indirectly for the accomplishment of the one object before us—the smashing of the enemy? The men at the front are waiting for the answer, and so are thousands of men and women here at home.

THE ONLY WAY

I say "the only way," and for the following reasons:—

1. If the men at the front know that they have got the nation at their back, there need be no fear lest they will ever lose one iota of the glorious spirit which, in spite of lack of guns, has so far kept the enemy from our gate. They will wait, and wait gladly, for what they so sorely need, if only they know that at last this business is being taken seriously in hand.

2. It is the only way, for only so can our Commanders-in-Chief at sea and in the field lay their plans of campaign with any certainty that they will be able to carry them out. As it is now, it is simply a matter of fighting as best you can from hand to mouth. When the Government knows that they can call on all the resources of men and material, then, and then only, can they lay their plans for certain production at definite times. Only so can they be able to tell the Commanders-in-Chief what they can expect, and when.

3. It is the only way, because it is the height of impudent folly to imagine that we are as a nation so miraculously endowed by the Almighty that we, and we alone of all nations in the world, can prosecute such a war as we are engaged

in to a successful issue without calling on the whole resources of the nation. At present we are treating it as a sort of "side show" to the real business of life, which must be kept going "as usual." Besides, it is not playing the game by our Allies. They are keeping nothing back; we are.

4. It is the only way, because only so will the nation get the greatest efficiency out of its individual members. As it is, many men are now serving at the front who ought to be serving at home, and *vice versa*. The present method of "go or not as you please" is utterly haphazard and unbusinesslike, and therefore hopelessly inadequate.

5. It is the only way, because an essential factor in the successful prosecution of the war is that the right spirit should animate not only the men at the front, but the nation at their back. It is only the right spirit which will be able to bear the strain and see this thing through to a finish.

To-day the right spirit is lacking because the conscience of the nation is uneasy. As individuals we do not know whether we are doing the right thing or not—whether we should go on with our ordinary work or offer to go and fight. We are afraid of indulging in wholly innocent amusement. We are afraid even of having a really healthy laugh—somehow we feel it would not be right. People are getting gloomy and depressed, not because they have any fear as to the ultimate end of the war (they do not know enough about the real situation for that), not because they are not ready to face, and face gallantly, the sacrifices which war has laid upon them to make, but because their consciences are not at rest. You cannot have the right spirit if your conscience is uneasy.

A NATION UNDER ORDERS

That is why the men at the front have the right spirit. They are so gloriously cheery because their consciences are at rest. They know they have done and are doing the right thing. They have made the great surrender. They have burnt their boats behind them and put themselves under orders. Nothing matters except to "do their bit" when they are told to. When they are not wanted they have no silly scruples about enjoying themselves, the best they can. When the whole nation knows itself to be under orders, and knows that it is doing the right thing, we shall see the same spirit of gay surrender at home; and this spirit is essential. All we want is a lead, and a strong and fearless lead.

But will the nation stand it? Politics again! Well, if it won't, it will have to stand something infinitely more distasteful before very long. But of course the nation will stand it. The nation will welcome it with both hands, once it is given a lead, once all are treated alike, once it is told the truth—not half-truths, which are worse than lies, but the real truth—that though we are holding the enemy through the indomitable spirit and the reckless self-sacrifice of our troops, we cannot and never shall be able to crush them until we provide our fighting men with a preponderance of munitions of war over and above the apparently ample and undiminished supply of the enemy. Advancing a few yards, or retiring a few miles, or merely holding the enemy—this is not going to win the war. It may produce a peace in the long run; but it will be a peace made in Germany and not of British manufacture.

The nation will welcome national service because the temper of the nation is different from what it was. Recent events have clearly shown, even to the most phlegmatic, that we are in a perfectly real sense up against the Devil incarnate. What else is it when we are fighting against an enemy who will stop at nothing, however mean and cruel and disgusting—an enemy who will use gas, sink Lusitanias, put arsenic in running streams, and sow disease? Mere abuse won't tame this Devil or drive him out, but a nation serving will. National Service will be welcomed once the nation learns the truth that thousands of the finest and most gallant lives that the Empire has ever produced are being thrown away because the nation has not yet realized that it is at war.

There is only one way to make the nation realize this fact, and that is by bringing every member of it under the direct orders of the State for one purpose, and one purpose only. Nothing else matters to-day.

Yours faithfully,
MICHAEL FURSE, Bishop of Pretoria

On the day that Furse's letter was published, Asquith addressed concerns about the progress of the war by reconstituting his government as a coalition, with Lloyd George at the head of a new Ministry of Munitions.

BATTLE SHOCK

26 May 1915

SIR,—YOUR MEDICAL Correspondent, in an article in to-day's issue, makes kindly reference to the hospital at 10, Palace-green opened for officers suffering from battle shock—due to the foresight of Dr. Maurice Wright. I should like to report progress, as the public were good enough to trust me with £10,000 to start, and run, this hospital, and many people have written since to ask me about it. The hospital, after it became known, has always been full, and so insistent has been the demand for further accommodation that we were compelled to start a second hospital. This was not easy to do in London, as the absolute essentials to successful treatment are complete quiet and isolation. The difficulty was solved by the most generous gift by Mr. R. Leicester Harmsworth, M.P., of his furnished house, Moray Lodge, Campden-hill. The conditions are ideal—a large house standing in lovely grounds of four acres or more. This has now been opened for 33 patients. More than 100 officers have passed through 10, Palace-green, and with but very few exceptions all have recovered from the effects of this shock of battle. Dr. Aldren Turner, acting for the Director-General, has completed an organization so that the officers are sent direct from the front to Palace-green, which has been very helpful towards their recovery. I have money enough to run the two hospitals for nine months more. I feel sure that the public will not allow this work to stop for want of money.

Yours truly,
KNUTSFORD

———◆———

"THE TIMES" IN THE TRENCHES

CONTENTS BILL RIDDLED WITH GERMAN BULLETS

1 June 1915

A soldier writes from "somewhere in France" under date May 25:—

Knowing that the German Press were rather dilatory with the news, we took the liberty of hanging your bill of 21st, "Italy Declares for War," over the front of our trench breastwork, where it could be read with ease by about 1,000 yards of German lines. Never did your *news* get such a *cutting up*. The board was riddled with shot, but after 24 hours it is still readable. We carried that board about seven miles to let them have the truth, and if you will let us have a good "leader" on your bill we'll be pleased to repeat the dose as it's sure to have a good effect.

A BLACKSMITH'S OFFER

5 June 1915

SIR,—I HAVE BEEN a subscriber for a daily copy of your valuable paper since the price came within the limits of a working man's weekly wage. Being blacksmith to trade, I am deeply concerned about how I can be made use of at the present time. For 20 years I was employed between two of the largest locomotive engine builders in Glasgow as angle iron smith, dome maker, flanging and piecing plates, also welding boiler barrels, and lately for a number of years I have been doing all kinds of general smith work and repairs. Although in my 50th year I am quite able for a good day's work. Surely I can be of some use in serving my country in this great national crisis. I am willing to do anything or go anywhere if only I can serve and feel that I am of use. I hope some scheme of national service will be put in operation which will include working men like myself, who would be quite able to do their bit and relieve younger men for more active service.

A WORKING BLACKSMITH

AN ILLUSTRATION

8 June 1915

SIR,—WITHIN THE LAST week the foreman on a farm adjoining mine in Perthshire, who is married and has five children, of which the eldest is eight, has been induced by the recruiting agent and the Government allowances to enlist. It is impossible to replace a man in such a responsible position under present circumstances except by bribing away another farmer's servant. On his judgment the ingathering of the crops in proper condition largely depends, as well as other work. His enlistment undoubtedly will mean a reduction in the value of the produce of the farm this year and a reduced area under cultivation next year. I ask what is the good of appeals from the Board of Agriculture to farmers to increase the area of land under cultivation if the recruiting authorities are permitted to act in this way. From a national point of view the want of organization of which this incident is an illustration is folly, and if persisted in may be properly described as madness.

Yours faithfully,
ERNEST MOON

BASIL MOON

9 June 1915

Sir,—It may interest many to know that the example of superb bravery, described in the enclosed extract in a letter in *The Times* of to-day, under the heading "An Officer's Courage," was displayed by an officer, the late Sec. Lieutenant Basil Moon (son of Mr. Ernest Moon, K.C., Counsel to the Speaker), who only joined the Army last August.

Yours truly,
ROBSON

The following is the passage to which Lord Robson refers:—

"During the attack, I am sorry to say, I lost two out of my three subalterns (the fourth has not yet returned). Poor old Roy was shot through the body after we had got about half-way, and though we quickly got his wound dressed and moved him back on a stretcher, he died in hospital the same night. Basil was simply magnificent all through; as soon as Roy (who was bomb officer) was wounded, Basil went up to the front and by his coolness and courage helped materially towards the success of the affair, and at last, when all our bombers had been killed and there was just the chance that the Germans might bomb us back again before we could block the trench, he picked up a rifle and ran along their parapet, picking off the German bombers until an exploding bomb blew the lower half of his face off. Even then he had sufficient strength left and sufficient thoughtfulness to write me a note and send it by messenger saying that he was sorry he was 'out of action.' Poor old chap, he was full of pluck right to the end."

THE MOBILIZATION OF INVENTION

11 June 1915

SIR,—WE HAVE RECONSTRUCTED our Government and it is not for an innocent Englishman outside the world of politicians to estimate the advantages and disadvantages of the rearrangement of the House of Commons. But there is a matter beyond the range of party politics which does still seem to need attention and which has been extraordinarily disregarded in all the discussion that has led to the present Coalition, and that is the very small part we are still giving the scientific man and the small respect we are showing scientific method in the conduct of this war. I submit that there is urgent need to bring imaginative enterprise and our utmost resources of scientific knowledge to the assistance of the new-born energies of the Coalition; that this is not being done and that until it is done this war is likely to drag on and be infinitely more costly and infinitely less conclusive than it could and should be.

Modern war is essentially a struggle of gear and invention. It is not war under permanent conditions. In that respect it differs completely from pre-Napoleonic wars. Each side must be perpetually producing new devices, surprising and outwitting its opponent. Since this war began the German methods of fighting have been changed again and again. They have produced novelty after novelty, and each novelty has more or less saved their men and unexpectedly destroyed ours. On our side we have so far produced hardly any novelty at all, except in the field of recruiting posters. It is high time that our rulers and our people came to recognize that the mere accumulation of great masses of young men in khaki is a mere preliminary to the prosecution of this war. These masses make the body of an army, but neither its neck, head, nor hands, nor feet. In the field of aviation, for which the English and French temperaments are far better adapted than the German, there has been no energy of organization at all. There has been great individual gallantry and a magnificent use of the sparse material available, but no great development. We have produced an insufficient number of aviators and dribbled out an inadequate supply of machines. Insufficient and inadequate, that is to say, in relation to such a war as this. We have taken no steps to produce a larger and more powerful aeroplane capable of overtaking, fighting, and destroying a Zeppelin, and we are as far as ever from making any systematic attacks in force through the air. Our utmost achievements have been made by flights of a dozen or so machines. In the matter of artillery the want of intellectual and imaginative enterprise in our directors has prevented our keeping pace with the German improvements in trench construction; our shortness of high explosives has been notorious, and it has led to the sacrifice of thousands of lives. Our Dardanelles exploit has been throughout unforeseeing and uninventive; we have produced no counterstroke to the enemy's submarine, and no efficient protection against his improved torpedoes. We have still to make an efficient use of poison gas and of armoured protection in advances against machine-guns in trench warfare. And so throughout almost the entire range of our belligerent activities we are to this day being conservative, imitative, and amateurish when victory can fall only to the most vigorous employment of the best scientific knowledge of all conceivable needs and material.

One instance of many will serve to show what I am driving at. Since this war began we have been piling up infantry recruits by the million and making strenuous efforts to equip them with rifles. In the meantime the actual experiences of the war have been fully verifying the speculations of imaginative theorists, and the Germans have been learning the lesson of their experiences. The idea that for defensive purpose one well-protected skilled man with a small machine-gun is better than a row of riflemen is a very obvious one indeed, but we have disregarded it. The Germans are giving up the crowding of men for defense purposes (though the weakness of the national quality obliges them still to mass for attacks), and they are entrusting their very small and light machine-guns in many cases to officers. They have, in fact, adopted as their 1915 model of trench defence the proper scientific thing. Against this we fire out shrapnel and hurl our infantry.

Now these inadequacies are not incurable failures. But they are likely to go on until we create some supplementary directive force, some council in which the creative factors in our national life, and particularly our scientific men and our younger scientific soldiers and sailors, have a fuller representation and a stronger influence than they have in our present Government. It is not the sort of work for which a great legal and political career fits a man. That training and experience, valuable as it is in the management of man and peoples, does indeed very largely unfit men for this incessantly inventive work. A great politician has no more special aptitude for making modern war than he has for diagnosing diseases or planning an electric railway system. It is a technical business. We want an acting sub-Government of scientific and technically competent men for this highly specialized task.

Such a sub-Government does in effect exist in Germany. It is more and more manifest that we are fighting no longer against that rhetorical system of ancient pretensions of which the Kaiser is the figure-head. In Flanders we are now up against the real strength of Germany; we are up against Westphalia and Frau Krupp's young men. Britain and France have to get their own brilliant young engineers and chemists to work against that splendid organization. Unless our politicians can add to the many debts we owe them, the crowning service of organizing science in war more thoroughly than they ever troubled to do it in peace, I do not see any very great hope of a really glorious and satisfactory triumph for us in this monstrous struggle.

Very sincerely yours,
H. G. WELLS

THE NEXT GENERATION

22 June 1915

SIR,—AS A SLUM WORKER and member of an L.C.C. Care Committee may I crave space for a few burning words? No one who has at heart the moral and physical welfare of the next generation can witness without dismay the appalling increase of "drinking" amongst the women of the poorest class. Let anyone who doubts this look at the unprecedented number of cases of women had up for drunkenness in our London Police Courts. The money which the Government is pouring out so lavishly upon soldiers' and sailors' dependents is in many instances being shockingly and shamefully wasted. There are many families who go dinnerless on Mondays, when the women draw their pay and often remain in the publichouse from 11 a.m. till late in the afternoon. A young soldier's wife who was explaining the black eye she had got the day before told me that it was not that she cared for the drink, but the "company" and the "treating." She had recently been troubled by a visit from the S.P.C.C. Another, who before her husband went away was considered a respectable woman, is now doing two months' hard labour, and I have had to help toward the support of her six little children. Scores of working men who are themselves moderate drinkers have said to me, "Why don't they close the pubs?" If the sale of drink can be limited to help on the output of munitions why not also for the moral and physical welfare of the mothers and the coming generation?

I am yours faithfully,
A SLUM PARSON

PICTURE PALACES

5 July 1915

SIR,—IF THE WAR LOAN is to have any chance with the "working class," at least in the Midlands, the compulsory closing of picture palaces will become an absolute necessity. These are probably a more serious menace to the nation now than even drink. With the opening of the National Register there need be no hardship to those employed at the picture shows. But there will be a bad shortage on 5s. vouchers so long as the money is spent every week in these places.

Believe me yours, &c.,
"BLACK COUNTRY" VICAR

7 July 1915

SIR,—IN ANSWER TO YOUR anonymous correspondent a "'Black Country' Vicar" I beg to forward you a few facts concerning the cinema and the war. We have received the personal thanks of his Royal Highness the Prince of Wales for the assistance we have rendered the National Relief Fund. We have proved a rich ground for recruiting, and with our "war topicals" have stimulated many a dull imagination; the Belgian Red Cross Society use a film entitled "War is Hell" to assist in the appeals they make in cinemas. One firm (Messrs. Walturdaw, Limited) have prepared a film at a cost of several hundred pounds to stimulate recruiting, and this they are lending free and also supplying 1,000 sheets of pictorial printing to advertise it, the only condition being that a recruiting sergeant is permitted to address the audience. The Ministry of Munitions has now approached the Exhibitors' Association and asked its help to advertise the call for workers to enrol for the production of munitions of war. In conclusion, Sir, I would suggest that money might be saved by abolishing the collection box.

Faithfully yours,
H. W. LEDGER, Royal Picture House, Egremont, Cheshire

THE WOUNDED FROM THE DARDANELLES

9 July 1915

SIR,—I NOTICE THAT questions have been asked in the House as to the adequacy of the medical arrangements in connexion with the British Forces at the Dardanelles. I have recently visited—in company with the respective officers in charge and with the concurrence of the general officers commanding and directors of medical services—the military hospitals at Malta, Cairo, Alexandria, Port Said, and Mudros. I have been given the opportunity of seeing, in the freest possible manner, all the arrangements made in the Mediterranean area for the reception of the sick and wounded from the Dardanelles.

I can say, without hesitation, that these arrangements are adequate. The supply of beds is adequate, and there is still a large number of beds unoccupied. There are plenty of doctors, nurses, and orderlies. There are at the chief centres a number of operating surgeons of the highest class, drawn from the leading hospitals of England and Australia. Eminent consulting surgeons, whose names are famous throughout the medical world, are stationed in those districts where the greater numbers of wounded are collected. The Royal Army Medical Corps has maintained the high reputation it has earned during this campaign, while of the vast Colonial Medical Corps I can use no stronger terms of praise than by saying that the Australian Army doctor has done as well as has his comrade in the fighting line. The work of the Australian Red Cross Society has been simply magnificent.

The number of casualties has been—as the Press has announced—very great, heavier, I imagine, than was ever anticipated. Owing to the sudden arrival of large convoys of wounded there have been periods of severe pressure and of urgent stress, just as there were during the early days of the campaign in France. These dire emergencies have been met heroically and with no little success, especially when it is remembered that the distances are great, that communications are not too easy, and that the difficulties in connexion with transport have been often unsurmountable.

Yours faithfully,
FREDERICK TREVES

THE WOMEN OF FRANCE

12 July 1915

SIR,—HAVING JUST RETURNED from France, where I had the honour of spending half an hour alone with General Joffre, the good fortune of paying a visit to Reims, and the inspection of a large workshop for the making of shells, I have brought back one outstanding impression—namely, the spirit which obtains amongst the women of France, and the use to which it is being put in all directions. The burning patriotism and the willingness to work in every home, from the highest to the lowest, is an inspiration, and the women over the water have sworn to take their part in expelling the Bosch from their country. For the exceptions among their mankind who, on whatever pretext, refuse to offer their lives, they have, and are not ashamed to manifest, a withering contempt.

Apart from statistics, which is the province of experts, the employment of women in the manufacture of munitions and in a thousand ways liberating men to serve at the front affords a practical sermon, the neglect of which on our part at this crisis amounts to madness. There is in France a wave of female enthusiasm and of consecrated passion which the State recognizes as well-nigh its chief asset in the termination of the war. At a single word of pessimism or murmuring, women are ready not only to take umbrage, but to denounce the offender as a traitor to the public weal. Their sacrifice and their courage are beyond all praise, and they constitute a driving force which sends men to the trenches with a song on their lips and a smile on their faces *pour la Patrie*. They are also prepared, without the smallest self-consciousness or snobbery, to tuck up their sleeves, to economize, and to labour without complaint, exhibiting as to the manner born a democratic zeal which rises far beyond politics, and is bound to prove irresistible. All this they are ready to do *sans bénéfice*, though if they earn in the process, they are grateful and save every penny for the conduct of the war.

What I desire to impress on the authorities is that the moment has come when women not only should, but must, have their chance of service, and that of national prejudice or of selfishness on the part of trade unions and employers there must be an immediate end if victory is to be assured. Neither money nor party should stand in the way, and I am absolutely convinced that the hearts of Englishwomen are panting to express their practical devotion precisely as much as those of their French sisters. No finer message could be sent to our Allies than that of a mighty procession of women on Saturday next, discarding all caste and class, banishing previous conceptions of false modesty, and uniting without one dissentient voice in a defiant claim to take their part in the present struggle for life and honour. You will then find that recruiting goes up by leaps and bounds, that the question of shortage of labour will be enormously solved, and, above all, that there will be lit throughout the land a flame which will burn up every form of self-interest, provided that it be not only used but commanded by those to whom are entrusted the destinies of the realm.

When General Joffre suggested to me that it must be difficult for us actually to feel the war so long as our country was free of invasion, I knew in my heart that it could be brought home mainly by the imagination of women. Later, when at the doors of the Cathedral of Reims, I uncovered before the statue of Jeanne d'Arc, which has up till now escaped every shell as by a miracle, I remarked to a French soldier who had driven me through the lines, "Rest assured history will repeat itself, and not for the first time, the cause of freedom and religion will owe its salvation to the sex intended by Heaven to constitute the soul of humanity."

HUGH B. CHAPMAN

Joffre was the Commander-in-Chief of the French forces.

THE COMMON CAUSE

12 July 1915

SIR,—THE VICTORY WON for Britain by a great Boer General brings to memory the words of a Canadian officer, spoken when the first Canadian contingent passed home through London at the time of the Boer War. This officer, French of blood and speech, spoke with burning love of that England which had subjugated his Canadian forefathers; he told of the hour when officers and troopers together had stood before Windsor Castle and looked through tears upon her—a women frail and aged, but Victoria their Queen—who was to every man the symbol of that England he had been ready to die for; and he ended by saying:—"I tell you, in 10 years from now, the Boers will volunteer to fight for Great Britain in the same spirit as we are fighting for her to-day." Perhaps these prophetic words of tribute to England's genius for Empire, so strangely in contrast with the hatred called forth by Prussia in the breasts of French, Polish, and Danish subjects, lose none of their point because they are repeated by the daughter of a Dutchman who became an ardent Englishman and was given burial in St. Paul's.

I remain, Sir, faithfully yours,
LAURENCE ALMA TADEMA

The victory referred to was gained in Namibia by Jan Smuts, later prime minister of South Africa.

SEVEN WEEKS' HOLIDAY

22 July 1915

SIR,—IN YOUR EXCELLENT leading article on "The Example of Parliament" in to-day's issue you ask the question, How will Mr. Asquith's announcement of a six weeks' holiday to Parliament strike the soldiers in the fighting line? I have recently returned from an eight days' visit to Rouen, where I met in the Base Camp a number of members of the oldest regiment in the City of London, who have now been for over 10 months fighting in Belgium without having had any home leave at all. These men had just recovered from slight wounds received in the fighting in front of Ypres, and were about to rejoin their battalion. Not one of them complained of his treatment, yet who could blame them if their answer to the question you put was somewhat wanting in that respect for our rulers which all good soldiers and citizens alike wish to retain.

I am, Sir, your obedient servant,
FATHER OF TWO SOLDIERS

EXPERIMENTS IN ARMOUR

22 July 1915

SIR,—YOUR RECENT ARTICLES regarding the use of armour for protecting soldiers are of interest to me, as I have for some months been experimenting on steel corselets or cuirasses and helmets for our men.

The problems of protecting the body and the head are distinct. I have been unable to find a steel of such strength as to stop a bullet fired at moderate range, which would not prove too heavy for a soldier to wear for any length of time, and even if it were obtainable, the force of the impact of the bullet would appear to be so great as to knock the man down, certainly to give him concussion, and probably to break his neck. The alternative, therefore, remained of providing a corselet which, while unable to stop bullets at moderate range, would be sufficiently strong to stop shrapnel and spent bullets, and at the same time light enough to wear. This can be done, but experiments have shown that, while affording protection against shrapnel, the direct bullet at moderate range, which under other circumstances might pass completely through the body with little injury, would carry fragments of the plate into the body and probably cause a mortal wound. Thus, while there would be a gain in the prevention of wounds from shrapnel and spent bullets, there would be an equivalent loss in the increase in serious wounds from bullets fired at close or moderate range.

As regards steel helmets, the case is different, as—although a few exceptions have been reported—a bullet which pierces the head will probably prove fatal. If, therefore, one can give protection against shrapnel and spent bullets, while at the same time there is no corresponding increase of mortal wounds through the steel being carried into the head, there is here an undoubted opportunity for invention. This opportunity is also the greater because nothing could have been devised more unsuitable for active service than the present military cap, which makes the wearer easily discernible owing to its straight lines, which gives little ventilation, and which affords no protection against sun or rain. A form of headgear which can remedy all these defects, and at the same time supply a steel protection sufficient to stop shrapnel, while light enough for comfortable wear, is the object at which I have aimed, not altogether, as I believe, without success. Beyond this, however, the matter rests with others.

Yours, &c.,
EDWARD R. DAVSON

AT NOON TO-DAY

4 August 1915

SIR,—THE HEARTS OF millions of the King's subjects will go out to him in loyalty and devotion during the hour of solemn intercession at St. Paul's on Wednesday. We are not a demonstrative people, but is it not possible for once, upon an occasion so unique and momentous, to cast aside our reserve? I venture to suggest that the hundreds of thousands of people who will be attracted to the Royal route not by curiosity, but by a compelling desire to show their profound attachment to their Majesties in this hour of national and Imperial crisis, should after the service march back to the Palace and there join, in the name of the entire nation, in singing the National Anthem. It would be an impressive token, good for Germany to know, of the nation's absolute accord and of its unswerving devotion to the King as the interpreter of its mind and will in this Holy War. At the time of the intercession service tens of thousands of Civil Servants, like myself, will be engaged in our duties in numberless Government offices in London. Might not we, too, set the conventions at defiance and at the noon hour pour out of our rooms into corridor and landing and "join the choir invisible" of St. Paul's in a verse of "God save our gracious King"? Why should not 12 o'clock on Wednesday be "National Anthem hour" all over the United Kingdom—in public office and home, in factory and workshop, in church and school, aye, and market-place? Such a combined outpouring of the nation's spirit would powerfully cheer the King and Queen in this the gravest crisis in their reign, and by it the nation would do justice to its feelings of loyalty and patriotism.

Yours faithfully,
PRO REGE ET PATRIA

"ON LEAVE AND TIRED"

7 August 1915

SIR,—I SHOULD LIKE TO offer a suggestion which I think will appeal to many of your readers who own motor-cars. A large number of men on leave from the front arrive home on short leave by trains arriving in London very early in the morning (several hours before trams and omnibuses are running), and consequently these men, loaded with their heavy kit, have frequently to walk several miles to their home or at the best a few miles to a London station from whence they proceed to their destination. It would be a kindness, very much appreciated, if owners of motor-cars would meet these trains and convey these weary heroes to the nearest point towards their destination.

Yours obediently,
EBER

SOME WEDDINGS AT ST. GEORGE'S

7 August 1915

SIR,—TO AN OLD CURATE on active service at St. George's, Hanover-square, over a quarter of a century ago your article on Mr. Charles Maisey, the parish clerk, was extremely interesting.

In that retrospect much stress is laid upon the grand functions at St. George's, but no hint is given of the tragic seamy side of life which the church attracted 30 years ago, and of which we curates were the witnesses. The rector, then a canon of Windsor, only officiated if requested. We took the ceremonies, he the fees. A certain proportion I might classify under three heads—(a) tragic; (b) sordid; (c) humorous.

The morning after my first wedding I was interviewed by a detective, who was anxious to know if I thought the bridegroom mad! "No more mad than other bridegrooms," I replied. The unfortunate man had shot himself after the ceremony. Letters from interested relatives followed, intimating that it would be greatly to my benefit if I could assert that the bridegroom looked mad. I could only repeat my answer to the detective. Here was a tragedy in a sordid setting, of which I had only touched the fringe.

One cold winter's morning an old man of 70 years sat warming his wrinkled hands at the vestry fire while close by stood a beautiful girl-bride of some 18 summers in the care of her mother. Presently the old man's relatives enter and object to his marriage (by licence) with the young bride. In the inner vestry the question is put—on what grounds? Answer—Because it is possible, and very probable, that the fair young girl is the old man's daughter! Doctors Commons had to decide, but here is a good example of the seamy, shady side of life and its unions of which St. George's a quarter of a century ago saw so much.

Finally—my last example—the humorous. A wedding by licence at 2.30 p.m., a well-known man in the district to one of the most beautiful widowed peeresses of the day. At the appointed time the organ was pealing forth appropriate music, a small crowd hung about the doors, for the vergers had whispered the news, reporters were on the *qui vive* and the well-groomed bridegroom was alert and expectant. Alas! the clock struck 3, and no bride. Sympathy profound went forth to the depressed and broken bridegroom. Two mornings later the same man was in waiting to be married before London was up at 9 a.m. Until 10 a.m. I, the long-suffering curate, waited, and then, offering my sympathy to the utterly dejected bridegroom, I departed. I have long since withdrawn that misplaced sympathy, because the lady had never given her consent!

Do you wonder that we curates objected to the extension of the marriage hour to 3 p.m. without remuneration? Yet without a whimper we endured the imposition of three solid hours of marriage ceremonies into our work and our Saturday half-holiday. What would the trades unions have said and done?

Yours faithfully,
CHARLES KENT

HUNS AND SARACENS

13 August 1915

SIR,—IN *THE TIMES* OF the 2nd inst., which has reached me to-day, your Correspondent in New York quotes an article in the *New York Times* in which the following passage occurs:

"A thousand years from now the awful story of violated Belgium will be read by schoolchildren . . . as children read to-day of the Hun and the Saracen."

Permit me to say that to compare the German soldier of to-day with the Saracen is to do the Saracen a very grave injustice. The armies of Mahomet did not make war on women and children nor destroy defenceless cities. On the contrary, the famous "Law" of Ali, nephew and son-in-law of the Prophet, expressly forbids these iniquities, and Abu Bekr, successor of Ali in the Khalifate, thus summed up its chief tenets in an address to his troops which might serve as a model to any general to-day:—

"If God gives you the victory do not stain your swords with the blood of those who submit, nor with that of children, women, or weak old men. When marching through the enemy's country do not cut down trees, nor destroy his palms and fruit-trees, nor ravage nor burn his dwellings, but of them and of his cattle take only what you may require. Destroy nothing without necessity; occupy the cities and fortresses, and only destroy those of them which may give shelter to your adversaries. Be merciful to the vanquished and humiliated, and God will be merciful to you. . . . Let there be no falseness nor double dealing in your treaties and dealings with the enemy, but always be faithful, loyal, and honourable, and keep your word and your promise. Do not disturb the peace of monks or of hermits, nor destroy their dwellings; but put to death the enemy who resists under arms the conditions imposed upon them."

Six hundred years or so after that "Law" was promulgated the co-religionists of the men commanded by Abu Bekr resisted for eight months the flower of the Castilian Army in the ancient Moslem stronghold from which I write, and in the detailed accounts of that long siege given by the Christian chroniclers no single incident is recorded which stained the Moslem arms.

My nephews write from the Dardanelles warning me not to believe all I hear about the "degenerate Turk, for he is a fine fighter." A fine fighter means, I take it, an honourable one. And the question arises whether the atrocities of which we hear in Armenia and elsewhere are all to be placed to the credit of these Mahomedans, or whether there has not been among them, as there has been practically all the world over, during 40 years of secret preparation, an inculcation of the German conception that might is right, carried on with a view to using these "fine fighters" as Germany willed when her "day" should come.

Be that as it may, it would be most unjust that our schoolchildren should be taught to class the Saracen knights of the Age of Chivalry with the German barbarians of to-day.

Yours, &c.,
ONE OF THE AUTHORS OF "ARABIC SPAIN"

———◆———

BLACK SANDBAGS

30 August 1915

SIR,—WILL YOU GIVE me space to say that no sandbags I have handled can be called white? Hessian jute, which Miss Tyler uses and I use, is a good earth colour, and black bags here and there are very effective in confusing the sight for snipers. It is disheartening to see in this morning's papers that the supply of sandbags is quite adequate to the needs. It may be from the War Office point of view, but I have a stack of letters from the front imploring me to send them. The men in our York hospitals tell me the need far exceeds the supply, and the cry is universal, "Never mind socks; never mind shirts; send sandbags." I have got the North worked up, and thousands are being made. Trusting you will help the cause by publishing this letter and saving the present good output from collapse.

I am yours, &c.,
EDITH MILNER

SIR,—I HOPE YOU WILL find space in your columns for the following quotation from my husband's letter, received a few days ago from the front:–
"You asked me to say whether sandbags are of any use. They are, but, unfortunately, we deal in very large numbers of them. What would be most useful would be black ones. Is it possible to dye them? The German trenches are very cute, they are like a chess-board and you can't see which is loophole and which is not, on account of the black and white. You probably get a man firing all day at what he thinks is a loophole, and it is really only a black sandbag. You can imagine how much easier it is to see a man's head over just a plain yellow sandbag trench than over one which is black and white. I don't know if the sandbags can be dyed or not, any strong black material would do. The Germans even use the bolsters out of ruined houses. A few black sandbags would go a long way, whereas a few of the ordinary colour would only be a drop in the ocean. You can't get black sandbags from Government stores."

Yours truly,
B. N.

LITERATURE FOR THE TRENCHES

30 August 1915

SIR,—I TRUST THAT you will allow me to explain to your readers the scheme which you announce to-day for supplying good literature to the soldiers who are in the trenches, or elsewhere out of the reach of books. The scheme has been warmly welcomed and commended by many officers and privates. They well know those "dreary, doubtful, waiting hours" which make up a great part of a soldier's life, and they know also that the appeal of the best things ever written, in verse and prose, is not diminished but enhanced by the new setting lent to them in war. Our fighting troops think more of England now than they thought of her when they were at home, and the familiar delights of peace have a new meaning for them. Mr. Lionel Curtis, who, I believe, first suggested your scheme, has told me that for him one of the great moments of the South African War was the reading of Bacon's Essay on Gardens, from a copy of the Essays which someone chanced to have by him.

Books cannot be taken to the trenches; they are too heavy, and soldiers have not the time to read a book from cover to cover. What is wanted, and what you have generously undertaken to supply, is a numerous and various selection of the best passages, grave and gay, from English verse and prose, to be printed on flyleaves or broadsheets, and sold in mixed sets at a very low price. One of these broadsheets can be enclosed in a letter, without adding to the cost of postage. Whole assortments of them can be sent to officers and distributed according to taste among the men of their command. I believe that hardly anyone who knows war will be found to deny that an opportunity of this kind would be an immense boon to thousands of our soldiers.

Patriotic literature and the literature of war will have their place in the scheme, along with other kinds, but it is these other kinds, perhaps, that are the more important. Soldiers do not desire, in their hours of relaxation or fatigue, to concern themselves chiefly with the heroics of war or the technical lore of their profession. They want rest and distraction. I do not know that any principle of selection can be laid down, except such principles as are common to all good literature. The extracts and selections will be as various as possible. Some of the broadsheets will give sundry passages from a single author; others will put together the utterances of sundry authors on a single subject. Some will contain only one long passage; others will contain several shorter pieces. Everything that is good will be eligible, and all good literature has in it a soul of peace and sanity. Among the early numbers planned are:—

The Song of Deborah.

Bacon's Essays on Death, on Revenge, on Adversity.

Dickens's description of the game of cribbage played by Dick Swiveller and the Marchioness.

Cobbett's description of his ride through the Winchester country.

Pericles' Speech to the Athenians, and Froissart's description of the Black Prince in Spain.

Four of the best poems on the present War.

Izaak Walton on the song of birds and on trout-fishing.

It is plain that a list of this kind can be carried on indefinitely through hundreds of numbers. It will be a fine library of a new kind, and it is safe to say that very few of the pieces which it reprints have ever before enjoyed the double privilege of refreshing a soldier's mind and lighting his pipe.

I confess I like the idea of this library; apart from its main use, it seems to me to symbolize the cause for which we are fighting. The Germans are right when they call us frivolous, if it may be permitted in the name of politeness to assume that by frivolous they mean playful. They are right; we have playful minds, and they have not, so that we are often embarrassed in our converse with them. They are full of a simple unquestioning faith in Germany, in things German, in the great deeds they have done and the great deeds they are about to do, in all that is large, heavy, solid, and persistent. They think of these things, if their own account is just, relentlessly and eternally, without mitigation or fatigue. They do not want Heine in their trenches; there is a danger that he might not be serious. We could not think of ourselves as they do, magnificently, for years together; someone would be sure to laugh. We are not very good at hating, and we do not believe in hate. We continue to believe in life, and in the variety and surprise of life. If we submit ourselves to rigid discipline, as we are quite willing to do, it is not that we wish to be like them, but that we hope to save life from being crushed under their machine. We believe in freedom, and we mean to keep it. We will fight as long as we can stand, so that the world may still be a place where spontaneous and playful persons, especially women and children, may lead a life free from fear. There is no better expression of freedom, in all its senses, than English literature. I can almost imagine an intelligent German officer trembling and growing pale when he finds it in our trenches. Here is the explanation, which he has so long sought in vain, of why it is that our brothers from all the English-speaking world are at one with us, heart and soul. Here is their inheritance; why should they give it up for the bribes of a foreign drill-sergeant? By this token we shall conquer.

I must return to the practical question. The main problem is how to secure the gradual and steady distribution of the broadsheets. I venture to hope that an army of voluntary helpers may be found, willing to treat literature as kindly as they have treated the sister of literature, tobacco. It would be a good thing to put batches of the broadsheets within reach of any of those thousands, or rather millions, of letter-writers who are now writing to the front. Some more ambitious helpers may perhaps be willing to undertake the regular supply of a battalion or a regiment. I am no expert in these matters, and must leave it to you, Sir, to expound the details of the scheme. By discussing it with men who understand the conditions, I have been convinced that the thing is worth doing, and can be done.

Yours faithfully,
WALTER RALEIGH

NATIONAL SERVICE

4 September 1915

SIR,—NO TRUER THING has been uttered in the present discussion on National Service than Mr. H. G. Wells's reminder that the essential difficulty we have to face is not one of principle, but one of suspicion—the suspicion that National Service is to be applied to the bodies and lives of the common people and not to the profits and privileges of the rich and influential. I do not believe that to be the intention of a single advocate of National Service. But as the suspicion, however ill-founded, exists, it is the duty of all of us who urge National Service to make it clear beyond doubt that it is no one-sided or class service we are asking for.

For my part, at any rate, I understand National Service to mean that in this hour of danger the nation shall have the right to make use, to whatever extent it may require, of the lives and property of all its members. National Service, as I understand it, means the right of the nation to the personal services of every man or woman among us in that work for which we are most fitted, without regard to wealth or rank. If there be any peer's son or millionaire's son who has not yet taken the opportunity of the past year to qualify for the command of men, his place is in the ranks as a private soldier, and his duty will be to obey the mechanic or farm labourer who joined last year and by his capacity and courage has won his stripes or his commission. It means the right of the nation to take or control the property of all citizens to any extent or in any way which the necessities of the war demand. If any section of employers is making special profits out of the war let the nation take those profits. If any section of workmen make use of the opportunity of a depleted labour market to exact higher wages at the expense of the community let the Government fix wages or tax them as may be most expedient. If there is any industry that can subserve the needs of the war, let the State control it, directly or indirectly, in whatever way the best results may be achieved. If there is any industry or trade that is non-essential the State should not hesitate to curtail it by taking away its labour or taxing its product. If there is any trade union rule or practice that stands in the way of efficiency of production let it be suspended. If the Government needs money and cannot get enough by voluntary loans, let it raise its loans by compulsion, at whatever rate of interest it chooses to fix, or without interest at all, if that should seem a preferable form of taxation. If it wishes to reduce consumption, let it put us all on equal rations of necessaries, and tax all luxuries, and all incomes above subsistence level, to any extent which the occasion demands.

When Mr. Wells, however, proceeds to denounce "ownership" in general, to decry the inefficiency of our manufacturers, and to urge the nationalization to our main industries, he is, I submit, wandering beyond the issue to which we should, for the present, confine ourselves. How far the principles of compulsory personal service, or of direct national ownership or indirect national control of industry, should extend in normal times is a matter which we can well afford to discuss, and differ on, when we have to take in hand the task of reorganization with which we shall be faced after the war. For the moment we can all be agreed that there is no sacrifice of life, of property, of social privilege, or of political or industrial prejudice that it is not worth making during this war to enable us to come out victorious from the struggle.

I am, Sir, your obedient servant,
L. S. AMERY

THE MIDDLE CLASSES

10 September 1915

SIR,—THE LETTER SIGNED by Sir Frederick Milner, which you favour with large print, is both unjust and insulting to that middling order of Britons which, I expect, forms the bulk of your readers. The "curled darlings" of the leisured classes (as he styles them) have certainly come forward nobly in this war; and so, we believe, have the working men. But the dark contrast which he sees in the response from the middle classes, though effective rhetorically, has no existence in fact. The middle classes have also come forward magnificently, and frequently at a heavy financial sacrifice. Let him ask information of his doctor, his lawyer, his stockbroker, and such like representatives of these classes. They could no doubt tell him of many families of this middling order the whole of whose male members of military age are, like his own relatives, serving their country. But probably it would never occur to any of the elder members of these families to write to The Times to say so. It is not necessary, in order to rebuke "slackers," to vilipend the bulk of the educated classes of Great Britain.

Yours respectfully,
A. KENNEDY

NEWS OF CASUALTIES

28 September 1915

SIR,—THERE IS ONE complaint that is daily growing more general against the War Office; I refer to the delay in giving news to relatives of those who are killed or wounded. My case, I believe, is only a typical one. On the 16th inst. the mother of a young Territorial received official notification to the effect that he was wounded, but no particulars were given as to the nature of the wound, whether slight, serious, or dangerous. On the same day, however, letters were received from other members of this regiment in the Dardanelles to their friends giving full details of the death, an hour or two after he was hit by a shell, of this same boy. In the town where the boy lived his mother would be one of the last persons to hear of his death; even to-day there is no further official news.

Yours faithfully,
C. H.

NIGHT CLUBS

4 October 1915

SIR,—THE MAGISTRACY, THE Government, and a portion of the public appear to be waking up to the fact that the numerous night clubs of London, far from being comparatively reputable places of recreation for people in need of healthy distraction, are for the most part the haunts and hunting grounds of sharks and loose women, whose business consists of exploiting the follies and weaknesses of those who are induced to visit them, and that the existence of these places in war-time is a danger not only to the individuals who resort to them, but also, through them, to the nation.

The London Council for the Promotion of Public Morality has for some months past had several of these places under observation, and, from the information laid before me as president of the council and chairman of its executive committee, I do not hesitate to say that the continued existence of some, if not most, of these so-called clubs is a danger to the capital of an Empire at war. Some of the clubs which have been under observation have recently been closed; others remain open. I am aware that the police authorities are in a position of considerable difficulty with regard to these matters. They often know that an evil exists to which they would gladly put an end, but for want of legal evidence of overt acts they have to stand aside.

Lord Kitchener, in his advice to the men of the Expeditionary Force, impressed upon them the importance of avoiding the particular temptations which men find in these night clubs. Is it too much to ask of the authorities, civil and military, that they should, in these critical times, combine and use the great powers which have been conferred upon them to deal drastically and resolutely with those who run places of recreation or entertainment in such a manner as to make it impossible for our young soldiers to visit them without having these temptations thrust upon them?

I am placing before the authorities all the evidence which we have accumulated in the office (37, Norfolk-street, Strand) of the council, which represents all religious denominations in London.

Yours faithfully,
A. F. LONDON

The writer was the Bishop of London, Arthur Winnington-Ingram.

THE TERMINOLOGY OF MUNITIONS

9 October 1915

SIR,—MAY I CRAVE A little space in your columns on behalf of our mutual friend the man in the street? He is sore troubled just now in the matter of munitions, and in his misguided zeal, for on this subject, the blind, who with alacrity load their brethren, are many, he has blundered into singularly inappropriate technicalities. The most unsuitable of these perhaps is shrapnel, with which he appears to be obsessed. Every one is wounded by "pieces of shrapnel." The walls of buildings on which Zeppelins have dropped bombs are pitted with "bits of shrapnel"; these, *par parenthèse*, being for the most part stones out of the concrete floors. A folded newspaper saves a man's life who would otherwise have been killed by "fragments of shrapnel." In short, this name, from which as much comfort appears to be derived as from that blessed word Mesopotamia, has now come into use as a synonym for *mitraille*. To the gunner mind this is a strange misappropriation of terms, since a shrapnel is the only shell which does *not* break up. Named after its inventor, Lieutenant (afterwards Lieutenant-General) Shrapnel, of the Royal Artillery, it consists of a cast-iron or steel case surmounted at its point by a fuze, and having at its lower end or base a small charge of powder, the remaining space being packed with bullets. The powder charge, when ignited by the fuze set to its appointed time of flight, blows out the bullets, but the case goes on entire, the fuze, a diaphragm or disc separating the bullets from the powder, and a small tin pot in which that charge is contained, being the only "fragments."

Such fragments as do wound and kill people are those of common shell which have stout steel bodies and are filled with a high explosive. These burst into many and jagged pieces, and, unlike the shrapnel, which shoot their bullets out to the front in a cone, are distributed in all directions, even to the rear of the burst. It is true that the Germans have a high explosive shrapnel in which trinitrotoluene takes the place of the resin which in our shells is run in amongst the bullets, but the fuze is said to be a very complicated one, and the presence of a detonator necessitated by the high explosive renders its use dangerous, since a premature burst in the bore would entail the destruction of both gun and detachment. For this reason, probably, it does not appear to have been much used, while I can personally testify to a very large number of the ordinary shrapnel cases having been sent home as trophies from both fronts, mainly as receptacles for smaller articles.

Again, our American friends have added to the difficulties of the man in the street by referring to metal cartridge cases as "shells," and in consequence one sees in an illustrated paper a row of very obvious cylindrical cartridge cases described as "Shells for the Front."

Cotton, too, has been a *bête noire.* "Scientists," he plaintively says, "differ as to whether it is absolutely necessary for high explosives, so what am I to think?" Well, as a matter of fact, they do not. Cotton is absolutely necessary for the charge of the gun. It has nothing to do with, and is not needed for, the bursting charge of the high explosive common shell. This is a tar product, be it lyddite, melinite, or trinitrotoluene. Compressed guncotton, however, is used for the bursting charges of mines and torpedoes.

There is another subject which hardly comes under this heading, but with regard to which both the man in the street and the writer would be glad to obtain information. Will any well-informed German, of whom it would appear that there is a considerable number in this country, tell us where are the fortifications of London?

Yours, &c.,
DESMOND O'CALLAGHAN, Maj.-Gen.

A VISIT TO VIENNA

18 October 1915

SIR,—AN ENGLISH FRIEND here at The Hague to whom I, a Dutchman educated in England, was relating my experiences in Germany and Austria last week, suggested that I should send them to your great newspaper. They may prove useful, and if they find a place therein I shall feel honoured.

Business of a private nature took me to Vienna and back. I was especially asked by the English in that city to communicate with English people and to request that such courtesies as can be extended to enemies be shown to Austrians in England. Your Government will find on investigation that the English in Austria are being well treated. Austrians say, "We are at war with Italy. The conflict with England is Germany's war." I was present at a small dinner party in a public restaurant in Vienna at which two Englishmen and their wives were guests, and on my remarking to them, "I understood that all English people here had to be at home by 8 o'clock," one of them replied, "I have been in bed since 8 o'clock—officially. As you see, it is now half-past 11." There were a number of Austrian officers and others in the restaurant who knew perfectly well that the party was mainly English and, in fact, we spoke English. Hungarians, I am assured, are even more lax with the English, who are supposed to be interned by them

Vienna is very gay at the moment, and many of my Viennese friends almost apologized for it. "We have been through such agonies of depression," one of them observed, "that now we are victorious we are letting ourselves go a little."

The Austrians have now absolute confidence in their ability to win the war, by the aid of their big brother Germany. But they like the Germans less now than before. They say that they do more than half the work, and Germany gets all the praise. They are very proud of the success of the Austrian troops in Russia.

Bread is quite plentiful in Vienna, though there is a shortage of many commodities, and one aged Austrian lady who had lately left England for Vienna greatly regretted her change. Passing from the pleasant Austrians to the bitter and exultantly confident Berliners is not pleasing to the inhabitant of a neutral State.

Berlin, like Vienna, has passed through many changes of feeling. I was there rather more than a year ago when Berlin was in the depth of depression, which was only relieved by the fall of Antwerp. To-day every German with whom I came in contact was openly exultant. While one part of the nation is concentrated on finishing the war, many of the higher authorities are preparing organization for after the victory. There have been conferences of bankers, manufacturers, agriculturists, and others, so that whether the war ends in one, two, or even 10 years, Germany will instantly proceed to commence to recover her industrial position.

Except for the bread cards, it is difficult to realize that Berlin is at war. The bread card is enforced with the utmost rigidity. In company with a German friend I had to make a flying visit to an hotel at Fürstenwalde. We had both forgotten our bread cards, and each had to go through the form of taking a bedroom and paying for it, as though we were really staying at the hotel, before we could get a bread card for the day. During luncheon my German remarked, "I wonder what that miserable, hiding British Fleet is doing. Round in Ireland, I suppose, as usual." "Our bread card trouble to-day," I replied, "is the answer to that question. But for the British Fleet we should be getting good, honest wheat bread without all this ticket trouble." My answer convinced, but exasperated.

Knowing that a short time back I had been in England and was there on September 8 during the Zeppelin raid, I was asked by every one I met as to whether England was not terrified, and as to the total destruction of Liverpool-street Station. I assured them that I had been in London on the night of the raid, but that I had hardly heard anything of it, that I had never heard that Liverpool-street Station had been destroyed, that the whole affair was regarded rather like a firework display at the Crystal Palace. The children of my host had stayed up the following night to see the next raid, and when it did not take place were just as disappointed as though the weather had been too wet for fireworks.

So confident are Berliners, that English and French newspapers are now freely on sale everywhere. A banking friend of mine, speaking of his perusal of your Press, remarked, "I see that the Englanders are still going on with their weekends as usual—from Mr. Asquith downwards, I suppose? Does anybody work yet in England?" I told him that it seemed to me that business was going on very excellently in London. "And do they not work on Sundays yet?" he asked. "Do they not know that we Germans are working doubly during the war, so as to achieve success?"

In addition to the delusion that the English are in terror of Zeppelins and that the English Fleet is afraid of coming out, there is the constantly repeated statement, made too by men in high places in Berlin, that members of the British Government have had conversations in regard to peace with certain persons in London. I was continually informed that members of the British Government have made "approaches" on this subject.

I replied on this point in every case that I did not believe such a statement had a vestige of truth in it. It is believed as a fact in high quarters in Germany, none the less, and anyone understanding the Prussian character will realize the avidity with which a chance remark of any prominent Englishman to any neutral or other in London would be seized upon and accepted as a sign of fear.

One recalls that the Prussians say, "When a man shows fear, hit him harder, and finish him." Peace conversations, therefore, would mean fresh military efforts on the part of Germany.

I have seen it stated that the anti-English feeling in Germany is diminished. That is untrue.

I see it stated in your newspapers that Germany is short of many things. The only shortages of which I could hear were of indiarubber, woollen garments, and Havanna cigars. Germany is obviously importing certain supplies through neutral countries. You are not strict enough.

The ease with which I could purchase *The Times* and *Le Temps* in Berlin so speedily after publication shows how readily reading matter can be introduced. Though excessively unpopular in Germany, *The Times* is closely studied, and as vigorously abused.

I enclose my card, and beg to remain,
Your obedient servant,
ANGLO-NEUTRAL

----◆----

THE EXECUTION OF MISS CAVELL

19 October 1915

SIR,—IF EVER A CHALLENGE rang out to the chivalry of our young men of military age not yet enlisted, it is surely to be heard in the dastardly execution of an Englishwoman at the hands of an enemy for whom self-respecting nations in the future can have but one feeling, absolute abhorrence. By this crowning tragedy of cowardice, the enemy has murdered not only a woman in cold blood, they have also murdered chivalry, so far as their nation is concerned. What will be the answer of those "nearly two million of unmarried men who could enlist without disaster to the munition supply or the national industries"? If chivalry and manhood are not extinct in them, they will make their answer as one man. Lord Derby and the trade unions will then have their task made easier. The call is a voice from the grave—the voice of Nurse Edith Cavell from that execution-yard in Brussels. She being dead yet speaketh.

Yours, &c.,
JOCELYN HENRY SPECK

THE LAST SURVIVORS OF TRAFALGAR

21 October 1915

SIR,—THE 110TH ANNIVERSARY of the Battle of Trafalgar, occurring at the height of the Great War, provides a suitable occasion for recording the names of the last survivors of the British, French, and Spanish vessels engaged in the battle. Probably the last British survivor, and certainly the last officer, was Lieutenant-Colonel James Fynmore, R.M., who died at Peckham on April 15, 1887, aged 93. He was a first-class volunteer on the Africa—a battleship which suffered so severely in her action with the Intrépide that she nearly foundered in the great storm that followed the battle. Colonel Fynmore entered the Marines in 1808 and retired 40 years later. He received the medal for Trafalgar granted in 1848, and was the son of Major (then Captain) James Fynmore Senior Officer of Marines in the same ship at Trafalgar.

The last French survivor was Louis André Manuel Cartigny, who died at Hyères on March 21, 1892, aged 100. He was a powder-monkey on the Redoubtable and was slightly wounded. He was taken prisoner and remained a captive on board the hulks at Plymouth and in the war prisons at Dartmoor and Stapledon for some years. On being exchanged, he returned to France and was attached to the "Seamen of the Guard," with whom he was present at Napoleon I's adieu to the Grand Army in 1814. During the last years of his life he was the landlord of a Café at Hyères. Napoleon III decorated him with the Legion of Honour and Queen Victoria sent a wreath to be placed on his grave.

The last Spanish survivor was Gaspar Costela Vasquez, who died at San Fernando, Cadiz, in April 1892, aged 104. He was present at Trafalgar on the Santa Ana. For many years he lived in the Convalescent Hospital of the garrison at San Fernando. His funeral was attended by the principal officers and men of the naval and military forces and of the Marines.

It will thus be seen that the last Englishman survived the battle 81 ½ years, the last Frenchman and last Spaniard 86 ½ years. It is not improbable therefore, that one or two of the naval veterans of the Great War of to-day may survive till the 21st century.

I am, Sir, your obedient servant,
N. KYNASTON GASKELL

THE PRESENT CRISIS

28 October 1915

SIR,—THE PRESENT CRISIS is the gravest we have had to meet since the war commenced. No Government has ever had so loyal a trust reposed in it. The Press, the people, and Parliament have all supported it. Before the Coalition took place the Opposition had completely effaced itself. The only criticism has been the criticism of the members of the Cabinet, who have admonished one another. The axiom "Trust the Government" having been observed, the time has arrived to trust the people.

The country is bewildered, and anxiety is increasing as to the conduct of the war. The members of the Cabinet do not trust one another, and continue to make statements mutually contradictory.

From the first I objected to the Coalition, and sent our leaders my reasons for my objections, in writing. The Coalition was always a compromise, and involved the danger of having no alternative in the event of catastrophe or reverse. Therefore, if circumstances arose in which democracy thought it had been betrayed or misled, and if the Government then fell there would be no alternative Administration. The result might be dangerous confusion at a moment of a definite crisis in our life as a nation. However, when the Coalition was formed, I supported it with all the energy at my command.

The conduct of the war has now produced the situation which was anticipated. The public are extremely anxious, and are rapidly becoming angry. Democracy is not easily controlled if it gets an idea into its head that the Government have mismanaged affairs, or that the Government have deceived them. The policy of muzzling the Press and the House of Commons, the policy of mystery and silence, and of withholding the truth from the people, has produced a state of affairs which may provoke so strong an ebullition of feeling that the Government will have to go, with nothing ready to take its place. The country is not satisfied with the conduct of the war, and it wants to know the truth. The truth has been withheld before the war and during the war.

The Censorship does not prevent news getting to the enemy, but the manner in which it is conducted prevents our own people hearing the truth when the news is not good. Our people are not cowards; if they heard of a reverse it would make them more determined to see the war through to the end. They have been informed on several occasions that our arms have won brilliant victories, the real facts of the case being that we have suffered something much more resembling defeat. It is unwise in a great emergency such as exists at present to treat the people like children. It is impossible to confuse the public and at the same time to enlist enthusiasm. The country wants a strong clear lead, with a definite and decided policy, and a Government that will govern. The people are vainly waiting for orders.

War requires quick decisions and prompt actions. Both have been singularly wanting since the war commenced. The policy of "wait and see" is fatal to success in war. Owing to indecision and vacillation, the Government has, on every important occasion, been too late. Ministers, having no initiative of their own, wait for public opinion to drive them; and at the same time Ministers withhold from the public the information without which they cannot form a just opinion.

We did not stand by our friend Serbia until too late. We neither stand by our friends nor stand up to our enemies. We attempted to bribe Bulgaria by offering her other people's property, thereby copying German methods; and we attempted to bribe Greece by offering a portion of our own property, and we necessarily are humiliated when Greece refuses to accept it.

If we continue our present procedure we shall head straight towards disaster before the latent energy of the nation has been awakened. Recriminations and deploring the past are not of much use at the present moment, except in so far as they prevent the recurrence of crass mismanagement. That mismanagement is partly the result of amateur strategy, and of political control of the executive. Thousands of our best have been lost both ashore and afloat because the politicians assumed the executive. The war up to now has been controlled by politicians, not by men who have studied and understand war. The Dardanelles expedition is a case in point. It has produced the present serious complications in the East and the Balkans, which involve great danger to ourselves. It has opened up the whole Eastern question, when all that was required was concentration in the West. Why are misstatements made to the country about the Dardanelles? Why did the former First Lord of the Admiralty say months ago that we were "separated only by a few miles from a victory such as the war had not yet seen"? Why did the Under-Secretary of State for Foreign Affairs state that we were "within a little of a great success which will have an enormous effect in all parts of the world"? Both of these statements induced the public to believe that we were within an ace of getting to Constantinople. The public were deceived. If we are to win the war certain matters must be settled at once. It is not a question of days, but of hours. We are in a crisis which means life or death to us.

Why are not drastic measures taken to secure all the Germans in our midst, naturalized and unnaturalized? Why do we not at once commandeer all German land, money, securities, &c., throughout the Empire? It is presumed we are going to win the war. If so, we can compel the Germans to refund all that they have taken from British subjects. The Order in Council of March 11, 1915, ordained that *all supplies* were to be prevented from reaching Germany. But on October 19, 1915, the Under-Secretary of State for Foreign Affairs stated that "the Order in Council of March 11, 1915, did not affect the validity or operation of any of the conventions or instruments referred to"—*i.e.*, the Declaration of Paris, the Declaration of London, 14 Hague Conventions, and all juridical niceties.

Why has the defence of London been neglected up to now? The First Lord of the Admiralty, after 14 months of war, declared that the system of defence was wholly inadequate. The defence of London appears to be administered on similar lines to the Censorship—divided responsibility, nobody knowing who is really responsible.

Why have not the Government taken up the question of the rise in prices of food and coal, in order to prevent exorbitant prices being charged to the poor during the crisis?

With regard to recruiting: Why does not the Government tell the country the truth? Why are we not told how many men they want and by what time, and for what branches they are required? If the voluntary system fails it will be quite a year before any other system can produce the men necessary to go to the front. The present scheme is to last six weeks. It will take two months to pass a Bill and before any men can be joined under the new system. It will take at least eight months to train the men, as we shall be short of non-commissioned officers and others who were available to teach the Kitchener armies.

At this moment the Government has no policy and no objective. The late Attorney-General left the Cabinet because there was no policy and no decision on any point. Only three men in the Cabinet have shown that they realize the intense gravity of our position. The Minister for War warned the country to be prepared for a three-years war; the Minister of Munitions made a speech the gravity of which cannot be overrated; the late Attorney-General resigned rather than stay in a Cabinet that had no policy. We began the war with two great assets, the Fleet and our wealth; the second asset is being squandered by millions without business supervision or adequate return. We shall soon be bankrupt if this goes on.

We blundered before the war, and have been blundering ever since. What else could happen when the war is being managed by politicians, and not by men who understand and have studied war? We have a Cabinet of 21, only one of whom understands anything of war. The administration, continuance, and successful conclusion of the war is the only question of vital moment to the country and the Empire at the present time. Twenty-one people—a debating society—(20 of them politicians) are totally unable rightly to control the war; the results of their administration up to date are ample proof that they do not understand anything about war. We can only beat the Germans by fighting; talking is useless.

There ought to be six or seven men who understand war to control the war and do nothing else, on the same principle as the German General Staff. The three men who show that they understand the gravity of the position— the Minister for War, Minister for Munitions, and the late Attorney-General— should be among the number.

A frank and careful statement should be made by the Prime Minister surveying the whole war, and letting the people know the truth. Everything that the enemy knows should be told to our own people. We cannot go on as we are doing without shaping straight for disaster.

I have the honour to be, Sir, your obedient servant,
CHARLES BERESFORD, Admiral

The massive British offensive at Loos had recently come to nothing and resulted in heavy losses, while the Central Powers, now joined by Bulgaria, were routing the Serbs.

A MISSING POET

3 November 1915

SIR,—MY EXCELLENT FRIEND, Professor Seippel, of Geneva, who is a fervent supporter of the Entente Allies, has asked me to bring to your notice the melancholy and mysterious fate of the poet, Max Dauthendey. The professor assures me that this unfortunate lyrist is "wholly innocent of the crimes of his country." I confess that, however blameless and elderly a German poet may be, his fate at present leaves me cold. Still, Max Dauthendey is a writer of some celebrity, and I consent to repeat his story, simply because it seems somewhat interesting. It appears that early last year, Dauthendey, who is between 50 and 60 years of age, started on a journey round the world. He was in the Moluccas when the war broke out. Thence he fled, I know not why, to Java, and thence to Sumatra. Arriving there, he rushed into the interior and vanished. Since then nothing has been heard from or of him. In Switzerland, where it appears that he has crowds of admirers, a sort of society is being formed to search for him. But as Switzerland lies high and dry, all his partisans can do is to beg the maritime nations to be on the look-out for him. It would seem to be the business of the Dutch, if of anybody. But *The Times* is always hospitable, and perhaps you will not mind saying that if any ship's captain, sailing through the Straits of Banka, sees an elderly poet being chased by a rhinoceros, that will doubtless be Herr Max Dauthendey.

I am, Sir, your obedient servant,
EDMUND GOSSE

AN ENGLISH HOSPITAL FOR FRENCH SOLDIERS

6 November 1915

SIR,—I HOPE IT MAY not be thought inopportune, at a time when our own wounded have so heavy a claim on us, to plead, if you will allow me, for an English hospital for French soldiers. The hospital at Arc-en-Barrois is one of those which serve the Army of the Argonne. The continuous fighting in that region has kept it busy all the year; and as early as February pressure necessitated the fitting-up of an auxiliary hospital, separately maintained, which has been used for convalescents. Of late the number of serious cases has increased, and the French Government has decided to have no convalescents any longer so near the front. The taking over of this annexe of 70 beds for the seriously wounded means a large increase of expenditure, and funds are urgently needed. Having had the privilege of serving for a short time in the hospital, I can testify to the value of its work, generously appreciated by the French authorities, and also to the exceedingly sympathetic relations between the patients and the English staff. What it meant for the staff to realize at first hand the splendid spirit of France, I need not say. But when I was bidding good-bye to the wounded soldiers, I could not but be deeply touched by their cordial words. One with tears in his eyes said, I shall never forget these days. Always and everywhere I shall tell people that the English are "braves gens," that England is a true friend of France. Vive l'Angleterre! Another—one of many— writes that England henceforth will be his "seconde patrie." These soldiers are drawn from every part of France. Few of them knew anything of the English before. They thought of us probably with the mistrust of tradition. Now an abstract prejudice gives place to a warm human experience. Over and above, then, the actual work of the hospital, there is this filtration into how many homes scattered over broad France of a changed fraternal sentiment of good will; something fluid and imponderable, but worth more, surely, than many official protestations. How much may this not count for in the future! Those who love France, who feel the debt all Europe owes to her, who understand how precious a gain among all these miseries of loss is the experience of human sympathy and friendship between the two great nations, will not willingly, I am sure, let this work come to an end for lack of support. Five pounds a month will maintain one of the 180 beds. A regular monthly contribution is a specially appreciated form of help; but any donation will be gratefully received and should be sent to the hon. treasurer. B. Martin-Holland. Esq., C.B., at 68, Lombard-street.

LAURENCE BINYON

Though then volunteering at a French hospital, Binyon was also a poet. His lines beginning "They shall not grow old", first published in *The Times*, would become synonymous with acts of remembrance after the war.

"THE TIMES" AND THE CRIMEA

8 November 1915

SIR,—YEARS AFTER THE Crimean War Sir W. H. Russell wrote to Gortchakoff and asked him whether the letters to *The Times* from the Crimea had helped the Russian Army. Gortchakoff answered:—

"Your admirable letters were as agreeable as they were well written; my cousin used to send me the papers from Warsaw, and I read them regularly, but I am bound to admit that I never received any information from them, or learned anything that I had not known before."

In 1894 Sir Evelyn Wood wrote to Russell:—

"In my article I am chastising you with scorpions, but still you will mind this the less, that I say, truly enough, that it was you who saved the remnants of our Army. See the *Fortnightly* 1st of next month; this will be balm, indeed, though seriously I always think that the present generation of soldiers has no idea of what you did for their fore-elders in saving the remnant of those who were allowed to starve, or next door to it."

I am, Sir, your obedient servant,
J. B. ATKINS

MR. CHURCHILL'S PLACE

15 November 1915

SIR,—MR. CHURCHILL's resignation, regrettable as it is, has at least this advantage—that it affords an opportunity of taking into the Cabinet some non-political man of business.

Such a man, if only for purposes of retrenchment, would be invaluable. He would, moreover, help to make this Government a national Government, which it cannot be so long as it is a mere collection of party politicians. And, indeed, we want a little new blood.

ROSEBERY

THE HOME SECRETARY AND "THE TIMES"

26 November 1915

SIR,—YOU HAVE STIGMATIZED as it deserved the dishonest answer given by Sir John Simon to a question in the House of Commons yesterday. You might have added that, so far as my articles are concerned, they have one and all been submitted to the Press Bureau, over which this lawyer now presides, and that they have been mangled, bowdlerized, or censored out of existence at the sweet will of this incorrigibly inefficient branch. These articles should be headed:— Revised and Edited by Sir John Simon and his minions; and if, as this Minister alleges, they assist the enemy, the only course open to Sir John is to resign, as he is convicted out of his own mouth of the inefficient performance of his public duties.

I have been subjected to the attacks and misrepresentations of the German Reptile Press and the Ananias Agency of Wolff for many years past. These attacks culminated in the impudent demand made by the late Baron Marschall von Bieberstein, on his arrival in England, and doubtless at the Kaiser's instigation, that I should be dismissed from the editorship of the *Army Review*. The Baron doubtless confused the Bosporus with the Thames, and he received from Colonel Seely, then Secretary for War, a crisp answer and a suggestion that his Excellency should mind his own business.

I am quite accustomed to German abuse, which is to me a matter of the utmost indifference. But I must express my surprise that a Minister of the Crown should aid and abet these machinations against me and your journal by disingenuously suggesting as Russian opinion an opinion that was not Russian at all, and by failing to tell the House of Commons that his Press Bureau had passed every line that I have written in your columns.

I am, &c.,
YOUR MILITARY CORRESPONDENT

Simon, the home secretary, had confused for a Russian newspaper article a French one claiming that *The Times* was hostile to the government – as indeed it was. Its military correspondent, Charles á Court Repington, had undermined Asquith with his reports on the shortage of munitions.

CARPET-SLIPPERS WANTED

27 November 1915

SIR,—THOSE OF US WHO are out at the front are constantly asked by the good folks at home to tell them what the men in the trenches really need in the way of comforts. Judging by the number of inquiries which I myself have received, there are a large number of people at home only too anxious to help us, but a little perplexed as to the best means of doing so. To all such may I suggest that the making of carpet-slippers would provide a really satisfactory outlet for their benevolent energy? The ordinary infantryman is only allowed one pair of boots. In weather such as we have now with us in the trenches this pair of boots is always wet. Even when we are taking our rest in billets behind the trenches the men have only too often to sleep in their wet boots. In the trenches themselves this is inevitable; but when men are not in the trenches they could, and most certainly would, wear warm carpet-slippers, and bless the hands that made them. And many would be saved from that dreadful malady "trench feet."

I am told by my elders that not many years ago the making of carpet-slippers was quite a fashionable pastime for young ladies. Could not the ancient pastime be revived? Many, I know, are tired of making socks and mufflers. Slippers will give to such a new interest. There is scope in the humble carpet-slipper for the artistic; there is opportunity for the least skilled. Above all, there is real "comfort for the troops."

I am, Sir, yours truly,
SUB.

DIRKS FOR TRENCH FIGHTING

29 November 1915

SIR,—As HAVING FOR more than a year urged upon my military friends the need for some more close-acting weapon in the trenches than the rifle with bayonet attached, and observing that in France this matter is being attended to officially, I desire to call attention to one or two important points. When the soldier jumps down into a trench full of enemies—as he must do when charging, unless he remains above to be shot—he is no longer able to use rifle or bayonet to advantage. He is like a man in a close crowd, who cannot draw back his weapon so as to make it effective. Accordingly we read of men taking off the bayonet to use it by hands, and also of men resorting to their fists. Now it is plain:—First, that the bayonet alone, being a long weapon, is not handy for use in a crowd; second, that the rifle and bayonet should be kept together, as proper bayonet work may become necessary at any moment.

Everything points to the advisability of a short knife or dirk being at instant command when the jump into the trench is made. And this not for thrusting forward as in striking a blow, but for back-handed action, the arm being swung with the blade projecting—a dagger action in fact, which is much the quickest and most effective way of dealing with an enemy who is close up to you. I notice that in a weapon devised for use by the French, the idea of a thrust-blow instead of a swing-blow has been adopted, there being a loop-handle, and the point projecting from the back of the knuckles. This is not a good arrangement. I suggest that the soldier should have a short knife, ready to be whipped out in an instant by putting it in a small leather case sewed high up on the left breast, close to the armpit. The mode of use would be to have it out just before jumping into the trench, and to swing it into the face of the nearest man, and as rapidly as possible into the faces of as many men as can be reached—no stabbing at the body. The purpose should be to "flabbergast" your man more than merely to wound. A "job" in the face is the most effective way of getting in first, which is everything in a hand-to-hand struggle, and the most disconcerting injury.

I am, &c.,
J. H. A. MACDONALD

"THE TIMES" AT THE FRONT

6 December 1915

SIR,—"THE TUMULT AND the shouting dies," but before Sir John Simon's unsuccessful counter-attack is entirely forgotten, one statement should not go unrefuted. Sir John Simon accuses *The Times* of depressing the troops at the front.

In a sense he is right. We should doubtless have continued more cheerful had we known that every miner in South Wales was working his hardest, that no shipwright on the Clyde was deliberately losing time, and that the politicians, all party animosities forgotten and all salaries willingly relinquished, were labouring unitedly in public and practising the most rigid economy in private, for the better prosecution of the war.

It was not the fault of the "Hide the Truth" Press or the "Hide the Truth" statesmen that we were undeceived.

"There was no shortage of munitions." And as we heard our batteries fire the two rounds to which they were restricted, and waited for the inevitable 30 or 40 in return, we tried to persuade ourselves that behind it all there must be some deep strategic reason which we could not fathom.

The Times upset this—never very comfortable—optimism; but it got us shells. It told us the truth, and it was not the fault of *The Times* that the truth was unpalatable. But however unpalatable, the men at the front could stand it, and infinitely preferred it to the reports of those continued Russian successes (two officers, 216 men, and a machine-gun captured, and the like) which culminated in the fall of Warsaw.

We were, indeed, depressed at the strikes, at the failure of recruiting in spite, or perhaps because of, the contemptible methods employed, at the demand for war bonuses and unprecedented wages, at the unprecedented waste of them, at the continuance of Lord Haldane in public life, and of Germans of military age at large in England and at the general rottenness of taste and feeling in a country which can amuse itself with "Charlie Chaplin" in days like these. Those of us who got home wounded had our depression confirmed. But nothing so depressed and irritated us as the professional optimists. Sometimes a feeling of intense depression would settle on one, and of black despair of England over facing facts or even words. "No compulsory service"—compel men to serve by threats and insults—but "no compulsory service"; that was the attitude that really depressed and sickened us—that, and the general eagerness to believe any palpable lie if only it were pleasant. The Turks were murdering the German officers, the Greeks were coming in on our side, there were peace riots in Constantinople, Bulgaria was coming in on our side, the Germans were starving and nearly annihilated, we were through the Dardanelles, or, if we weren't, it didn't matter—anything. That is the national state of mind which the professional optimists have engendered. And I hope that they and Sir John Simon are pleased with it.

For us they need not be anxious. We are not depressed by the truth. Let us know what we have to do and we will do it the better for knowing the difficulties. Nor is this merely the officer's point of view. We know the men as no politician ever has or ever will know them, and I say confidently that there is hardly a man in France who is not grateful to *The Times* for speaking out.

I am, Sir, your obedient servant,
WOUNDED

***It will perhaps avoid hostile misrepresentation if we state at once that this letter reaches us, entirely unsought, from an officer who is quite unknown to us except by name. We print it (though it obviously gives an exaggerated picture of conditions in England) as a type of many which have reached us within the last few days. It is impossible to give space to them at a time when far more serious issues are at stake than political intrigues against *The Times*; but we are none the less grateful to the writers.

THE COUNTRY AND THE WAR

13 December 1915

SIR,—I BELONG TO THAT large section of "silent public" which usually leaves the talking alone. I look in vain to the House of Commons for three things—

1. Light upon a war which, as the days pass, seems to be becoming less and less of a war "of the people" (viz., by direction, through the usual channels by which public opinion makes itself heard), in proportion, as the sacrifices asked of the people grow.

2. An example set in economy which might raise the people's House a little in the common estimation.

3. The relegation of party animosities and ties to a pit as bottomless as is the feeling of the country bitter that its central council should have so failed to act as the true mirror of the Empire, throughout these dark days.

Yours truly,
WILLIAM DEEDES

THE VOICE OF A SCHOOLBOY
RALLIES THE RANKS

14 December 1915

SIR,—MAY I SAY ONE word in reply to the letter of a "Public School Master," which appears in *The Times* of to-day (11 December). As an old headmaster, I am not likely to underestimate the value of school discipline. But long experience has convinced me that we keep our boys at school too long. And, as to the commissions to boys, Clive sailed to India at the age of 17; Wolfe, "a lanky stripling of 15", carried the colours of the 12th Regiment of Foot; Wellington was ensign in the 73rd Regiment at the age of 17; Colin Campbell gained his commission in the 9th Regiment of Foot at the age of 16. We keep our boys in leading strings too long.

I am, Sir, your obedient servant,
JOSEPH WOOD

SUNDAY VARIETY SHOWS

15 December 1915

SIR,—THE CORRESPONDENCE column of *The Times* may be regarded as the Forum of our modern world, in which the individual may deliver his soul; and I ask indulgence as I express my deep concern, which I believe is shared by many others, at the increasing facility with which the authorities are giving special permission for Sunday variety shows. I will not take your space for the production of evidence, but I think the fact will be generally admitted. A very large number of theatres are also opened on Sunday evening for musical selections and entertainments, to raise funds for charitable objects. Now, the serious question arises, whether under the special exigencies of the war, society is not quietly removing ancient bulwarks, which have been for our national safeguarding in many a stormy period of the past, and setting up precedents of a very undesirable character. The question could, of course, be argued on the need of periodic rest, and the report recently presented to Parliament by the Health of Munition Workers Committee is greatly to the point on this aspect of it; but I frankly argue on the highest ground possible and ask, can we as a nation afford to trifle with or set aside those religious sanctions and observances, which are being seriously encroached upon by these innovations?

Of course, if the majority affirm in this sense, one must quietly await and desire the turning of the tide back to more serious views of life. But is this the time to make the great exchange? This war, unlike other wars, is essentially one of ideals, the clash of spiritual forces, the shock of two differing types of civilization; and that side will win which is most closely allied with the evolving purpose of the Almighty. Is it wise at such a time, when the destiny of the world's future is trembling in the balance, for this nation to surrender to the seductive call of amusement and pleasure hours which our fathers reserved for the further alliance of the human spirit with the eternal and divine reinforcement? Believe me, Sir, I am no kill-joy, and am only eager to conserve the highest welfare of our nation and enable her to front and master the unexampled difficulties of the situation; and I urge the arrest of further encroachments on our Rest-Day.

Yours sincerely,
F. B. MEYER

16 December 1915

SIR,—I THINK DR. F. B. MEYER may be under some misapprehension as to the greatly increased number of Sunday performances that are being given in war time. Previous to the war, he may not be aware that concerts and entertainments were freely given on a Sunday, and on that day the picture palaces plied, as they do now, a roaring trade. The actual increase in the numbers of such entertainments due to the war is, I believe, inconsiderable, and the fact that any such increase has been accompanied by the payment of substantial sums to various war charities may perhaps at the moment be held to justify their existence. It is true that the conditions under which entertainments are given on Sunday are strangely anomalous. Whilst it is permissible to give a symphony of Beethoven or a variety entertainment or to exhibit scenes of wild buffoonery and lurid passion on the cinematograph, it is forbidden, for however worthy a cause, to perform on a Sunday a play of Shakespeare. Such a state of things is typical of the shifty humbug with which, in this country, we approach problems of this kind. Whether the spiritual and religious enthusiasm of the community is going to be better kindled by spiritualizing or abolishing Sunday entertainments, or whether, from the point of view of the Churches, deeper causes underlie the whole question, is another matter. But is it the time, when many such entertainments are helping substantially war funds, and giving harmless entertainment to many soldiers on a Sunday, to raise the question of their restriction? If such restriction is to come it must be general and deal with all forms of Sunday entertainment, charitable or not, indiscriminately.

Yours very truly,
H. B. IRVING

SIR,—WITH GREAT RESPECT to the Rev. F. B. Meyer, who, in a letter in *The Times* to-day, writes objecting to any form of Sunday amusements in London, might I inform you that there are a large number of strangers here from far parts of the Empire who know nobody and who have no opportunity for amusement other than that afforded by Sunday entertainments of some sort? I have heard it suggested again and again by those who, like myself, are strangers in this vast city that some effort should be made to make Sunday a less trying day than it is for those of us from overseas.

Yours faithfully,
CONVALESCENT CANADIAN OFFICER

FRENCH SARDINES AND OTHER

18 December 1915

SIR,—IN HIS INTERESTING letter on the importance of discriminating between imports from our Allies and from other foreign countries, Mr. de Maratray rightly refers to the value of the sardine fishery as one of the principal industries of Brittany; but he makes a slip when he says that "sardine fishing has become principally a Norwegian and a Portuguese industry." That sardines are caught off the coast of Portugal as well as of Brittany is undoubted. But recent legal proceedings (Rex v. Angus Watson and another) have conclusively proved, to the satisfaction not only of the late Sir John Dickinson, but of the King's Bench Division of the High Court (the Lord Chief Justice, Mr. Justice Darling, and Mr. Justice Avory), that the sardine is not caught—and does not exist—in Norwegian waters; and it has been finally determined by the highest Court in this country that the fish hitherto sold as "Norwegian sardines" are sprats, and not sardines, and have no right to be sold under the name of "sardines," even when qualified by the term "Norwegian."

Yours faithfully,
CHARLES E. FRYER

LIVINGSTONE'S GRAVE

20 December 1915

SIR,—THE GREAT MPUNDU tree, which for over 30 years served to mark the place where my father's heart was laid to rest by his native followers, near Chitambo's old village, on the banks of the River Lulimala, North-East Rhodesia, was replaced some years ago by a concrete monument, near which is a small cottage for the use of visitors. In this cottage was placed a visitors' book, which has been carried off, by some one probably who valued the blank pages more than those containing the unreplaceable collection of signatures, and these have been lost.

I have been paying a few months' visit to my son and daughter, stationed here, and have been to the monument. It was very interesting to go along a part of the actual route by which my father must have travelled the last day of his life, to the village of Chitambo, where he died; and also to meet some old men who remember his coming to their village, and who were able to give us some interesting details of that time. But I was disappointed to find in the present visitors' book scarcely a dozen names, although many more have been to the spot, and it has occurred to me to ask, if I may, through your columns, whether some of those who have visited, either the present monument, or in older days, the tree, would be so very kind as to write me giving names, designations, and if possible, dates of visits. By this means I am in hopes of recovering as far as possible some at least of the lost names, and so having a record of them, although only copies, in the present book. I need not say how grateful I should be to anyone who will give me any assistance in my search.

As I am on the point of starting on my homeward journey letters should be sent to me at my home address of Clachbheo, Nethy Bridge, Inverness-shire.

I remain yours sincerely,
A. MARY LIVINGSTONE WILSON

CHRISTMAS IN GERMANY

24 December 1915

SIR,—MANY ANXIOUS thoughts will be turned to Germany this Christmas and to our fellow-countrymen, combatants and non-combatants, imprisoned there. Perhaps you will allow me, therefore, to give your readers the latest information I have received, important letters and messages having reached me this very week. There can be no doubt at all that the general treatment of the prisoners steadily improves as our men become more and more resourceful, gaining the confidence and respect of those set over them. The food question, of course, still remains very serious, as we can quite well understand, and individual non-commissioned officers are as tyrannical and unkind to our men as they are to their own. No vigilance apparently can prevent this evil, however careful their superiors may be.

Mr. Williams, our Chaplain at Berlin, assisted by Mr. Flad, of the London Jews' Society, also in Anglican Orders, is doing his best to give the ministrations of our Church in every camp, and there are in addition now no less than 40 English-speaking German Lutheran clergy, giving regular services of a simple character which, though they do not of course include Holy Communion, are very greatly valued. The Roman Catholics have had no difficulty from the first in receiving the ministrations of their Church, and there has been a priest in actual residence at Ruhleben all along. There will be, I feel sure, bright and cheering services—there are excellent bands in most places—in every camp in Germany this Christmas, and, for all who desire it, opportunities of receiving Holy Communion.

It is much to be regretted that the German Government does not, as yet, see its way to allowing us of the Church of England more than those two clergy, though we have offered that others, if admitted, should be interned and share the lot of the prisoners in every way. It would be a great boon, for instance, if we could have a resident English clergyman in Ruhleben, where there are 5,000 prisoners of all classes, and very special opportunities.

Next let me say, for the information of readers of your paper abroad, especially in Germany and Scandinavia where many untrue reports have been circulated, that the War and Home Offices are doing their utmost to give the prisoners of war in this country just what we should value for our own countrymen abroad. By the appointment of the War Office I have now been for some months superintending the social and religious ministrations in every Prisoners of War Camp in Great Britain and Ireland. We have five Lutheran pastors at work, as compared with our two clergy in Germany, and there will be Holy Communion for both Catholics and Protestants in every camp this Christmas season. Our commandants have shown the greatest anxiety, in their letters to me, to secure these privileges, and the War Office have issued their permits immediately and readily, not only for the German pastors, but for our own clergy, members of the Free Churches, of the Salvation Army, and anyone indeed of whom we could feel that they could be of any real use, while the Cardinal Archbishop and his brother Bishops have seen to the services of their Church.

The Y.M.C.A. still do all in their power to mitigate the lot of the prisoners, and the Friends Emergency League carry on their valuable educational work. I can honestly say therefore, from personal visiting, in the course of which I have moved freely about amongst the prisoners, when, if they had any grievance, I am sure they would have told me, knowing that a great part of my work has been in Germany, that everything that can be reasonably and conscientiously is being actually done to prevent prisoners of war in this country from deteriorating in their manhood, mentally and physically, morally or spiritually; and one can only hope that this will have its effect, in time, in improving the conditions of life for our unfortunate fellow-countrymen abroad. I on my part, from all I hear, am not without hope that it will.

I am just sending more service-books to Germany for our countrymen. I should be grateful if I could have another thousand or two. They cost, with carriage, about £8 a thousand; I should be glad indeed also if I could add a portable organ or two. These, with carriage, cost about £5 each.

I am, Sir, yours truly,
HERBERT BURY, Anglican Bishop for North and Central Europe

A WOMAN'S LETTER FROM BERLIN

28 December 1915

SIR,—THE ACCOMPANYING letter, which has reached me indirectly from a lady in Berlin, may interest readers of your journal. It gives a good deal of new information as to life in the German capital, and, incidentally, entirely corroborates and adds later information to the views of your "Neutral Observer," whose articles attracted so much attention about 10 days ago.

I am, your obedient servant,

X.

... On the whole, my experiences in Berlin are almost as interesting as those opening days of the war when T— and I were in Paris. Slightly, but distinctly increasingly, we are all beginning to feel rather like a besieged population. There is not the least abatement in the confidence of the Germans that they have won the war, but there is increasing annoyance and irritation because the Allies are so slow in asking for peace. Irritation is also arising against the women of the lower classes here in Berlin and in other German towns whose ridiculous and despicable desire for butter, culminating, as you know, in butter and other riots, is making the official classes thoroughly ashamed of them. In the first few days of the war Paris was a city of queues. People were waiting in long lines for passes and permissions of all kinds. Berlin is now a city of queues, I counted a score of them the other day during a short walk. These queues are of people waiting for the microscopic amount of butter and other commodities allowed to each inhabitant. There is every effort to put the best foot foremost in Germany at all times, but especially now. This butter craze, however, seems to be beyond the power of the authorities to suppress.

The state of affairs here is difficult to describe, for the Germans are adepts at make-believe and are always posing before that world. The shops have been filled with people and the people have been buying Christmas gifts. This I know, for I saw them. Wertheim's was crowded. The tableaux which form an attraction of their Christmas bazaar were almost entirely devoted to the war. One will amuse you, as it represented a Zeppelin raid on London. It was most realistically produced. There was an exact model of a Zeppelin, with searchlights shining upon it from Trafalgar-square. Suddenly the roof of one of the houses opens and an Englishman with, as usual, side whiskers, long teeth, and check suit, rises slowly and elevates a long telescope from a roof top. Directly he catches sight of the Zeppelin he pops down and disappears from view! This clockwork representation was the chief feature of the bazaar, and must have pleased hundreds of thousands of people.

Small change is getting very difficult to obtain in shops, and one is now usually given change in postage stamps. The authorities say that owing to the great extension of German territory there is not enough German coinage to go round, and that is way we must be content with postage stamps. But B— tells me that it is due to the nickel and copper famine.

B— and I, though our sympathies are not German, rigorously adhere to the rule of two *fleischlose* (meatless) and two *fettlost* (fatless) days per week. A good many of our wealthy neighbours, however, dodge the law by buying in advance and storing. Servants are sent scouring the city for extra butter and sometimes bring home with great pride an extra quarter of a pound. We are getting very much accustomed to a diet largely composed of fish salad, potatoes, tinned asparagus, stuffed tomatoes, sea and fresh water fish, sauerkraut, macaroni, and spaghetti. I lunched at the Esplanade on Wednesday with the two — boys, who had come in from Potsdam to skate with their cousins. There was no sign of any deficiency in the menu. I asked for milk with my coffee, to see if they had it, and obtained it easily. The hotel was quite full on account of the opening of the Reichstag. It was difficult to believe that Berlin was at war. All the places of amusement are apparently doing well. Large numbers of officers and men are on leave from the various theatres of war just now, and assist to fill such entertainments. But one feels the whole thing to be unreal.

I see speculations in the English newspapers as to German losses in killed, sick, and wounded. People here say they are four millions, a large number indeed, but not yet sufficient to make great impression on a population of 70 millions, especially as the medical arrangements are so efficient that men recover speedily.

My feeling is that the Germans, though convinced that they have won, are rather war weary, the women particularly. The present situation to people like ourselves is merely interesting. To those of limited means the daily trials of life must be intensely annoying.

We had, of course, to give up our motor many months ago. Now we must either walk, which in the blizzard season in Berlin in never pleasant, or take a taxi. Taxicabs have lately adopted spring wheels to obviate the need for pneumatic tires. They are not a success. We had a severe shaking the other day while going to call on the von —'s. There, by the way, I heard the almost incredible story that, in order to get much-needed glycerine, dead bodies have been medically treated successfully in more than one war zone. This may be only one of the extraordinary rumours one hears every day, but it was told me with all seriousness. That which I do know is that the —'s have been informed by the authorities that the roof of their house, which is made of copper and has only been built two years, will shortly be required. They take the matter very seriously, and I do not wonder, for it is a charming home, and will not be improved by a wooden roof.

On Sunday we had an extra Hindenburg Day, for nailing the great statue. I think I told you in my last letter that this wooden colossus was erected just in front of the Reichstag, and the Germans with their unaccountable mania for putting nails into heroes are allowed in return for certain payments to hammer a gold nail into the orders on the breast of Hindenburg, a silver nail into his sword, or an iron nail elsewhere. To give the movement a fillip we had bands playing all round the statue on Sunday. It was amusing to see fat Fran F—— mounting the platform and solemnly hammering in a silver nail amidst the electric illumination while the band was playing.

The introduction of German fashions has, of course, been a hopeless failure. I frankly told T— that I would rather be divorced than be seen in the gowns and hats portrayed in the German mode journals!

The French and English better known fashion journals are obtainable in several *Buchhandlungen* in town.

England is, of course, still the chief enemy, but the Americans are a very good second. The Italians are said here to be fighting well, and some officers in our circle are loud in their praise of the fighting quality of the English, especially of the army they met at Mons, which they frankly admit did much to change the whole situation, and to convert a war that they thought would last for at the most a few days into the present wearisome tragedy. The economic situation changes imperceptibly but certainly. It cannot improve, and must assuredly grow worse.

"THE TIMES" AND THE WAR

29 December 1915

SIR,—AS TIME GOES on, and the eyes of our people are being slowly but surely opened to the intense seriousness of this life-and-death struggle in which we are locked with Germany, this war to the knife, in which one or other must bite the dust, the nation is beginning to feel the boundless debt of gratitude which it owes to *The Times* for its persistent courage in stating the unvarnished truth with regard to the progress of the war and our past deplorable shortcomings, which have been so clearly and so bravely expressed, as far as the all-important question of munitions supply is concerned, by Mr. Lloyd George. We cannot lose this war; our sea power must throttle Germany in the end, as it did Napoleon—that is, if the freedom of the Fleet is not curtailed by any too strict observance of those ghastly and to us dangerous fiascoes. The Hague Conference and the Declaration of London, which were so justly ridiculed by Germany, though accepted with hypocritical compliance with her tongue in her cheek; by the inexplicable tenderness towards our brutal enemy by politicians and by lawyers' law, which as regards the war should be consigned to the bottomless pit for its duration.

The only possible reason why we were justified in not accepting conscription, as other nations did, was because the German Emperor was believed to be a determined supporter of peace and a friend of Great Britain, as he declared himself often to be, and the firm belief that we should not be involved in a great Continental struggle. These two beliefs have vanished into thin air, and if we are to emerge triumphant from this war we must insist that absolute freedom of action is given to the Navy, and that, should Lord Derby's scheme not produce a sufficient number of young unmarried men to make good the enormous wastage in the Army caused most by the Gallipoli "gamble," conscription should be at once established, as it ought to have been 16 months ago, directly war was declared with a powerful "nation in arms."

The Times has from the commencement of the war courageously advocated these two vitally important measures, and has shown itself, as it has during all our great struggles, regardless of party and politics, and devoted only to the cause of the Empire and the total crushing of our deadly and eternal enemy—"macte esto virtute."

Your obedient servant,
ALFRED E. TURNER

1916

———◆———

THOUGHTS FOR NEW YEAR'S DAY

1 January 1916

SIR,—THE DAWN OF THE New Year irresistibly impels us towards retrospection and introspection. There are grave lessons to be learned and new resolutions to be formed. As we look back wonderingly through the shadows of the past 17 months, we find much to cause pride and rejoicing, but also much to arouse bitter regrets. Our Navy has accomplished more than even extremists of the Blue Water School dared to expect. It has shown resourcefulness beyond all praise. Our young commanders of submarines have seized every opportunity which offered, with skill and daring worthy of the traditions that Nelson bequeathed, and nothing has miscarried that has been left to the discretion of the Service afloat. Silence fell upon the Grand Fleet when war began, and landsmen in the Allied countries may not yet realize that it is the firm base upon which our and their operations securely rest. We may well say with the young military officer who gave his life at Ctesiphon and whose touching letter was recently published in *The Times*, "God bless the Navy."

The old, solid, highly-trained Army, which helped to save France at the great crisis of the war in August and September, 1914, has almost passed away; but at least 2½ millions of citizens have freely responded to the call of patriotic duty, and the annals of no country can show such a record. The raising, training, and supply of these masses of men constitute an achievement for which the War Office deserves full credit. Of the stormers of Badajos in the second siege Sir John Jones wrote:—

"The efforts of British troops occasionally set all calculations at defiance, and when a few years shall have swept away the eye-witnesses of their achievements of this night, they will not be credited."

This may, with equal justice, be said of the heroes who forced the landings on the Gallipoli Peninsula, and whether in Flanders, Gallipoli, or on the banks of the Tigris and Euphrates, British and Indian troops have endured trials far exceeding those of the Peninsular War. No improvised army has ever been called upon to undergo more searching ordeals, and none has shown greater aptitude and devotion. Canadian and Australasian troops, newly raised, have given proofs of valour never excelled. Even the new artillery units have surprised all who understand the exacting requirements of their arm, and have learned in months what we believed could be acquired only in years. Britons—always war-like, if unmilitary—have displayed fighting powers never approached in scale, or exceeded in quality, in the stormiest periods of their long history. The Dominions, lightly knit to the Mother Country in time of peace, but inspired by devotion to one Sovereign, one flag, and shared ideals, rose instantly to meet a common peril, and now stand grimly determined to throw their all into the scales of war. The Princes and Chiefs of India have given lavishly of their men and treasure to the great cause which they feel to be their own. For all this and more we have reason for supreme thankfulness as we look back through the war-swept vista of 17 months. So far the calculations of the German Great General Staff and of the affiliated Professors have been falsified.

Yet, as we survey the past, a sense of failure may come to us. The sacrifices have been so great, and the apparent results so disproportionate. To-day, on the Western as on the Eastern front, we can discern no near prospect of a decisive military success. At Salonika, we are preparing to defend positions which the enemy is not anxious to attack. The line of the Suez Canal must still be strongly held. On the banks of the Tigris we anxiously await the relief of the isolated British-Indian force which has most gallantly resisted a far superior enemy.

It may seem that the effect of the long and meticulous preparations of the Germans for aggressive war has not yet spent itself. In September last, however, it became clear that the Central Powers were not in a position to attack little Serbia, and that it was necessary to call in Bulgaria to administer the "stab in the back." At the present time the enemy's offensive depends upon the subsidized assistance of Turks and Bulgars, which has limits and must constitute a drain on German resources. Meanwhile, the economic situation in all enemy countries is becoming difficult, and the winter months will aid the Allies, whose resources in men and armaments are steadily growing, whose stern fixity of purpose is more than ever assured, and whose civil populations are not suffering from present over-strain. So much we may note as we seek to peer into the future. The immense efforts and sacrifices of the Allies have not been in vain, and must tell heavily in the coming year.

It is when we reflect upon the conduct of the war in all its branches that we find subject for regret and lessons to be learned. We were forced into conflict, not only with armed nations, but with the most powerful machine of government that the world has ever known. Our political conditions were such that Government had become dependent for motive power upon the electorate, which, so we have been told on high authority, was not interested in preparation for war. The grave warning of 1912 had passed unheeded and was withheld from the public. Aptitudes in domestic controversy, forensic arts, and official methods based upon the theory of continued peace became suddenly unserviceable. We had none of the memories which crowded darkly upon the French nation in August, 1914, and served to unloose a flood of burning patriotism by which France was transfigured. The British people, when at length "the day" dawned, had the direst need of leadership and found it not. To political conditions, methods, and habits of thoughts we owe the mistakes and the delays, the wavering and the incertitude which have marked the conduct of affairs in the greatest crisis the country has ever known. If, in the sight of our Allies, we did not appear to rise quickly to the full measure of this world conflict, the cause was not due to inherent defects of character, but to the want of enlightenment and direction. The handling of the Navy in regard to enemy imports, the treatment of the questions of internment, finance, and State economy, and postponement of measures for the provision of munitions and for instituting a National Register arose from the inability of Government to realize the inexorable needs of war and to take the prompt action to which the normal training of Ministers and the administrative machinery where alike opposed. Decisions waited until outside pressure was brought to bear and the co-ordination of the work of departments accustomed to independence was slowly and imperfectly affected. Even in the case of far-reaching military operations, our method of arriving at conclusions, judging from the revelations made public, were ill-conceived and unlikely to result in wise counsels. In no branch of knowledge need we admit inferiority to the Germans, and in military matters we had the advantage of comparatively recent experience; but the neglect to use the best brain power at our disposal was manifest during the first six months of war, when every day was important, and lingered to a later period. From the strategic point of view the Germans gained inevitably from the central direction which made their Allies the tools of a military policy happily not free from errors. We and our Allies have at length arranged to share in councils, where full discussion will be possible and sound views as to military action may be expected to prevail.

The main sources of past weakness are plain, and they can be removed if we earnestly undertake the task. For the whole nation there is only one object, compared with which all others—the political legacies of days that have gone—are trivial and irrelevant. For the sake of many thousands of gallant lives that have fallen, and of the bitter sorrows and suffering that remain, we must enter on the New Year with resolutions strongly forged in the fierce fires of war. Heavy sacrifices have come to us in 1915, but also inspiring memories of devotion, cheerful endurance, and true patriotism among all classes. If only real leadership, based on trust of the people, and organized methods are forthcoming in 1916, we and our true Allies, in growing strength, may fight on with calm confidence "until the day break and the shadows flee away" in the light of victory and peace.

I am, Sir, yours obediently,
SYDENHAM

AN INJUSTICE TO INVALIDED MEN

1 January 1916

SIR,—THE WASTAGE OF our armies through wounds and sickness has been so great that the War Office finds it necessary to issue stringent orders against the discharge from the Army of invalided men, should their state of body promise any capacity at all for further service. Not rarely they are sent back to the front when their war-worn bodies and minds need above everything some space of quiet life and some chance for recuperation at home. Large numbers of those who patriotically left civil employment and endured the risks and hardships of active service are now after having been wounded or nervously shattered at the front being returned to military duty. Many instances might be given. Here is one. A "New Army" soldier, picked up wounded and unconscious after a catastrophe, finds himself after three months again in the front trenches. His officer there, experiencing that he is unfit for such a place, insists on his withdrawal. The man is now passing through a renewed period of tentative military convalescence. In times of peace men of the kind I am speaking of would certainly be discharged from the Service. Had their casualties occurred by civil accident, monetary compensation by statute would ensure them a convalescence in their homes.

By what excuse of conscience can the service of these men to fight again despite their want of health be claimed by a State which yet hesitates to claim military service from sound men who have not yet served at all? Sound men who in many cases are reaping profit from the advance of civil wages and the sacrifices already made by these brother citizens, who could be invalided if there were sound men to take their place. The State is, indeed, burdening beyond all limit of endurance backs in many cases already broken. And at what cost of money! Such service is the most uneconomical of all. But there are things worse than want of economy. Of the illogicalities of our voluntary system the consequential injustice of none impresses more than does this one the unbiased onlooker who at first hand meets the pathos and the tragedy of its results.

I am, Sir, your obedient servant,
C. S. SHERRINGTON

A WORKING-CLASS VIEW

1 *January* 1916

SIR,—THE FOLLOWING extract from a letter received by me, unsolicited, from a working man constituent may be of interest as showing, as many of us in contact with working men know, that conscription would meet with a much larger measure of support from the working classes than some of the trades union leaders would lead the public to suppose. Stating that he has two sons in the Army, he continues:—

"I have another son about the age to join the Army, but he is not going to join until conscription is put in force, which will put them all on an equal footing. Perhaps my view of the way conscription would be voted for may interest you. If conscription for the period of the war only were put before the people I think all those who have sons or brothers in the Army would vote for it, while those who have sons who are shirking their duty are in favor of the voluntary system. As a working boilermaker, employed here and in Cardiff, I come in contact with a large number of working men, they all agree this war must be won by us, and conscription is the only logical solution of the difficulty."

Yours faithfully,
ALFRED MOND

Mond, then MP for Swansea, was an industrialist who would later create ICI. Some politicians feared imposing conscription on working-class men who, not being property owners, did not have the vote and hence no perceived reward for their sacrifice.

MULES AND THEIR TREATMENT

3 January 1916

SIR,—I SEND YOU AN extract from a letter which I have received from an officer at the front, and I hope you may find it sufficiently interesting and instructive for publication:—

"You asked me to tell you about our mules. We have 50 of them, and they have been with us since March last. We did not look forward to them at all. The truth is, not one of us knew anything about them, and I came across no one at the time who did. Our men, many of them unaccustomed to animals of any kind, were frightened of them. They arrived at night and led us a real dance. They had just come from America, and were thoroughly upset by their voyage and many handlings. Many, of course, were entirely unaccustomed to harness or to being ridden, and all were in very poor condition. Many were unshod, others were shod on forefeet only, and all were covered with lice. One man was savaged, and several were kicked on the first day, but I made up my mind to try nothing but kindness in dealing with them. I have never allowed a twitch to be used, or a mule to be hardly treated by beating, nor have I allowed them to be put in stocks when being shod. Kindness has paid in a wonderful way. Our mules let us do what we like with them. There are still one or two timid ones, but we have no difficulty in harnessing, shoeing, or handling, and they are the most willing and sensible of beasts, except when they are up against a load which they cannot move, and in that case they jib. I have always fed them on maize in preference to oats, because it is the food they were brought up upon in Argentina, and I have had no disease of any kind. Indeed, I was congratulated the other day in having the best-conditioned mules in the division, not a poor one amongst them, in spite of the hard work which a field company under present conditions finds for them to do."

I remain, Sir, yours truly,
CECIL CHAPMAN

LIKE FATHER, LIKE SON

10 January 1916

Sir,—Reading again the memoirs of Lord Byron's publisher, John Murray—a book worth returning to even amid the allurement of current literature—I come upon a passage that shows there is nothing new under the sun, not even the proclivities of an otherwise civilized nation that made possible the brutal ravaging of Belgium and the suffering imposed upon French towns and villages held in the grip of the Prussians. Within a month of the Battle of Waterloo John Murray made a trip to Paris. The Allied Armies having finally defeated Napoleon were marching on the French capital. Mr. Murray reports that "the Prussians, billeted on the population, were particularly outrageous in their demands, pillaging, devastating, and destroying in the provinces wherever they came all that they cannot use or take away, even to burning the houses of the inhabitants upon whom they had lived." Respecting the conduct of the British troops, "there is but one universal sentiment of admiration. Their forbearance has been exemplary, equal to their courage, and extends to the most inferior private." One hundred years later these passages might without variation of a word have been written in correspondence from victims and eye-witnesses in Flanders and in France. Indeed, I have read in the columns of *The Times* reports absolutely identical in purport.

Yours faithfully,
HENRY LUCY

OUR NEIGHBOURS' EXAMPLE

26 January 1916

Sir,—May I echo Lord Redesdale's final remark in his letter of the 19th inst.? How grand are the Frenchwomen!

Yesterday, not far behind the shell area, I met a frail French girl, not more than 17 years old, very nearsighted, but ploughing industriously with two large horses. The operation seemed to tax all her strength. Arrived at the end of the furrow, I asked, was there no one to help her. "Non, M'sieur. Mon frère est à la guerre." Is it not too hard for you? "Non, M'sieur," with an air that seemed to say, "It is hard—but I don't mean to admit it." And she started on the new furrow. She had no time for idle conversation. Certainly—How grand are the Frenchwomen!

And the men also play their part! To-day I overtook a miner making his way home across the fields. As we were some distance from any mine I asked him had he come from the nearest one—some four miles distant. "No, I come from B—," and he mentioned one quite seven miles away. How long does it take you to do the journey? An hour and a half. What are your hours of work? Twelve hours—three hours extra to our peace shift, owing to the war. So you have 12 hours' work and three hours' walking every day? Yes. That is a good deal! In war all is hard—with a cheery shrug, and we parted.

Certainly—How grand is the French nation!

I have the honour to be, Sir,
Your obedient servant,
A COLONEL OF GUNS

GERMAN SLANDERS ON
BRITISH TROOPS

1 February 1916

SIR,—WHEN THE GERMANS either have committed or are about to commit some barbarous outrage, it is their practice to accuse us of some similar outrage. In support of this may I refer to evidence which I have recently taken for the Belgian Government, and which is summarized in the 21st report of the Belgian Committee on violation of the Laws of War? The witness was an educated Belgian lady, of unimpeachable character. She had heard that a train of wounded was coming into L— Station, and went there to see if she could render help. In one truck seven wounded British soldiers had been placed. Two had died in the truck, but their bodies had not been removed. There was a soup kitchen at the station. A German corporal brought some soup, showed it to the wounded men, and then took it away, saying, "Not for you English swine." The men were crying out for water. A German private brought some water, showed it to them, and then threw it over them. The lady after several struggles succeeded in bringing some water to the poor fellows, and was duly punished for her offence. On previous occasions we have had somewhat similar accounts of German brutality from members of the Belgian Red Cross.

We had some interesting evidence about Miss Edith Cavell from a Franciscan Father. He told us that she was in no way connected with the Belgian committee for aiding the escape of prisoners of war. Anything that she may have done was done out of womanly sympathy for individuals who came to her for help, and she well knew the fate that awaited them if she did not give that help.

I am, Sir, your obedient servant,
M. D. CHALMERS

THE ZEPPELINS

LESSONS OF THE LAST RAID

4 February 1916

SIR,—THIS LAST ZEPPELIN raid has cleared the air. There may be difficulties from the aircraft point of view in reprisals. I am not behind the scenes and do not know. But as regards policy there can be none. We have too long displayed a passive and excessive patience.

We all remember Gray's noble line, "To scatter plenty o'er a smiling land." For "plenty" read "bombs," and you have the Prussian ideal. To scatter bombs over a countryside, to destroy indiscriminately the mansion and cottage, the church and the school, to murder unoffending civilians, women, children, and sucklings in their beds, these are the noble aspirations of Prussian chivalry, acclaimed by their nation as deeds of merit and daring.

Let them realize this triumph, let us bring it directly to their hearts and homes. Let us unsparingly mete out their measure to themselves. Nothing else will make them realize their glories. And the blood of any who may suffer will rest on their Government, not on ours.

ROSEBERY

GRAMOPHONES IN HOSPITALS

12 *February 1916*

SIR,—I WRITE AS ONE with experience. I have been wounded six times in this campaign and four times in earlier. I do not differentiate my experiences by the nature of my wounds, the skill of the surgeons, or the charm of the nurses, nor even by country, be it France, Flanders, Africa, or the Farther East, though in all of these have I lain in hospital. No, Sir, there is another matter of far more "arresting" significance than any of these that distinguishes our modern, enlightened civilization from the dark, uncultured wars of old. I refer, you will have already guessed, to the presence of the gramophone in all hospitals and most aid-posts, and it is to the donors of these that I make my appeal, and my appeal is, "Give no more." In one hospital from which I have been recently "evacuated" the chief medical officer had the temerity, brutality, lack of culture, call it what you will, to limit the hours of music on the gramophone from 8 a.m. to 8 p.m. Consider the state of the sick and suffering, of those mangled, sleepless patients, who, used elsewhere to unlimited musical alleviation, were here allowed only 12 hours of this musical culture. But the generous donors of gramophones may well say, if this be the measure of the popularity of our gifts, why in the name of all the Nine Muses do you cry, "Give no more"?

Most generous but most thoughtless race; who is it who rule the world? The healthy, dominant, strong, or the worn and weary? And in the hospital world it is the same. It is the small former class, deficient perhaps of little fingers or great toes, who ceaselessly supply these musical gifts with endless "records," to the distress of their prostrate comrades, too ill to protest, too weary to make a fuss, who accept this last form of culture, not as a blessing nor with a blessing, and who fail to recognize in it—

ea sola voluptas
solamenque mali

It is this that makes me add my one appeal to the countless number that beset your readers, and say, "For gramophones give no more."

A PART WORN COLONEL

From *The Aeneid* of Virgil: "That was his sole delight and solace in his woe."

SOLDIERS AND MORPHIA

16 February 1916

SIR,—THE RECENT PROSECUTION at Folkestone for the sale of cocaine to Colonial troops prompts me to suggest the danger of sending small quantities of morphia to men at the front. I have recently been shown what appear to be small silver matchboxes, which can be obtained from well-known jewellers and silversmiths in the West-end. In reality these matchboxes, which are provided with a chain for suspension round the neck, contain three tubes filled with tablets of morphine hydrochloride. The idea is that when the wearer is wounded he can place a tablet on his tongue and so obtain relief from pain until he is attended to. This scheme is very well-intentioned on the part of both the jewellers and the kind friends who buy the matchboxes; but, unfortunately, the men have in many instances been tempted to take the tablets, not to diminish pain, but to act as a stimulant after fatigue. I have been told by medical officers that the number of cases of morphia-habit that have arisen from this practice is becoming serious. It is generally admitted that the Royal Army Medical Corps is an efficient service, and the public can well leave the wounded to its attention. Morphiomania is a terrible malady, and the small amount of good that may come from the purchase of the matchboxes cannot compare with the harm that is already coming from it.

I am, Sir, yours faithfully,
H. C. ROSS

ARMY NURSES

17 February 1916

Sir,—I met an Army nurse a few days ago who, after serving many months of strenuous work in the Eastern Mediterranean, had been invalided with enteric fever. She spent two months in hospital in London, along with other sick nurses. She spoke of one of their chief "amusements" during that monotonous time, and that was watching the lines of motor-cars brought by kind people to a military hospital close by to take out wounded and convalescent officers and men. But nobody ever came to take them out. Now, we ought not to overlook our nurses these times. I wish some of your readers could see them at work, sometimes under the most adverse conditions. They are simply magnificent. I have myself worked along with them during the strenuous fighting days of August, and nobody who has ever thus been associated with them or has been a patient under their tender care can ever say too much of these splendid women. When we consider their marvellous and untiring energy and unfailing cheerfulness, and the miserable pittance a grateful country allows them, it is a wonder we do not try to give them a little more happiness when they are invalided back to us. Let us treat them at least as well as officers and men. They deserve it quite as much, perhaps more.

Yours, &c.,
R. A. M. C.

DISAFFECTION IN KERRY

25 February 1916

SIR,—MR. JOHN REDMOND has issued a further appeal to the manhood of Ireland to do its duty and fill up the reserves of our gallant Irish regiments. I fear much that this appeal will fall on very deaf ears in this county of Kerry. Recruiting in this county, with a population of some 165,000, is dead. Many causes have helped to kill it. The open and avowed pro-German, anti-recruiting, Sein Fein element has been allowed to spread and to spread until every village in Kerry is rotten with it. In May last I warned his Excellency the Lord Lieutenant that if meetings openly anti-recruiting in their objects were allowed to be held in this county trouble would surely follow. The reply from Dublin Castle reads:— "If any breach of the Defence of the Realm regulations occurs, it will be dealt with by the competent military authority." On February 6 a recruiting meeting was being held in Killarney. A Sein Fein mob, headed by a band, marched up and down through this meeting, with the usual accompaniment of booing and yelling. This riotous mob was led by one of the justices of the peace for County Kerry. This man is still a justice of the peace and, I suppose, likely to remain one. A personal representative of his Excellency the Lord Lieutenant was present at this Killarney meeting, and I have no doubt reported fully to the authorities. Mr. Birrell, who seems to live mostly in England, says, "All's well in Ireland, pass me on my £4,000 a year."

Truly yours,
MORGAN O'CONNELL

Augustine Birrell was chief secretary for Ireland, in effect the minister responsible for it. He was soon to be castigated for not taking firmer action to prevent the Easter Rising.

THE FUNERAL OF HENRY JAMES

4 March 1916

SIR,—THE GROUP OF FRIENDS, a large company, who gathered in Old Chelsea Church this afternoon, must have included several whose thoughts went back, like mine, to the mysterious and poignant story which Henry James contrived to publish 25 years ago, after it had knocked in vain— incredible revelation—"at half a dozen editorial doors impenetrably closed to it." Some of us must have thought that "The Altar of the Dead" of our wonderful friend has been found in the beautiful old dim church of All Saints which stood almost at his door, and into which, he too burdened with unutterable regrets, often silently slipped. As we stood round the shell of that incomparable brain, of that noble and tender heart, it flashed across me that to generations yet unawakened to a knowledge of his value the Old Chelsea Church must for ever be the Altar of the Dead.

No man has awakened greater loyalty or penetrated so many shy spirits with affection. But we want to proclaim to the sensual world that when the war with Germany broke out he ceased to be merely the idol of an esoteric group. He became a soldier; he belonged to England. No one has suffered more in spirit, no one was more tensely agitated by the war, than Henry James. Not that he doubted of our victory, which was to be his victory. In the deadliest trances of the night he never questioned the end. But his nature was like a violin-string, and it was strained until it snapped.

He was a supreme artist; but what we must remember and repeat is that he was a hero. He belonged to a neutral nation that he was attached to by a thousand ties. Yet he broke them all to devote himself, heart and brain and vibrating nerves, entirely to his passionate love of England. He was a volunteer in our great cause. Quite in the beginning of August, 1914, he said to two English friends, "However British you may be, I am more British still." He has died before we celebrate the catastrophe of wickedness, and perhaps it is as well, for his great heart might have broken with joy in the midst of the huzzas.

But let those who knew Henry James and those who knew him not approach the Altar of the Dead with reverence, for he was an English hero of whom England shall be proud.

I am, Sir, your obedient servant,
EDMUND GOSSE

WOMEN ON THE LAND

13 March 1916

Sir,—In your leader upon the employment of women you say that the chief step is the offer of adequate wages. The custom of employing women upon farms has never quite ceased in the north, but the supply of women is undoubtedly affected by the competition of munition work. I pass no opinion as to whether munition workers are extravagantly paid; I only know that farmers cannot compete with their wages. Three girls have gone from adjoining farms here; they expect to earn at least £2 wages per week. They are trained dairymaids and milkers, but totally inexperienced in mechanics. The present waste of skilled training is unfortunate. At one and the same time I was receiving from a Labour Exchange advice to take outside women on my farm; from another Labour Exchange requests for the character of my cowman's daughters for munitions; and my little general servant was being canvassed to go on the land (from which I should presumably have been removed to do the housework). I have worked on it for years and love it; but I still feel some sympathy with the perplexity of the farmers. Harm is being done by the ridiculous and vulgar photographs which appear in the Press. I am perfectly ready to employ the right sort of woman. French women and North country girls have found it possible to work in a short petticoat, and they have not required the theatrical attractions of uniform and armlet to induce them to do their duty.

Yours truly,
A WOMAN FARMER

MISMANAGEMENT IN MESOPOTAMIA

15 March 1916

Sir,—Your leading article in this morning's issue on "Mismanagement in Mesopotamia" will be welcomed by all who, like myself, are personally interested in this campaign and have known for a long time past of the deficiencies to which you now call attention, but have hesitated to give expression publicly thereto, in the hope that adequate measures, however belated, were at last being taken by the Indian Government to correct them. It is quite time, however, that the public were made aware of the serious state of things to which you now direct attention.

The Indian Government appear to have had no ideas beyond the small frontier expeditions to which they are accustomed and to have ignored the fact that the enemy in this case are provided with the most modern weapons of war and, under the instruction of their German masters, are skilled in every device which the long trench warfare on the Western front has developed. The Indian Army is composed of splendid fighting material in a high state of efficiency, and its highly trained staff will compare most favourably with that of the British Army in the West, but the Indian Government have failed to make the best use of it, reducing its efficiency by parcimony in essential details, and wasting it by the incorrigible British habit of sending a boy to do a man's job. Even at the very beginning—at Basra in December, 1914—the supply of dressings and bandages gave out at once, and yet but two months ago the medical staff at Atnara had no bandages and had practically run out of antiseptics and anæsthetics, the wounded often had no change of dressings for four or five days, there were not nearly sufficient blankets. For 2,000 wounded preparations had been made for 200, and so on. Surely after 15 months' campaign something must be very wrong for such a state of things to be possible. Then as regards artillery, there does not seem to have been an adequate conception of the requirements. Imagine sending to Mesopotamia from Gallipoli mountain guns which had already fired 10 times the number of shells that are supposed to represent the life of a gun! If what remains of the gallant 6th Division—Townshend's Invincibles, who were sent up "in the air" on an impossible task without support, and have now been for over three months beleaguered in Kut—are left there until it is too late, the public will demand that the responsibility for such a disaster shall be brought home to the right quarters.

There is much matter for very pertinent questions in Parliament, which meets to-day, and I trust that members interested in India are giving full attention to the subject.

FORTITER

Much of the British force in Iraq, sent there to protect British oilfields in Iran, had become besieged at Kut by Ottoman troops. A relief effort had recently failed.

————◆————

THE CASE FOR A GENERAL ELECTION

21 March 1916

Sir,—Recognizing to the full the high sense of patriotic duty which prompted the leaders of the Unionist Party to enter into the Coalition, we have given that Coalition Government the utmost support that conscience would permit. Support ceases to be useful when misgiving spreads itself throughout the nation.

The nation is learning more and more that the Coalition Government contains elements which will not coalesce. From the first—almost avowedly—there have been divided counsels. These come together only by compromise; and a policy of compromise, however convenient in peace, is fatal in war. One day Lord Selborne attacks Lord Derby, the Government's recruiting agent, and bluntly declares that not Lord Derby's advice, but his own, should be followed. Lord Derby tells us that if Lord Selborne's views are those of the Government, he must resign. One day we are told that groups of married men are to be called up. On Tuesday the order is cancelled. On Wednesday Lord Kitchener tells us that the married men must presently be called. On Thursday Mr. Long tells us that there is no divergence of opinion and makes a vigorous defence of his own and his colleagues' honour, which had never been impugned. No; there is no charge of bad faith; only of dire lack of cohesion and of firmness of purpose.

In other spheres it is the same. As to our economic policy after the war, we have lately heard some ringing words of leading and of guidance; but they have not come from our own rulers. With them there is only procrastination, compromise, non-commitment.

We are often told from the Treasury Bench that there is no alternative to a Coalition Government. It is not a peculiarly manly or comforting argument; but it may be true. Does it follow that a Coalition Government must be constituted on the present basis? Surely concentration of purpose is possible only if Government is in the hands of a few men who can sink for the time their divergent principles. Half-a-dozen men might do the nation's behest. A promiscuous company of 23 is—what we see and lament. Are we sure that we have got the best of the youth, the energy, the courage, that are available? We listened last week to faltering apologies and halting explanations as to our military organization. It was another atmosphere when, on Friday night, the Prime Minister of Australia proved to the Pilgrims that the Empire possessed a man with foresight to discern, courage to lead, and forcefulness of personality to arouse enthusiasm. Amongst our chosen 23 and their long string of Under-Secretaries—selected with a due balance so as to adjust party claims—do we find any echo of that personal and compelling touch?

What wonder that increasing numbers are asking, Why not try the wholesome effect of a General Election? An appeal to the nation might clear the air, and save us from dangerous cabals. One thing would be all to the good: in an election now the party caucuses would have a minimum of influence. In the fixed purpose of the national will we have a splendid asset. It might be well to let it have free play.

I am, Sir, your obedient servant,
HENRY CRAIK

Derby had presided over a voluntary scheme intended to shame men into joining up. Conscription for single men under 41 had been imposed at the start of March, prompting the resignation of the home secretary. Married men were added in May. Ireland was exempt.

PROVISIONS LEFT BEHIND BY CAPTAIN SCOTT'S PARTY

27 March 1916

SIR,—IN VIEW OF THE fact, as stated in *The Times* of to-day, that there will be anxiety as to the food supplies available for the Ross Sea section of Sir Ernest Shackleton's Antarctic Expedition, you may be glad to publish these lists of provisions left in January, 1913, by Captain Scott's last expedition. They are compiled from the official lists which I have here.

At Cape Evans, where 10 men are stated to be left, Captain Scott's hut was left in perfect condition, with stove, bed, tables, &c., and the following provisions:— Sledging biscuits, 1,906lb.; pemmican, 780lb.; sugar, 546lb.; chocolate, 180lb.; cocoa, 456lb.; flour, 3,700lb.; jams, 1,470lb.; lard and margarine, 608lb.; oatmeal, 1,302lb.; dried vegetables, &c., 954lb.; biscuit, 1,488lb.; various other foods, 706lb.

The stores also included plenty of salt. A considerable amount of provisions was left ready for use in the hut, apart from those mentioned in the above list.

At Hut Point, 13 miles south, where Sir Ernest Shackleton's party would arrive, there is the old Discovery Hut, with a blubber stove, sledging provisions complete for four men for 20 weeks, with 520lb. sledging biscuits and 15 large cases of "cabin" biscuits. Also pemmican, 200lb.; cocoa, 48lb.; sugar, 250lb.; flour, 210lb.; oatmeal, 210lb.; lard, &c., 110lb.; dried vegetables, 300lb.; with some butter, salt, tea, sardines, and other luxuries.

Communication between Hut Point and Cape Evans over the newly-formed sea ice was possible in 1911 and 1912 during the first two weeks of April. Large numbers of seals and penguins can be killed, and meat and provisions will always keep fresh if properly stored.

I hope the publication of these particulars may lessen anxiety.

I am, Sir, yours faithfully,

A. CHERRY-GARRARD, British Antarctic Expedition, 1910-13

SUNDAY MUNITION WORK

30 March 1916

SIR,—THREE TIMES NOW has the Health of Munition Workers Committee warned the Government of the evils of working seven days a week, but so far nothing has been done in the Government factories. The first time the trade unions took the matter up and got a promise that Sunday work should be stopped. The second time the Government appealed to the "controlled" establishments to abolish Sunday work. This time you have published the third warning from the committee with the sub-title "Overwork a Source of Waste." There are now thousands of middle-aged and old men in the Arsenal quite unused to factory life; also many discharged soldiers unfit for active service by reason of wounds or illness, to say nothing of the number rejected or obviously unfit for military service. What a horrible waste of money it is to pay these men extra for working on Sunday when 12 hours a day for six days in the week is already beyond their strength. This consideration ought to appeal now that every one is advising every one else to economize. Then to bring these tired men here on the seventh day thousands of other tired workers on railways and trams and hundreds more in canteens are also compelled to work seven days in the week. And all this energy is wasted, if the report of the committee is to be trusted. After nearly a year of canteen work, first at the Royal Small Arms Factory and afterwards at Woolwich, I am certain they have understated the case, and that the harm done to the efficiency of the workers proves that the output must suffer.

Yours, &c.,
CANTEEN WORKER

CONSCIENTIOUS OBJECTORS

4 April 1916

Sir,—As I read of the handling of conscientious objectors by some local tribunals, I am visited by some painful fears. The Act of Parliament under which these men were recruited provides in explicit terms that the conscientious objector to war is to be exempt from service. Now I have no wish to screen cowards or shirkers; if such there be, let them be exposed. But that there are among us conscientious objectors, all agree. The Friends are such, and are exempted. There are others outside of that body, in the Church of England for example—in spite of the Thirty-nine Articles. Need any man be ashamed of interpreting the Gospel as did Tolstoy? Such a man may be useless for war, but he may be a useful citizen. We want prophets and visionaries, and we shall need them still more. The will or capacity to take an enemy's life is not the only element in good citizenship. At all events, the honest objector is safeguarded by the law, let him enjoy its protection.

Is the nation, in its military zeal, slipping into the old vices of intolerance and persecution? Conscience is a sacred thing. Is private judgment to be swept wholly aside in time of war? As I read these reports I am set thinking of the rough treatment of Faithful by the Court in Vanity Fair, as described by John Bunyan, or of the trials of heretics by the agents of the Inquisition. "What chance would Christ have to-day?" wrote Mabel Dearmer bitterly from Serbia: "Crucifixion would be a gentle death for such a dangerous lunatic."

If I felt that what I have written could in the least degree hamper our Government in the victorious prosecution of the war I would not write it. But it is perilous to trample on conscience; we must not try to deprive the honest objector of the protection secured to him by the law of the land.

Yours, &c.,
EDWARD: LINCOLN

The writer, Edward Hicks, was Bishop of Lincoln.

ECONOMY IN DRESS

4 April 1916

SIR,—A WELL-KNOWN firm, typical of the fashion world, has just issued a spring catalogue. At least seven yards more stuff is required on every dress than was the case last year. May we ask who is responsible for the setting of these fashions, and whether it can be really true that we are asked to economize in clothes? Is every patriotic woman to protest to her dressmaker, or doesn't it really matter?

Yours truly,
PERPLEXED

"DOMINION" HOSPITALS

7 April 1916

Sir,—Orders have been issued from time to time to medical officers in hospitals in the London area to transfer all their "Dominions" wounded who are fit to be moved to special hospitals, for New Zealanders, Australians, Canadians, and South Africans respectively. The same order of segregation applies to convalescent hospitals near London.

The advantage, however, of mixing up "Dominions" and British wounded in the same hospitals is very great. The men fraternize and meet one another's relatives, and lifelong friendships are being made on all sides, which will be of value in the days of emigration to come. The influence for good of the "Dominions" men amongst the men of Great Britain (particularly among the poorer class of London born and bred Tommy) is very noticeable. Medical officers and nurses are unanimous in their praise of the conduct of these "Dominions" men in hospital, and particularly of the Anzacs from Gallipoli. I know of many cases where good influences are at work through this admixture. The "Dominions" man himself seems to be more than satisfied and pleased with his treatment in our hospitals, and strongly objects to being transferred.

The advantages of segregation are purely administrative; but the difficulties attaching to the opposite system have been overcome in the past and I feel sure can, with a little care and attention, be satisfactorily dealt with in the future. From the point of view of the welfare of this country—to enlarge and open its eyes to an Imperial view of things in the future—and for the good of our Dominions and emigration after the war, these new regulations, I feel earnestly, require serious reconsideration.

Yours, &c.,
A MEDICAL OFFICER

GERMAN CHANCELLOR ON PEACE

11 April 1916

SIR,—IN THE COURSE OF a speech delivered in the Reichstag on the 6th inst the German Chancellor made the following remarks on the conditions of peace:—

Let us suppose, I suggest, that Mr. Asquith sits down with me at table to examine the possibilities of peace, and Mr. Asquith begins with a claim for the definitive and complete destruction of Prussia's military power. The conversation would be ended almost before it began. To these peace conditions only one answer is left, and this answer our own sword must give. ... The enemy wants to destroy united free Germany. They wish to put Germany back to what she was during past centuries, a prey to the lust of domination of her neighbours and the scapegoat of Europe, beaten for ever in the domain of economic evolution even after the war is over. That is what our enemies mean when they speak of the definite destruction of Prussia's military power.

For three reasons this remarkable utterance is worthy of attention. First, because it represents what the German Government wishes the rest of the world to believe. Secondly, because it probably embodies what the vast majority of Germans themselves believe. Thirdly, because so long as the Germans continue in this belief the difficulties of concluding peace will be almost insuperable.

I am aware that in present circumstances there is little to be gained in bandying words with our opponents. I am also aware that it would at present be altogether premature to discuss the possible terms of peace in anything approaching to detail. I cannot help thinking, however, that it would be advisable that some authoritative notice should be taken of the German Chancellor's statement, if only to show to the rest of the world, and also possibly to such Germans as still have ears to hear, not only what we are but also what we are not fighting for.

I am not aware that either Mr. Asquith or any other responsible authority in this country has said anything which can be contorted into a desire to aim at "the complete destruction of Prussia's military power." I am quite certain that they have never said that they wish to destroy a "united Germany." They certainly cannot have said that they wish to destroy a "free" Germany, for Germany is not and never has been "free," in the sense in which we are accustomed to use that word. Had Germany enjoyed freedom, it is possible that the devastating war which Herr von Bethmann Hollweg so much deplores would never have occurred.

So far as I know, no one in this country wishes to destroy the "military power" of Prussia. The military strength of Prussia always has been, is now, and probably will continue to be very great. None in this country would object to its maintenance, provided that they could feel some definite assurance that it would be used for legitimate purposes and would cease to be an abiding menace to the rest of the world. What they object to is that this vast military power should be in the hands of an absolutist Sovereign, only responsible to himself, who is apparently guided by a number of people whose views on the sanctity of international engagements and of State morality are wholly at variance with those held by every other civilized nation. Herr von Bethmann Hollweg would have been nearer the mark if he had said that we wish to destroy, not the military power of Prussia, but the militarist party dominant in that country. There is a very great distinction between the two objects.

My own views as regards the main object for which we are fighting may be embodied in three simple propositions.

The first of these is that there can be no prospect of a durable peace so long as uncontrolled Junkerdom reigns supreme in Germany.

The second is that any change in the direction of bringing Junkerdom under effective control must be the work of the Germans themselves. Even if the Germans were completely vanquished it would be a fatal error to endeavour to impose from without any internal reforms on Germany. The capital error made at the time of the Declaration of Phillnitz must not be repeated.

The third is that we need not and should not continue the struggle for mere military glory, or to humiliate Germany, or, in the German Chancellor's words, to obstruct "the economic evolution" of Germany, or even to avenge the cruel misdeeds perpetrated by the German Army with the consent and approbation of its commanders. But we cannot, in justice to ourselves, to the rest of Europe, and to posterity, lay down the sword until the Germans are converted, and until they wake up to the fact that their present policy and system of government constitute a curse both to themselves and the rest of the civilized world. No such conversion can take place until the complete failure of their system is rendered so clear to whatever sane elements remain in Germany as to encourage them to throw off the yoke of Junkerdom and again to enter into the comity of civilized nations, from which they are now banished.

I remain, Sir, &c.,
CROMER

CROMWELL ON WAR

15 April 1916

SIR,—IN MORE THAN ONE respect Cromwell resembled the officers of our new Armies. He was not a soldier by profession. He had acquired from reading some knowledge of the European wars of his time, but all that he knew about fighting he learnt while he was fighting. His original qualification for the command of a troop of horse was his active habits, his knowledge of horses, and his power of dealing with men. What distinguished him from other officers of the same class was his complete devotion to the cause and his concentration of all his powers on its success. He never wrote about the art of war; his principles are revealed in his letters as he worked them out, one by one, under the pressure of events.

First, the necessity of swift action. "It is happy to resist beginnings betimes." "Our motion must be exceeding speedy, or it will do no good at all."

Secondly, the necessity of united action. "It's no longer disputing, but out instantly all you can." ... "You may help forward in sending such forces to us as lie unprofitably in your country. ... The enemy may teach us that wisdom who is not wanting to himself in making up his best strength for the accomplishment of his designs."

Thirdly, the necessity of getting all the men possible. "I know it will be difficult to raise thus many in so short time, but let me assure you, it's necessary, and therefore to be done."

Above all things energy was essential, alike in the field and in the council. "We have some amongst us much slow in action; if we could all intend our own ends less, and our own ease too, our business would go on wheels for expedition." "There is nothing to be feared but our own sin and sloth."

He could not infuse his own energy into others. "Weak counsels and weak actings undo all," he complained, and urged on Parliament a change of men as well as measures. "It is now a time to speak, or forever hold the tongue. The important occasion now is no less than to save a nation, out of a bleeding, nay, almost dying, condition, which the long continuance of this war hath already brought it into; so that without a more speedy, vigorous, and effectual prosecution of the war we shall make the kingdom weary of us, and hate the name of a Parliament. ... If I may speak my conscience, without reflection upon any, I do conceive if the army be not put into another method, and the war more vigorously prosecuted, the people can bear the war no longer, and will enforce you to a dishonourable peace."

The change was made, and in a year the war was practically over. Is it necessary to point the moral? One historical situation never exactly resembles another, but in all wars Cromwell's words are true that "weak counsels and weak actings undo all."

Yours faithfully,
C. H. FIRTH

———◆———

ANZAC MEMORIAL SERVICE

17 April 1916

SIR,—WILL YOU ALLOW ME a small space in your valuable paper to put before the public the fact that there were a great many British troops engaged in the first landing on April 25, 1915, at the Dardanelles? I see in your paper a service is to be held in memory of the Anzacs who fell in the landing. There were more British troops engaged, and their casualties were three times as heavy. The great landing seems now to be entirely claimed by the Anzacs, whereas I venture to state that, had it not been for the 29th (Regular) Division, the East Lancashire Division, and the Naval Division, no landing would have been made. One never reads the paper without seeing some word of praise for the Anzacs, and quite rightly too; but what is said of the thousands of heroes lying forgotten between Morto Bay and "Y" Beach? Nearly the whole of the 29th Division, one of the finest divisions of the Regular Army, lies there; surely something might be done to perpetuate their memory. I am sure his Majesty the King would like those fallen ones who have served him for many years in far distant lands honoured by their fellow-countrymen.

Yours, &c.,
A SURVIVOR OF THE 29TH DIVISION

THE GALLIPOLI LANDING

25 April 1916

SIR,—ALL THOSE WHOSE great privilege it was to have been with the 29th Division in Gallipoli will be rejoiced to hear of the memorial service to "Anzacs" to be held at Westminster Abbey to-day. The admiration of the division for the Australians and New Zealanders was unbounded, especially, when some of them were landed on Cape Helles and made their magnificent charge on May 8 through the trenches held by the 88th Brigade, to which part of the 86th had been attached. I heard many of the officers say afterwards that it was an unforgettable sight. With three cheers for Australia they rushed forward, utterly fearlessly, against an absolutely murderous fire from the Turkish machine-guns, rifles, and guns.

As chaplain to the 86th Brigade, which was first to land on Cape Helles and covered the landing for the rest of the division, I knew many of the officers and men who lost their lives that day. To anyone knowing the circumstances that landing must rank as one of the greatest achievements in our military history. It entailed the sacrifice of more than half the brigade. The 2nd Royal Fusiliers landed on X beach under cover of the guns of the Implacable without a casualty, though they lost very heavily later that day. The 1st Lancashire Fusiliers made their memorable landing on W beach, afterwards known as Lancashire Landing in their honour, losing over half their men. The 1st Royal Dublin Fusiliers and the 1st Royal Munster Fusiliers landed at V beach from the River Clyde, losing so heavily that when I joined the Dublins a few days later there was only one officer and a little more than 200 men left. The brigade had achieved practically the impossible. Many felt that the effecting of the landing against the tremendous difficulties which had to be encountered was the first real victory we had won in the war. Some of us would have liked a memorial service to the 29th Division to have been held on the first anniversary of their landing, but, though it was tentatively suggested, it seemed impossible to arrange. I had prepared my diary, with various accounts by officers in the 86th Brigade both alive and dead, for publication at this time, but the military authorities have delayed its publication, and I hope that those who had helped me and were looking for it will see this letter and understand why it has not appeared after having been announced in your columns. I merely write this letter in order that the relations of those who fell may not feel that they have been forgotten, though nothing has been done officially by way of a memorial to them.

Yours faithfully,
O. CREIGHTON C.F.

THE TROUBLE IN IRELAND

2 May 1916

SIR,—GOVERNMENT WAS doubtless aware that mischief was brewing and knew the ringleaders concerned. But if these traitors had been arrested and punished before they had committed any overt act of rebellion a storm of protest would have been raised by ignorant, prejudiced, or weak-kneed people. The blame should come in if and when Government fails to punish adequately the responsible leaders—not the dupes, but the men who have led them astray.

I am, Sir, &c.,
WILLIAM LITTLE

SIR,—IT IS WITH BITTER feeling I read in your paper of the rebellion at my home (Dublin). It is indeed a horror to think that my dear ones at home are in danger of being killed by my own countrymen. The same men for whom I have been fighting in Gallipoli. I trust the English will see that the full penalty of the law is carried out on all rebels taken prisoners. In conclusion, I may add it is some consolation to know that Irish regiments are making fame for themselves at the present moment at Hulluch.

Private G. V. POULTON, No. 15878, 7th Royal Dublin Fusiliers

The Easter Rising had taken place in Dublin in the last week of April, as republicans began the armed effort to end British rule of Ireland.

CONSCRIPTION IN IRELAND

3 May 1916

Sir,—May I, as an Irish Nationalist and a Radical, in both cases in the most extreme senses of the terms, but always subordinating both my Nationalism and my Radicalism to what I believe to be in the best interests of the Empire, now express the hope that there will be no more of this most damnable policy of waiting and seeing, and that conscription will be at once adopted, in its most drastic form, not only for Great Britain but for Ireland? I could quote scores of instances, within my own personal knowledge, of glaring inequality of sacrifice, sufficient to convince the most conservative adherent to ancient prejudices of the utter inequity of the present system in England, but I wish in this letter to confine myself to Ireland.

Over nine months ago I remonstrated strongly with one of the acknowledged leaders of the Irish Party in the House of Commons on his opposition to the application of compulsory military service to Ireland, pointing out to him that the Irish people are a nation of soldiers, that they would one and all welcome the chance of being trained as such, and that their alleged antagonism to compulsion came, not from their own hearts, but from the instigation of their political leaders, some of whom, of sufficient standing and ability to influence the whole party, equally failed to appreciate either the inclinations of their own countrymen or the effect that their military services would have on the Empire at large. I am forbidden to quote fully the reply I received, but its main argument was that any attempt of the nature I suggested would cause bloodshed and have disastrous consequences, not only in Ireland but in America and in the Colonies.

Well, I, as an Irishman, do not believe it would have caused bloodshed then or at any time. But if it had, would the blood shed have been one tithe of that which has been poured forth in torrents in the Dublin shambles during the horrors of the last week? We do not yet know, may perhaps never know, the numbers of the poor misguided youths, with hearts full of patriotic fire and of what I shall call the spirit of Christian Bushido, that puts country above everything, who have given up their young lives; but hundreds must have fallen. Every one of these youths was a possible O'Leary, and if conscription had put him into the ranks, trained and equipped, with the other O'Learys already there, he would last week have been fighting at Hulluch with the same reckless bravery as that with which, ill armed and untrained, he has faced the troops of England at the barricades of Dublin. It is not yet too late. A hundred and fifty years ago rebel Highland clansmen were converted into Highland regiments. Give the surviving Dublin rebels, who are already or soon will be prisoners, the chance of joining the Imperial Army. Form them into new Dublin or Leinster regiments, and there will soon be an Irish brigade that will emulate the most glorious deeds of the Irish regiments of the past or present wars, and with this example before them the rest of their countrymen will not raise one word of protest against sharing any obligations that are equitably imposed on other citizens of the United Kingdom.

Yours faithfully,
JOSEPH H. LONGFORD

———◆———

DUBLIN—THE NEXT PHASE

5 May 1916

SIR,—A DISQUIETING RUMOUR is prevalent here that the officials at Dublin Castle are anxious to dispense with martial law, and to take up the reins of government again at an early date. I desire to say two things.

First, martial law is the only security for life and property at present in the City of Dublin. The danger, which has been much graver than the Government will admit, is by no means past. If the Prime Minister thinks otherwise, he is as badly informed as he was when he told the House of Commons that the rebels had no machine-guns. Many armed rebels are at large in Dublin still, and the danger of another rising can only be averted by the adoption of the sternest measures. As I write there are snipers on the roofs trying to shoot any officers that they may see. This is not the time for amnesties and pardons; it is the time for punishment, swift and stern. And no one who lives in Ireland believes that the present Irish Government has the courage to punish anybody.

Secondly, in place of Mr. Birrell we ask that we shall be sent a man, who will reside in the country which he is paid to rule, and a Secretary of State who will do his best, without fear or favour, to help and not to hinder the police.

Yours, &c.,
JOHN DUBLIN

THE DUBLIN DAMAGE

11 May 1916

SIR,—WHATEVER PLEAS MAY be advanced for providing compensation for the damage sustained in the recent disturbances in Ireland, no good cause can be shown why the taxpayers of Scotland and England should contribute.

Messrs. Birrell and Redmond have admitted that it was owing to their anxiety that the British public should be led to believe that all was tranquil in Ireland that a policy was favoured which failed to deal effectually with growing disloyalty.

It is too much to expect that the British public, which was to be hoodwinked and misled (in the interest of this disloyalty), should be invited to pay the damage. Such a proposal is well calculated to create a rapidly increasing bitterness against the Government amongst the entire population of Great Britain, which had no sympathy with the Sinn Fein movement—a population whose soldiers and officers have been foully murdered in the streets now awaiting reconstruction.

Your obedient servant,
J. A. SWETTENHAM

———◆———

THE RATION ALLOWANCE

16 May 1916

SIR,—THE RATION ALLOWANCE of Tommy Atkins has been reduced from 1s. 9d. to 1s. 7d. a day. Now the pay of a private soldier is 1s. a day, or 7s. a week; and his ration allowance when on leave was formerly 1s. 9d. a day, or 12s. 3d. a week—making a total weekly income of 19s. 3d. upon which to house and feed himself. But now the ration allowance having been reduced to 1s. 7d. a day—that is to 11s. 1d. a week—the private soldier home for a few days from the front has no more than 18s. 1d. a week upon which to live. It leaves the private soldier cold when you talk to him of farms in the future and take away his bread to-day.

Yours, &c.,
A TEMPORARY TOMMY SINCE 1914

THE GREAT NAVAL BATTLE

7 June 1916

SIR,— I AM AFRAID THAT the real significance of the great naval battle is in danger of being missed by our own people and foreign nations. The Germans, after their manner, issued and spread over the world their false bulletin before it was possible that the facts could be known. It is clear that this bulletin had little relation to the truth; but it secured a start, and it enabled Germany to proclaim a victory and to indulge in rejoicings greatly needed to dispel the growing depression, but utterly unwarranted by anything that had occurred in the North Sea.

The broad features of the tremendous conflict, as I understand them, are these. Sir David Beatty's squadron boldly engaged an enemy's force between two and three times as strong as his own, held it, and inflicted very severe losses. His three battle cruisers were unfit to engage battleships except at long range, and were—so we had been informed—specially designed for that purpose. The conditions of the action forced upon these vessels the alternative of retiring or of fighting at relatively short ranges, and there could be no question as to which course a British commander would choose. The loss of our three battle cruisers, thus circumstanced, was inevitable, and the three armoured cruisers were obviously unfit to engage the enemy's battle cruisers at any range. The fragile destroyers seem to have acquitted themselves nobly. As at Coronel, the light was unfavourable to our gunners, and this disadvantage increased as the afternoon drew on. But for the four fast battleships attached to Sir David Beatty's command he would have fought against absolutely overwhelming odds. As it was the enemy's superiority was overpowering, and only 11 British battleships were ever engaged, some of them probably after the Germans had begun their retreat.

It may be thought that the flinging of a fraction of our forces against the whole German High Seas Fleet was a rash proceeding; but at least it was a supremely gallant action, and it must be remembered that, if it had been delayed, the Germans, informed of the position of the Grand Fleet by their Zeppelins, would most probably have retired before they could be effectively attacked. If so the severe punishment which has certainly been administered was due to Sir David Beatty's decision.

Already it is clear that many important lessons can be learned from the battle. With them I am not now concerned; but it seems vital that, in our sorrow for the heavy loss of our splendid officers and men, we should not lose our sense of perspective. We shall not know the full extent of the German losses till the war is over, if then. The German Government will see to that; but I shall be surprised if they are not equal to or greater than our own, in spite of the great inferiority of our forces engaged. Meanwhile, it is already plain that the British

Navy has never achieved a finer feat than that of last week. It has magnificently demonstrated its power to hold the sea, and our Allies will note the fact. The gallant men whose loss the nation mourns have not died in vain. They have added a shining page to our naval history, upheld the best traditions of Drake, Hawke, St. Vincent, and Nelson, and they have finally disposed of any hope that the enemy may have entertained of contesting our sea supremacy. *Requiescant in pace*, and in the love and admiration of their countrymen.

I am, Sir, yours obediently,
SYDENHAM

The Battle of Jutland was the only major engagement of the war between the British and German fleets, and the last in history to be contested mainly by battleships. Debate continues over its outcome, widely seen as indecisive.

———◆———

LORD KITCHENER

7 June 1916

SIR,—I WOULD LIKE TO be among the first to place a wreath on the noble and stainless memory of Lord Kitchener. Only last Thursday Dr. Clifford, Rev. J. H. Shakespeare, Dr. Garvie, and I were favoured with a long interview with him on the subject of the conscientious objector. It would not be fitting to give premature publicity to his proposals; suffice it to say that we left him vastly relieved and feeling that a satisfactory settlement was within view. One was struck with his splendid physique, his manly bearing, his unaffected manner, his quick apprehension of difficulties and ready resourcefulness. It seems impossible to realize that his great personality is withdrawn at this great hour of our need. He was the Bayard of the 20th century—without fear and without reproach.

Yours truly,
F. B. MEYER

Kitchener, the secretary of state for war and a former Commander-in-Chief, had died when the ship carrying him to Russia for talks struck a mine.

THE LATE SISTER AUGUSTINE

27 June 1916

SIR,—IS IT TOO MUCH, now when the Roll of Honour daily fills so large a space, to ask you to spare a few lines more to the memory of a remarkable Englishwoman, whose death your Correspondent at Bukarest has just chronicled—Sister Augustine of Salonika?

For some 40 years Sister Augustine Bewicke had lived in the Balkans; she spoke six or seven languages with singular fluency; she was the friend and confidante of men and women of all classes and nationalities. Her little room, with its rows of bottles and masses of books and papers, in the outer court of the Convent of St. Vincent de Paul, saw a strange variety of visitors—Turkish soldiers, Bulgarian komitadjis, American missionaries, Albanians, Italian pensioners, French schoolgirls, foreign Consuls, special correspondents, and, latterly, a stream of French and British officers. To all who came to her Sister Augustine had something to give; it might be a remedy—she enjoyed a peculiar sanctity among the Musulmans and Spanish Jews for her powers of healing—or it might be a bread ticket, or counsel or comfort, or the latest news or rumour, which always seemed to be brought first to her.

Sister Augustine had a boundless interest and delight in life; she had a bright intelligence, a gaiety of heart and ease in conversation, a charm which would have made her a notable member of any society; she had a burning sympathy with the oppressed, and a radiant, absolute confidence in the ways of Almighty God which made her fearless for herself and for others. Her superiors, with the wise discretion which characterizes the Order of St. Vincent de Paul, allowed her a remarkable degree of liberty. She would ask a general permission beforehand for all the unusual things she might wish to do during the coming week.

The happiest days of her life, even in old age, were spent in journeys for relief work to the villages; rough mountain roads, snow, or rain, or burning sun, miserable quarters at nights, hostile Greeks or Turks, nothing daunted her if the people could be reached and helped and comforted. I recall her joy when she was allowed to nurse a case of black smallpox in a hovel where no one else would go, and her unflagging spirits when she worked, almost singlehanded, in a hospital of sick and wounded through a cruel winter in Kastoria, and I remember her courage in confronting high Turkish officials to ask for mercy for prisoners or justice for the oppressed. It was wonderful to see this aged nun, her pale face, lit up by her ardent dark eyes, below the white papillons of her Order, her rosary in one hand, her ancient cotton umbrella in the other, addressing the assembled Council of a Kaimakam or a group of Bulgarian insurgents, or, it might be, the formidable Hilmi Pasha or Enver Bey himself. She was a privileged person to whom every one must listen and whose petitions were seldom refused.

Sister Augustine had strong views on Balkan politics; few people understood better than she the mentality of the Balkan peoples. Her stories were admirably told and coloured with the kindly humour which serves best to interpret so much that is strange in the Near East. She was the life-long friend and champion of the Bulgarians, but she always said that the curse of ingratitude and faithlessness had been laid on them from the beginning of things; she—almost alone of the Europeans who witnessed the strange pageant of the Young Turk Revolution in Salonika—remained unmoved and foresaw that the Young Turk would be even as the old.

The last letter that came to me from her—only a few weeks ago—gave a graphic description of a visit she had paid to the British lines, when my husband had the honour to escort her—a day of intense enjoyment and interest to her. "I think there is no Englishwoman who would not envy me," she wrote.

It is well that she should go while her powers were still unimpaired, but it is the passing of a vivid personality and of a real power in the Balkans.

I am, yours faithfully,
ELLINOR F. B. GROGAN

THE CURE OF BURN WOUNDS

29 June 1916

Sir,— In the course of a recent visit to France on behalf of the French Wounded Emergency Fund I saw many French hospitals, but none quite so interesting as that of St. Nicholas, in Paris, where Dr. Barthe de Sandfort is carrying on his wonderful treatment of burn wounds. Much is heard of it in conversation in Paris, but, so far as I could learn, hardly any English surgeons had visited the hospital; and, in view of the number of our own men who have sustained, or will sustain, burn wounds, you will need no apology for my request to be allowed to state what we saw.

The St. Nicholas Hospital is in Rue Ernest Renan, Issy-les-Moulineux (near the Porte Versailles). We arrived there about 9.30 a.m. to see the morning dressings, and were received by Dr. de Sandfort. At present there are between 50 and 60 patients in all stages of treatment, so that we could compare the ghastly new cases with those approaching discharge. Photographs of each patient on reception and after five, 10, and 20 days enabled us also to follow the cure of individuals. The treatment, which is applicable to frostbite as well as burns, is a simple one. After the wound is cleaned liquid paraffin wax at a temperature of 100deg. C. is sprayed over it; the whole surface is then covered with light cotton gauze, over which cotton wool is plentifully applied and lightly bound on. The treatment is repeated every 24 hours. The first application removes the pain, and as the bandages come away quite easily the subsequent dressings cause none—indeed, one of the men with terribly burned head, hands, and body actually fell asleep in our presence while being dressed. Thus, though the sights are ugly to the non-professional eye, the evident painlessness of the patient enables one to look upon them with composure. Next to the relief of pain, the most remarkable feature of the treatment is its success in restoring the skin to its normal condition in nearly all the cases where the patient has been brought into the hospital soon enough. We saw a case of late reception after ordinary hospital treatment in a field ambulance, where the skin was and would remain badly scarred; this we could compare with other cases of early reception where the facial skin was completely restored, the photograph on reception showing in each case something like a blotched death-mark. As Dr. de Sandfort says, there is developed "une cutinisation parfaite sans rétraction cicatricielle."

Every British doctor who goes to Paris ought to see the St. Nicholas Hospital; he will find Dr. B. de Sandfort and his enthusiastic assistants ready to explain the whole process, and eager to extend to the British wounded the benefits which they have conferred on their own countrymen.

I am, Sir, your obedient servant,
ALBERT GRAY

MAINTAINING THE STATE

7 July 1916

Sir,—Your short article to-day, "A Policy for Conscientious Objectors," suggests depriving the conscientious objector of the right to vote. It is interesting to note that statutory exclusion from the franchise is here recognized for what it really is—a punitive measure of considerable severity. You add:—"They [the conscientious objectors] cannot reasonably claim any voice in the management of the State if in the last resort they are not prepared to maintain it"; and you conclude by saying that you "see no practical reason why supporters of woman suffrage should demur." Neither do I, if it is recognized that there are other ways of maintaining the State besides fighting for it. For men between 18 and 45 the best way of maintaining the State at this moment may be (and in my opinion is) to fight for it. But no one dreams of disfranchising men who happen to be past military age. We suffragists believe that the work of women towards maintaining the State is just as essential as the work of men, and has been for countless generations as faithfully fulfilled. If we look at recent experience, can anyone say that women of all classes have not on the whole set the wellbeing of the State in front of all considerations of private interest? And this, according to a book which is now on every one's lips, is the supreme test of citizenship.

Yours obediently,
MILLICENT GARRETT FAWCETT

JUSTICE FOR OUR HEROES

10 July 1916

SIR,—I WOULD LIKE TO draw the attention of your readers to another instance of the niggardly way in which our gallant men are treated by the authorities. I can put the case best by an actual illustration. I have three cases in hand of a similar nature.

Sergeant Waller served his country faithfully and well for 21 years. He was in possession of the long service medal, the good conduct medal, two medals with clasps for war service. His character throughout his service was exemplary. He retired with a modest pension of 1s. 10d. per day. He obtained a good post as storekeeper, where he was enjoying a comfortable income. When the war broke out and Lord Kitchener appealed to old non-commissioned officers to come forward and help their country in her need, Waller, like the true Englishman he was, gave up all his prospects in life, prepared to go through hardships and dangers for the country he had served so well. He persuaded a young storeman to come with him. Curiously enough, both the sergeant and his recruit were knocked out at the same time, and as both were totally incapacitated they received the full pension of 25s. a week. Naturally the sergeant supposed this would be in addition to the pension of 1s. 10d. a day he had already so honourably earned. To his dismay, however, he was told that his old pension was to be merged in the new pension of 25s. per week now granted, so that the man who had served his country for 22 years was to have the same pension as the young man who had served for less than one year.

This, to my mind, is an intolerable injustice, one of the many cruel injustices inflicted by the Royal Warrant, which I hope to live to see burned and an intelligible and human code substituted for it. Is there a man or woman in this country who would grudge this gallant man the miserable pittance of 1s. 10d. a day he had earned after 21 years' service? Even with this addition he would be in a far worse position than when he gave up his business, and, mind you, he is now a broken and incapacitated man. I do trust some member of Parliament will take up this matter vigorously, and have this monstrous injustice put right. Incidentally, I may say the pension authorities are trying to do this disabled man out of the 4s. a week due to him as sergeant, and 2s. 6d. a week for each of his young children, but I mean to get this put right.

It is perfectly intolerable the way these gallant men are treated. I am utterly worn out in my efforts to get them justice, and pretty well heart-broken too.

Very truly yours,
FREDERICK MILNER

WOMAN SUFFRAGE

18 July 1916

Sir,—If the Committee on Registration is appointed, and finds, as it is bound to find, that its real subject-matter is the franchise, the country will, I think, be fully prepared to include in it the woman's vote. There is no antagonism between the women's case and that of the soldiers who have lost qualification. A new register would be a mockery if it left out the armies; it would be equally unreal if, in view of all that has happened since the war broke in on the nation, it omitted half the community.

The Times has not been slow to record the part that women have played in the war. Without it there could have been no nation in arms. The armies could not have held the field for a month; the national call to arms could not have been made or sustained; the country would have perished of inanition and disorganization. If indeed it be true that the people have been one, it is because the genius of women has been lavishly applied to the task of reinforcing and complementing the genius of men. So far as I know, the qualities of steady industry, adaptability, good judgment, and concentration of mind which men do not readily associate with women, have been conspicuous features of their service.

This was not surprising to those who knew the long travail of their apprenticeship to public life; their work in education and local government; their skill in the professions open to them; the unselfishness of their choice of hard and uninteresting detail; the freshness and conscientiousness with which they joined themselves to the work of directing or being directed. The excellence of this self-training appeared in August, 1914, and the country now knows that it has at its disposal not an emergency service, but a permanent and varied enrichment of its energies, when they are again restored to the normal uses of civilized being.

There has, I am sure, been a real process of conversion in regard to woman franchise. The Government and the House of Commons have only to reflect this change of opinion and temper.

Yours, &c.,
H. W. MASSINGHAM

BODY ARMOUR

19 July 1916

Sir,—The introduction of the steel helmet and the undoubted life-saving properties it possesses has started an agitation for body armour, which agitation, I fear, is the work of well-meaning people entirely unacquainted with modern war conditions. The British soldier carries into action between 56lb. and 63lb. of clothing and equipment, a weight which can only be carried because his body is properly ventilated. If he is presented with body armour weighing between 4lb. and 8lb. (which I believe is about the weight manufactured by private enterprise) and then has to wear his very heavy load over it, I fear his efficiency would deteriorate about 80 per cent. and his discomfort increase about 400 per cent. We must also remember that the great majority of wounds are caused by machine-gun fire at close range, that the machine-gun bullet makes the cleanest of clean wounds (as I can personally testify), and that by placing an inadequate shield between the bullet and its victim we simply get a very much worse wound and jagged splinters of the shield carried into the wound. It cannot be too greatly emphasized that the shield which a soldier could carry would be absolutely inadequate; ¼in. hardened steel will stop a bullet at 200 yards. Anything less will not. A suit of this would weigh about 40lb. for the front of the body.

I am yours truly,
WOUNDED IN THE PUSH

The lethal properties of artillery shrapnel had persuaded all armies to adopt steel helmets instead of their traditional leather or cloth caps.

THE CANADIANS

28 July 1916

SIR,—I ENCLOSE PART OF a letter from an English Staff officer at the front in France about the splendid bravery of the Canadians.

"The Canadians have done wonderfully well, and we are proud to be fighting with them. The way they fought to get back their lost trenches was a lesson to every one, and we all shall never forget it. They are a most hospitable, self-denying lot, and will share their last crust of bread and drop of water with any one of us if they think we need it. I have the greatest admiration of them after the recent fighting."

Yours faithfully,
TENNYSON

In common with all sides, the Canadians would suffer heavy losses in the Battle of the Somme.

THE UTILITIES OF A CHANNEL TUNNEL

7 August 1916

SIR,—ONE OF THE POSSIBLE utilities of a Franco-British Channel tunnel, which has not yet, I believe, been mentioned, is the increased facility it would afford for direct telephonic communication between Great Britain, France, Switzerland, and Italy. There are at present two English Channel telephone cables, each with twin circuits, which, by the method of usage called phantomizing, can be made equivalent to three circuits each. These cables are, of course, subject to the possibility of injury, like all submarine cables, and repairs might be costly and take time. If, however, the Channel tunnel were constructed with proper provision for it, a large number of telephonic and telegraphic cables of a certain type could be laid in it which would afford greatly increased means of intercommunication at a less cost than by equivalent submarine cables. If these were extended by suitable coil-loaded aerial lines, telephonic communication could be established between the principal cities in Great Britain and those in France, and possibly Italy. Having regard to the far closer commercial relations which will exist between the Allies in the post-war period, this improved intercommunication will be of the greatest advantage.

I submit, therefore, that in any plans for such a tunnel ample provision should be made for telephonic and telegraphic cables of the latest type for long-distance working.

I am, &c.,
J. A. FLEMING

———◆———

TASK FOR MR. SAMUEL

8 August 1916

SIR,—WHEN MR. HERBERT SAMUEL was at the Post Office he greatly increased the number of cab ranks and stations whence cabs could be called by telephone. His scheme has not been a success, since drivers prefer to distribute themselves at other cab ranks or to parade the streets in the hope of being called by whistles. Now that Mr. Samuel is at the Home Office he could complete his reform by prohibiting cab whistling except between stated hours. There are over 400 entries in the current London telephone directory of cab ranks, &c., connected by telephone. If whistling was prohibited drivers would be compelled to resort to these places, whence those who have access to telephones could call them and where those who have not would be able to find them. As a member of the medical profession who knows what an enormous help this administrative reform would be to us in our efforts to help shell-shocked and wounded soldiers back to health I earnestly appeal to Mr. Samuel to carry it out without delay. It is clearly quite useless to appeal to the public not to whistle for cabs as long as this is the easiest way to call them.

Yours, &c.,
LAURISTON E. SHAW

THE RUHLEBEN CRUELTIES

10 August 1916

Sir,—Mr. Layton, an Englishman, one of the leading dentists in Brussels, was seized by the Germans in defiance of the Geneva Convention, and along with other professional men was carried off, in 1914, to Ruhleben, where he contracted nothing worse than chronic bronchitis through exposure and neglect. He has lately been released after protracted representations by the Geneva authorities and the Foreign Office, and writes as follows to a correspondent who had interested himself in his case:—

"I would have liked to explain to you [before proceeding to France] the inhuman and disgraceful treatment meted out to the prisoners in Ruhleben, more especially the criminal neglect of the doctor in charge during the first part of the imprisonment, the want of food, the unnecessary cruelty in many ways, insomuch that I had the absolute conviction that as the Germans could not shoot us they desired to destroy us mentally and physically as much as possible. This is so true that the *Nord Deutsche Allgemeine Zeitung*, about the month of October, officially informed the German public that we would not be allowed to have any means at our disposal that would render our internment supportable. This and more I would like to tell you, because I know it would get to the right channel, which some day will be able to give us the justice which we have learned to be our birthright as Britishers."

Your obedient servant,
M. H. SPIELMANN

"FILMING" THE CABINET

23 August 1916

Sir,—Whatever may be the motives which led to the proposal to "film" the Cabinet, and whatever the immediate use to which the film might have been put, it must surely be remembered that the cinematograph has a much more important function than that of providing music-hall "turns." It is now perfect as an instrument of historical record; and its productions may have a value for posterity not very much below that of a State document. Posterity, it is true, has not at present done anything for us; but, despite Sir Boyle Roche, it may eventually do a good deal, and it is an imperative duty to provide it with such historical material as it may have a right to demand from us.

A film of Pitt's first Cabinet would be a document not only intensely interesting to the curious, but of great value to the student of character and manners, and of the greatest value to the teacher of history. Every event of public importance which can be filmed ought to be filmed, for the benefit and instruction of those who come after us; and, whatever we may think of the performances of the Cabinet, it is difficult to imagine anything that would more enchain the mind of a future age than a moving photograph of the representative public men of both parties who held the administration of Britain during the greatest war of all time. Our great-grandchildren will not thank this generation if it misses the opportunity of using this new invention to hand down to them a legacy of such surpassing interest.

There is, indeed, very little to be said for exhibiting at street "cinemas" a film showing the Cabinet "in action," but the formation and preservation of records by cinematograph of the chief events of a time so literally "epoch-making" as the present ought surely to be accepted as a matter of course, and might well form the work of a special department created for the purpose; and a meeting of the war Cabinet is certainly one of those events.

I am, Sir, yours faithfully,
F. T. DALTON

ONE-HANDED GOLF

29 August 1916

Sir,—I was extremely interested in your reference to one-armed golfers in to-day's edition of *The Times*. Before the war golf was my favourite recreation, and is so still in spite of having lost my left hand. Through the kindness of a friend who placed his golf tutor at my disposal during part of my sick leave, in about four months I have got a 20 handicap. Anyone who knows the Formby course, Lancs, will realize the length of my drive when I inform them that at different times I have cleared all the first bunkers from my tee shot. Some critics say I play the wrong way. I use right-handed clubs and take an ordinary forward drive.

They say I ought to use left-handed clubs and stand on the opposite side of the ball and play a back-handed stroke. Different opinions as to this point would be very interesting.

It is true that the weight of the clubs is a most important feature for one-armed players, and I have chosen my clubs mostly by weight, and got what I consider a good combination, though probably with more practice I should alter them again. However, if any of your one-armed readers would like the benefit of these particulars I should be delighted to give them. I don't believe in the indented grip. I persevered with it on my mashie for some time, but found no benefit at all. An ordinary sticky grip is quite satisfactory and the club never slips. It is a most delightful feeling to know that in spite of having lost a hand one can have an excellent day's sport at golf, and I am sure after the war there will be many very interesting competitions between one-armed and one-legged crocks and so on. What a fine scheme it would be to have a war crocks' amateur championship and let it follow the ordinary amateur championship; but perhaps the complete men would find there was so much more interest taken in the incomplete men that they'd be jealous. However, something interesting, I feel sure, will come along, and in the meantime we'll apply sticky grips to the Huns.

Yours faithfully,
W. H.

MR. BERTRAND RUSSELL

5 September 1916

Sir,—Mr. Bertrand Russell's view of pre-war diplomacy is not mine, and it is very far from yours; nevertheless, I hope *The Times* will allow me to protest against the military edict which forbids him to reside in any part of Scotland, in Manchester or Liverpool, or on the greater part of the English coast. Such an edict is obviously aimed at a man who may justly be suspected of communicating with the enemy, or of assisting his cause. Mr. Russell is not only the most distinguished bearer of one of the greatest names in English political history, but he is a man so upright in thought and deed that such action is, in the view of every one who knows him, repugnant to his character. It is a gross libel, and an advertisement to the world that the administration of the Defence of the Realm Regulations is in the hands of men who do not understand their business. Incidentally, their action deprives Mr. Russell, already debarred from entering the United States, of the power of earning his livelihood by arranged lectures on subjects unconnected with the war. *The Times* is the most active supporter of that war; but its support is intelligent, and it speaks as the mouthpiece of the country's intelligence as well as of its force. May I therefore appeal to it to use its great influence to discourage the persecution of an Englishman of whose accomplishments and character the nation may well be proud, even in the hour when his conscientious conclusions are not accepted by it?

Yours, &c.,
H. W. MASSINGHAM

The philosopher's outspoken opposition to the war led him to be prosecuted and to lose his position at Cambridge University.

OVERSEAS SOLDIERS IN LONDON

12 September 1916

SIR,—AS AN EXAMPLE OF the time wasted, wrong impressions gained, and money scattered uselessly, may I mention two cases?

Five Canadian soldiers in London for two days standing opposite Big Ben. They had never been in London before, and never may be again. Overhearing their conversation, I found they thought Big Ben was Westminster Abbey, and they were arranging to take a train to see Buckingham Palace. As a second instance, yesterday I found seven Australians in the Charing Cross Tube reading a list of stations. "Can I help you?" I asked. "Yes, M'am; we've been here half an hour and we want to go to Mme. Tussaud's." " I'm afraid Mme. Tussaud's is not open on Sunday; but all men in uniform are admitted free at the Zoological Gardens," and I put them on their way.

These men, and thousands more, may never see London again. They have come from distant lands, and some day they will go back to talk about "the old country." Would it not be possible to open everything in the way of museums and public buildings to these men freely on Sundays, and for more ladies and gentlemen than are already doing so to take them round to see our sights? The dark days of winter are coming, and although much is being done, surely we might try and do a little more. There are still thousands of elderly ladies and gentlemen past the age of washing dirty plates at canteens who might volunteer to sit at turnstiles at interesting buildings while others showed the men round on Sundays, so as to save these soldiers wasting time, and money, and precious hours.

Let us try and do something more to save these Canadians, Australians, and South Africans, to whom we owe so much, from wandering helplessly about. I shall be glad to receive any suggestions by post.

Yours truly,
E. ALEC TWEEDIE

THE DISCHARGE OF SOLDIERS

13 September 1916

Sir,—There is a matter of grave and urgent national importance that would seem to call for immediate attention unless the Government are to be again found guilty of being "too late" and "unprepared." I refer to the question of dealing with discharges when this war is over. Unless immediate steps are taken to frame some practical scheme for this purpose, there will be undoubtedly severe hardship and hopeless chaos. I speak with knowledge, having had personal experience of the chaos that reigned during the "enlistment" period in the earlier months of the war. It will be remembered that recruits came in so rapidly that it was impossible, under the system and organization that then prevailed, to deal with them properly. There was overcrowding, with the inevitable result (in many cases fatal) of sickness (measles, spotted fever, mumps, scarlet fever, &c.) and exposure. That was a minor matter, in some respects, compared with the chaos that reigned in the pay offices in dealing with questions of separation allowances and allotments; the result in these cases being that numberless families were left temporarily destitute, except for what their enlisted relatives could spare them out of their seven or eight shillings a week pay—and even that was not always possible, because in hundreds of cases men were sent overseas almost immediately, and their families were reduced to appealing for assistance from the various charitable organizations throughout the country. The whole cause of the mischief was "unpreparedness." One could not blame the pay offices or the regimental depots. Under the system in force they could not possibly cope with the sudden rush with the inadequate and already overworked staff at their disposal.

If this was the state of affairs when men were enlisting by the thousand week after week, what may one expect after the war when men will have to be discharged by the hundred thousand, and when they will all be wanting to get home again at once? It may sound simple enough to the ordinary civilian to say to a man: "You are discharged! You can go!" But there are a hundred and one details to be gone into in the Service before a man is discharged.

Properly speaking, every man should be discharged through his regimental depot, and the "discharge" consists, among other things, of the following measures:—

1. The regimental paymaster has to be notified at least 10 days before the discharge can be carried out, in order that any outstanding charges against the man's account may be taken into consideration in computing the balance due to or by him.

2. He will have to be accommodated in barracks or billets until his documents are completed, including the man's signature to the correctness (or otherwise) of those documents.

3. He will have to be fed while he is there.

4. He will have to hand his kit (clothing and equipment) into store, being debited for such deficiencies as he is adjudged responsible for.

5. He will have to be issued with civilian clothing in lieu of his Service dress.

6. He will have to be given a railway warrant to take him home.

7. Arrangements will have to be made for special trains to take away the large number of men being discharged.

8. The railway authorities will have to be notified in plenty of time to make the arrangements.

These are a few of the essential points that strike me at first sight. No doubt there will not be much difficulty in dealing with discharges at infantry and cavalry depots, but where the R.A., R.E., A.S.C., and R.A.M.C. are concerned the work will be stupendous. And unless the question is fully gone into now, and proper arrangements made to cope with the situation, there will, as I say, be hopeless chaos and confusion.

I make the suggestion that men should be "demobilized" by units as far as possible, scattered over England, clothing depots and clerical staff being first of all put in working order. The war gratuity (£5, I think) due to each man would at any rate keep him for a short time until the regimental paymaster could forward him the balance due to him, but there is always the danger of towns, such as Aldershot, being overcrowded, and opportunities for hotel and lodging-house keepers to overcharge, if large numbers are allowed to accumulate in one town or district.

The magnitude of the task of carrying out these discharges appals one, and, as the work will in all human probability be thrown on the shoulders of those who have been doing the same sort of work since the beginning of the war at home (without "mention" or "reward"), the mental and bodily strain on these "willing horses" can be more easily imagined than described.

I am yours faithfully,
REGULAR OFFICER

BROKEN SOLDIERS

16 September 1916

Sɪʀ,—I ᴀᴍ ᴡᴇʟʟ ᴀᴄQᴜᴀɪɴᴛᴇᴅ with the methods employed at the command depots for restoring serving soldiers to health. The views of the Army on men who are no longer useful fighting units are common knowledge. It falls to my lot, as a member of the London War Pensions Committee, to interview the men after discharge, and I can from personal experience endorse every word in your article and leader of Thursday. I see in *The Times* of to-day that Mr. Cyril Jackson, vice-chairman of the War Pensions, &c., Statutory Committee, shares your views. The mental attitude of the discharged disabled soldier is somewhat peculiar, and for that reason as well as on purely physical grounds it is most desirable that he should be kept in the Army until he has, as far as may be, ceased to be disabled and learnt to fend for himself. The Army has broken the soldier and the Army should mend him. Many of the cases which one sees are piteous, and unless something is done for these men, and quickly, there will be an unprecedented outburst of public indignation.

Yours faithfully,
M. SOPHIA JEVONS, M.A., M.B., B.S.

The Times had argued that soldiers whose injuries were deemed incurable and who had sunk into depression should not be allowed to return to civilian life in a state of apathy.

GERMAN JEWS AND THE WAR

21 September 1916

SIR,—LORD NORTHCLIFFE's recent account of an interview with a German Jewish man of business on the war corroborated an incident which has come under my notice.

A young American lady of Jewish origin was describing her recent visit to some family connexions in Berlin—people of considerable financial importance. As she had passed through England on her way, they were inquisitive about what she had seen, and when she informed them that, as far as she could see, there had been no damage by Zeppelins, they were completely incredulous, and an elderly aunt was positively angry. They were also under the impression that food was as scarce in Paris as in Berlin; that very few ships were able to reach England, and only those flying the Dutch or American flag; but they have no doubt that Germany would conclude a separate peace with either England, Russia, or France before the end of the year. They pay no attention to copies of the *New York Sun* which reached here during her visit, declaring that the United States were as guilty as England in bringing on the war. They were so obsessed with the idea of the certainty of German victory that she found it difficult to endeavour to explain facts favourable to the Allies which had come under her own notice.

My informant was an exceedingly intelligent, charming young woman, and said she was quite glad to get away from relatives who hitherto have been extremely fond of her.

Yours obediently,
ANGLO-SWISS

THE V.A.D. NURSES

21 September 1916

Sir,—I was delighted to read the excellent article on the Nursing Profession you published on Monday, and I venture to ask for space in your columns to suggest another reason why the supply of V.A.D. nurses is inadequate. Is the public aware that nursing in a V.A.D. military hospital is so expensive that only the woman of independent means can undertake the work? Of course, the V.A.D. member expects no salary, but it seems grossly unfair that she should have to provide her own uniform, pay her own laundry bill (a fairly heavy item for a nurse), and even, in many cases, have to pay for the food she receives while she is on duty. No accommodation is provided for the V.A.D. nurse at her hospital; if, under exceptional circumstances, she is permitted to "live in," she is obliged to pay for food and lodging! Members can leave their detachments, on receiving permission to do so from their commandant, and they can generally obtain employment under much better conditions at the big Army hospitals, if they are willing to "sign on" for a considerable time. Fortunately for the voluntary hospitals, however, very few of their nurses care to desert them, and so the supply of workers is kept up somehow. But in order to ensure a sufficient number of recruits to the Voluntary Aid Detachments, and, above all, on the principle that the labourer is worthy of his hire, one feels that it is enough to ask these noble women to spend their time and strength in the care of the wounded without burdening them with such heavy financial expenses in the discharge of their splendid work.

Yours, &c.,
H. E. SALMON

REFRESHMENT FOR CENSORS

25 September 1916

Sir,—Even the joy of (legitimately) reading other people's letters must pall when it reaches a matter of many thousands a day, and in any case it must be, both mentally and physically, an exhausting occupation. The clever linguists who are very properly occupied these days in delaying our correspondence, and that of our enemies, in the Censor's Office are working long hours and at high pressure. Luncheon time is practically their only breathing space; yet what an uncomfortable occasion it is for them! Not only is there no place on the premises where food can be obtained—so that the tired and the weak are compelled to walk about the streets in all weathers, doing battle for a bun in the already overcrowded teashops of the neighbourhood—but there is no room in the building itself where even a private sandwich can be devoured in peace. Here, surely, is a splendid opportunity for the establishment of a small canteen, where decent food might be purchased at a reasonable price. If the authorities are unable or unwilling to establish a buffet of this description themselves a contractor might come to the rescue, as at the British and the Victoria and Albert Museums. The crowds which daily issue from the Censor's Office should make an enterprising restaurateur's mouth water. Winter is approaching and the health of a number of delicate women is at stake. This must be my excuse for venturing to call attention to their necessity.

I am, Sir, yours obediently,
PHILIP BURNE-JONES

OFFICERS' WIVES

2 October 1916

SIR,—IN VIEW OF THE fact that the war is obviously with us for a very long time, I venture to raise *de novo* the question of the rule whereby officers at the bases in France are not allowed to have their wives out to live with them. Such officers are in one sense living practically under peace conditions, in that they find their own billets and that their work is not affected by any question of presence of the enemy. Many of them have very long hours and arduous work with no possibility at present of freshening up their minds for their work by a change of thought, and I submit that if they were allowed the privilege of having their wives out to live with them they would be the gainers not only from a personal but even from a public point of view. Safeguards and restrictions to prevent the abuse of the privilege could very easily be arranged.

Your obedient servant,
OFFICER'S WIFE

SMOKING IN HOSPITAL

4 October 1916

Sir,—Sir Thomas Fraser in his letter on Tobacco for Soldiers raises a question which has been widely discussed. There are two schools of expert opinion, that which believes that tobacco is detrimental and that which regards its benefits as being greater than any ill-effects it may produce.

The question has not yet been decided. Meantime we may agree that excessive use of tobacco is bad, just as excessive use of any other commodity is bad. This by no means commits us to the view that our men should not have their smokes, nor yet to the view that they do receive an excess of tobacco.

If one thing is more certain than another it is that enormous comfort both of mind and body comes with a pipe or cigarette when the smoker is in a tight corner. Tobacco at the front has a moral value which simply cannot be ignored, and it may be asked whether any ill-effects it possesses are equal to or even comparable with ill-effects of shock and strain and stress which cannot be eliminated, and which tobacco does so much to mitigate.

War is not a health cure. The chief danger of war, speaking medically and putting actual wounds on one side, is its terrible effect on nerves. Practically the whole Army is of opinion that in tobacco it possesses a means of counteracting this nervous strain. In the absence of definite evidence to the effect that this belief is ill-founded, are we to take from our fighting men the comfort they rely upon and desire so wistfully?

In so far as it concerns the patient in hospital, Sir Thomas Fraser's letter should be weighed carefully. There is no doubt that many sick soldiers spend most of their time smoking—especially their recreation time out of doors. This may well be a great evil, and it is not evident that steps have been taken to cope with it.

I am, &c.,
M.D.

ZEPPELIN AND BALLOON

5 October 1916

Sir,—It may be of interest, now that the remains of the Zeppelin are on view in the Honourable Artillery Company's grounds near Bunhill-row, to recall the fact that it was from this spot that a large crowd witnessed the ascent of the first balloon ever launched into the air in England. It was sent up by Count Zambeccari in 1783. The following year from the same place, known then as "Artillery Garden," the more ambitious Lunardi actually went up in his balloon, and as it proved too small to carry the friend who was willing to risk his life, he took up a dog, a cat, and a pigeon with him. It is an apt sequel that the greatest air monster of modern times should now be lying there.

Yours truly,
ALICIA M. CECIL

TWELVE-HOUR SHIFTS

24 October 1916

Sir,—May I beg for a few lines in your valuable paper to correct an impression which has arisen from the report of a speech of mine at the Women's Institute last week, where I spoke with respect to Woolwich Arsenal, as this is the only place about which I have any information or right to speak? The popular impression is that I, and coupled with me Mr. Rowntree, approve of 12-hour shifts for women. This is not the case. We deplore the fact that war exigencies make it an impossibility to act otherwise just now. An eight-hour day would mean the employment of one-third more women, and it is only because this is impossible we put up with the 12 hours. What I do say, and what I think Mr. Rowntree agrees, is that owing to the fact that these women are earning good money and can provide themselves with good clothes and good food, the 12 hours up to the present has done them little harm, but I most emphatically state that to keep the women at these long hours permanently would be a national disaster from the point of view of the national future.

Every one interested in the welfare of women munition workers is watching this point of the 12-hour day most anxiously, to assist in shortening it where possible, and to make these hours as easily borne as possible by having good factory conditions, good travelling facilities, good housing, and excellent canteen provision. The Health of Munition Workers Committee, under Sir George Newman, have concentrated on this, and where an eight-hour day is possible it is in practice, but where impossible, by means of the aids to health mentioned above, the work is helped and physical conditions made as good as they can be to avert as much disaster as possible. Never for one moment could Mr. Rowntree or myself agree other than that a 12-hour day is one of the many regrettable war necessities which must end the moment peace is declared.

Yours faithfully,
LILIAN C. BARKER, Lady Superintendent, Royal Arsenal

THE VICTORIA CROSS

30 October 1916

SIR,—IN YOUR ISSUE of to-day appears the interesting record of the posthumous bestowal of the Victoria Cross on an officer whose father had received it 17 years ago.

The first name in the list of the gallant 15 recipients is that of Lieutenant-Colonel J. V. Campbell, Coldstream Guards. I shall esteem it a favour if you will allow me space to state that his father, my Staff officer, Captain the Honorable Ronald Campbell, Coldstream Guards, was killed in 1879, when performing an act of extraordinary courage in my presence, and for which, as I reported officially, I should have recommended him for the Cross had he survived; an officer and a private who followed him received the Cross.

More appreciative views of noble deeds have now amended the rules of the coveted Order.

Your faithful servant,
EVELYN WOOD, F.M.

MISS HOBHOUSE AT RUHLEBEN

31 October 1916

SIR,—IT WAS WITH feelings of regret that I read in your issue of October 18 a letter from that ardent propagandist, Miss Emily Hobhouse. As stated in her letter, this lady visited Ruhleben camp and Dr. Weiler's sanatorium, where I was then interned, in the month of May or June this year. She was escorted by a German officer, and travelled under the auspices of the Berlin War Office, who made every effort to suppress her identity. During her visit she commented on the excellence of the *Kriegsbrot*, of which she ate a minute portion in public, and pronounced it most beneficial for the digestion—a remark which I cannot believe even Count Reventlow himself would have endorsed. She described the dingy villa, where we were packed like sardines in a tin, and which made a mockery of the word sanatorium, as a delightful spot, and declared it almost made her wish to be ill that she might dwell in such a place. She made several more equally fatuous and disingenuous remarks, such as that the British Government was to blame for the small number of civilian prisoners exchanged; but I hope I have written enough to show how little credence should be placed in the statements of a witness who can arrive at such very definite conclusions after a wholly inadequate examination of the facts.

I am, Sir, your obedient servant,
RETURNED RUHLEBENITE

GERMAN SUBMARINE POLICY

1 November 1916

Sir,—As chairman of the Select Committee of the House of Commons on Shipping Subsidies which sat in 1901 and 1902, and made an exhaustive inquiry into British shipping conditions and foreign subsidized competition, I should like to add my firm support to the policy of requiring in the terms of peace compensation, as far as possible, ton for ton and ship for ship for Allied merchant vessels destroyed by enemy submarines. The researches and report of the committee made it clear, even 15 years ago, that German efforts to undermine our trade by taking advantage of our hospitality and "open door" system were extremely insidious and deliberate, and it is certain they will not slacken after this bitter war. The German method of quoting very low through rates provided transport was effected on German steamers in the East African Levant, and other trades from inland places in Germany to ports in these countries or similar Naboth's vineyards, was rendered practicable by the cunningly-devised German shipping subsidies, and had the effect of subsidizing German export trade and manufacture at the expense of British trade, even to British colonies. More recently, before the war, the German and Austrian Governments have controlled and stopped at their frontier stations emigrants to America because they held passenger tickets by British ships. This pre-war spirit is bound to be accentuated after the war, and it will be immensely aided if German submarines have so crippled and sunk the Allied and neutral mercantile marine that German merchant vessels, emerging unscathed from their harbours of refuge or from internment in the United States, can dominate the world's reviving commerce. German submarine action against Allied and neutral shipping can be checked in two ways—one is by our Navy, which has shown the utmost skill; the other is by announcing our determination to exact "ton for ton" reprisals as a condition of peace. Germans understand reprisals; let us speak plainly in a language they comprehend.

Your obedient servant,
EVELYN CECIL

THE AWARD OF HONOURS

2 November 1916

Sir,—About a month ago the *London Gazette* printed two dispatches from the G.O.C. in Egypt relating to events in that country during the first six months of 1916. The first dispatch was narrative; the second contained a long list of names of officers, mostly well known in Whitehall, whose services were specially brought to notice. From the first dispatch it was apparent that practically the only fighting in the period dealt with was a "regrettable incident" last April, whereby we lost several hundred men. It is safe to say that the great majority of the officers mentioned never, throughout the period in question, heard an enemy shot fired, and that they were actually safer in Egypt than are we in London nowadays.

Now let us turn to another theatre of this world war. Two years ago—on November 2, 1914—a small, indeed, an utterly inadequate, British-Indian force disembarked at Tanga, in German East Africa. The enterprise was unsuccessful, as might have been foreseen by those in London who planned it had they paid the slightest regard to relative strengths. The official veil of secrecy still remains tightly drawn over Tanga, but enough is known to make it possible to assert with confidence that never have British officers, confronted with the most adverse conditions, acquitted themselves so well. Rightly enough a number of names were sent in by the G.O.C. as deserving of recognition—even if such recognition were no more than a mention in dispatches. But the expedition was an Indian one; it numbered not one single name familiar to Whitehall, and the dispatch was never published. Some of the officers mentioned lost their lives on that occasion, others have since been killed, or have died of disease or been invalided, and the mention in dispatches which is so much prized has never been awarded to them. It is difficult to see why this dispatch should not be published. True, Tanga was a failure. But then so were Gallipoli and quite a number of other enterprises, the participators in which have been copiously rewarded. The feeling amongst officers of the Indian Army is very strong that they have no "look in" nowadays, and this feeling is one which the India Office would do well not to disregard, because it is far-reaching in its effects. The *moral* of troops suffers seriously when officers of all grades feel that, because they belong to the Indian Army, their services have little chance of being recognized. That such a feeling does exist anyone can ascertain and its effects are deplorable. Mesopotamia is at one with East Africa in feeling how badly Indian Army officers have been treated.

SENEX

SWEATERS

10 November 1916

Sir,—Many of your readers ask how their promised 10,000 sweaters are going. Well, Sir Edward Ward, omniscient and industrious, is packing 7,000 for Mesopotamia, 2,000 are here being classified, the remaining 1,000, and more, judging by the letters, are on their way to me. So we haven't done so badly; I admit I hadn't allowed quite enough time for delays, inevitable in these days, but I still wonder what the connexion is between the glory and grandeur of the Somme and the difficulty of procuring needles No. 7 in Slodgecumb-in-the-Mud. But the main thing is that the promise is kept in the spirit if not in the sweater, and that the men, our incomparable men, will have this little offering of ours before the snow.

My correspondents are not less curious, actively and passively, than heretofore, "Will you please write an explanatory history of the sweater movement to allay suspicions?" Madam, in the whole story of criminal derangement, did you ever hear tell of a diseased lust for accumulating 800 sweaters a day in a garret in the Temple? And what is the scientific name for a morbid passion for buying 10,000 half-penny stamps to acknowledge them? I believe you are still haunted by the spectre of the elderly, alien, female enemy in the Mile End-road, deriving enormous profits from the sale of your sweaters to her compatriots.

One sweater is, I fear, irretrievably lost. To a venerable lady whose honoured hands have knitted for the men on every front I wrote, "If you thought well to stitch a card on the sweater giving the age of the knitter [it was something over 90], the happy warrior who wears it will be happier still." All very decorous and well intentioned, but I spoiled the effect by putting my message into the wrong envelope. It was not well received—and the Army is a sweater short to-day.

I have done the best I could with the acknowledgements, but there are still 176 unidentified parcels. I give what particulars I can of these in your personal column to-day, but I may say that your advertisement manager is not half so agreeable as yourself, Sir, and this is an expensive process. So will ladies add the kindness of clear and complete cards to their good sweaters?

I approach the delicate ground of the future of sweaters. While the London County Council, or it may be the Lord Chancellor himself by this time, are making up their minds what is to be done with my vile body, I am correctly forbidden to make further appeals. The fact is my application for registration was late—I was turning the fire escape into a sweater chute that afternoon.

* * * * * *

The above represents the most eloquent paragraph ever composed on the need of sweaters all the winter through, and the excellence of the printed pattern I have here for distribution. Shall I awake in Pentonville if I ask your readers to take it as read? I had almost forgotten—the sudatrix presents her duty, and, to my great relief, your readers' conduct is considered not otherwise than satisfactory.

Yours faithfully,
JOHN PENOYRE

WOMAN SUFFRAGE

A PLEA FOR MATURE CONSIDERATION

17 November 1916

SIR,—THE OPPONENTS OF female suffrage have neither the wish nor the intention to violate the truce which, by common consent, holds good for the present in respect to all contentious questions connected with national policy. But inasmuch as it appears likely that the matter will come under the consideration of the conference now sitting under the presidency of the Speaker, they are desirous that no misapprehension should exist as to their attitude.

It has now become abundantly clear that, as we have always anticipated, it will be impossible to settle this important question by the adoption of any such compromise as that which was embodied in the measure known as the Conciliation Bill. For all practical purposes, it may be said that there are only two alternatives. One is to maintain the existing law, under which women are unable to vote at the election of members of Parliament. The other is to sanction universal suffrage for all men and all women. The adoption of the latter course would involve increasing the electorate from some seven or eight millions to about 24 or 25 millions, of whom more than half would be women, their majority amounting, it is believed, to about 1,350,000.

A large number of those who before the war were opposed to female suffrage, whilst fully recognizing the very valuable services rendered by women during the present national crisis, are unable to admit that recent circumstances are of a nature to justify any serious modification of the conclusions at which they have previously arrived. They intend, therefore, when the proper time comes, to offer, by all legitimate means, the most strenuous opposition to the extension of electoral rights to women, and they cannot be parties to any attempt at a premature and unauthorized solution.

Among others who have hitherto opposed woman suffrage, there are no doubt some—represented among the names given below—who are disposed to think that the experience gained during the war has introduced some new elements into the case, which will require careful consideration.

We may, however, state with the utmost confidence that both sections of opinion are equally convinced that the present Parliament has no moral right to deal with the matter. It has to be remembered that the male electorate has never as yet pronounced any definite opinion upon it, and that as regards women there are a large number who do not wish for the vote, while others go so far as to protest very warmly against the burden of voting being thrust upon them. Without expressing any positive opinion on the very difficult question whether this matter can best be decided by means of a referendum, we hold strongly that it should certainly not be decided until after a General Election, conducted in normal circumstances, has taken place; further, that before any such General Election occurs, the electors should be warned by responsible statesmen of the issue which awaits their decision. In this conviction all the signatories to this letter are at one.

We are, Sir, &c.,

SARAH BOYCE
E. M. BURGWIN
BEATRICE CHAMBERLAIN
FLORA FARDELL
LILY FRERE
M. E. JERSEY
MARGARET H. MACMILLAN
V. MONTROSE
ELLEN F. PINSENT
GLADYS POTT
CATHERINE E. ROBSON
MAUD TREE
H. S. WANTAGE
MARY A. WARD

BRYCE
EDWARD CLARKE
HENRY CRAIK
JAMES CRICHTON-BROWNE
CROMER
CURZON
A. V. DICEY
JOHN GRETTON
GEORGE HAMILTON
H. HENSLEY HENSON
CHARLES HOBHOUSE
W. W. JACKSON
RUDYARD KIPLING
LOREBURN
H. J. MACKINDER
JOHN MASSIE
EDWARD A. MITCHELL INNES
JOHN MURRAY
WEARDALE

TRAINING OF THE DISABLED

18 November 1916

SIR,—MANY WILL REJOICE that *The Times* is pleading the urgency of the question of the training of disabled soldiers. Nothing that this country can do can ever make up for that which these men have done for us, but no effort should be spared to liquidate the debt as far as possible. As one who has been brought in contact with many men permanently disabled, may I suggest that two steps should be immediately taken. First of all it should be made perfectly clear by the highest authority that if a disabled soldier learns a trade and earns a good wage it will not in any way affect his statutory pension. We know this is so, but official announcements on the subject are obscure, and soldiers have heard of Crimean heroes being allowed to finish their days in the workhouse, and there is a certain amount of distrust in their minds. A very clear official pronouncement would clear the air and encourage many disabled men to learn a trade suited to their impaired powers. The second point is the necessity of an immediate amendment of the Employers' Liability Act to meet the situation. It is impossible for employers to take the heavy risk of employing partially disabled men who cannot be covered by insurance. Would it be possible for the State to take over the liability in the case of these men?

I am, Sir, yours faithfully,
B. STAUNTON BATTY

AFTERNOON TEA

24 November 1916

Sir,—There seem to be two entirely different sides to the argument against 5 o'clock tea—namely, the extravagant and the economical side.

To pay 2s. for 5 o'clock tea is, no doubt, an outrageous luxury, when all that can possibly be wanted to support the inner man can be obtained at some of the best clubs in London for 6d., which it is to be presumed leaves a margin for a reasonable profit; but if people cannot drink tea except with an accompaniment of sugared cakes and indifferent music, the question assumes a different aspect. These accompaniments are no doubt convenient for hotel-keepers and restaurateurs, as they attract people to their restaurants at tea time not because they are hungry and want a meal, but because they want indifferent music and society, which could very well be economized. There are, on the other hand, many people who get tea at any time between 1 and 6 because they are really hungry and want it, and even for the well-to-do it is a long time to go from 1 o'clock until 8 or 8.30 without anything to eat. The fact seems to be that extravagant teas, like extravagant dinners, are the fashion in order to put money into the pockets of the expensive hotels and restaurants. If an excellent four-course dinner with perfect cleanliness and first-rate waiting can be obtained at a French restaurant in the Soho district for 1s. 9d., why pay 21s. for a smart dinner at an up-to-date hotel? It may not be known that at some of these hotels champagne is sold in ginger-beer bottles and liqueurs in teapots in order to evade the economical regulations!

As long as this sort of thing is allowed to continue there does not appear to be much hope of improvement.

I am, Sir, yours faithfully,
AN INVETERATE TEA DRINKER

SPINAL CARRIAGES

27 November 1916

Sir,—Can you very kindly grant me a small space in your columns to appeal for gifts of spinal carriages for the use of our wounded soldiers? Many of these men lie in hospital looking out of the windows when they might be out enjoying the air and seeing fresh scenes, simply because there are no means by which they can be taken out of doors in a recumbent position. I feel sure that laid up in store rooms, out of use, there must be many of these carriages, which might be made the means of affording much relief and enjoyment to men who are unable even to sit in a bath-chair, and consequently have to remain indoors week after week and month after month. I have had the pleasure of observing the joy which can be introduced into the lives of these helpless men by the provision of such carriages, and I would like to see every hospital equipped with them. I should be delighted to hear from anyone who has a spinal carriage which could be given to a hospital.

Yours truly,
WINIFRED PORTLAND

GIRL WORKERS AT WOOLWICH

30 November 1916

Sir,—Many of the girls at the Woolwich Arsenal are working from 7 to 7, night or day, with short intervals allowed for meals. Many of them have to travel considerable distances to and from work, and in bad weather have often to walk. All this they willingly put up with, though many of them feel better work would be done were the hours of work shorter. But they do feel they should not have to stand in the rain for nearly an hour, after the long tiring day or night, waiting for their wages. They have made protests, but the stupid people in authority continue to ignore them. As a medical man, I cannot conceive a better way if one wanted to develop pneumonia.

There seems to be a great deal at the Arsenal that requires the attention of the "Welfare" ladies, if such have really been appointed.

I am, yours, &c.,
F.R.C.S.

A TUBE INCIDENT

6 December 1916

SIR,—ON SATURDAY EVENING last, at 5.15 o'clock, a friend and I were coming down the spiral staircase at the Charing-cross Embankment Station; we were puzzled by a curious, irregular "thump," "thump," "thump" preceding us from below, of which we could not see the cause; nearly at the bottom we came upon two wounded soldiers, with only two legs between them. The perspiration was pouring off their faces as they painfully and laboriously hopped from one step to the next below, carrying their crutches. We, of course, helped them to the bottom and put them into the train. We then ascertained that they were just out of hospital and were on their way "home," one to Manchester and the other to Liverpool. Knowing the number of steps at Euston Tube Station, my friend and I decided we must, of course, see them safely through (we were on our way home after a week's hard work), so we each took one of these poor boys and supported them down the three flights to the lift, then up the long flight to the L. and N.W. station, where they were at all events on level ground. They were so pathetically grateful for this trivial service, mere boys, and oh! so plucky and so cheery it made one's heart ache, but surely there must be hundreds of leisured women, who would be only too glad to take these poor maimed heroes to the station from the hospital and see them safely and comfortably into the train instead of allowing them to get there as best they can. I do not know what hospital these two boys came from, but I cannot say how dreadfully it hurt us to think they should have this additional suffering after they had already gone through so much.

Yours faithfully,
M. E. S.

POPULAR DESIDERATA

7 December 1916

Sir,—May I venture to place the following views before you? The Cabinet has resigned.

What the country requires is an able Executive, consisting of our best soldiers, sailors, and business men. For example—Sir J. Jellicoe, Sir W. Robertson, Lord Devonport, Sir O. Philipps, the President of the London Chamber of Commerce, and two good Labour men, with power to add to their number, who should see:—

(a) That there are sufficient heavy batteries to destroy utterly all the German artillery and save the present heavy losses when our infantry make attacks.

(b) Who will blockade the whole of Europe, including neutrals, and by so doing cause an effective blockade of the enemy to take place.

(c) Who should see that sufficient heavy guns are immediately produced, so that our merchant ships shall be able to sink all hostile submarines.

(d) Who should compel the immediate construction of at least 1,000 standardized merchant ships (to be in addition to those already building) to secure an adequate supply of food and raw material for munitions for England and her Allies.

I have the honour to be, Sir, your obedient servant,
NUNBURNHOLME

Asquith, undermined by leaks, splits in the government and attacks in the press, had resigned and was to be succeeded by the more decisive-seeming Lloyd George.

THE FOOD REGULATIONS

7 December 1916

Sir,—Had the academic theorists who sit in authority at the Board of Trade over our national housekeeping condescended to consult any mere daily practitioners of a somewhat difficult art they might perhaps have abstained from inaugurating a new source of public extravagance and waste of good material. From the point of view of economy a more wasteful expedient than the two-course and three-course luncheon and dinner could hardly have been devised, as most housekeepers on a large scale could have satisfactorily demonstrated. The abolition of the *entrée* and other attractive adjuncts, which serve up the leavings of yesterday's meat, poultry, or game, fruit or vegetables in so attractive a disguise as to render serious economies on expensive solid courses unnoticeable and unsuspected by the ordinary diner, will merely transfer to the pig-tub or the tout at the back door a mass of valuable foodstuffs and increase the sum of daily purchasing requirements. Had the official powers in Whitehall contented themselves with applying the price limit to meals served in public places as has been done by the military authorities, their announcements would have met with a different reception this morning from the chorus of somewhat edged feminine laughter from critics everywhere who have to run their own houses very much on the price-limit system, but unhampered by such unfortunately inspired decrees as to the methods of economical achievement.

I remain, Sir, your obedient servant,
HOUSEKEEPER

Britain, which imported most of its grain, had been hard hit by the U-boat campaign. Restrictions were gradually introduced and it became illegal in restaurants to eat more than two courses at lunch or three at dinner.

A MINER ON SACRIFICE

12 December 1916

SIR,—IN AS MUCH AS the Government have taken over the control of the South Wales coalfield, it would be very interesting and instructive to know what will become of our army of miners' leaders and their subordinates during the period of such control.

The deserving charities in our midst are very numerous, therefore it would be hardly playing the game to keep such a large number of our servants (British subjects) unemployed. If they would be acceptable for military service, all well and good, but on the contrary they should certainly, and without further delay, play the manly man, and cut coal, slow rubbish, or do any other work of national importance, as the circumstances nowadays really warrant more deeds and fewer words.

Our monthly Federation subscriptions should be forthcoming as usual; but the amount hitherto allocated for salaries and expenses of our agents, &c., should be diverted to more deserving causes, such as Red Cross, &c., during the period of this ghastly war. We have heard a great deal from time to time about the joint audit of our employers' books; has it ever dawned on our leaders and fellow workmen that the Government could also compel us to submit the Federation accounts to the scrutiny of a competent authority? Apparently our leaders have been playing too much with fire, and have now reaped their well-deserved reward. It is high time that the constant agitation and the "anything-to-justify-my-existence" policy by third parties should cease, and the sooner we as miners meet our respective masters face to face and thrash out any grievances which we may have the better it will be for all concerned. There is indeed, a growing discontent as to the extreme attitude of our leaders, and I am confident that if the foregoing suggestions could be brought into immediate operation the South Wales coalfield would cease to bear the unenviable reputation of being the hotbed of agitation and strife which it enjoys (?) at present.

When the great cry going up from the heart of the nation is for sacrifice, and more sacrifice, is it patriotic, nay, is it honourable, that we as miners should be wholly wrapped up in our little selves and branded by the whole civilized world (excepting Germany) as renegades and trailors—*A oes heddwch?*

Yours faithfully,
OLD AND EXPERIENCED COLLIER

The traditional challenge of the druids at important ceremonies: "Is there Peace?"

THE WOMAN WHO WORKS

19 December 1916

Sir,—Your suggestive article and "Colonel's" letter thereon will be welcomed by all who have dreaded the wholesale entry of women into the labour market unprotected by trade union membership. This is hardly the time to discuss the reason why so many are unprotected, but the result is painfully clear to the most imaginative, when questions crop up in the House of Commons similar to that put by Colonel Lord Henry Cavendish Bentinck concerning a certain controlled firm in Southampton, where women over 18 commenced work at 2d. an hour, to be increased after a year's service to ¾d.; the weekly wage averaging 10s. 10d.—13s. with overtime. I have before me some examples of low wages paid to women, employed wholly or partially on Government work, that tell the same tale.

Safety fuses.—11s. a week, now raised to 13s. by arbitration.

Linen cloth.—Government award of 2¾d. per hour to certain day workers.

Electric firm.—Day rates commencing at 2d. an hour, rising after a year's satisfactory service to 2¾d. an hour.

N.B.—52 hours' week at 2d. an hour—8s. 8d. 52 hours' week at 3d. an hour—13s.

The War Emergency Workers' National Committee reported that there are, "notwithstanding all the Government's declarations, still thousands of adult women on Government orders, and many of them legally forbidden to leave their employment earning less than 2d. an hour or 15s. a week; the trade boards have not yet revised their scale of wages anything like in proportion to the rise in cost of living." Committee issued Dr. Leonard Bill's report, founded on April prices, that 2s. 1½d. a day (or 14s. 10½d. a week) should provide sufficient and adequate food. And in *The Times* of September 25 the following significant paragraph appeared:—"The provision of proper meals for the workers is an indispensable condition for the maintenance of output on which our fighting forces depend, not only for victory but for their very lives."

Perhaps, a beginning might be made by the Government securing at least for all workers with controlled firms wages enabling them to procure "sufficient and adequate food" and ensuring, too, that it be an illegal condition of employment for a controlled firm to demand from a prospective employee a signed declaration that she will not join a trade union. Then, indeed, may woman with safety to herself, and to the man she may be displacing, "regard the whole field of labour as her province."

Yours, &c.,
BARBARA TCHAYKOVSKY, M.D.

A SOLDIER ON PEACE

27 December 1916

Sir,—The cry to demand of the enemy "unconditional surrender" coming from a man sitting before a brazier in a safe dug-out—or even in an armchair at home—might be superficial. A few days ago I visited a post in the front line trenches at 6 in the morning. The sun was due to rise just before 8 o'clock. A mist was doing its best to clear out the last traces of snow. Trenches were muddy, conditions very bad, everything uncomfortable. One man acted as sentry and three others were near him, so to speak, resting, waiting their next turn of duty. As I mounted the fire-step alongside the sentry and looked out into the dark the hasty thought passed my mind that externally viewed these men in such conditions appeared to have nothing to live for. "Well, how are things here?" I asked. "Oh, rather cold, sir, but all right." "Do you get all the latest bits of news along here?" "Yes, sir, I think so. We have heard about the peace." "And what do you think of it?" "Well, sir"—and I felt instinctively as he spoke that the subject had been debated during the night, and the vote was unanimous—"we don't think it right. We must finish beating the Boches first." I wonder whether German papers would please copy.

I am, Sir, yours truly,
ON LEAVE

1917

———◆———

TOO MANY PHEASANTS

5 January 1917

SIR,—I AM AMUSED (as well as annoyed) when I read all about this growing of vegetables, and then go out and look at my own big vegetable garden, where I see numerous upstanding stalks, entirely denuded of leaves, and realize that they represent curly-greens, brussels sprouts, &c., which ought to have been consumed this winter by human beings, but have instead been enjoyed by my neighbours' pheasants! There is a perfect plague of pheasants, for there has been no one to shoot them for two seasons. If the Government would give every one possessing a gun leave to shoot them, there might be a chance for the vegetables.

I enclose my card, and remain, Sir,
Yours obediently,
SUSSEX

CAPTAIN SELOUS

10 January 1917

SIR,—I MAKE NO CLAIM to be associated with Fred Selous in his hunting experiences, but as one of the very few left who knew him intimately in the old days in far-away Africa I will ask your leave to say a word in his memory. There have been many mighty hunters in the story of Africa, but, to those who really know, there has not been one to approach Selous as the king of his craft. My wife and I, with our little son, were with him at Inyati, in Matabeleland, in those troublous days in 1883 and 1884 at the time of "the great hippopotamus case" which, most unjustly, caused Selous's first break with Lobengula, and we shared the danger of that time together, spending an anxious Christmas Day in 1883 not knowing what each day might bring forth.

The name of Fred Selous has been a veritable beacon light to all hunters and travellers in Central Africa. Hunters, traders, and missionaries alike loved him. His courage, his skill, his generosity, and his manifest honesty were the talk and the pride of what was then known as "the Far Interior." Years have passed since those days, but even to-day the African continent rings with his fame, and the name of Fred Selous stands for all that is best and straightest in South African story. I can conceive no death more fitting to him than that which he has met: going forth at the age of 64 to fight for his King on the veld which he loved so well, and where his name was held in such abundant honour.

Yours faithfully,
RALPH WILLIAMS

MILITARY HONOURS

11 *January* 1917

Sir,—The New Year's Honours List must have gladdened the hearts, not only of those decorated but also of the nation, which must now realize that there is to-day no delay in rewarding those who fight splendidly in our cause. Cases of disappointment there must be, men overlooked who have done distinguished service. But this is inevitable in all human chances.

It seems desirable, however, that the attention of the Government and the public should be directed to the lot of some of our grand fellows, whose case is most unfortunate, and whose record, though known, remains unrecognized and unrewarded. At Château d'Oex and Mürren are to be seen many of our officers and men who have fought splendidly and have been desperately wounded, many of whose deeds are well known and freely recounted in the camps, but no one of whom has a piece of ribbon on his khaki coat. They are prisoners, and fall under what is understood to be the rule that no soldier who has been made prisoner by the enemy is eligible for reward until, after his release at the close of the war, he can "justify his surrender." The necessity of rule regarding surrender to the enemy can readily be understood, especially in the case of unwounded men. But in many cases is not the severity of the wound evidence enough of the cause of surrender? Note how otherwise the rule might apply. Two comrades fight throughout the day with well-recognized valour. Towards night both are desperately wounded. The one has just sufficient strength to crawl back to our lines, is carefully tended in our hospitals, very properly petted on convalescence, and receives without delay the Cross for his gallant conduct. The other, equally, possibly even more, deserving, is left unconscious on the field, supposed dead, and is raked in, in a helpless state next day, or perhaps two days later, by one of the enemy's search parties. Even if his wounds are properly cared for, he has on convalescence to undergo all the horror of a German prison camp. Later on, if he is fortunate, when suffering from terrible wounds and odious ill-treatment in the prison camps, he is permitted to come here into Switzerland a prisoner and exile, debarred from rewards or promotion, whilst his juniors decorated and promoted pass over his head.

Our French Allies treat such cases differently. In this neighbourhood are large numbers of French *internés*. These have not all been overlooked in the New Year's distribution of decorations, and I have been able to congratulate some of my friends on receiving the Cross or promotion in the Legion of Honour. It would be well if this lead were followed in the case of some of our dear fellows whose record is well known, and whose conduct has been the talk of the camps since their imprisonment. But this must be done quickly, otherwise, in some cases at least, the severity of their wounds and the odious ill-treatment in the prison camps may not admit of their lasting to see peace restored, and thus to have the opportunity necessary to "justify," forsooth, their so-called "surrender" whilst in a helpless state to the enemy's search parties.

Yours, &c.,
J. H. RIVETT-CARNAC, late I.C.S., Colonel Volunteers and Aide-de-Camp to King Edward VII

———◆———

WOMEN AS GARDENERS

12 January 1917

SIR,—MAY I ASK YOUR courtesy in bringing to the notice of your many readers the urgent need there is for more educated women to come forward and be trained as gardeners? The kitchen gardens of both small and large gardens could well be carried on by five or ten women, assisted by one man, and by this means many elderly but still vigorous men gardeners would be released to help the farmers. There are in England many young women who are good at hockey, golf, and lawn tennis. Will they give one moment's consideration to the fact that it is the produce grown on the land which gives them the vigour, energy, and activity which they display in taking part in those games? Without this food grown on the farms, without milk provided by the herds of cows, without cheese and butter, bread and eggs, where would be their strength? Where, too, would be the enduring fortitude of many thousands of active civilian and military workers? Will they, therefore, not come forward and go through a course of training as gardeners, thus releasing men for the Army and the farms? Let me remind these ladies of Mr. Prothero's words:—"It is my sincere conviction that it may be on the cornfields and potato lands of Great Britain that victory in this great war may be lost or won." Here, then, is a prospect of patriotic work for young women, fully equal in importance to that of munition factories—something which could help the whole nation, an object which all young athletic English women should join in. The call of the land has come! Do not let it be carelessly pushed aside this time.

Yours faithfully,
WOLSELEY

TAXATION OF CAPITAL

15 January 1917

SIR,—IN MY FORMER communication I mentioned that the notion of taxing capital generally, though illusory, was reasonable compared to the existing practice of taking two citizens with precisely the same income, and exacting from one a bearable percentage of that income whilst compelling the other to pay the whole of it twice over. This remark seems to have conveyed to some of your correspondents, including even my new disciple Mr. Marriott, that I regard a levy on capital as absolutely reasonable. I do not even regard it as possible. Mr. Marriott is quite right in his contention that it would disappear by depreciation in the process. But there is something more fundamental in that phenomenon than more depreciation; and since there seems to be some danger that an attempt at it may be made, either directly or in the guise of what is called taxation of values (land values for example), I had better try to make the situation even clearer than Mr. Marriott has left it.

There is one thing that the most energetic Government of practical business men cannot do even if its omission means defeat in the field; and that is, take from a citizen within the space of a financial year what he does not possess and cannot procure because it does not exist and cannot within that period be produced. I take that to be self-evident.

Now let me ask, What is a millionaire capitalist? Many people think he is a man with a million pounds in his pocket. He is not: he is only a man with £50,000 a year. Tax his million at the current rate of 5s. in the pound income-tax *plus* 3s. 6d. supertax, and the collector will demand from him more than eight times his entire income for the year—three hundred thousand odd pounds. He will simply reply, "I haven't got it."

But the practical man of business will stand no nonsense of that kind. He will say, "You haven't got it; but you can get it. All you have to do is to instruct your stockbroker to sell your income of £50,000 a year, and he will get you a million for it before you can say Jack Robinson."

Fantastic as the operation seems, it is not impossible under certain conditions. The first is that the millionaire's investments have been so widely distributed that he can sell out without throwing upon the market a huge block of shares in any one concern: a condition that would checkmate most of our industrial millionaires. The second is that all the other millionaires and investors generally are going on just as usual, buying and selling neither more nor less than the average. But this is just what would not happen as the result of a general tax on capital. All the other capitalists would be selling out at the same moment to pay the collector; and the consequence would be not merely depreciation, but zero, a total disappearance of the capital values owing to the fact that all the capitalists would be trying simultaneously to sell to one another, not the existing produce on which they were living for the year, but the as yet non-existent produce of next year and many succeeding years as well. Now, even in a world which lives, as ours does, mostly from hand to mouth, it may be possible, as an isolated transaction, to sell £50,000 worth of the wheat or coal or hardware of 1920 to a very rich man, because he can afford to wait for it. But you cannot put your hand on the entire harvest and output of that year in 1917-18 for immediate consumption at the front. Yet that is exactly what a tax on capital would attempt. It is flatly impossible. Within certain rather narrow limits you can defer consumption by tightening your belt. You cannot anticipate consumption on any terms. The wheat must be grown and the bread baked before you can eat it and fight on it. At most you can borrow spare wheat from the current harvest of the neutrals. You cannot borrow wheat that is not yet sown or grown from anybody.

What we call a capitalist is simply a person for whom we have agreed to earmark, year after year, a certain share of our national income in consideration of his having deferred consumption of part of his income at some past period when we needed the spare money for starting elaborately equipped industries. For a while his contribution is represented by machines and steel rails and so forth; but they soon wear out, and have to be renewed out of the income of the concern; all that is left of his advance being his claim on that income. The fact that now and then he can sell his claim to X for as much as, or perhaps more than, it cost him, and that X may, as an isolated case under a pressure peculiar to himself, sell it to Y, and Y to Z, and Z to A, and so on, until it has become the subject of a hundred fresh individual investments, does not multiply it by a hundred nor alter the fact that it remains a claim on the future and not, except as to the current year, a body of immediately consumable goods. In other words, you must tax income because there is nothing but income to tax. The depreciation foreseen by Mr. Marriott would be the outward and visible sign of the discovery that, "Where there is nothing the King loses his rights."

The point is one of pressing importance, because the war has driven us into a phase of collectivist activity which we have confided to a great extent to experienced men of individualist business. Now it happens that collectivism has always been one of the hobbies of experienced men of business who have made large fortunes. From Robert Owen to Joseph Fels, a long string of them might be named. A great deal was expected from their practical good sense and knowledge of men and affairs; but the truth is that in collectivism they were all incorrigible Utopian failures, with the single exception of William Morris, who was a poet forced unto business by the inadequacy of the people who had devoted their lives to it. We already see how the practical man of business having experience of the fact that an economy can be effected in a counting-house by cutting down the office boy's joy rides, infers that a public economy can be effected by hampering the locomotion of the whole nation at a moment when facilitation of transport both for men and goods has reached a value that would probably justify us in doubling the number of trains and abolishing fares. This pseudo-practicality is precisely of the kind that may lead its possessors to conclude that because an isolated individual or firm can "realize his capital" and spend it in shooting, a whole nation can do the same.

Let us suppose that Sir Douglas Haig comes to Mr. Lloyd George, or General Hindenburg to Herr Bethmann Hollweg, with the assurance that with unlimited munitions and men he can win the war. And let us add the further terrifying supposition that the statesman answers the soldier as a practical man of business as follows:—"First, you will understand, we must win: that goes before everything. Now, as to our resources, let me see. The national income before the war was estimated at £2,000,000,000. How much capital does that represent? I will take it at 5 per cent., because, though many of my friends get much more than that, still, as a cautious practical man of business, I will put it at that moderate figure. I therefore, being pledged, always as a practical man looking facts in the face, to the last shilling of our money and the last drop of our blood, have at my disposal £40,000,000,000 ready capital under the hand of the Chancellor of the Exchequer. And I daresay I can borrow a lot more if the worst comes to the worst. You can lay your plans accordingly. Are you satisfied?" The soldier points out that owing to the prodigious impulse given to production by the war the national income must have at least doubled since 1914, and that the capital now available must therefore be nearer a hundred thousand millions than thirty thousand. The statesman congratulates him on his practical knowledge of business, and admits that that is so. The soldier proceeds to plan his spring offensive on the assumption that he has a hundred thousand millions ready money to play with. In the middle of May, he surrenders at discretion; and all the practical statesmen are torn to pieces by an infuriated patriotic mob in Palace Yard.

Let nobody think that this is a joke. It is a quite possible mistake; and if it is to be made at all, I hope it will be made by the Imperial Chancellor, and not by our Prime Minister.

Yours truly,
G. BERNARD SHAW

OUR SMALL BIRDS

31 January 1917

SIR,—BEAUTIFUL WAXWINGS are in England again, as usually happens when severe cold is brought to us by continuous east winds; and why should civilized people kill them? About 12 years ago, in a similar winter, you permitted me to record, under the heading "A Rare Bird Not Shot," the pleasant fact that a Norfolk gamekeeper, gun in hand, had watched with interest a waxwing feeding on the scarlet hips of the wild rose—a sight, to my mind, worth walking far to see—and had not tried to shoot it. This was in spite of the fact that his titled employer prided himself upon his vast collection of rare birds shot upon his estate. One result of my letter was as pleasing as the incident, for a generous reader of *The Times* sent me a guinea to present to the gamekeeper. If, by publishing this, you extend its application to the present time, will you kindly allow me also to enforce it by asking whether any bird-killer or stuffed-bird collector can justify, on scientific or any other civilized grounds, his action in killing or adding to his collection a waxwing that has been driven to seek asylum in Britain? Many of the killers and collectors seem to glory in their achievements, judging by "records" in their Press; yet if you, Sir, would enlarge their publicity by a "pillory," giving the names and addresses of all known killers and collectors of waxwings during this immigration of the beautiful, fearless birds, you would go far to stamp out these shameful practices altogether.

Yours, &c.,
E. KAY ROBINSON, Editor, "Country-Side Leaflet"

SKATING ON THE THAMES

1 February 1917

Sir,—A propos to your notice of the upper Thames being frozen in places, and of "a tandem and trap" having been driven over the Serpentine in 1891, it is perhaps worth recording that in turning over an old MS. book of translations the other day I came upon one of the skating scene in Wordsworth's "Prelude," underneath which I had written (in Latin, which I will spare your readers) that it was made "after I had skated on the river from Sandford to Oxford with a friend and three Radley boys, in February, 1855." In the intense cold of that winter an Oxford man drove a trap from Folly Bridge, Oxford, to Kennington island and back.

WILLIAM WOOD, D.D., *ætat* 88

PRE-CRIMEAN VETERANS

OLD CHELSEA PENSIONERS

2 February 1917

SIR,—DURING THE LAST few months death has been taking its average toll of the inmates of this institution, and among them were three notable veterans, the last survivors of pre-Crimean wars in the place, and probably anywhere else.

The oldest, William Adams, aged 94, took part in the Battle of Punniar, fought in the Gwalior War of 1843, and at Moodkee in the Sutlej War of 1846, where he was shot in the knee and crippled for life. In spite of this he could get about fairly well up to the last few months, and he earnestly hoped he would live to see the Germans "done in." The other two were both 90, James Hales, 10th Foot, a survivor of the storming of Mooltan and the Battle of Goojerat in the Sutlej War, a cheerful and garrulous old man, who followed the doings in the present war of his old regiment, now the Lincolnshire, with keen interest. The third, William Clark, 24th Foot, was at Chillianwala in 1849, where the regiment was terribly cut up, losing 25 officers and over 500 men, a record which was cut some 30 years later when it was practically annihilated at Isandhlwana.

There are still nearly 40 Crimean men here, but they are all 80 and upwards. One of them, Trooper James, Royal Dragoons, must be almost the last survivor of the heavy cavalry charge at Balaclava, still very fit and well.

I am, Sir, yours faithfully,
N. G. LYTTELTON, Royal Hospital, Chelsea

THE FREEDOM OF THE SEAS

7 February 1917

SIR,—I OFFER TO YOUR readers the following free translation of a part of Fichte's famous account of Napoleon, all of which is good reading, especially at the present moment. It was written about 1813. Some Germans think it the best piece of historical prose in their language:—

"Ecquipped with these two elements of heroism, a calm perspicuity of intellect, and a firm will, he [Napoleon] might have become the benefactor and liberator of mankind if but the slightest inkling of the moral vocation of humanity had been granted to his soul; but such a perception never broke on him, and he became, therefore, for all time an example of what these two qualities can effect of themselves unaided by any spiritual intuition. For of them was built up the edifice of his thought, whence he judged the whole human race to be a blind lump of force, either altogether stagnant, or quickening in disorder and perplexity to intestine strife; and be judged that neither should that stagnation be—for it should be movement; nor should that movement be disorderly, but should direct itself to one aim; and he thought that along the ages rare spirits were born here or there, destined to give direction to this mass, the like of Charlemagne, and of none other but himself after Charlemagne; and that the inspiration of these master-spirits was the highest thing of all, the verily godlike and holy, the first principle of motion in the world's history; and that for this, all other aims, whether of security or pleasure, should be sacrificed outright; for this, all forces in motion; for this, all life whatsoever be impropriated; and that to oppose its activities were a rebellion against the highest law of existence. In himself, he thought, this universal law appeared with the new order of things as he would work it out, within a Culture-state beneath his sovereignty. And the most immediate indispensable tool of his ordinance was at this moment "The Freedom of the Seas," as he said, but thereby intended the "Overlordship of the Seas" in his own hands; and for this most important aim, determined by his world-law, all the happiness of Europe must be sacrificed, all its blood flow—since for that purpose only was it there; and this mighty world-plan, which indeed overstretched the scope of one lifetime, should be carried on after him by his dynasty, so long as until, may be in another thousand years, another inspired hero might spring up, a new incarnation of the type of himself and Charlemagne."

I would not add remarks; but what Buonaparte, with some assistance from Fichte, really accomplished was to unite the German-speaking peoples. It will be of wholesome historical significance if his imitator should succeed in uniting the English-speaking races; and it will not be his fault if he fails.

ROBERT BRIDGES

SOLDIERS IN LONDON

10 February 1917

SIR,—THE LETTERS WHICH pour in upon me testify to the fact that the conscience of England is aroused over the shocking state of affairs that has arisen. The conscience of England may well be aroused. Presently she may stand at the bar before the sister nations, who will ask her, "How have you cared for the boys who were sent to help you?" It will not be easy to find a reply. If we answer, as the Bishop of London has done, that some of them were themselves "looking for trouble," that will not, I think, condone the fact that all of them were placed under conditions of provocation which no men should be asked to endure. "The pavement outside is blocked by the women lying in wait; they push open the windows in broad daylight and try to call the men out—they even force their way inside. The police seem powerless though there are plenty of them about." What can we say to the Colonies when we are reproached for such a state of things as that? We can only make the miserable reply that our own youth has been sacrificed as freely and as needlessly as theirs.

With all possible respect to the Bishop of London, I am of opinion that his suggestion of making venereal disease a military offence would be most dangerous in practice. The man would naturally conceal his condition; he would get worse from want of treatment, and would end by total disablement. In the case of the man I can only suggest that the exhibition to him during his training of a few medical pictures depicting the exact effects of advanced venereal disease would have a distinctly chastening effect. I am clear also that the act of a man who, knowing that he has such a disease upon him, risks the spread of the infection should be made criminal and heavily punished.

The case of the women is different. I cannot clearly follow the Bishop when he uses the word "Christian" in order to support one form of coercion as against another. It does not appear to me to be relevant, and it complicates what is already sufficiently complex. Strictly speaking, one might say that it was not Christian to turn the women out of the warm, well-lit halls into the winter streets. Many of us have our doubts how far moving the women from one point to another can have any effect save that of contaminating new areas. As to the alleged total failure of concentration it is remarkable that nearly all Continental countries (Christian nations, by the way) continue to use the system. I think that it would be fairer to say that it has partially failed, and that this failure is due to venal police and lax administration. I can never believe that a disease, moral or physical, which is quarantined, or even partially quarantined, is not more wisely treated than a disease which is allowed to spread without a check.

But, the present condition needs a more speedy and drastic remedy. These women are the enemies of the country. They should be treated as such. A short

Bill should be passed empowering the police to intern all notorious prostitutes in the whole country, together with brothel keepers, until six months after the end of the war. All women found to be dangerous should be sent to join them. They should be given useful national work to do, well paid, kindly treated, but subjected to firm discipline at the hands of a female staff. So a curse might be changed, for a time at least, to a blessing, the streets of London would be purified, and our conscience would be clear in that we had done our utmost. "I was ready to give his body for the King, but I am giving his soul as well," cried an agonized mother. We cannot let such words be said in vain.

Yours faithfully,
ARTHUR CONAN DOYLE

SPARROWS AND RATS

17 February 1917

SIR,—MR. CATTLE'S LETTER about rats is most timely, but we are in even greater danger from sparrows than from rats. The case against them is proved up to the hilt by the Carnegie Trust investigations and otherwise. They not only destroy and damage crops, but also drive away really insectivorous birds. Sparrows do, of course, eat a certain quantity of phytophagous insects, *e.g.*, wireworms and daddy-longlegs, but they do not become carnivorous until gorged with vegetable food, and the innumerable investigated cases show traces of insect food in only 4 per cent. On the contrary, from careful estimates I find that 3,000 sparrows will consume at least a peck of grain per acre per day, and they certainly waste as much again when the grain is mature.

Ignoring, then, the waste on the field, the harms done to grain that is sprouting or milting, and the robberies from the stack, the threshing-floor, quays, warehouses, stables, and nosebags, and assuming that all the grain is nothing better than average good oats (at 1s. 10d. a peck to-day), sparrows cost us, on our 8,000,000 acres of grain, £800,000 per day during the time the grain is mature!

More damage than ever is to be feared this year because of the larger amount of suburban land being brought into use, and this raises a further point. The fine work done—*e.g.*, by the Wirrall Farmers' Club and the Epping Sparrow Club—has failed only because of the impossibility of coping with the millions of sparrows that migrate from the towns. It is of vital importance, therefore, that an immediate and simultaneous crusade should be made against these pests in town and country alike. The work should be taken up by all local authorities and carried through in some definite weeks, and a capitation fee should be offered. On this point failure and success elsewhere, *e.g.*, on such "suburban" arable land as is normal in Belgium and New Jersey, are convincing. I suggest 6s. per 100 birds (or eggs) to be delivered to the nearest sanitary depôt or police-office.

Yours,
L. W. LYDE

ETON WAR MEMORIAL

19 February 1917

SIR,—WE ASK OUR brother Etonians to subscribe to a fund in memory of their schoolfellows who have given their lives for their country.

The chief object of the Fund will be to enable the sons of fallen Etonians to be educated, like their fathers, at Eton. Accordingly we propose that, after providing for a permanent and visible record at Eton of those who have fallen, a capital sum should be set apart for the above purpose. When, by the allocation of a sufficient amount, that purpose is fulfilled, the surplus would be devoted to the creation of an Endowment Fund to help Old Etonians, who could not otherwise afford it, to provide an Eton education for their sons, or to some other similar object to be hereafter determined. The administration of the fund will be vested in a committee representative of the Provost and Fellows and of Old Etonians.

A large sum will be required; the College have undertaken to contribute to the fund; and it is hoped to raise at least £100,000. A circular letter giving full details will shortly be sent to all Old Etonians, as far as possible.

We are, Sir, yours faithfully,

ARTHUR	CAVAN
ALEXANDER OF	JAMES W. LOWTHER
TECK	ARTHUR JAMES
LANSDOWNE	BALFOUR
ROSEBERY	EDMOND WARRE
CURZON	

Eton was the only school to lose more than 1,000 former pupils to the war.

NEW SOURCES OF FOOD

19 February 1917

SIR,—HITHERTO THE FOOD Controller has shown, as far as we can judge by the daily Press, little originality either in his suggestions for diminishing the amount of food consumed or for providing new sources of food.

A few years ago the number of dogs in Great Britain was 1,871,619, excluding puppies, and puppies eat quite a lot. As these statistics were based on the dog tax, I think we may safely assume there were at that time at least 2,000,000 adult dogs in England, Scotland, and Wales. One naturally omits Ireland, although the voracity of Mr. Flurry Knox's hounds is proverbial. Each of these 1,871,619 dogs ate on an average about ¾lb. of food per day, over 4,500 tons a week. Not all of it, but still a considerable part of it, was fit for human consumption. The majority of our dogs are comparatively useless, and the masters of foxhounds have already set an example in diminishing their numbers. I submit a very considerable amount of food useful for human beings might be saved by either rationing or destroying a certain percentage of our dog population.

Again, I gather from the suggested restrictions put on the weekly consumption of bread by the Food Controller that there is a shortage of starch in the country, and yet we have an enormous supply, almost an unlimited supply, of starch in the underground stems or rhizomes of the common bracken-fern, *Pteris aquilina*. Starch from this source is used for food in many parts of the world. Thirty years ago I remember eating bread or cakes prepared from it in the Canary Islands. A closely allied species of fern, hardly to be distinguished from *Pt. aquilina*, is the Australian *Pt. esculenta*. It is, as its specific name implies, used as food, and it is a well-known fact that the Māoris of New Zealand—a very fine race—nourish themselves on starch from a similar source. The young fronds of the bracken, cooked and served like asparagus, make an excellent green vegetable course. Bracken requires no expensive seeds, no planting, no manuring, no weeding, and no tending in any way. The underground stem, packed with starch, is simply there, asking to be taken.

The Departmental Inquiry or Grouse-disease, which sat a few years ago, took a great deal of evidence on the question of the bracken in Scotland, and it is difficult to decide which class of men had the worst opinion of this graceful fern. The sportsman who shot grouse showed that its spread destroyed the young heather, and the farmer complained bitterly that it destroyed the grass of his sheep-runs. So that by utilizing this form of farinaceous food we should be helping the farmer as well as providing food for the hungry.

I am, Sir, yours faithfully,
A. E. SHIPLEY

NATIONAL SERVICE AND INCOME-TAX

23 February 1917

SIR,—NATIONAL SERVICE, voluntary or compulsory, will rule the coming year. May I ask how the Government is dealing with income-tax procedure?

A barrister, solicitor, writer, or other professional man, has earned in 1915, 1916, 1917 (say) £4,000, £5,000, £3,000 respectively, and will have to pay in (say) February, 1918, 5s. at least in the pound on a statutory income of £4,000—a matter of £1,000, *plus* supertax. In February of 1917 he responds to Mr. Neville Chamberlain's appeal and does national work at (say) £300 a year. Is he in February, 1918, to find this £1,200 or so of taxation out of his £300, besides living and perhaps keeping a family on it? If he has been patriotic he has given or invested all his surplus income these last years for purposes of the war, and has no balance at his bank. There must have been hard cases of this kind already since income-tax has run so high, but with national service they will be greatly multiplied.

The only reasonable demand, of course, in these days of high tax is payment on net income for the year. The difficulty, I suppose, is the postponement this entails in collection—net income for the year ending April, 1918, could not be known and paid on till during that same April at earliest, whereas the present payment on statutory income is made in the previous January or February. The Government, however, can surely not contemplate that those who voluntarily respond to its appeal for national service, or those whom it forces to respond, shall find themselves in such a fix.

So, much for while the war lasts. But even when it ceases income tax will be as high as ever, and the same hardship will fall on professional men overtaken by illness, or by the disorder, shall we say? of wanting to do work for a year which will not bring in any money. For instance, they may conceivably desire to write poems and plays or paint pictures which they know to be unsaleable, or may devote themselves to microbes or the slums for the benefit of mankind. And I suggest that such efforts, rare enough and not without their use, should not be discouraged for want of a little extra elasticity in income-tax procedure.

Yours truly,
JOHN GALSWORTHY

MR. WILSON AND CONGRESS

28 February 1917

SIR,—IN OUR PRESIDENT's latest address to Congress, as I see it, we get a picture of Wilson the man as distinguished from Wilson the statesman. Wilson the statesman appeals to Congress to empower him to act strictly from the American standpoint; Wilson the man states that he is concerned fundamentally, not about American property interests, nor yet about the lives of American citizens, but about "those rights of humanity without which there is no civilization." Wilson the statesman, lacking the power to compel, must persuade; Wilson the man enunciates the great faith that is in him.

Wilson's championship of American rights, it may be said, is distinctly militant, while his championship of human rights is merely pious. Might not one go a little wrong here? Is it sure that declared American hostility to the Teutonic Alliance would be a harder shield of freedom than will be American "armed neutrality"? We want our ships to carry food and munitions to the forces of right. If "armed neutrality" can protect this traffic, why substitute for it the doubtful aegis of destroyers? As for the Dutch, the Scandinavians, other neutrals, if Britain's vast Navy, here in European waters, with an incomparable *personnel* born to the sea, cannot deflect, or cannot deflect wholly, German torpedoes from their shipping, how can we?

Of course, if Germany, right and left, begins to sink our ships, the power of our neutrality to serve democracy will have vanished. Then, in my opinion, there will be no puzzled councils in America as to what the interests of free humanity demand we shall do.

Our ships, we hear, are not sailing. Even President Wilson, with a touch of scorn, refers to many American ships remaining "timidly" in port. But, I daresay, if many of our ships are in port, many also are on the water, with valuable cargoes for the Allies. Can one imagine an American shipowner calling the reporters down to the docks, and saying, "Here is the good ship Hunsbedamned, loaded with 16in. guns, putting to sea at 2 o'clock to-day for Havre, speed 12 knots"?

From an old and able friend in Indiana I received this morning a letter in which he says:—"We all are watching our German-American friends closely." It would be safe, I fancy, to wager heavily that President Wilson has directed, and is directing, shrewd glances in the same direction. Not, in all likelihood, that he questions the patriotism of the body of German-American citizens, but that he feels somewhat less than easy concerning the possible conduct of a few Germanistic stalwarts in the larger German-American communities.

If we must make war, we want no social fissures in the United States, any more than you wanted them in Britain. If, and when, our country takes the fateful step, Wilson wants a public temper so hot throughout America that it instantly will burn to ash any revolutionary unrest, or any opposition by pacifist die-hards. Why? Because if our Government, in existing circumstances, struck for freedom, with a clashing nation behind it, it would be in danger of doing freedom the greatest disservice it ever has suffered at the hands of its friends.

I am, Sir, yours faithfully,
EDWARD PRICE BELL

———◆———

SUBSTITUTION OF WOMEN

1 March 1917

SIR,—THE LORD CHANCELLOR, speaking in the House of Lords last night on the Solicitors (Qualification of Women) Bill, said:—"To introduce women as competitors with men was to aggravate the situation in this country by displacing men who might be the breadwinners of families." As it had been pointed out that the shortest possible period of qualification was three years and the normal period was five years, we have here an opportunity for the discussion of an economic question in the most detached form. No one can do necessary work of any kind without taking a place which some one else would otherwise fill. If the argument that women by doing necessary work are injurious because they are taking other people's jobs be sound, then each workman engaged in necessary work of any kind, although excuse might be found for him on the ground of his necessities, is an injurious person, and the real benefactors are the inmates of our prisons, who are helping others to find employment by wearing clothes and eating food and occupying buildings, while in many cases at least they are not taking away anyone else's opportunity of finding employment by doing work that he might do. It may be difficult in each case to follow the effect on each particular interest, but economists are surely right in thinking that the more efficient workers of all kinds we have engaged in rendering necessary or useful services the better will it be for the prosperity of our people as a whole. I do not of course, write for the purpose of criticizing the Lord Chancellor, for whom I have the highest regard, but for the purpose of dealing with a line of thought which is very usual, and which has, I think, to be fought out, as it might prejudice our appreciation of women's labour, which is, in my belief, a great national asset in war and in peace wherever it can be carried out with profit rather than injury to the women themselves.

I am, &c.,
ROWALLAN

ABSENTEEISM AT WOOLWICH

2 March 1917

Sir,—I have been lodging, in order to be near canteen work at Woolwich, with a workman's family. The husband is exempted from military duty in order to do piece work in a large factory controlled by Government. He constantly stays away from work for a day, sometimes for a whole week, idling at home. He is quite a steady man, only lazy, and no compulsion being put upon him to work regularly he just does enough to keep his family in moderate comfort, though he could earn a very large wage, and save money, as his thrifty, capable wife, with a young family coming on, would be so glad if he did. She says that many of the workman at his place are far worse in this respect than he is, sometimes taking a whole fortnight off work and just living from hand to mouth. Why is this sort of slacking allowed when workers are so much needed, and when these men have been exempted from soldiering to do this work? How glad their wives would be if they were obliged to work full time, and then they would all have had savings to put in the War Loan, instead of just paying their way, and often not even that.

Yours faithfully,
M. M. M. S.

FISH EXPORTS

3 March 1917

Sir,—The reply to "Ex-Inspector of Coastguard and Fishery Officer" is that there is no known method of dealing with the huge catches of herrings as they come in, except by salting. Small quantities can, of course, be preserved in tins, but it would be impossible to deal with the gluts in this manner. The herring is a fish which rapidly deteriorates when once out of the water, and the only effective way of preserving the bulk of the catch is by salting. As the working classes of this country refuse to use salt fish, and as it is not good enough for our German prisoners, the curer must export. After all, the exported fish brings back other commodities in exchange. Smoked herrings, or "reds," are very much appreciated by our men in France, as I know from personal experience, and if introduced into the Army rations they would be very popular, besides being the means of replacing other forms of food. "Red" herrings are at the present time the cheapest form of food we have; it is portable and easily handled; 60lb. weight would contain 250 to 300 smoked dried herrings—enough to feed 200 men.

Yours, &c.,
FISH CURER

AMERICA AND ENGLAND

FAST RIPENING SYMPATHY

5 March 1917

SIR,—I ENCLOSE (IN case you think fit to print them) some extracts from a letter written to me by a friend in America, of high academic position, widely respected for his abilities and character. The state of American feeling described in the letter has since ripened fast.

I remain yours very faithfully,
GEORGE OTTO TREVELYAN

I have not had the heart to write to you before. I have been so downcast that I could not trust myself to write; but, at last, our Government has been brought to the point which it should have reached 18 months ago. Von Bernstorff has been sent away and Gerard has been called home. One good thing has been accomplished by these delays. The German-Americans are resigned to the President's action, if not pleased with it. The long campaign against disloyalty has had the result of making them see that policy, if nothing else, counsels them to be acquiescent. Many of them have come to see, too, that Germany is like a fine horse, ridden by a demon-rider; and that its terrible guide must be brought low before civilized life can go on. Our entry on the scene may mean little to you, but it means a great deal to us. I hope that you in England understood that most thinking men here felt, as Bonar Law expressed it, that what President Wilson longed for England was fighting for.

* * * * * *

Before I close this letter there is one matter which I wish to let you know, and to make very clear. You Englishmen are so generous that you may not have thought much of the fact that for a long time American sympathy, as a whole, went out more to France than to you. Within the last three months there has been a great change. The sympathy for France has not lessened, but there has been a great welling up of sympathy for England. One manifestation of it is the desire to do something for the English wounded, for the English orphans, for any good cause in England. But England has gone her fine, proud way—asking nothing, making no complaint, but doing her whole duty without a murmur. Suddenly it has dawned on people here that England, too, is suffering, that this noble strife of hers is tearing her very heartstrings, and drawing upon her every resource. Everywhere I go, not only here among my friends, but out in the State among business and professional men, I am asked, "What can I do for England?" The spirit is there to do many things, if only the avenues were open. Whether England wants this aid or not, it will, I am sure, be gratifying to you to know that the spirit is here.

My own great effort is to foster the friendly feeling between the English and the American people. In that friendship only do I see any practical way for the realization of the widespread desire to attain a permanent peace. I have little hope in leagues to enforce peace, or other artificial devices not founded on the everlasting rock of human nature.

After much debate, America would declare war on Germany on April 6.

———◆———

SUGAR FOR JAM

26 March 1917

SIR,—MAY I HEARTILY endorse "Country Residents'" letter in your to-day's paper? In view of Mr. Prothero's statement, my household has voluntarily been using only about one-third of its sugar ration, the surplus being carefully noted and obtained from London to be "hoarded" for fruit preserving. We have 20 apple and pear trees and 10 stone fruit. Many of these are old trees and very prolific, but are not keeping sorts; there is also a good quantity of small fruit. Unless preserved, much of this crop must be wasted, as last year, when I made no jam, and, in spite of giving away large quantities, nearly half a ton had to be fed to fowls. Sugarless preserving is impossible, on account of cost and the difficulty of obtaining corks and bottles. Local greengrocers who are also market gardeners will only buy the pick of the fruit just when they need it, but they have been so hardly hit by the calling up of their men it is unfair this year to sell or give away locally, while the cost of transit and distance from station prohibits sending to hospitals, troops, and friends often. I would also remind Lord Devonport that no firm pays railway carriage on goods of less than £2 value, and this does not include carrier. Naturally, therefore, country housekeepers buy in bulk, and all have store cupboards, as village grocers cannot afford to stock heavily things not in daily use in rural districts; also in most of these shops dry goods are getting scarce, therefore it is a help for those who can afford to do so to import these. Railway transit is, however, very uncertain, and delays often occur, so six weeks' supply is none too much to have in reserve. In view of this, I trust Lord Devonport will see his way to making some concession in such cases, as it seems most unfair thrift and unselfishness should be penalized and the produce of our gardens wasted at such a time.

Yours truly,
ANOTHER COUNTRY RESIDENT

PROPORTIONAL REPRESENTATION

30 March 1917

SIR,—THERE SEEMS TO be a very general failure to grasp the importance of what is called—so unhappily—Proportional Representation in the recommendations of the Speaker's Conference. It is the only rational, honest, and efficient electoral method. It is, however, in danger of being thrust on one side as a mere fad of the intellectuals. It is regarded by many ill-informed people as something difficult, "high-browed," troublesome, and of no practical value, much as science and mathematics were so regarded by the "practical" rule-of-thumb industrialists of the past. There are all too many mean interests in machine politics threatened by this reform, which are eager to seize upon this ignorant mistrust and use it to delay or burke the political cleaning-up that Proportional Representation would involve. Will you permit me to state, as compactly and clearly as I can, the real case for this urgently-needed reform—a reform which alone can make Parliamentary government anything better than a caricature of the national thought and a mockery of the national will?

The essential point to grasp is that Proportional Representation is not a novel scheme, but a carefully worked-out remedy for universally recognized ills. An election is not the simple matter it appears to be at the first blush. Methods of voting can be manipulated in various ways, and nearly every method has its own liability to falsification. Take the commonest, simplest case—the case that is the perplexity of every clear-thinking voter under British or American conditions: the case of a constituency in which every elector has one vote, and which returns one representative to Parliament. The naïve theory on which we go is that all the possible candidates are put up, that each voter votes for the one he likes best, and that the best man wins. The bitter experience is that hardly ever are there more than two candidates, and still more rarely is either of these the best man possible. Suppose, for example, the constituency is mainly Conservative. A little group of pot-house politicians, wire-pullers, busy-bodies, local journalists, and small lawyers, working for various monetary interests, have "captured" the Conservative organization. For reasons that do not appear they put up an unknown Mr. Goldbug as the official Conservative candidate. He professes a generally Conservative view of things, but few people are sure of him and few people trust him. Against him the weaker (and therefore still more venal) Liberal organization puts up a Mr. Kentshire (formerly Wurstberg) to represent the broader thought and finer generosities of the English mind. A number of Conservative gentlemen, generally too busy about their honest businesses to attend the party "smokers" and the party cave, realize suddenly that they want Goldbug hardly more than they want Wurstberg. They put up their long-admired, trusted, and able friend Mr. Sanity as an Independent

Conservative. Every one knows the trouble that follows. Mr. Sanity is "going to split the party vote." The hesitating voter is told, with considerable truth, that a vote given Mr. Sanity is a vote given for Wurstberg. At any price we do not want Wurstberg. So at the eleventh hour Mr. Sanity is induced to withdraw, and Mr. Goldbug goes into Parliament to misrepresent us. That in its simplest form is the dilemma of democracy. The problem that has confronted modern democracy since its beginning has not been the representation of organized minorities, but *the protection of the unorganized masses of busily occupied, fairly intelligent men from the tricks of the specialists who work the party machines.* We know Mr. Sanity, we want Mr. Sanity, but we are too busy to watch the incessant intrigues to oust him in favour of the obscurely influential people, politically docile, who are favoured by the organization. We want an organizer-proof method of voting. It is in answer to this demand, as the outcome of a most careful examination of the ways in which voting may be protected from the exploitation of those who work elections, that the method of Proportional Representation with a single transferable vote has been evolved. It is organizer-proof. It defies the caucus. If you do not like Mr. Goldbug you can put up and vote for Mr. Sanity, giving Mr. Goldbug your second choice, in the most perfect confidence that in any case your vote cannot help to return Mr. Wurstberg.

There is the cardinal fact in the discussion of this matter. Let the reader grasp that, and he has the key to the significance of this question. With Proportional Representation with a single transferable vote (this specification is necessary because there are also the inferior imitations of various election-riggers figuring as Proportional Representation) it is *impossible to prevent the effective candidature of independent men of repute beside the official candidates.* Without it the next Parliament, the Parliament that will draw the broad lines of the Empire's destinies for many years, will be just the familiar gathering of old Parliamentary hands and commonplace party hacks. It will be a Parliament gravitating fatally from the very first towards the old party dualism, and all the falsity and futility through which we drifted in the years before the war. Proportional Representation is the door for the outside man; the Bill that establishes it will be the charter to enfranchise the non-party Briton. Great masses of people today are utterly disgusted with "party" and an anger gathers against the "party politician" as such that he can scarcely suspect. To close that door now that it has been opened ever so slightly, and to attempt the task of Imperial Reconstruction with a sham representative Parliament on the old lines, with large masses of thwarted energy and much practical ability and critical power locked out, may be a more dangerous and disastrous game than those who are playing it seem to realize at the present time.

I am, &c.,
H. G. WELLS

GREAT BRITAIN AND RUSSIA

2 April 1917

SIR,—I HAVE READ with great pleasure to-day's telegram from your Petrograd correspondent of his address to the Soldiers' Committee at Pskov. It is of interest that it was suggested to him to visit other committees of the Army in order to explain to them Great Britain's attitude towards the new Russian Government. If the British Government would send immediately a small delegation of three or five men to visit the Russian capitals and other large cities to express its good will to the new Government of Russia, it would not only lend support to the national cause and to the cause of the Allies, but would earn the eternal gratitude of the Russian democracy. This new proof of Great Britain's sympathy with the Russian nation would further cement the union of the two nations and make Russia even more determined in their struggle against Prussianism.

Yours faithfully,
DR. L. SEGAL

Riots and numerous attacks on the apparatus of the state had led to the abdication of the Tsar and the formation of a provisional government. Meanwhile, Lenin had returned from exile.

ILLNESS AT OSBORNE

3 April 1917

Sir,—I should like to add my support to the letter of "Paterfamilias" in to-day's issue of *The Times* on this subject. My boy returned to the college on January 18 "in the pink of condition," and now, alas! he is no more. I believe at one time there were more than 280 boys in sick bay. I would suggest a searching inquiry, first, whether the medical staff is sufficient to cope with this number, and, second, whether the nursing staff is sufficient. It is wicked to send over 500 boys of the best blood of the country to the college unless they can receive proper care and attention in the event of sickness. Is there no one in Parliament willing to bring this matter before the powers that be?

A BROKEN-HEARTED MOTHER

Sir,—I have just spent the winter in the Isle of Wight in close vicinity to the Naval College, and watched with keen interest the course of this term's illness. My interest was particularly keen because for many years previously I was matron at one of our largest public schools, and had the management of large numbers of boys. For years past we have been accustomed to reading in the Press of large numbers of cadets at Osborne suffering from infectious complaints—numbers far greater than occur at the public schools. From my own observation of boys of school age, I have noticed that boys under 15 are specially liable to illness, and that after 15 they are either immune or, when ill, are strong enough to recover rapidly. At a public school the boys range from 13 to 19, and it may be said that the majority are past the delicate age. At Osborne all the boys are under 15. It has always seemed to me that the initial error is the Assembling of 500 boys of the delicate age in one place and in very close proximity. The open dormitories, the crowd in Nelson Room, and perhaps especially the closely-packed mess room, where the cadets assemble for meals and evening prayers, no doubt assist in spreading infection, while the very strenuous life of hard work and long hours may well induce the fatigue that is a predisposing cause of illness. A public school with such a death rate would soon cease to exist, as parents would decline to send their boys there but Osborne is a Government Department and is difficult to convince, while the cadets' parents would seem to be powerless.

Yours faithfully,
LATE PUBLIC SCHOOL MATRON

BOAR HUNT AT THE FRONT

12 April 1917

AN OFFICER SERVING in France writes:—

We are out of the line for a time now and have just had a great boar-hunt.

We got the men to beat a wood for us, while four of us lined up outside with drawn swords. Presently out came the old tusker, followed by his sow, two three-quarter-grown, and two half-grown, all in single file led by the old boar. The major and I got well away and rode through the young ones after we had gone half a mile, left them behind, and went after the others. At the top of the hill we got close on to the bigger four. We were then on hard going where the sun had not reached; my horse slipped and sat on his haunches. The two three-quarter-grown broke to the left into a small wood; the old ones kept straight on, making for "A" wood. Then came a frozen hill to go down; the major got down well as his horse had frost cogs on. I slipped most of the way down, then kept wide on the major's left. He got to the wood not more than 20 yards behind the boar and almost on top of the sow.

I rode straight on, expecting to see him going away, but he got lost in the wood. We again picked up the boar's line, but finally lost in "B" wood. On the way home we ran into the two three-quarter ones, evidently trying to join the old boar. We had a really fine ten minutes. The sun had thawed the surface of the ground, and the going was good. I made the running and was on their heels just waiting to stick one, when I tried to follow a right-angled jink too quickly, and over we went, horse and self—an imperial toss. The pig got away a few hundred yards further on by charging straight through a barbed-wire fence. The wires were only 9 in. apart; he snapped the two bottom ones—*some* animals, are they not? Best day's sport for years.

AFTERNOON TEA

A MEAL TO BE ABOLISHED

21 April 1917

SIR,—YOU WERE GOOD enough to publish a letter from me in November last, urging, as a preliminary step towards compulsory economy in food consumption, that all caterers should be prohibited from selling food or drink between the hours of 3 and 6 p.m.

For that letter I was very severely criticized by those who, like myself, had the afternoon tea habit, and more often than not their criticism took the line that I would inflict a great hardship on the working classes, and particularly on the working women. My suggestion applied only to unnecessary eating between midday and evening meals, not to the class whose tea constitutes the evening meal. The restriction would cause discomfort, as does the breaking of any habit, and in many cases it would mean inconvenience, and it was from the class who were not prepared to make even this sacrifice that the howl was heard in November. I heard no protest from the working women.

Now I find that the unnecessary consumption of food at "afternoon tea" is being condemned in the Press right and left, and finally the Food Controller has adopted certain restrictive measures as to the types of food which may be consumed. But what does it amount to? The latest restriction recognizes, and therefore encourages, the consumption of 2oz. of breadstuffs during the three restricted hours between the midday and the evening meals.

For some time the Food Controller has been urging upon the country the absolute necessity for rigid economy. He has put the situation as to food supply before the nation in the sternest possible manner. Mr. Kennedy Jones urges the people to eat 1lb. of bread less per week than they are accustomed to do. The appeal to eat less bread is excellent, but is it, in the light of experience, likely to be effective, having regard to the fact that it is very difficult so to regulate one's consumption as to be aware of reduction, and having regard also to the very human tendency to demand equality of sacrifice? The cooperation of the British public has never been in question, but compulsory Order would in a measure ensure equality of sacrifice.

We are asked to consume 1lb. less of bread per week, while we are by law permitted, which is tantamount to being encouraged, to consume 14oz. of breadstuffs per week during the period of the three restricted hours between meals. It is this inconsistency that causes doubt as to the actual necessity for rigid economy in the minds of those who cannot understand the position to be so serious as stated. The necessity does exist, and as I urged in November, I reiterate that half-hearted measures in dealing with the situation are ineffective and dangerous.

I read in a newspaper of the 13th inst. a reply by the Food Controller to a Sunday school official, as follows:—

"With reference to your inquiry of 7th inst., I am directed to inform you that a letter has been sent by this Department to all churches, chapels, and similar bodies in reply to inquiries as to the holding of annual Sunday school treats, teas, &c., to say that in view of the necessity of conserving our national food supply the Controller considers that all such entertainments as those which involve the consumption of food should be discontinued."

I think that when one comes to realize what the annual Sunday school treat means to the children, and that is, the poor children of the country, one feels it is demanding from the weak a sacrifice entailing a very minute advantage as compared with the results which would be obtained if the stronger members of the community temporarily gave up their afternoon meal.

The situation is, indeed, grave when we must abolish the red-letter day in thousands of juvenile calendars, and a comparison of the saving effected by the discontinuance of the annual Sunday school treats with the saving effected if the adult population of the country were put to a little inconvenience would be, in similitude, as a pebble to a pyramid.

Yours faithfully,
BURTON CHADWICK

BREAD AND ANIMALS

CUT DOWN HORSE-RACING

25 April 1917

Sir,—Mr. Alfred Watson, in a letter published by you to-day, mentioned me as a supporter of horse-racing to-day because as at present conducted "it is not a question of sport, but simply of the preservation of the all-important horse-breeding industry of which racing is an indispensable branch." I should like to reply to what appears to me as a misleading implication in his statement of the case. Most people agree that the horse-breeding industry, in which we are pre-eminent, must be maintained. To ensure this it is necessary to allow oats for brood mares, for horses at the stud, and for yearlings. These classes are not affected by racing. Racing is only essential in a year such as this for the 20 or 30 first-class three-year-olds, so that their degree of value as prospective stallions and mares may be decided, and this would be achieved if the five classic races only—or the substitutes for the five classic races—were run at Newmarket. Of course on the day the classic races were run there would be, say, two or three races for two-year-olds, so that the stamina of youngsters might be tested. But even here, if the entrance fees were fixed at a high figure for these races, the number of entries would not be large. Thus the 4,000 horses now in training would be cut down at once to about 80 or 100 horses, and the saving in oats would be, if not large, at all events of real value in the present circumstances. Brood mares, stallions, yearlings, and the 80 or 100 horses which might be entered for these five races, ought to be strictly rationed, and the other horses should either be turned out to grass or killed. In view of the fact that our stocks of oats at the present rate of consumption may be completely exhausted before another harvest, it would appear to me urgently advisable, even in the interests of horse-breeding, that the course I suggest is adopted. May I add that I have not raced a horse this year, and I do not intend to do so?

Yours, &c.,
KENNEDY JONES

THE NIGHTINGALE

1 May 1917

SIR,—I HAVE NOT noticed in your columns, or elsewhere, notification, common at this time of the year, of the return of the nightingale. Punctually at break of day I have for fully a week heard this bird singing in a garden overlooking the Channel, situate in a locality which, lest I should convey information useful to the enemy, I will distantly allude to as "somewhere on the south coast." The melodious notes always have a plaintive undertone. Just now, probably subtly influenced by the carnage going on day and night across the water, I find in them a distinctly deeper sadness.

Yours faithfully,
HENRY LUCY

RATIONING—TWO SYSTEMS

1 May 1917

SIR,—IF AND WHEN rationing is established in this country, would it not be well to adopt either of the two systems which have proved successful in France? The first of these is a card showing the maximum amount to which the holder is entitled each week. Every purchase has to be entered on the card, and signed for by both purchaser and tradesman. Purchases within the maximum may be made at any shop. By the second system customers can only deal at one shop. The tradesman keeps the list and must not supply casual purchasers. The penalties for infringement under both systems are heavy enough to act as a real deterrent. In the opinion of French people the first system is the better of the two.

I am, Sir, yours &c.,
MARIE BELLOC LOWNDES

NAVAL STRATEGY

MR CHURCHILL EXPLAINS HIS APPROACH

5 May 1917

SIR,—SIR REGINALD CUSTANCE is mistaken in thinking that I have at any time failed to advocate the need of offensive action by the Navy. The sentence which he quotes from a magazine article, which dealt exclusively with the relations of the British and German Battle Fleets as exemplified in the Battle of Jutland, cannot be judged apart from its context or the limited scope of the argument in which it was used. Both the Boards of Admiralty over which I had the honour to preside during the present war maintained a continuous aggressive action against the enemy. From the fight of August 24 onwards the Heligoland Bight and the German and Belgian coasts were repeatedly raided, always with risk, frequently with success. The enemy's cruisers and armed merchant raiders in all parts of the world were sought out and destroyed till not one remained at sea. Even the Königsberg, sheltering in the recesses of the Rufiji River, was cut out by monitors dispatched for that purpose. The naval attack on the Dardanelles, however else it may be viewed, was a naval offensive of the highest degree. The first German submarine campaign against merchant shipping, which began in March, 1915, was encountered by measures and devices mainly offensive in their character, and was so completely quelled in the months that followed that it was precipitately assumed that that danger was past. Further, the Board of Admiralty which quitted office in May, 1915, had prepared whole fleets of ships, largely immune from torpedoes, whose sole object was to play their part in a definite scheme of offensive war. The responsibility for the paralysis of the naval offensive lies in no small degree with those whose senseless outcry at the loss of a few obsolete ships checked naval enterprise, and quenched Admiralty initiative, with the result that, for almost two years, no single aggressive act, apart from the Battle of Jutland (which I hold in principle to be aggressive) has been attempted. Sir Reginald Custance knows how strongly his military conceptions of naval strategy, as apart from his views upon *matériel*, appeal to me, and I am the last person on whom he should seek to fasten his present quarrel.

In conclusion, I may perhaps be permitted to quote the following passage from the speech which, with good knowledge of the position, I felt it my duty to make on the Naval Estimates of March, 1916:—

"In a naval war you must always be asking about the enemy—What now? What next? You must always be seeking to penetrate his mind, and your measures must always be governed and framed on the basis that he will do what you would least like him to do. My right honourable friend (Mr. Balfour) showed that the late Board had surmounted some of the very serious and difficult dangers at the beginning of the war, but one he did not mention. The menace of the submarine attack on merchantmen was overcome by measures taken this time last year of an extraordinary scale and complexity. But although the German submarine campaign has up to date been a great failure, and although it will probably continue to be a failure—here, again, you cannot afford to assume that it will not present itself in now and more difficult forms and that new exertions and new inventions will not be demanded, and you must be ready with your new devices before the enemy is ready with his, and your resourcefulness and development must continually proceed upon a scale which exceeds the maximum you expect from him. I find it necessary to utter this word of warning which for obvious reasons I should not proceed to elaborate.

There is another matter which I cannot avoid mentioning, though I shall do so in language of the utmost precaution. A strategic policy for the Navy purely negative in its character by no means implies that the path of greatest prudence is being followed. I wish to place on record that the late Board would certainly not have been content with an attitude of pure passivity during the whole of the year 1916. That is all I say in a matter of that kind." (*Hansard*, March 8, 1916.)

Surely, in view of the foregoing facts, it is rather a far-fetched undertaking to attempt to involve the Board of Admiralty which left office two years ago in the responsibilities of the present grave situation.

I am, Sir, yours faithfully,
WINSTON S. CHURCHILL

COOKED RHUBARB LEAVES

11 May 1917

SIR,—I NOTICE THAT soda was one of the ingredients added to the rhubarb leaves which are supposed to have been the cause of the Rev. W. R. Colville's death. The rhubarb leaves are most probably quite harmless, but common washing soda is a deadly poison, and the symptoms that the family suffered from were caused by the soda. If very little is used a dull headache and slight nausea are the result, if more is put in violent sickness, pains and faintness are the result, and even death. Common washing soda is the refuse of glass, and is quite unfit to be used in food, but, unfortunately, is frequently added to vegetables, from the palace to the cottage, as the cooks do not distinguish the very great difference between bicarbonate of soda and common washing soda.

Yours truly,
D. ROLLESTON

15 May 1917

SIR,—IN REFERENCE TO a letter which appears in your issue of to-day, will you permit me to make the following remarks? Sodium carbonate or washing soda is not a "deadly poison" and is not a poison at all in the ordinary sense of the word. To produce even mildly unpleasant effects such large quantities would have to be used in cooking as would render the cooked vegetable quite uneatable. Washing soda is not the "refuse of glass" and has not necessarily any connexion with glass. Cooks very rightly do not distinguish between bi-carbonate of soda and washing soda, since if equivalent quantities are used the result is precisely the same, that is to say, the bicarbonate of soda becomes converted on boiling with water into sodium carbonate. Washing soda is merely sodium carbonate in a crystalline form.

With regard to the food properties of rhubarb leaves, there appears to be but little information available, but the rhubarb plant contains appreciable quantities of a salt of oxalic acid (which is a poison), and I think that the public would be prudent not to eat the leaves until some more definite information as to their qualities as a food product is forthcoming. It seems possible that different persons may exhibit marked idiosyncrasies in connexion with this material.

A. CHASTON CHAPMAN

RECRUITS UP TO 50

15 May 1917

SIR,—IN ABOUT 12 WEEKS I shall be 47. In much less than 12 months I shall have completed—I am ashamed to say—a quarter of a century at the Bar. To-day, I observe, I am invited to join the Army at a shilling a day. Meanwhile, I am informed that more than one barrister of military age is engaged as a "volunteer" at Whitehall on a pound a day. This is only hearsay. But I can go a little beyond hearsay. Six months ago I made (not my first) attempt to do work for which I was fitted in a Government office. I was ushered into a room containing three legal-looking gentlemen (whether barristers or solicitors or only students I know not) all obviously under 35. I was asked my age. When I responded "46" a shiver went round this select assembly at the idea of another man of military age finding shelter in that Temple of Peace. I make no complaint. I merely venture to ask, through your good offices, these young gentlemen a question. If this war continues till October—and I see no reason why it should not—the reservoir of the 41–50 men, for what it is worth, will have certainly run dry. Press and politicians will look for a new source to tap. Possibly these young people will help us with suggestions. Shall we take the men from 50 to 60? Or a better way might be to subject the twice-discharged invalids to a third comb out. Or possibly they might prefer to invite women to volunteer to protect their billets in Whitehall, with their pound a day. Like Miss Rosa Dartle; I merely want to know.

Yours, &c.,
BARRISTER-AT-LAW

Rosa Dartle figures in *David Copperfield*.

PET DOGS

31 May 1917

Sir,—I am a lover of dogs, and therefore I keep none in London. But in the row of 19 houses, one of which I occupy, there are at least 23 dogs. In one house alone there are four, if not five. I ask you to imagine the state of the pavement and doorsteps in front of and near that house (my own is very near it), after the pack has been turned out for its morning and evening run. My cook keeps her particular strip of pavement clean by means of a stout-handled mop and a pail of water, which she uses for prevention rather than cure. But some of my neighbours appear to be less fortunate in their cooks; and, whenever my wife or I go out, we must pick our way and hold our noses. Shortly before his loss in the Titanic, Mr. Christopher Head, then Mayor of Chelsea, issued a very sensible appeal to the inhabitants of his borough to keep up the level of health by keeping down the number of their dogs. There was a violent outcry against him, for these "lovers" of dogs lay claim to more sensibility than other mortals. In truth, they have less. They are sentimentalists, and, like all sentimentalists, are both callous and cruel. It is useless to tax their dogs, for such people have more money than they should be trusted with. It is useless to speak or write to or at them, for the annoyance of their neighbours is a matter of indifference if not of amusement to them. Yet since the distant days in which Mr. Christopher Head appealed solely in the interests of health and cleanliness, a new and more powerful argument has come to hand. The keeping of unnecessary dogs is now, as we know, one of many means of helping the Germans to win the war. Taxation, appeal, reproof being all futile, I suggest that the occupants of every house where more than one dog is kept should be compelled to exhibit in each of their front windows an attractive placard, bearing in emphatic letters the legend "Pro-German; Anti-British." It would speak no more than the truth, in fact if not in intention. And the street-boys might be left to do the rest.

I am, Sir, your obedient servant,
ARGUS

THE ATTACK ON FOLKESTONE

4 June 1917

SIR,—IT IS VERY EVIDENT that the recent destructive aeroplane enemy raid on this town was merely a trial and experimental trip. Apart from the damage said to be effected by the falling of our own anti-aircraft shells, it appears that four kinds of bombs were used:—(1) Shrapnel to burst and scatter low overhead; (2) penetrating 60-pounders for demolition and destruction; (3) incendiary; and (4) with sensitized contact-fuses to explode, say, on touching a roof. Now, the Germans will require to know exactly the individual results for future developments. Who in this town furnish this information; and how do they do it? The town has been howling since war began to have the matter of aliens properly treated; martial law was objected to by the town authorities because their pockets would be affected.

Yours truly,
H. K. GORDON, Lieutenant-Colonel (retired)

THE WARMEST MAY

4 June 1917

SIR,—IN QUICK SUCCESSION to the coldest April I have to record the warmest May since the establishment of observations here in 1858. The mean temperature on the Glaishor stand for May, 1917, has been 59.1deg., or 5.1deg. above the average; April was just 5deg. below its average. The memorable hot summer of 1868 was introduced by a May with mean temperature 58.9deg., and was thus only cooler by a hairsbreadth than the month we have just enjoyed. Last month, however, had a mean daily maximum temperature of 71.4deg., which is 1deg. higher than in 1868, although the hottest day reached only 83.9deg. on the 27th, as against 87.6deg. in May, 1868. The extreme warmth apparently affected quite a small portion of England, the month having been cooler all round London, and even below the average temperature in parts of Scotland.

Old London records seem to prove that since 1703 warmer Mays than that of 1917 occurred on seven occasions—viz., in 1833, 1811, 1809, 1808, 1804, 1788 and 1784; but only in 1809 did an extremely warm May follow, as this year, an extremely cold April.

Yours sincerely,
HUGH ROBERT MILL

PRINCE KROPOTKIN'S FAREWELL

8 June 1917

Sir,—May I ask you kindly to give me the hospitality of your columns for sending a farewell to the British nation and expressing my heartfelt thanks for the friendly reception I found in this country since the days when I landed on these shores in 1876 as a quite unknown stranger down to the present day, when I leave here so many personal friends? Their touching friendship has contributed so much to relieve the gloominess of a long exile that I deeply regret the impossibility of expressing my thanks personally, and it would have been out of place, at the present time, to organize farewell meetings.

I regret it the more as I wished to express my gratitude, not only for the kindness which I and my family found in England, but also for the sympathy that Russia, and especially Young Russia, found with a considerable portion of this country's population and its political leaders.

Those of us who have lived it through will not forget the energy with which our friends and the Labour organizations altogether took the defence of every Russian refugee whose extradition the Tsar's Government tried to obtain, in order to establish a precedent, nor the contempt with which the British nation as a whole treated all attempts at obtaining an extradition treaty. And we shall not forget the friendly support which we found each time we appealed, be it for the relief of a famine (especially in 1891), the relief of exiles in Siberia, the expression of sympathy with the attempt at throwing off the yoke of autocracy in 1905, or a vigorous protest against the atrocious repression that followed this attempt.

Another token of the sympathies which the advanced movement in Russia awakened here was the mass of letters of congratulation with the Russian Revolution, and expressions of hope for its full success, which were addressed to me lately as to one of the oldest Russian refugees.

Having been able to answer only a very small portion of these letters, I take this opportunity to express my own and my countrymen's thanks for the expressions of sympathy they contained. And, in common with the great bulk of the Russian nation, I can only say how happy I am to see my mother country standing in one camp with the Western democracies against the Central Empires.

There are moments in the life of mankind when certain general ideas, prepared by a slow evolution of the minds, suddenly get hold, with an unprecedented clearness, of the great masses of men. Such a movement takes place now, when it becomes quite evident that, in this war, two different civilizations come in conflict. One of them—the Western one—striving to achieve Progress through a steady growth of its inner forces, economic and intellectual, and the other returning to the obsolete ideals of outward expansion and enrichment through conquest.

Russia, happily enough, threw in her lot with the Western current, and I earnestly hope that the efforts now made to lure the Russian nation into the wake of the German servants of Conquest will not succeed. The great bulk of the Russian nation see that such a step would bring back the misrule of a pro-German Tsar and the reconstitution of the Holy Alliance in the shape of the Three Emperors' Union. And I feel sure that Russia will continue to fight so long as the Germans themselves do not recognize the criminal mistake they have made in favouring the "World Empire" schemes of their rulers.

In my wife's and my own name I beg our friends to forgive our taking leave of them in this way. They know the feelings we carry in our hearts in leaving this country.

I am, Sir, yours truly,
P. KROPOTKIN

———◆———

A BLACKBIRD AT WYTSCHAETE

16 June 1917

SIR,—AFTER THE WYTSCHAETE Ridge had been taken on the 7th, my servant told me that when going across in the evening he had found a blackbird sitting on its nest in the German front-line trench. I could not believe it was true, but this morning, having a spare half-hour, I got my servant to take me to the place, and, sure enough, there was the nest with five warm eggs in it. It was in the side of a communication trench leading back from and about 15 yards from the original German front line. After waiting a few minutes the bird came back and sat on its nest, taking no notice whatever of us. The nest is about 3ft. off the ground level. I may add that one of the big mines had been exploded within 120 yards of the spot, making a crater large enough to accommodate a good-sized house! There were also large shell holes within a few yards of the nest. It sounds incredible that the bird should have practically ignored the battle, but I saw it with my own eyes and so did other officers.

Yours faithfully,
BRITISH OFFICER

WHAT IS "PROFITEERING"?

21 June 1917

SIR,—DR. A. SHADWELL's important and useful letter in *The Times* of to-day deserves serious attention. He distinguishes between two kinds of "profiteering" according as one is or is not responsible for the rise in prices which gives the opportunity to the profiteer. The former case, he says, is "criminal" (under war legislation?), the latter is not criminal, and the difference, he adds, is "moral," as well as "legal and practical."

What, then, is the "moral" duty of the seller in these cases? The duty of the seller is to supply the public with that which is needed and good for the public as cheaply as he can, taking only such profit for himself as is proportionate to the labour spent by him and by his workmen for that end; and "proportionate" means such as will support them in their rank of life with due provision for old age. The less work he does, the less gain he deserves. Anything beyond this gain is "profiteering," and it should be the business of Government to check and control it by making the books and accounts of contractors, and firms accessible if required for audit or examination. If it is soldiers' duty to die rather than fail their country, why is it not the duty of the merchant or artisan to suffer rather than take advantage of his country's straits to make profit beyond his earnings? Not till the Churches make up their minds on this, which underlies almost all the crucial questions of to-day, will our civilization be consistent with either morality or religion.

I am yours obediently,
H. E. LUXMOORE

THE ENGLISH REGIMENTS

26 June 1917

SIR,—I READ WITH MUCH interest, and not a little amazement, your Correspondent's article on "Welsh Troops at Messines" which appeared in your issue of June 22. Far be it from me to criticize his very true remarks on the dash and courage of the Welsh troops. The daylight raid, of which he speaks, which I watched from the front line, was one of the most magnificent things I have seen done in this war. But I do not see why the Welsh should be selected for special mention, and all the English county regiments which did most magnificent work passed over in silence. Moreover, the work which was done by my own regiment, an English south county regiment, is actually ascribed to the Welsh. One battalion of them went over to the left of "Nag's Nose" (not Nag's Head), and so missed the mines altogether. The other battalion, which did cross the Nag's Nose, went over behind us, and was just leaving the support line as the mines went up. My company was the first into Hollandscheschuur Farm. I was wounded there before the Welsh got near it. Why is it that the doings of the Welsh and the Scots, and the Irish, and the Canadians, and the Australians and the New Zealanders should all be heralded abroad with trumpets, and the doings of the English county regiments, which are the backbone of the Army, should go unrecorded?

W. S.

CHILDREN IN TRAMWAY-CARS

29 June 1917

Sir,—Much has been said recently on the subject of the increase in juvenile crime and the behaviour of children in the streets, more especially young girls. We have heard from members of the London County Council and others of what After-care Committees should do to help these children. There is another side to the question. What is the Council prepared to do? The country has called every one, including children, to work in this time of stress. Many children are readily shouldering burdens too heavy for them to bear, there are few After-care workers to be found, and these do not get all the support they might expect from the Council under whom they are supposed to be working. Many of the children have long journeys to get to their work, and have used the Council's tramway-cars. To get the advantage of cheap fares from most outlying districts they must take a car before 7.15 a.m. This frequently brings them to Central London an hour or more before the business houses open. An unnecessary hour is thus added to their working-day—not an unimportant matter. With children of 14 or 15 an hour with nothing to do may easily become the hour for "juvenile crime," or what, if public school boys were concerned, would be called "getting into mischief." On cold or wet days the danger to health is obvious. It is a fact that these children cannot afford, on their small earnings, to travel by ordinary cars, for if they are crowded out of workmen's cars no return fares are now available; thus the evil does not end with the long morning wait; the difficulty is as acute at the end of the day. To save fares, many of the children start to walk home from the City and West End, hoping to catch the car for the last part of their journey. Is it surprising that they do not always go straight home? What does the London County Council do to try to save them from temptation? This question has been raised before the Highways Committee, not once or twice, but repeatedly, by many After-care Committees and nearly every public body that has the interest of children at heart. The Committee has been asked to extend facilities for special fares for working children on all cars, or to run workmen's cars to a later hour, but have refused to take any action. Why? Because the tramways are commercial enterprise and, it is said, must be run on business lines, so as to show a good return to the ratepayers of London. Is the financial position of London in such a parlous condition that the children's halfpennies are more valuable than the welfare and health of the younger members of the working population? I believe the opinion amongst ratepayers will be far ahead of that of the London County Council.

Yours truly,
MURIEL WILSON, Hon. Secretary of a Care Committee and Member of a Juvenile Advisory Committee

"THE MOTHER OF CHILDREN'S HOSPITALS"

3 July 1917

SIR,—THE AIR IS FULL of schemes for the preservation of child life and the instruction of mothers in the science of motherhood. Among all the proposals for carrying out this most laudable and momentous national work, we have seen no mention of the first enterprise in this direction, which has been carrying on the work with ever-increasing efficiency for 65 years. In 1850 Dr. Charles West had the foresight to realize that there was no institution for the special study and treatment of children's diseases, and he founded the Hospital for Sick Children in Great Ormond-street, which was opened in 1852. The value of this hospital is so well proved and recognized that we need not dwell upon it; suffice it to say that over a million cases have been treated there, and some thousands of mothers have been instructed in the rudiments of motherhood.

And now amid all the new proposals "the Mother of Children's Hospitals" is practically left to starve. At the present moment we are in debt to our bankers for £7,500 to pay for the bare necessities of maintenance, and we are at our wits' end to know how to carry on. How great is the need of the work is proved by the fact that, whereas in 1914 over 83,000 cases were treated in the hospital, the number rose in 1915 to over 105,000, and in 1916 to over 118,000. We plead that it is better to support an old institution of proved efficiency than to spend large sums of money on new ones which may not prove equally efficient, and we most earnestly appeal to the public to help us.

We are, Sir, your obedient servants,
ARTHUR LUCAS, Chairman
JOHN MURRAY, Vice-Chairman

GOVERNMENT FROM SIMLA

5 July 1917

SIR,—THE SEGREGATION OF the Government of India during the greater part of the year in a remote mountain station, to which your article of July 2 calls attention, has become an increasingly serious matter since the change from Calcutta to Delhi as the cold-weather headquarters of the Imperial Government. This alteration of the seat of Government was generally approved by the British Press and public when it was announced. But most of those who had lived long in India, I believe, feel that the loss caused to good Government by this move far outweighed the alleged gains. There is, as your article under reference states, very little public opinion in India. But whatever enlightened and independent public opinion does exist is nearly altogether to be found in the Presidency towns, and more especially in Calcutta. The influence of a large non-official and independent European community there has occasionally in the past beneficially altered or modified proposed bureaucratic legislation. I have heard a civil servant holding high office express indignation because the Viceroy and his Council had allowed themselves to be influenced by the strongly-expressed views of the non-official community. He contended that mere merchants, traders, lawyers, and others, holding no office under Government, ought to be a negligible element when legislation was proposed or public measures of importance were contemplated. At Simla the public consists almost entirely of persons in the service of Government. No independent criticism or public discussion of Government action can reasonably be expected from them. The cold weather move to Delhi fixes the authorities amidst similar surroundings, supplemented by a military contingent, equally unable to become an important factor in creating an independent public opinion. The Commissioners' report on the Mesopotamian muddle does seem to suggest that a continuance of a system of what you call "hill-top Government" has become impossible. My signature can add no value, I know, to anything I write, because I was only an obscure observer of authorities and policies during 25 years of Indian service, most of which was spent in the plains. But I dislike writing anonymously, and therefore beg to remain

Yours faithfully,
WELBORE GRANTHAM

THE RAID OF SATURDAY

9 July 1917

SIR,—IT IS EVIDENT that the controlling minds in Germany, whoever they may be, are now relying on "frightfulness" by aeroplane. They have been led to it by the failure of hopes placed on (1) the military genius of Hindenburg, (2) the U-boat campaign, (3) the Russian Revolution and the Stockholm Conference, on which they have successively relied. They have been encouraged by the impunity with which these raids conducted and the hubbub in newspapers, which is to them evidence of perturbation and alarm here. The object is evidently to terrorize the public into submission or into a revolt against the Government. That is clear from the fact that the raiders do not seek to do military damage, but choose time and place where they can kill most civilians. And since the rulers of Germany are in a very tight place, with waning chances of escape from their doom, they will pursue the new campaign with the greatest determination and on the largest scale they can command, without regard to any other considerations. It is their latest and possibly their last hope.

Let us, therefore, be prepared to meet it. Two things are needed—(1) more restraint in word, (2) more energy in deed; less excited jabber and more purposeful action. What action? Obviously an efficient defence. The airships which were formerly entrusted with the same task were stopped not by reprisals, but by the crushing losses inflicted on them. And so it will be with the aeroplanes.

No doubt aeroplanes are more difficult to tackle than airships; that is why the Germans have resorted to them. But it can be done and must be done. It may take some effort and some patience—effort by the proper authorities and patience on our part; but surely we can supply both without kicking up such a hullabaloo, which only plays the German game by reviving the waning confidence of the German people. This is, I submit, the common sense of the matter. How it should be done it is not my business to say, being only

A CIVILIAN

SIR,—FROM THE COMMENTS which have appeared in a section of the London Press since Saturday morning, an agitation would seem to be afoot which is entirely in the German interest. There has been the usual outburst of indignation against Hun wickedness; and this does no particular harm, though it does no particular good, for you might just as well expect a swarm of locusts or a thunderstorm to pay attention to moral considerations as the Prussian Government. But there has also been a good deal of complaint of the inadequacy of the defences of London, and somewhat vehement demands for more and better guns and aeroplanes. And there has been a loud clamour for reprisals. In the last two there lurks considerable danger if the Government should fail in firmness and plain speaking.

1. The objects of the enemy in raiding London appear to be two in number. Their man object is to induce us, at a most critical point of our military operations in France and Flanders, to weaken our air forces abroad by withdrawing them for the defence of London. Their subsidiary object is to create a panic at "the nerve centre of the British Empire," which may induce us to sue for peace. The latter object we need not pause to consider. I doubt if the German Government really counts upon it (except with a view to heartening their own people), for they are probably well served by their intelligence department in this country. But their first object, which is a purely military object, may quite conceivably be attained, if the people of London allow their minds to be confused as to the main issues, and thereupon proceed to bring the wrong kind of pressure to bear upon the Cabinet and the War Office through leading articles and speeches in Parliament. If either Ministers or military commanders were to yield to a clamour of this kind, if they were to weaken our air forces in France in order to defend London, they would simply be playing the German game, and would accordingly deserve to be shot. If, on the contrary, they stand firm, it is the Germans who will have lost; they will have lost because they will have failed in their object of making us weaken our air forces in France and Flanders; and they will also have lost because they will themselves have wasted the efforts of their own air forces in those countries without achieving any military result.

It is stated to-day that 37 persons were killed and 141 wounded in this latest raid. I would ask my fellow-townsmen to consider seriously how much better this is than if the 20 aeroplanes which raided London on Saturday last, and all their flanking squadrons at sea, had been employed behind our lines from Nieuport to Péronne, and had killed and wounded an equal, or even a much smaller, number of soldiers. It may be a very shocking and disgusting thing deliberately to kill civilians; but lives of civilians are much less valuable in time of war than those of soldiers; and that Government which wastes its resources in killing civilians when it might kill soldiers makes a very bad bargain, unless it can thereby induce its adversary to weaken to a still greater extent his military dispositions at the critical point.

2. Precisely the same considerations apply to the question of reprisals. The best reprisal is the heaviest military blow. I can conceive of nothing weaker or more contemptible than to send our airmen off on long and hazardous expeditions without any military object, either direct or indirect, but merely in order to kill a certain number of children, women, and old men in the vain hope that the Germans will then cease from murdering our own civilian population. Before people write and talk so glibly about reprisals I wish they would look at the map. If they did so, they would understand that a German air-raider from the coast of Flanders takes just about five times less risk in attacking London than a British

air-raider from Arras takes in attacking (say) Cologne. The reason is clear enough. The German raids unobserved over the sea. When he is sighted off our coast he is within 40 miles of his objective—a matter of 20 minutes or thereabouts. The British raider on Cologne, on the other hand, has some 200 miles to fly overland. He is sighted at once. Warnings go forth in all directions. Enemy aeroplanes rise in front of him tier upon tier. He cannot hope for a surprise. He has to fight his way both there and back; four hours of it at the very least. Say we succeeded in killing two or three hundred civilians in Cologne, and lost, as we very well might, 25 aeroplanes out of 50 in achieving this result, how the Prussian High Command would chuckle and slap their thighs at having succeeded in inducing "these English madmen" to play the German game!

But by all means let us criticize where criticism may help to win the war. There can be no harm in insisting upon the need of shooting lessons. Nor can there be any harm in insisting also that the Air Board is deficient in energy, resourcefulness, business qualities, and, above all, in imagination and cooperation. But for heaven's sake don't let us waste our precious air forces, and the still more precious lives of our gallant airmen, by nervous clamour about the defences of London and insensate proposals for a ruinous policy of reprisals. After all, our soldiers in France are bombed and shelled most days in the week; surely London can stand being bombed now and again, if it realizes clearly that its own safety can only be purchased at the expense of the British Army, and by injury to the Allied cause.

Yours, &c.
WATCHMAN

THE AIR RAID

LESSONS OF SATURDAY'S ATTACK

10 July 1917

SIR,—THE TROUBLE ABOUT the Air Service is that neither the Government, the Army, nor the Navy realize that a new Service has arisen working in a new element. It seems absurd to have two reports when air raids occur, one from the Army, a land force, another from the Navy, a sea force, and none from the Air Service, the air force. We require a commander-in-chief of the air forces, with the same powers as those granted to the supreme naval and military authorities. The Air Service should be represented on the War Committee on the same plane as the Army and Navy. Cooperation between the three Services will be as easy as they are at present between the Army and the Navy.

G. MANERA, Lt.-Col.

MESOPOTAMIA AND LORD HARDINGE

23 July 1917

SIR,—NEARLY A DOZEN years have gone by since Parliament had the opportunity to hear expressions of Indian opinion at first hand. Unfortunately, there is no Indian now in either House of Parliament—an undoubted loss to the Empire as a whole. If any Indian were now in either House, no matter of what religion, province, or political complexion he might be, he would have been eager to testify in the Mesopotamian debates to the strength and unanimity of Indian admiration for and attachment to Lord Hardinge, and to condemn the ignorant attacks made upon him in some portions of the Press. My countrymen of all shades of thought feel that he has been most unjustly and ungratefully treated, and I am constrained to write on their behalf.

Lord Hardinge's work in India, both in peace and war, should be judged as a whole, and not alone by the temporary breakdown of military arrangements in Mesopotamia. Mr. Montagu himself, a statesman trusted and popular in India, and who knows India better than most people, accurately described him as the most popular Viceroy of modern times, and as showing himself, from first to last, a Viceroy upon whose sympathy and assistance Indians could rely. The hold that Lord Hardinge has upon the affection and gratitude of India has not been diminished by the findings of the Commission, and has been strengthened by the unfair attacks to which he has been exposed. The *Indian Social Reformer*, one of the most thoughtful and important of Nationalist Indian newspapers, and by no means given to flattery, has described the feeling of the people of India for Lord Hardinge as that of veneration—a very true description indeed.

The Mesopotamian breakdown was the inevitable result of the mistaken policy, so long pursued in relation to Indian military resources, actual and potential. Every well-informed man of the world knew, during the last 10 years, the inevitability of a war with Germany, and no attempt was made to adjust the prospective utilization of Indian military strength to such a contingency. The deliberate policy recommended by Lord Nicholson's Commission was to reduce the military expenditure of India to the lowest limits compatible with Indian safety from external landing and from internal commotion. Yet, when the moment of the world-crisis came, Lord Hardinge, rightly trusting India's profound loyalty to the Emperor and her indignant repudiation of German efforts to seduce her to revolt, sent the flower of the Indian Army to France, and it arrived in time to share in the glory of saving Calais. No request from England for help in any of the theatres of war was refused, and in a military sense India had been bled white before the Mesopotamia policy was completely changed by the decision of his Majesty's Government to authorize the advance to Baghdad. Lord Hardinge relied on his military advisers and on the unanimity of expert official opinion, both in London and Simla. His fault was one of too-generous response, considering the means immediately available, to the many calls made upon India. Even the chairman of the Commission has testified in your columns to the force of these considerations.

On the question of the use of private telegrams in relation to matters in which secrecy was essential, it may be remarked that this system was an old inheritance, and was not developed—much less was it established—by Lord Hardinge and Mr. Chamberlain.

Indian opinion heartily endorses the refusal of Mr. Balfour to accept the resignation, twice tendered by Lord Hardinge, of his present appointment. It asks that the malignant persecution of this statesman, who trusted and loved India and who inspired unbounded Indian sacrifices in the first half of the war, should cease; and it shares with Lord George Hamilton the view that time should be utilized not to belittle the great services of the ex-Viceroy, but to effect urgently-needed reforms in Indian administration.

I have the honour to be, Sir,
Your faithful servant,
AGA KHAN

KEEP YOUR MOUTH SHUT

30 July 1917

Sɪʀ,—Iɴ ᴛʜᴇ ᴄᴏᴜʀsᴇ of various journeys between France and England during the war, I have been painfully struck by the indifference shown by women passengers, some of them apparently returning from visits to their husbands on leave in Paris, to the notices, abundantly displayed in French restaurants, railway stations, and trains, warning passengers against talking about naval and military matters in public. This is, no doubt, partly due to the fact that only a small percentage of these ladies understand French, and partly to the familiar feminine inability to abstain from gossip. The result, in any case, is that I have on several occasions heard young women imparting to friends, in the slightly raised voice which they adopt when they think they know something specially interesting, details of harbour defences and the movements of troops which, even if they are inaccurate, they should never have been told in the first place, and in the second should not be allowed to repeat with impunity in a mixed crowd, of which all the passport formalities in the world cannot absolutely ensure loyalty. The remedy seems to be for the authorities to post large notices in English on the wharves where passengers congregate and on board the boats, and for anyone overhearing these indiscreet revelations to report the delinquents immediately on landing.

Yours faithfully,
BRITISH TRAVELLER

CABDRIVERS AND THE PUBLIC

31 July 1917

Sɪʀ,—Uᴛᴛᴇʀʟʏ ʀᴇɢᴀʀᴅʟᴇss, ᴀs usual, of any interest but their own, the London and Provincial Union of Licensed Vehicle Workers propose at this time, when traffic is congested and porters hard to come by, for the sake of avoiding the payment of two or three pennies a day out of their not inadequate earnings, to compel passengers to come out from the stations into the streets to get a cab. May I suggest that, if cab-hirers in return would unite in a determination to pay the cabman his precise legal fare to the uttermost penny, the union might learn that the public too have rights and also powers?

I am, Sir, yours, &c.,
A WORM BENEATH THE WHEEL

AN ACT OF WILFUL DEFIANCE

31 July 1917

I AM MAKING THIS statement as an act of wilful defiance of military authority because I believe that the war is being deliberately prolonged by those who have the power to end it. I am a soldier, convinced that I am acting on behalf of soldiers. I believe that the war upon which I entered as a war of defence and liberation has now become a war of aggression and conquest. I believe that the purposes for which I and my fellow soldiers entered upon this war should have been so clearly stated as to have made it impossible to change them and that had this been done the objects which actuated us would now be attainable by negotiation.

I have seen and endured the sufferings of the troops and I can no longer be a party to prolong these sufferings for ends which I believe to be evil and unjust. I am not protesting against the conduct of the war, but against the political errors and insincerities for which the fighting men are being sacrificed.

On behalf of those who are suffering now, I make this protest against the deception which is being practised upon them; also I believe it may help to destroy the callous complacency with which the majority of those at home regard the continuance of agonies which they do not share and which they have not enough imagination to realise.

LT. SIEGFRIED SASSOON

The poet's celebrated letter of protest was sent originally to the *Bradford Pioneer* newspaper and republished four days later in *The Times*, having been read out in the House of Commons. Sassoon, who had won the Military Cross in France, had been on convalescent leave after being wounded. He wrote the letter after deciding to refuse to return to the trenches. His friend and fellow war poet Robert Graves persuaded the authorities that Sassoon was mentally ill and therefore unfit to be court-martialled. He was treated instead for shell shock at Craiglockhart Hospital, Edinburgh, where he met and encouraged Wilfred Owen in his writing.

PRICE OF CHEESE

2 August 1917

SIR,—MAY I CRAVE the hospitality of your columns (as it seems useless to write direct to the authorities concerned) to draw attention to two important points regarding prices and make of cheese, both colonial and English? One is that the unfairly abused grocers, whom so many call profiteers, are not allowed a living profit on Government-controlled cheese, because though on paper they are supposed to get 2d. per lb. profit on cheese retailed at 1s. 4d., they do not get the weight that they have to pay for owing to the fact that many of the crates of New Zealand and other Colonial cheese have lost 7lb. up to 12lb. weight since they left the country of production, and they are only allowed 3½ per cent, margin to meet this heavy loss. The other point is that the English cheesemakers can make a lot more of their milk without the labour of cheesemaking. Therefore the make of English cheese will be very short indeed unless the limits are immediately raised. I speak from over 30 years' experience of wholesale trade. It takes a gallon of milk to make 1lb. of cheese and two gallons for 1lb. of butter. You may fix limited prices, but you cannot make farmers produce cheese unless it pays them. Therefore best cheese cannot be profitably retailed at 1s. 4d. or even 1s. 6d, per lb., or butter at 2s.

Your obedient servant,
JOHN WOOD

OFFICIAL STYLE

10 August 1917

SIR,—YOUR CONTRIBUTOR POKES good-humoured fun at certain eccentricities of official phraseology, but he would, I expect, admit that its characteristics are in the main inevitably determined by the conditions under which this branch of literature is produced. An official composition is the expression of the mind, not of any particular person, but of a body of men, and its style is therefore bound to be impersonal, calm, colourless, and sometimes even humdrum. A vivacious and piquant manner of writing is pleasant enough as reflecting the idiosyncrasy of a gifted individual; but for a Board or Department to attempt it would be absurd. Again, it is important for the spokesman of the bureaucracy not to give offence. Hence he "can hardly call a man a liar," or even "a fool." Hence also he must refrain, except on very rare occasions, from the use of irony or sarcasm. Lastly, an official document, if it takes the form of a general minute or set of regulations, partakes of the character of an Act of Parliament, and, as it has to provide for a great variety of cases and contingencies, cannot avoid generality and lengthiness of statements. Members of the public who write to Government offices seem to have developed stereotyped modes of expression of their own. If they are ladies, five out of six begin "Dear Sir, I am sorry to trouble you, but ..." Some excellent remarks on official style will be found in chapters 6 and 24 of Sir Henry Taylor's little book entitled—not very appropriately— "The Statesman."

I am, Sir, your obedient servant,
CIVIL SERVANT

GUNFIRE

A PARADOX OF AUDIBILITY

21 August 1917

SIR,—A PROPOS THE RECENT correspondence in your columns relating to the sound of gunfire in Flanders being heard in England, I now submit for the consideration of your readers a few conclusions arrived at as the result of 18 months' experience at the front. These facts are essentially of a more or less technical nature, but their appreciation is vital to a thorough understanding of the phenomena of sound in connexion with gunfire.

In the first place, there is a most fundamental and peculiar difference between the sound emitted by a gun and that of an exploding shell. By this I do not refer to the obvious contrast that most people are aware of between the clear boom or sharp crack of the gun and the irregular "crump" or "whoof" of the shell or bomb. When the gun is fired the sound wave produced is of a totally different nature to that produced by the burst of a shell. In the former case the impact of the gases leaving the muzzle, as it were, "strikes" the atmosphere in the direction in which the gun is pointed, but the burst from the shell causes a sound wave of uniform intensity all around, as the gases emanating from the high explosive are not confined in any direction, as is the case with the cordite of the gun, the only escape being at the muzzle. Every soldier who has been to the front knows that if you stand in front of a field gun or naval gun whilst firing even at a considerable distance (several hundred yards), the crack is painfully intense to the ears, and may even cause injury, whereas it is possible to stand close behind the gun with comparative impunity. In other words, the sound wave from a gun is more concentrated along its line of fire than elsewhere. No such difference is observable with a shell, its concussion being equally violent to the ear whether it explodes in front of or behind one.

Now the laws of sound say that the intensity of the sound emitted from a body grows less in proportion to the square of the distance of the ear from the source of the sound; in other words, at double the distance the sound is a quarter as great. This, of course, is identical with the laws of light, and applies perfectly to the shell, but not to the gun, in the same way as the ordinary law of the intensity of light will apply to a candle, but not to a searchlight, which concentrates its light along one path instead of distributing it equally all around. Hence, in fact, we are driven to the conclusion that the wave of sound emitted by a gun is closely analogous to the wave of light emitted by a searchlight. The intensity of the ray from a searchlight only diminishes gradually, and this analogy is borne out by the peculiar fact, familiar to those who have been in the trenches, that the German machine-guns, or rifle shots, always seem as loud, whether the width of "No Man's Land" is 70 yards or 500 yards. One of the most wonderful and, indeed, majestic of all sound phenomena in connexion with artillery—but which I have never seen described or even referred to, as, when first heard, the novice is unable either to explain it or decide upon its nature, and afterwards the ear becomes so used to it that it passes unnoticed—is the great "roll" that follows the discharge of a high-velocity gun. To hear this at its best one must visit part of the front where the contour is rugged, or where the landscape is well wooded, and where houses and other excrescences are abundant, as at Arras. The report of the cannon is followed at once and continuously by a majestic echoing roll that may be compared to a mixture of thunder and the music of a mighty bass orchestra. Now this rolling sound seems to travel forward as though it were following the flight of the shell, and is, indeed, mistaken by some for the actual sound of the shell.

The real explanation, however, is that it is a series of echoes from the thousands of heterogeneous excrescences in the surface of the landscape, each of which sends back its echo to the ear, the whole combining to form a continuous trail of sound. Now the fact that this continuous sound travels in the direction of the shell, and hence in the line of fire of the gun, also fits in with the searchlight analogy; as otherwise if the sound of the firing gun were not concentrated along its line of fire this chain of echoes would not appear to flow in any definite direction, and thus one of the most grandiose aural phenomena that the ear can receive would not exist.

Now the above considerations give rise to a remarkable and surprising fact, which, indeed, arises in theory and is borne out in practice. This is, that at a certain distance and upwards from the firing line the sound of the German guns will be greater than the sound of our own, because we are in front of the German guns but behind the British, and, although the latter are nearer to us, yet the sound of the former will appear louder and sharper because of the peculiar nature of the sound wave emitted from the muzzle of a gun, the noise being nearly all concentrated in the direction of fire. Thus, when approaching the firing line before a big attack the sound of the German guns often appears to preponderate over our own, giving one the apprehensive impression that the enemy's artillery is in superior strength to our own, and it is only in coming into the artillery zone that the British superiority is perceived. Another point illustrating this is the origin of the word "drum fire." This term (*trommel-feuer*) was first used by the Germans to describe the effect of our massed artillery on an unprecedented scale on the Somme. Now to the British, who were, of course, behind the direction in which their artillery was firing, this term would never have occurred, for to be behind a British bombardment there is but little resemblance to a drummer's tattoo, the whole sound being merged into a dull and heavy roar of guns; but to the Boche generals behind their lines every shot from the British guns would stand out as a sharp staccato note, the whole combining to give the impression of the rat-a-tattat of a mighty drum tattoo.

From these conclusions it will appear that the further one is behind the firing line the greater is the tendency for the sound of the German guns to preponderate over our own, although the latter may be in much greater strength, and the probability is that the greater part of the noise of firing audible on our coasts comes from the German artillery and not the British, although the sound of shell bursts may tend to modify matters.

GEORGE F. SLEGGS, B.Sc.

THE SOUND OF GUNFIRE

22 August 1917

SIR,—I HAVE READ with interest Mr. Sleggs's letter, "A Paradox of Audibility." He is a scientific man and I am not; but these few points may be interesting, though what he says is entirely correct as far as my knowledge goes, which is more practical than theoretical. I have had considerable experience now in France, and these few points have always struck me very vividly. While at Lydd I found struck that often by getting underground you could distinctly hear the sound of gunfire, whereas standing in the open you could not hear it. While in France I have noticed this rather interesting point: very often during a heavy bombardment you could not hear it at a certain distance, yet if you went farther back, and to a lower altitude, you could hear the bombardment quite distinctly. To my mind it appears that the sound of such bombardments is carried to a greater extent not by sound waves through the air, but by strata in the ground. The sound is passed through the ground, and if you happen to be on a different stratum you may not hear the gunfire, but if you are standing on a continuation of the same stratum as that on which the gunfire is taking place you will probably hear it quite distinctly, though much farther away. My most vivid experience of this was on the Somme. During one of the bombardments I was some 30 miles behind the line and could hear nothing, though I knew the bombardment was taking place. My errand necessitated me going to a village some eight miles farther from the front line, and when I reached there I was astounded to find that I could hear the bombardment distinctly. On my return journey I found that quite suddenly the sound failed until I was close again to the front, when I heard it by sound waves. To make sure of my doubts I made inquiries and found that the bombardment had not ceased for one minute during my absence. This firmly implies that the sound is carried more by the earth's strata than by sound waves through the air. May this not be a more plausible reason for the sound of gunfire in England? I would like Mr. Sleggs's opinion on this

A SOUTH AFRICAN GUNNER OFFICER

SIR,—SEVERAL OF YOUR correspondents have mentioned, as a new acoustical phenomenon, the fact that gunfire can be heard more clearly, in some circumstances, through the ground than through the air. This fact has been known for a long time. On the morning of the Battle of Waterloo Marshal Grouchy, with several of his Staff, was in a house at Sart-lez-Walhain at about 11.30 a.m. My father in his "Waterloo" (Chapter IX.) says that Grouchy had just sent off a dispatch to Napoleon announcing his position and what he proposed to do, when one of the staff walked in from the garden and reported that a cannonade was audible towards the west. My father goes on to say:—"Grouchy, Gérard, and several officers walked into the garden and listened in silence. Some of them placed their ears to the ground and thus detected plainly the muffled boom of distant guns." I have no doubt that other similar instances could be met with in military history. But we may go back to the days of Shakespeare for evidence of common knowledge of the fact that ground conducts sound well. In *Henry IV.*, Part I., Prince Hal, when he and Falstaff were taking part in the "Gadshill robbery" thus addresses the fat knight:—"Lay thine ear close to the ground and list if thou canst hear the tread of travellers."

Yours, &c.,
WYNNARD HOOPER

SIR,—I HAVE READ with interest Mr. Sleggs's letter on the sounds produced by the firing of high-velocity guns. His observed facts are in the main correct, but his explanation is incomplete and in many respects misleading. Many of the facts which I am about to indicate were established by Professor Mach many years ago; attention has recently been again directed to them, and papers on the subject by M. Angus and others have appeared in the *Comptes Rendus de l'Académie des Sciences* for 1915, as far as I remember.

First, for the facts, which anyone who cares to walk across the line of fire of one of our 18-pounders, or, better still, a 60-pounder, can easily verify. The sound produced by a high-velocity gun, as heard in front of the piece, is double, consisting of a sharp crack, which is very distressing to the ear, followed at an interval (which for the 60-pounder may be two or three seconds if the listener is in the line of fire) by a dull boom, which is the true sound of the firing of the piece. This boom is a much duller and heavier sound, which shakes buildings, but does not hurt the ear. The sharp crack is not produced by the gun directly, but by the shell during its flight, and then only if the initial velocity of the shell exceeds that of sound, as is the case with all modern guns. The double sound is never heard with a howitzer, where the velocity of the shell is low. The interval between the two sounds is greatest in the line of fire: as one walks to a flank it becomes less and less, until finally only one sound, that of the gun itself, is heard, the same sound that is heard behind the gun. The zone within which the double sound is heard is bounded by lines from the gun making an angle of somewhere about 45 to 65 degrees on either side of the line of fire, varying with the initial velocity of the shell and also with the angle of elevation at which it is fired, factors which also influence the magnitude of the interval.

An analogy which may make the formation of the shell-wave clear to the non-technical reader is offered by the ripples on the surface of still water. If a stick be dragged slowly through water, with a velocity less than that with which the ripples on the surface are propagated, a series of circular ripples will be formed, which spread out slowly, the stick being always within the circular ripples. If the stick is dragged with a greater velocity, however, a sharp, intense wave, shaped like the wave at the bow of a ship, will be formed, with its nose always at the stick and its sides running back from it. This corresponds to the wave of sound produced by the high velocity shell. The shell starts a sound disturbance at every point of its path, but, owing to its moving faster than the sound can travel out, it is itself always ahead of the spherical sound-waves produced by it in its previous path, and so drags with it a thin wave of compression, which is propagated as a sharp pulse of sound. The shell-wave is a surface shaped something like the pointed end of an egg, with its point always at the projectile as long as this is travelling with a velocity greater than that of sound. Such surfaces are often indicated in Captain Bairnsfather's drawings as accompanying his high-velocity shells. This surface touches somewhere behind the shell the spherical sound-wave produced by the gun itself, and, so to speak, fits on to it. Thus, as can easily be seen by sketching the two surfaces, anywhere outside a certain cone only one sound will be heard; anywhere inside, two sounds, the interval between them being greatest in the line of fire. The higher the velocity of the shell, the larger the interval. Anyone whose mess is in front of a 6in. naval gun will have a good opportunity of observing this. He will notice that it is not until a few seconds after he is deafened by the crash that the glasses begin to jump to the boom which is the true sound of the gun. Behind the gun his ears will be spared, but not his windows.

Another way of looking at the phenomenon may be indicated. If you are in the line of fire a shell coming towards you will be at one instant approaching you with the actual velocity of sound, since its velocity is continually decreasing. (Considerations of its height above the ground are also involved, but are omitted here for simplicity.) At such a moment it is travelling abreast with all the sounds it makes and all murmurs and whistles from its path will reach the listener at exactly the same time, and *not consecutively*. All these arriving at once add up to a very sharp crack.

My chief object is to emphasize the double sound; it is the shell-wave which is concentrated along the path of the shell, and not the sound of the gun, which spreads out in spherical waves, though very likely its intensity is somewhat greater in front than behind. But it is not the gun itself which causes the distressing crack, which will not be heard with a gun firing a blank charge. The double sound can be heard very distinctly with a rifle, too, and is often noticed by the marker. Photographs of a flying bullet have been taken with the aid of special methods of illumination by Professor Boys which actually show the sharp air-wave streaming back from the bullet exactly like the wave at the bow of a ship.

With German guns the two sounds can often be heard. The shell sound carries the farther, being directed, and also being originated in the air above obstacles such as trees, so that if only one sound be heard it is the "crack" and not the "boom." All Mr. Sleggs's facts as to the sounds heard on approaching and passing through the line of our batteries follow at once if the shell-wave be substituted for his supposed directed gun-sound. The phenomena are, of course, complicated by echoes, the whistle of the shell which reaches one from other points of its path *after* the crack, and other such minor things.

As regards the letter which appeared in your issue of August 22, zones of comparative silence are frequently observed with bombardments; for instance, some of the Somme bombardments of 1916 were heard better near Arras than at places much nearer. I suggest that this is probably less due to a propagation through the ground than to the well-known fact that, owing to layers of air of different temperatures and to winds blowing more strongly at a height than along the surface of the ground, sound-waves are distorted, so that they may curve away from the earth and down to it again, missing, or only reaching in less intensity, intermediate places. Such "zones of silence" have been observed in peace time with big explosions. Of course, bombardments can be very distinctly heard in dug-outs, but then the hearer is in a small enclosed volume of air which readily takes up the vibrations from the earth. I rather doubt if the outer air takes up much sound vibration from the earth when it is a question of distant bombardment.

Lest any should suppose that anything I have said might be of use to the enemy, I may mention that a good short account of most of the phenomena in question can be found in Winkelman's "Handbuch der Physik," in (I think) the second volume, "Akustik."

E. N. DA C. ANDRADE, B.Sc., Ph.D.

4 September 1917

SIR,—MR. GEORGE F. SLEGGS has quoted some interesting facts as to the transmission of sounds from Flanders, and in his letter of August 31 he inclines to the belief that there are facts which tend to disprove the conduction of gunfire by the earth rather than by the atmosphere.

I would like to recall a communication upon this subject, made as far back as 1888, by Jean Ingelow. She stated that many years before that the shepherds on the elevated and bare ranges of the Wiltshire Downs always knew by the sounds when the guns were being fired at Portsmouth—fully 40 miles distant to the south. The shepherds stated the sounds were chiefly heard whilst they were sitting or lying on the Downs—thus bringing their ears nearer to the ground. An aged vicar, who lived six miles from Marlborough, used to say that he frequently heard these sounds during his youth and middle age, and until they were pointed out to him by the shepherds he had not known what they were. When the shepherds called his attention to the sounds, he sat down with them and listened, and he discovered how regularly the sound was timed; this and the sudden bursts convinced his reason they could have been nothing else. The sound in this instance was described as somewhat like the distant unloading of stones from a cart or the remote rumbling of thunder, although not very similar to either. One of the vicar's neighbours, five miles from Marlborough, had often verified the shepherds' story, and, having taken an interest in it, proceeded to make observations as to what he himself could hear, and he often recorded that, when the London coach (in the old coaching days, before the days of railways) came into Marlborough (in the dead of night), he could hear it advancing up the hill on which Marlborough stands, and he could hear it stop at the principal inn to change the four horses.

The earth, as well as water, is a better conductor of sound than air, as may be perceived when a gun is fired at sea. If it is far off the flash is seen, and there is time to stoop almost to a level with the surface of the sea, when the ear will receive the report of the gun carried by water. After this another and a fainter report is heard, which comes by the air. Earth conduction is also supported by experience along the Mediterranean coast, the deep earth-groaning rumbling of earthquakes is perceived before the ground begins to quake, and some domestic animals show symptoms of this in abject fear, restlessness, and unmanageableness some time before the human ear detects the noise.

It is a matter of general observation that sounds are better heard in the night than by day; for instance, the humming of insects and the music of the nightingale—and these are not fancied notions. It is admitted that at night there are fewer other noises to interfere, but the presence of the sun in the day retards the propagation and the intensity of sounds by opposing to them currents of air of different densities, which cause partial undulations of the atmosphere through unequal heating of different parts of the ground. In this way the sound waves are broken up into different sections, which reach the ear at different times, and so lessen the distinctness and clearness of the sound. Added to these facts is the mental effort which is concentrated upon listening at night, which is intensified through the absence of other noises.

The human ear varies much in its compass in different persons. The average range comprises about nine octaves; very few persons can hear beyond four octaves above F in the middle of the keyboard of the piano. The human ear is as perfect a machine for the analysis of sound as exists in the whole animal kingdom—within its compass. The trained ear of a musician can detect a difference of one-thirtieth of a semitone, whereas an untrained savage fails to detect a difference of less than a semitone. We are powerless to alter the capacity for pitch or to extend the range of sounds, but we can do a great deal to increase the keenness of perception and to cultivate the ear as an analytic receptor by practice, direction, and mental concentration. The colour-blind cannot be cured, but the tone-deaf, in most instances, can. It is one of the surprises of the war that men who have suddenly become stone-deaf—a condition which occurs not often in the trenches, but most commonly behind the lines—have completely regained their hearing, and equally suddenly, by appropriate mental treatment.

The difference in the compass of the human ear and the difference in power of mental concentration probably account for the extreme variability of experiences recorded by your correspondents.

I am, Sir, your obedient servant,
ROBERT ARMSTRONG-JONES, M.D.

7 September 1917

SIR,—READING THE correspondence in your columns in the light of my own experience, I am convinced that there are two distinct sensations; one, the air concussion of the explosion of the charge from the gun; the other the earth concussion when the shell thumps on the earth. There seems to be strong reason for believing that the latter sensation is carried the further. I am even so bold as to suggest that the facts stated by Mr. Sleggs, in his letter in your issue of the 31st ult., tend to confirm the theory on which he throws a doubt. He distinguishes between two sounds heard behind the guns in Flanders, the one resembling a heavy blow as of a stone-hammer within the earth "that makes itself felt rather than heard"; the other a resonant "crump", louder and more obvious, transmitted by the air.

I can lay no claim to any scientific knowledge, but I have, my doctor tells me, a perfect and unblemished ear. On the hills near Crowborough I have observed what is undoubtedly and admittedly the result of gunfire at the front. I have observed it also near Maidstone on the occasion of a great offensive. It has been recorded at various spots round London. I have picked it most distinctly on the recent offensive in Flanders at two enclosed spots in Battersea Park, one of them the beautiful "old English garden", somewhat disfigured this year by a rather snobbish growth of vegetables. The "thuds" could be distinctly sensed in spite of the confused sounds of distant traffic. I found the parkkeeper, who is there in the quiet hours, was quite familiar with the phenomenon. I have heard the sound of artillery practice in different parts of the country, and this distant rumble, very like far-off thunder, is a sound quite distinct. On the still winter's day of Queen Victoria's funeral I was on Wimbledon Common, where the long "roll" of the guns in the Solent was clearly audible. This again was a sound bearing no resemblance to the short quick "thud" that is now "felt rather than heard" in England. Is it not a plausible theory that the terrible thumps on the earth by modern high-explosive shells, which make "craters", can be felt through the earth to a distance far greater than air concussions are carried?

I am, Sir, your obedient servant,
STUDIOSUS AUDIENDI

10 September 1917

Sir,—"Studiosus Audiendi" states in his letter published in your issue of the 7th inst, that he is convinced "that there are two distinct sensations; one, the air concussion of the explosion of the charge from the gun; the other, the earth concussion when the shell thumps on the earth." The concussion received by the earth when a heavy howitzer is fired at a high angle is far greater than that received by the explosion of a shell which forms a crater. The reason for this is that the main force of a shell explosion escapes upwards into the air, thereby reducing the amount of concussion received in the earth, whereas in the case of certain classes of guns when fired, the recoil received from the explosion of the charge and the resistance thereto from the heavy projectile impart to the earth a much more heavy blow, causing the sound to travel further through the earth.

I am, Sir, your obedient servant,
X.Y.Z.

SEPARATION AND DIVORCE

31 August 1917

SIR,—I OBSERVE THAT Sir Arthur Conan Doyle and others are about to address the Government, begging them at once to initiate legislation for the purpose of converting orders of separation, after the lapse of a certain time, into absolute decrees for the dissolution of marriage. It is also suggested in the same quarter that power should be given to dissolve all marriages which have been contracted between English women and German men. Let it be clearly understood that Sir Arthur Conan Doyle and those who are acting with him are turning their backs upon those principles which from the beginning have governed the members of the Christian Church in regard to holy matrimony. Moreover, I should have thought if there were one lesson more than another which this war taught us it was that the real welfare of mankind depends upon adherence to Christian principles, and that Sir Arthur Conan Doyle and his friends could hardly be doing a worse service to England than by advocating such legislation as is now proposed. Of this they may be assured, that throughout the length and breadth of the land all who have regard for the Word of God as given to us in Holy Scripture, and who feel how intimately the true welfare of the Empire is bound up with Christian teaching, will oppose any such legislation to the very utmost of their power.

I am, Sir, &c.,
HALIFAX

TEACHING OF DOMESTIC SCIENCE

4 September 1917

Sɪʀ,—Iɴ ʀᴇᴄᴇɴᴛ ᴀʀᴛɪᴄʟᴇs in the Press there have been presented the lines on which the young educated girl of the day might develop to her own advantage and that of the country at large. Certainly, imagination has been quickened, and, to take advantage of this new birth, new channels of activity must be provided, or much of the boundless energy of youth may be lost.

It is for the older generation to realize that every girl, like every boy, should have a profession, and that a thorough training in a subject, no matter what the subject may be, makes for development of character and in no way detracts from the finished whole. There is room in the world for all types, and scope for everyone with youth and health, opportunity, and encouragement at her back. Wealthy parents, no less than their poorer neighbours, will be wise to take full advantage of the careers open to women. Nursing, medicine, architecture, horticulture, banking, departmental work, teaching, give endless variety of choice, but the greatest of these is teaching, calling, as it does, for all the best qualities of heart and brain and hand.

Never was the cause of education so much in people's minds, never was there such a call to save to the uttermost the children of the nation bodily, mentally, and spiritually, and never were hopes centred so high as they are at the present time. Education has been for so long the Cinderella of the profession, badly equipped, badly endowed, nobody's child; but our eyes have been opened, and all classes are calling out for more light.

Among the many branches of educational work, none has deserved better of the public at large than that of domestic science. It is helping in this time of crisis in every conceivable way and has penetrated into every stratum of society.

On the women of this country no less than on the men is laid the necessity of fighting enemies of stern stuff—in the case of the women, want and hunger for themselves and their children, unless scientific knowledge is brought to bear on the question. The various food campaigns organized all over the country have done much to open the eyes of the people to shortage of food and the national defect of ignorance in cooking; but the trained people who are wanted to present the truth in a convincing and incontrovertible way are comparatively few in number, and many have been lent by education authorities to other departments requiring help in practical food questions.

There is needed at the present moment a large army of women qualified by training and natural gifts to undertake the teaching of domestic economy. The supply is not equal to the demand, even now, when for years the training schools have been pouring a steady stream of intelligent qualified women into the ranks of the teaching profession. Now when more, and still more, are required, the numbers coming forward for training are lamentably short. The facilities for training in cookery and domestic economy both in London and the provinces are ample, and are not at the present time being used to anything like their full extent.

I would, therefore, ask parents who are weighing the future of their daughters to consider whether they could not usefully be trained for such work as described above. Work in offices and banks, labour of all sorts (most of it of a transitory nature) are deflecting into blind alley occupations the girls on whom the educational future of the children depends. There is no one to sound the alarm. The terrible mortality of infants and children due to improper feeding is a scandal to our civilization and could be minimized, if knowledge of this important branch of education were more widespread.

The subject is worthy of grave consideration, and we are looking forward in the hope that in future more consideration may be given to the domestic subjects, both for their own educational value and for the sake of the race.

Yours faithfully,
M. LLOYD GEORGE

6 September 1917

SIR,—I HAVE READ with much interest, the letter from Mrs. Lloyd George published to-day. Perhaps your readers may in their turn be interested in the views of one who is at present training in one of the recognized domestic centres.

As it is very often necessary for a student to leave her home to attend one of these centres the total cost for a two years' course amounts to about £200, to put it at the lowest figure. The average salary on leaving the training school (if a post can be obtained) is about £80 per annum. The preparation for a business career in order to earn such a salary at the present time bears no comparison with the above. As Mrs. Lloyd George will see at once, it is largely a matter of £ s. d. Moreover, there are no bursaries in these training schools, not even of such a kind as would enable the best students to take a third year of training, and so fit themselves for higher work.

The shortage of food has affected the domestic centres as well as the ordinary household. It is impossible, under the present conditions, to get an adequate training, especially in cookery. It is true that students get many new ideas as a consequence of the war, but these are mere temporary matters. Education authorities are cutting down expense in this direction, as in every other (to their lasting disgrace). Staffs are depleted so that it is quite impossible to keep the subject on a decent educational level.

Mr. Fisher is going to insist on more domestic training as part of his new scheme. Unless he is prepared to ask for a sufficient sum of money to place the centres on a proper footing, to help the local authorities to pay proper salaries, and to provide pensions for domestic teachers, his scheme will fall to the ground. No amount of urging on the part of people of high position will be of any use unless these practical matters are dealt with.

It is, I think, unfair to urge girls to undertake this work at a time when statistics prove that there are not enough posts to go round.

Yours faithfully,
PRACTICAL EXPERIENCE

GENERAL KORNILOFF

13 September 1917

SIR,—A LETTER IN YOUR yesterday's issue from Mrs. Lethbridge appears to suggest that General Korniloff is the sole patriot in Russia at the present moment. The fact is that, so far as genuine patriotism and true love of the country are concerned, there is absolutely no choice to be made between Korniloff and Kerensky. No one who has viewed Kerensky's career impartially can deny this fact. Since the Revolution Kerensky's views on the efficacy of the idealistic Socialist programme have been totally shattered, and the terrible fire of experience he has passed through has served but to remove the dross and leave the gold. When, after the Revolution, the decree for the abolition of capital punishment was signed the paper was stained with Kerensky's tears—they were tears of joy. And yet it was Kerensky himself who four months later was willing to sacrifice all to secure the reintroduction of the death penalty for his country's good. What torture must have racked his soul to drive him to this step! And who dare impute self-interest or mean ideals to Kerensky? The truth is that Kerensky and Korniloff are equally necessary for the salvation of Russia. Each is incomplete without the other. They are two utterly unselfish men both striving for the same goal, but along different paths. The paths must eventually of necessity converge; the nearer they approach the goal the better they will understand one another, the differences will vanish, and the solution of the vast and intricate Russian problem is to be sought in the combination of the characteristics and abilities of a Kerensky and a Korniloff.

Yours, &c.,
PAUL DUKES

The Cossack General Lavr Kornilov (as it is now spelled), commander of the army, had attempted a coup against prime minister Aleksander Kerensky's provisional government. Lenin would seize power soon after. Paul Dukes was a musician working in Russia, but would later become a spy there for MI6, and be knighted for his exploits.

AMERICA AT WAR

17 September 1917

Sir,—So much stress is being laid on the material participation of America in the war that some Americans are apprehensive lest the far greater importance of the deep moral sympathy of their country with the cause of the Allies may to some extent be left out of account.

I hope, therefore, you will find space for the following extracts from a letter just received from a man of business in New York who may be trusted to reflect the sober and impartial view of his environment. May I add that I have not a single young relation, and do not know of a single young man among my friends, who did not volunteer the day we declared war?

I am, Sir, yours very truly,
EDITH WHARTON

"I have wished so often that you could be here in these striving times, for you would be so interested to see the gradual change that is coming in the minds and temperament of the people. You meet men in uniform, officers, soldiers, and sailors, everywhere, in the cities, villages, and country, and there is no question at all that the seriousness of the war is at last being realized. We are taking things as a matter of course that to me are very surprising in a country so accustomed to peace and so unmilitary. The draft is working smoothly, and, I believe, thoroughly, and I have heard of no disturbances anywhere.

"There is a splendid spirit of determination abroad which means to see this business through. It is very hopeful for the future spirit and character of the country, and is a sign of a real underlying intelligence of the perils facing us in the future, if Germany is not beaten, and of sympathy for what other countries have already suffered at her hands in the past.

"The reception that our troops have had in France, and our engineers in London, has been very gratifying to all, and has added much to the already strong feeling towards our Allies. I believe we are now passing through an awakening of a people that means to do its work thoroughly and from the highest motives. There are of course some 'blatherskites' and bounders; but what country has not suffered from them?"

FLOWERS AT THE FRONT

17 September 1917

SIR,—THE SUBJOINED LETTER has been received by the mother of a young officer in the Household Battalion, and was written from the fighting line in Flanders. It pleasantly varies the story of devastation daily transmitted from the front, and incidentally reveals the sort of young fellow who, in various degrees of rank, is captaining our gallant Armies. This one, impatiently awaiting the birthday that marked the minimum age for military service, went from Eton straight to a training camp, and in due course had his heart's desire by obtaining a commission. He followed close in the footsteps of an elder brother, also an Etonian, killed in his first month's fighting.

"In England there seems to be a general belief that nothing but every imaginable hardship and horror is connected with the letters B.E.F., and, looking at the three letters, people see only bully beef, dug-outs, shell holes, mud, and such like as the eternal routine of life. True enough, these conditions do prevail very often, but in between whiles they are somewhat mitigated by most unexpected "corners." The other day we took over from a well-known Scottish regiment, whose reputation for making themselves comfortable was well known throughout the division, and when I went to examine my future abode I found everything up to the standard which I had anticipated. Standing on an oak table in the middle of the dug-out was a shell-case filled with flowers, and these not ordinary blossoms, but Madonna lillies, mignonette, and roses. This vase, if I may so term the receptacle, overshadowed all else and by its presence changed the whole atmosphere, the perfume reminding me of home, and what greater joy or luxury is there for any of us out here than such a memory ?

After having duly appreciated this most unexpected corner I inquired where the flowers had been gathered, and was told they had come from the utterly ruined village of Fampoux close by. At once I set out to explore and verify this information. Sure enough, between piles of bricks, shell holes, dirt, and every sort of debris, suddenly a rose in full bloom would smile at me, and a lily would waft its delicious scent and seem to say how it had defied the destroyer and all his frightfulness. In each corner where I saw a blossoming flower or even a ripening fruit, I seemed to realize a scene belonging to this unhappy village in peaceful days. Imagination might well lose her way in the paths of chivalry and romance perhaps quite unknown to the inhabitants of Fampoux. I meandered on through the village until I struck a trench leading up to the front line; this I followed for a while until quite suddenly I was confronted by a brilliancy which seemed to me one of the most perfect bits of colour I have ever seen. Amongst innumerable shell holes there was a small patch of ground absolutely carpeted with buttercups, over which blazed bright red poppies intermixed with the bluest of cornflowers. Here was a really glorious corner, and how quickly came memories of home! No one, however hardened by the horrors of war, could pass that spot without a smile or a happy thought. Perhaps it is the contrast of the perfection of these corners with the sordidness of all around that makes them of such inestimable value. Some such corners exist throughout France, even in the front line trenches. It may not be flowers, it may be only the corner of a field or barn; it may be some spoken word or a chance meeting. No matter what it is if it brings back a happy memory or reminds one of home. It is like a jewel in a crown of thorns giving promise of another crown and of days to come wherein, under other circumstances, we may be more worthy of the wearing."

Yours faithfully,
HENRY LUCY

OVERWORKED WOMEN

17 September 1917

SIR,—A LETTER SIGNED "E. C." in your issue to-day is somewhat difficult to understand. It is a plea for a continuation of the state of things which only an ignorant and incapable employer would allow to exist.

Every intelligent employer has discovered that long hours of exhausting labour entail loss to the employer and not gain. In the case I have cited, not only did the workwomen earn more money with less fatigue, but the employer benefited by a decreased cost of output. The circumstances were perfectly normal and in no way exceptional. They are such as exist in every munition factory in the kingdom.

"E. C." admits that the working day which prevails generally is such that no ordinary woman can submit to it without making such serious demands on her reserve vitality as will leave her more or less bankrupt in the years to come, but that women are willing to make this sacrifice on the supposition that output depends upon it. It is the grossest error, but, unfortunately, it prevails in the minds of some employers as well as "E. C." Over-fatigue leads to nothing but reduced output. In the case I have cited, with a 54-hour week, the average loss of time per woman was 12 hours per week, reducing the effective week to 42 hours. When the week was reduced to 48 hours the loss of time was four hours per week, making the effective week 44 hours. This no doubt arises from the fact that over-exertion in the case of women has a more disastrous effect than in the case of men.

There are, I daresay, many incompetent employers who suppose that low pay and long hours mean cheap production, but experience shows it is the gravest error, and it simply demonstrates a want of capacity on the part of the employer. No one has the right to be an employer of labour unless he can, by his intelligence and industry, not only make a profit for himself, but also a reasonable living for those he employs.

The question of unskilled and semi-skilled labour presents some difficulties, but these difficulties are of short duration, especially as women are mostly engaged on repetition work, the skilful accomplishment of which does not take much time to acquire. The payment by results solves most of the difficulties appertaining to labour. It is the basis for the earning of the highest possible wages with the least possible fatigue, as well as the most economic cost of production, and it enables the unskilled labourer to participate in the higher earnings of the skilled. For example, in the case I have mentioned, the wages of the unskilled labour in the shop are increased *pro rata* to earnings of the skilled labourers, whom they assist. Payment by time, irrespective of result, is at the bottom of all labour troubles. Payment by result is the proper solution of all labour troubles.

"E. C." points out it is not possible to convince the employed of the good faith of employers. Perhaps the action of some dishonest employers in the past may have justified this, but to-day every decent employer sees that it is in his own interest, as much as in that of the working-man, that confidence should be established between them, and that they should both work cordially together to obtain the end to be arrived at—namely, economic production under conditions beneficial to both parties. The fate of both depends upon economic production, and economic production depends upon the brain capacity of the employer to organize manufacture, and not upon brainless incapacity supported by low wages and over-fatigue.

Your obedient servant,
F. L.

"NO CHILDREN"

4 October 1917

SIR,—IT SEEMS ALMOST incredible that at such a time as this the heads of families who are forced by present war conditions to live temporarily in furnished lodgings, apartments, or flats are frequently confronted with the tyranny "No children."

My own experience during over three years of war has been confined to parts of the East and South Coasts, and it would be, no doubt, interesting to hear of the experiences of others. But in my ken Southsea is, of all places, the worst. Last year there were difficulties for the married folk with "encumbrances." This year, when the flight of Londoners on account of air raids has augmented the number of winter residents at South Coast resorts, the state of things is a public scandal. One of the first questions the house agents ask is, "Have you any children?" and on an affirmative answer one is shown against many items in the register of lettings the note "No children." Other people, who presumably at least have some sense of shame (as is evidenced by their unwillingness for this kind of publicity), wait until the proposed tenant has had the trouble of inspecting the domicile, and then say, "Oh! I'm afraid I can't let if you have children." This is my wife's experience after wearying days of search for a suitable domicile for herself, three children, and a nurse, and at a time when many a mother is weeping for the loss, perhaps, of an only son, and when remorse adds to the grief of those who might have had larger families, and at a time, too, when the nation is concerned at the falling birthrate. The fact is that we are confronted with a very unpleasant class of people, who ignore the misfortunes of others, and, while accepting complacently the death or wounding of those who are fighting for them, themselves go in mortal terror lest a leg shall be broken from some rickety chair or a chance casualty be caused to some blatant wall-paper, and who pander to others of their kind, who put their fingers in their unsympathetic ears at the weeping of a child or the joyous laughter of a nursery. There is no redress, and all I (who gave up my business when the war started and joined up) can do is to register my scorn of these unnatural beings and my indignation that the income-tax which is muleted from my inadequate pay should go to the relief of their taxation.

Yours, &c.,
LIEUT., R.N.V.R.

6 October 1917

SIR,—I HAVE READ with interest an officer's complaint in your paper to-day. But I should like to say that there is another side to the question "No children"; and if your correspondent had let his house furnished as often as I have to a family with children he would not wonder that people are forced to say "No Children." Take my case. When war was declared my husband at once went on active service. My eldest boy was at Woolwich and the youngest at an Army coach; so, not caring to live alone, I let my house furnished and took up war work. What was my experience?

First, I let my house to a clergyman, wife, and three children, with very good references. Damage done in six months by children:—Two pewter plates, value 25s. each, cut with pocket knives and names scratched on them; old oak tallboy cut badly with knives; old Jacobean table, name carved on it. The furniture was valuable, old family stuff, and nothing could replace it or remove the names carved on the wood. The second let was to the wife of an officer on active service, and two children, little boys, with matches set fire to a large double bed and burnt linen sheets, linen pillow-case, and mattress; opened the door of an old grandfather clock and broke the springs and chain, also the hands of the clock. Being war-time I could not get such good linen sheets to replace the ones burnt. The third let was to a naval officer's wife with three children. Damage:—The children broke the springs of a sofa and entirely spoilt a fine old tray by using it to slide down stairs on, cut and scratched two fine old oak chests and a corner cupboard.

After that surely even "Lieut., R.N.V.R." will not blame me that I now say "No children" and since doing that I have had no damage done to my furniture. My house is now let furnished to an elderly couple, and, though they pay me very well for it, it would pay me better to let them have the house for £2 a week rather than let it for £6 6s. a week to a couple with children. If "Lieut., R.N.V.R." will only consider a moment he will soon realize how little ordinary wear and tear an elderly couple of 60 years take out of carpets compared with children, who are always running in and out with muddy boots, and banging doors, and never sitting really still on chairs and sofas. The ordinary wear and tear with children is three times what it is with an elderly couple. If I had continued to let my house to people with children, by the end of the war my house would not have been fit for me to live in. Personally, my own experience has been that the wisest people are those who say "No children" when letting their houses. I never mean to do anything else.

Yours truly,
AN OFFICER'S WIFE

CHEQUERS AND
"THE PRIME MINISTER"

9 October 1917

SIR,—AMONG THE NUMEROUS interesting points suggested by Sir Arthur and Lady Lee's munificent gift, there is one which may have been overlooked. Chequers is to be held in trust for the use of the great officer of State described in Sir Arthur Lee's memorandum as "the British Prime Minister" or simply "the Prime Minister."

As matters stand at present, this definition is sufficiently explicit. In a future that may not be remote it may be wanting in precision, and may even lead to some confusion. There are indications that the Cabinet, of which "the British Prime Minister" is the chief and presiding member, may in due course relegate one part of its powers to a Committee of Ministers concerned with Imperial administration and policy, and another part to a Committee of Ministers occupied with the affairs of the United Kingdom. To many observers it appears inevitable, or at any rate extremely probable, that this differentiation of function will eventually lead to formal separation, so that there will be one Cabinet or supreme Executive Committee for the Britannic System of Nations as a whole and another for the Kingdom, Dominion, or Union of Great Britain and Ireland. Each of these Councils would have its own chief or chairman, by whatever title he might be known.

In this event, who would be able to claim the user of Chequers under the terms of the trust? Would "the British Prime Minister" be the Imperial Chancellor or Empire Secretary of State, the head of the Ministry for Common Affairs; or would it be held that the phrase could properly be applied only to the Premier of the United Kingdom, the Minister-President of the British (domestic) Cabinet? The question seems so likely to arise, sooner or later, that it might be worth while to provide for its solution in the clauses of Sir Arthur Lee's patriotic and public-spirited trust-deed.

I am, Sir, yours &c.,
SIDNEY LOW

Lee, himself a politician, had given his country house, Chequers, to the nation to be used as the prime minister's residence.

TANKS VERSUS PILL-BOXES

15 October 1917

Sir,—The distinguished Head of a House at Oxford has sent me the following couplet, which I think you may like to publish:—
"Tanks v. Pill-boxes.
Victrix per campos Cisterna vagatur, et eece!
Viventes pilulas capsula capta vomit."
And this he has done into English as follows:—
"The Tank triumphant wanders o'er the fields
And living pills the captured capsule yields."

Faithfully yours,
TANK

THE FIRST BATTLE OF YPRES

26 October 1917

SIR,—WITH REFERENCE TO your statement in to-day's leading article that "it was the 2nd Worcesters who saved the day" on the memorable October 31, 1914, when the first battle of Ypres reached its climax, may I be allowed to suggest that the honours should be shared with the South Wales Borderers, to whose relief the Worcesters went? Horatius was honoured above all for having "kept the bridge," and to-day those who stand fast are surely entitled to as much credit as those who go to their relief. All the available evidence goes to show that after our line had been broken, and the 2nd Welsh, who were astride the Ypres-Menin road, had been shelled out, the Borderers on the left flank held their position, and from the north barred the advance of the enemy from Gheluvelt. Lieutenant-Colonel E. B. Hankey, who commanded the Worcesters, and was ordered by General FitzClarence to counter-attack and try to retake Gheluvelt, states:—"The General gave me a Staff officer (I forget his name), who went some distance to give me the direction of the right flank of the South Wales Borderers. I should like to add that I feel perfectly certain that by shoving us in at the time and place he did the General saved the day. If he had waited any longer, I don't think I could have got the battalion up in time to save the South Wales Borderers, and fill up the gap."

Other evidence that the Borderers were holding the advanced position may be gathered from the awards to Captain H. Conway Rees, of the Welsh Regiment, for successfully supporting the advance line with a company, "thereby relieving pressure on the Borderers"; and to Private Black and Corporal Pugh, of the Borderers, for "collecting unattached men and bringing them into the trenches" on the same day. The casualties also have a special significance. When the Commander-in-Chief inspected the Worcesters at Bailleul three or four weeks after the battle, they mustered nearly 600; of the Borderers there were only 225 survivors.

After a space of three years could not the War Office publish an authoritative account of the battle in order that its crucial importance may be more intelligently appreciated?

Yours faithfully,
JAMES A. WALKER

SIR,—NO MORE FITTING opportunity could be found than your proposed commemoration of the first battle of Ypres to repay a debt of gratitude which this country owes to Charles FitzClarence, V.C., who saved the day at Gheluvelt, 1914. At the time when the authorship of the order to the 2nd Worcesters to retake

Gheluvelt was definitely traced to Charles FitzClarence—the summer of 1915—the veto on the bestowal of posthumous honours prevented this great soldier and most gallant officer from receiving any recognition of the part he played in the first battle of Ypres. That veto no longer exists. Though FitzClarence's reward was the highest that this great Irish Guardsman would have desired, the knowledge that he had done his duty, surely the time has come for the country to see that his great services are acknowledged and rewarded as they deserve to be.

I remain, Sir, yours faithfully,
HUSCARID

ENFORCEMENT OF RATIONS

3 November 1917

Sir,—It is common knowledge that in many places the rationing orders are a dead letter. The number of people who do not heed them make it extremely difficult for the most loyal to obey them. Servants leave a house where the rations are kept to find numbers of places more accommodating. Custom flies from hotels and restaurants for the same reason. I propose that it should be incumbent on every one concerned to apply for the following form, which should be issued to them by the Government, and that those found disobeying the orders contained therein should be severely dealt with:—

"This book to be kept by every householder and every manager of an hotel, club, canteen, hostel, place of entertainment, and by every one supplying meals of any description, and to be produced on demand.

The weekly allowance of every person is 3½lb. bread (or corresponding quantity of flour), 2½lb. meat, ½lb. sugar, ½lb. butter, ½lb. tea. Accounts to be kept:— weekly quantities used of bread, flour, meat (including bacon, sausages, &c.), tea, butter, sugar; number of meals supplied weekly; bills for foodstuffs to be produced on demand.

Twenty-one meals is the weekly number allowed to each person. The total number of meals served will be divided by 21, and the amount of foodstuffs used should correspond to the number of persons thus served. Afternoon tea will not be reckoned as a meal in any place except aerated bread shops and places for afternoon tea only, where it will be reckoned that eight teas should go to each pound of bread, and 50 to each pound of sugar."

Anyone not producing these books on demand, falsifying the accounts, or exceeding the rations, allowed to each person, will be liable to fine or imprisonment.

ELLEN ASKWITH

Sir,—At Manchester last week, in a leading railway hotel, my morning cup of tea was served with four thick slices of bread and butter, although the latter were not ordered. On inquiry I was told most customers like it. At Melton the following day the midday lunch at a leading hotel was reminiscent of tenants' dinners in peace time. Every one was offered second helpings of meat, and bread was served in the loaf and no suggestion of restriction made. The next day a "pot of tea for one" was brought into my City office from a tea-shop accompanied by five large slices of bread and butter, each a quarter of an inch thick. With facts such as these, what is one to think, or how can one justify the appeals from the Food Department that most of us not only live up to, but try to impress on all around?

I am, Sir, your obedient servant,
R. D.

———◆———

WITNESS FROM ITALY

6 November 1917

SIR,—THREE WEEKS AGO we were the guests of the Supreme Command at Udine, and afterwards of a committee of distinguished Senators and Deputies at Rome. As representatives of the British Allied Parliaments Committee we were received with the greatest cordiality. Now that there is a pause in the tremendous events in the Italian theatre of war, we desire to express our gratitude to our hosts and our sorrow for the reverse, we hope and believe a merely temporary reverse, which has befallen their gallant country. Before the war Italy lay in the plain below a mountainous frontier held by the enemy. In two strenuous years, with great courage, skill, and industry, her soldiers and engineers forced their way into still unredeemed Italy through almost insuperable difficulties of mountain and gorge. We saw her army clinging to waterless and rocky heights, with a river gorge in rear athwart the lines of communication. It required no soldier's eye to appreciate both the magnitude of the achievement which had brought them thus far and the peril in which they still stood. They have now to defend themselves, and not only themselves but the whole Allied cause, on their own ground. The gloriously rich plain of Venetia is threatened with the barbarities of the enemy. In this hour of Italy's trial we feel it both a duty and a privilege to bear witness to what we have seen on the spot. The recent misfortune has not shaken our confidence in the Italian soldiers, nor will Germany succeed in her effort to break the *moral* of the Italian people. Italy came into the war in an hour which was dark for us, and through good fortune or bad she must know that we shall stand by her.

We are your obedient servants,

TREOWEN	AUBREY HERBERT
A. SHIRLEY BENN	GEOFFREY HOWARD
EVELYN CECIL	H. J. MACKINDER
F. W. GOLDSTONE	

The Italians had suffered a catastrophic defeat at Caporetto and little appeared to stand between the enemy and Venice.

"FIVE MILES FROM JERUSALEM"

28 November 1917

SIR,—I WONDER WHETHER it occurred to any chaplain serving with General Allenby's troops in Palestine to select for the text of his sermon of yesterday the second verse of Psalm cxxii., "Our feet shall stand within Thy gates, O Jerusalem"? Written an unnamed thousand of years ago it seems singularly apposite to the occasion.

Yours faithfully,
HENRY LUCY

British forces would occupy Jerusalem in early December.

VENEREAL DISEASE

SOURCES OF INFECTION

14 December 1917

SIR,—ONE RESULT OF the creation of our present great Armies has been to reveal the prevalence of venereal diseases in the male population of military age in Great Britain. Without giving actual figures, it may be stated that on any day there are now many thousands of soldiers in hospital and unfit for duty on account of these diseases. This is a highly regrettable fact, but from the point of view of public health it is a consolation to reflect that it is now possible to ascertain the actual prevalence of these diseases among men of military age, and also to treat them more effectively than in the past, since every infected recruit and every serving soldier who becomes infected is sent to hospital, where he is treated until he is either non-infective and fit for duty, or invalided out of the service, should this course become necessary.

So much for the adult Briton at the height of his physical and mental vigour—the father of a considerable percentage of the rising generation. It is humiliating and deplorable that in so many cases he should be infected with a disabling disease, with far-reaching results upon his future health, and possibly upon that of his wife and future children, but it is at least an improvement upon the past that he is no longer able to conceal his disease and so multiply the results of it indefinitely, but is compelled to undergo appropriate and adequate treatment.

Now, the overwhelming majority of these men (any 92 per cent. to 98 per cent.) have acquired their disease by irregular sexual intercourse—i.e. with infected women, not their own wives. Reflection upon this point naturally turns one's attention to the female side of the problem. Who are these women, and what steps are being taken or can be taken to deal with their condition, moral and physical? Systematic inquiry has so far given the somewhat surprising result that for every man who acquires his disease from a prostitute, four acquire it from a non-prostitute.

This is a highly important distinction: the former prostitutes her body for money—it is her trade; her wits are therefore constantly exercised to avoid infection, and if she becomes infected to get cured, or at least to avoid the consequences of infection; she is under a certain amount of supervision. She is a persistent parasite upon the body politic, and has been the despair of the social reformer in all countries and in all ages. However desirable it may be to deal with her effectively, it would seem obvious that it is four times as important to deal with the the non-prostitute, who is infecting four times as many men.

This latter class—the sexual free-lance—prostitutes her body not for money, not as a trade, but because she wants to do so, and has not sufficient chastity or self-control to restrain her natural appetites. Inquiries directed towards identifying her commonly show that the total acquaintance of the man with the woman who has infected him is limited to an hour or two; he knows neither her name nor anything else about her; he has paid her nothing, there has been no concomitant drinking, or excitement; it seems probable (chiefly from other sources of information) that she is generally a young woman who is employed in a shop, munition factory, or domestic service.

It would appear, therefore, that probably the greatest problem in the crusade against venereal disease is the sexual free-lance young women; the available evidence goes to show that as a class they are neither being treated nor controlled in their depredations; they ought to be the mothers of thousands of future British children, unless their sinfull careers have deprived them of this birthright, but at present they stalk through the land, vampires upon the nation's health, distributing and perpetuating among our young manhood diseases which constitute a national calamity.

Personally, I do not attach more blame to the woman than to the man with whom she sins, but, feeling convinced that, if we are to deal with the evil of venereal disease, the first essential is to recognize not only its existence but also its nature. I write to direct attention to this aspect of the problem, in the hope that the interest of the public may be still further aroused, and that possibly those who are working earnestly in any sphere of activity for the welfare and improvement of the nation may be helped by further evidence of the great problem that confronts them.

Yours truly,
M.D.

AFTERNOON TEA IN SHOPS

17 December 1917

Sir,—For the first time in my life circumstances impelled me yesterday to go into one of the great drapery stores and get a cup of afternoon tea in the restaurant attached to it. I was struck with the number of women aged presumably from 20 to 40 who were entirely engrossed in working hard to give tea, scones, &c., to hundreds of customers, who probably like myself, as I reflected with shame, had homes and servants of their own, and with a little foresight need not have applied to this extra and unnecessary labour. Why should not the *bona fide* traveller rule, or at least a *bona fide* customer rule, be set in action for drapery stores restaurants, and this labour be set free for Sir Eric Geddes's shipyards?

Yours, &c.,
GEORGINA H. POLLOCK

THE HALIFAX EXPLOSION

21 December 1917

SIR,—WITH REFERENCE TO the awful disaster at Halifax, allow me to draw the attention of your readers to the explosion at Santander, Spain, on November 3, 1893, which is the only similar case of the kind.

The Cabo Machichaco steamship, 1,213 tons register, with a general cargo—rails, paper, wine, petroleum, flour, &c.—entered the harbour, and the agent obtained permission to land 30 cases of dynamite and declared "no more on board"; but there were 33 tons in the fore-hold mainly No. 1 grade, 75 per cent. N.G., and nearly 20 tons in the after-hold, mainly No. 3 grade 30 per cent. N.G. She came to the sea embankment tied up to a short pier 33 yards long across its end, and situated 130 yards from the railway station and 200 yards from the front of the centre of the town. The 30 cases were landed, and soon after 1.30 p.m. the cargo was found to be on fire and people, including many notables of the place, thronged to the pier and embankment adjoining. At 4.30 p.m. the fore-hold exploded without exploding the after-hold, the engines, and boilers, and a good deal of cargo separating the two charges of dynamite in the two holds; yet the non-explosion of the after-hold was extraordinary. It was low tide, and at 4.30 the vessel lay in 15ft. to 20ft. of water. Her hold was submerged to the waterways. The captain, therefore, appears to have scuttled her where she lay, and this is an important difference between the Halifax and Santander explosions. In the latter case the force of explosion was directed to the zenith by the walls of water surrounding the charge, and the horizontal waves of air compression were reduced to minima. The conditions of the Halifax explosion are not yet published, but early Press records state that the crew were engaged in fighting the fire, and the attempt to scuttle the ship appears to have been postponed too long, thereby causing a much larger charge than the Santander 33 tons to have full effect in a horizontal direction above the water-line, and to cause the awful disaster that ensued on all sides. These effects alone show that the charge was not tamped for vertical action by scuttling ship. Houses were overturned in Dartmouth on the other side of the harbour and many lives lost; five British steamers in the harbour were damaged and two-thirds of their crews lost. On the other hand, at Santander steamers only 110 and 165 yards distant were practically unharmed, save for a few falling projectiles. In time an official expert report will give us the details of the Halifax explosion: quantity and quality of explosives, and of other cargo, if any; position in ship and as to water-line; position of ship in harbour when exploded; area of damage to structures and life—(a) by concussion, (b) by projectiles. Also the events preceding the explosion—viz., the fire on board, the collision with another steamer, the action on board and their sequence.

These details prior to explosion are, however, quite trivial compared with the broad fact that a steamer laden with H.E. of various kinds was allowed to enter harbour and wharf in front of a city with 50,000 inhabitants living chiefly in wooden houses that fall like a pack of cards from their want of weight to resist air concussion. At Santander 33 tons of dynamite well tamped to resist horizontal action killed 510 people and injured about 2,000; damaged many houses in the front of the town, and caused many fires thereby, although these houses were substantially built. At Halifax not only were the houses flimsy and weak, but they were built on the side of a steeply rising ridge, so that the stronger houses in front were only a partial protection.

Santander should have shown every one concerned with the city that Halifax was quite unsuited for an ammunition port, and that powder ships should have been prohibited from coming farther up the harbour than a line across, say, by York Redoubt, any import or export being worked by barges between the ship and the city.

Your obedient servant,
J. T. BUCKNILL, Lieutenant-Colonel

On December 6, a collision in Nova Scotia between two ships, one carrying munitions, had caused what was the biggest man-made explosion before the dropping of the atom bombs. Some 2,000 people were killed and 9,000 injured.

WINDOW DRESSING

28 December 1917

Sir,—Is it of any use to call attention again to the waste of precious labour involved in the window-dressing of shops? Does any one in authority ever pass along Oxford-street, Regent-street, High-street, Kensington, &c., at about 9.30 in the morning and take note of the wasted labours of young men as well as young women who are busy spreading temptation for the eyes of the foolish people who will, later in the day, flatten their noses on the windows? No shopkeeper can afford to give up laying his trap unless all are compelled to do so. If these displays were not allowed a good deal of unnecessary buying, which comes of incessant window-gazing, would also be prevented.

Yours faithfully,
Y. E. T.

———◆———

GOLF AND THE PLOUGH

29 December 1917

Sir,—Within a radius of 10 miles of Harrow Church, close to which I am writing, are at least 2,500 acres of land devoted to golf, and I have yet to see a single acre which has been ploughed up by the Golf committees who are in charge of them; a few sheep are sometimes grazed free on them, without any outlay or risk to the clubs. No land could be more suitable for the plough; its arable value is very high; almost all the hedges and ditches have been filled in (thus allowing the tractor the long straight run which is the ideal for economical ploughing), the bunkers could be filled in quite easily, and the courses are well drained for crops of wheat or oats. What is the use of applying compulsion to the farmer to plough out his grass land when he can see all around him thousands of acres still devoted solely to sport in this fourth year of war? If anyone still harbours the delusion that golf is not being regularly played I can show him courses which are almost as well patronized at week-ends and holiday times as in July, 1914. Why should not each club be compelled to plough out 20-30 per cent. of its acreage, and for the period of the war reduce the number of holes from 18 to 15 or 12?

Yours faithfully,
FIVE HANDICAP

THE GERMAN HAND IN RUSSIA

31 December 1917

SIR,—THE IGNORANCE AND misunderstanding here at home of events in Russia, caused partly by the various censorships, partly by the interested and misleading statements of the factions concerned, suggest to me that, with your permission, I should endeavour in the simplest language to disentangle the skein of cross-purposes that is responsible for the confusion of some of the ideas adopted by the Special Conference of the British labour Movement. I venture to think that the facts set forth below substantiate the argument that the "management" of the Russian Revolution was "made in Germany." I also contend that it was essentially anti-national and anti-Russian.

Mr. Henderson demands the destruction of "militarism ... universally." Now that is just the sort of talk that the Leninites indulged in. The Germans like it. It suits their book, because it encourages pacifist tendencies among the peoples that Germany has set out to conquer. It is notorious—and has been proved by documents in the possession of M. Kerensky's Government, part of which have been published—that Germany commissioned and financed Lenin to go to Russia in order to sow disaffection in the Russian Army. For Germany wants to abolish "militarism" in other countries. She has succeeded in Russia, for a time at least. She would like to do the same in England, France, and America. But she will take good care to keep her own army in fighting trim.

Mr. Henderson lays particular stress on the renunciation of post-war economic designs against Germany. That is, above all, what Germany wants. And Lenin's "Government" is even now engaged in opening the Russian market to Germany. Once it is "opened" to her she will soon make good all the losses that she has sustained in her war of aggression.

While I was with the Russian Armies in Galicia last summer a German officer, taken prisoner, disclosed a very interesting and significant fact. As early as last May—two months after the Revolution—the Germans had turned many of their mills back to peace production to prepare for the economic flooding of the Russian market. So sure were the Germans then that Lenin and their other agents would bring Russia to a suicidal surrender. The conquest of the Russian market will vindicate German militarism in the eyes of the German people. One of the most substantial reasons for which they went to war was to subordinate Russia to themselves, commercially as well as politically.

Mr. Henderson's references to the effects of the ignoring by the British Government of "warnings" which he gave them after his visit to Russia in July do not specify the nature of these "warnings," nor does he explain the fact that in July the Russian Armies had been checked in a victorious offensive by the pro-German propaganda of Lenin and his associate, and the Russian Treasury had already been milked dry by the Soviet under their direction.

"We all of us recognize that the evil effects of Germany's policy of aggressive militarism and world domination must be destroyed," says Mr. Henderson. But his economic arguments tend the other way—they help to promote German militarism. He came to Petrograd a convinced opponent of the Stockholm Conference idea—the "moral and political factor" that he now be lauds. He expressed his disapproval of the underhand manner in which the invitation on this Conference had been issued by the Soviet. He even spoke rather strongly about the Russian Revolutionaries in general. But instead of his "converting" them they "converted" him. Quite unknown to himself, Mr. Henderson while in Petrograd lived in an atmosphere created by these people, who were then in the background.

When I met Mr. Henderson there he was completely overwhelmed and upset by his surroundings. The initial circumstances of his arrival had not been propitious. The Leninites not only searched his apartment and stole his papers—to ascertain whether he was really a Socialist leader or merely an agent of the British Government, but, it may be amusing to recall, their myrmidons also took his clothes, which was excusable inasmuch as the members of the Soviet themselves were suffering from a shortage of garments, due to the decreased output of the textile mills.

It will doubtless shock and pain him to be told that some of the ideas he has advocated were "made in Germany." He is even perhaps unaware that they recall with pathetic coincidence the Soviet platform promoted by Lenin, not less than the *desiderata* so easily pressed by the German "negotiators" at Brest-Litovsk.

We know—or should know by this time—the source of the Bolshevist inspiration. But many of us are still deluded by the "ideals" of Russian revolutionaries. Now, it is all very fine to talk about these worthy people as being convinced exponents of "democracy." The Revolution has taught us—if we are capable of learning anything from the misfortunes of our neighbours—to put not our trust in words, but to judge persons and parties by their acts and the results that accrue therefrom. And since Mr. Henderson has appeared before the British Labour organizations as the exponent of Russian revolutionary "ideals," let me state a few facts of which he probably has no cognizance.

I have said that the so-called "Russian" Revolution was anti-national. Here are these broad and unchallengeable facts:—

First. The Revolution was not the work of Russian Labour or miscalled "democracy." There has not been a single revolutionary leader of any note in Russia who comes under either of these arbitrary classifications. The Lenins, Trotskys, Kerenskys, Skobeleffs, Tehernoffs, Tehkheidzes, and Tseretellis are men of the middle class, lawyers, university graduates, &c., and well-to-do. As a revolutionary movement it has been essentially *bourgeois*, both in the composition of its leaders and in the incentive they offer to their followers, namely, to possess themselves of property. The upheaval in Russia differs as a revolutionary movement in all respects from the French Revolution. In France the *bourgeoisie* enriched themselves at the expense of the nobles. In Russia a section of the *bourgeoisie*— the revolutionary *intelligencia*—is helping to transfer property to the proletariat. It is the doctrine of *"enrichissez-vous"* applied to the masses.

Secondly. The Russian Socialists are divided into two distinct camps—one pro-German, the other pro-Ally, one appealing to industrial, the other to agricultural, Labour. The former are Social-Democrats of the German type, the latter are a preponderantly Russian faction known as the Socialist-Revolutionaries. To these have adhered large numbers of the idealistic and unpractical *intelligencia*, believing in the Utopian doctrine of land nationalization which forms the basis of the party programme. In practice, under the inevitable influence of demagogue extremists who ever dominate revolutionary movements, it has assumed the form of land-grabbing at the expense of landowners, large and small, with attendant consequences. Similarly the Social-Democratic theory of the nationalization of industries has resulted in the grabbing of mills and the complete paralysis of work.

Thirdly. The large majority of the Russian workmen and peasants—all the national and industrious elements in the country—are in opposition to the pro-German extremists who under the direction of German agents have converted the Russian Revolution into a German machine.

Fourthly. The German Revolution in Russia has been carried out by Lenin and his associates with the aid of (*a*) ignorant and undisciplined reservists who did not wish to fight, (*b*) of workmen who had been deceived by their leaders into believing that they could live without working by the plunder of capital, and (*c*) of rustics deluded by the dream of free lands for all. And, I may add, we find the Soviets, or councils of workmen's, soldiers', and peasants' delegates—a sort of revolutionary Parliament—composed of "workmen" who did not work, of "soldiers" who did not fight, and of "peasants" who did not plough.

Organized and financed by Germany, the Leninite revolution has naturally been directed towards the goal desired by Germany: the conclusion of a separate peace, involving complete surrender of Russia's independence, politically and economically.

I pointed out the inevitable consequences of Soviet rule 10 months ago, a few days after that body—which, in Mr. Henderson's view, still represents Russia— had taken charge of affairs in Petrograd. Pacifists in the House of Commons ventured to challenge my statement. Events have answered them. The elections to the Constituent Assembly, carried out under every conceivable method of aggression from the German Bolshevists, have yielded a substantial majority against them, *i.e.*, against the chief arbiters of the so-called "Russian" Revolution, and yet Lenin and his partners proceed—as they have done throughout—to carry on the German business in Russia.

Though Mr. Henderson was in Petrograd last spring and summer, he failed to see what was going on under his very eyes. Let me recall some of the principal features of the German programme as it was then being carried out by the Bolshevists under the auspices of his friends in the Soviet:—(a) It (the Soviet) destroyed discipline in the Army and Navy; (b) it proclaimed the formula "no annexations, no indemnities" in order to convey to the minds of ignorant soldiers the futility of carrying on the war; (c) it plundered the Treasury, scattering hundreds of millions sterling among its supporters in the various committees and among the demoralized soldiery, so that Russia became financially impotent to resist German aggression; and (d) when, a spite of all these German-made contrivances to dishearten Russia, her armies in the south-west began their offensive in July, in failed to check the Bolshevist propaganda that finally crippled them as a fighting force.

All this was done while the Bolshevists were, so to speak, in the background, though in reality directing the Revolution according to German plan. As soon as they came out into the open they began their "peace negotiations." Need it surprise us to learn that Herr Warburg, the German paymaster to the Bolshevists, is now living in Petrograd? Or that British and American travelers are intercepted by M. Trotsky? Or that Admiral Kaiserling is a guest of honour in the Bolshevist capital arranging for a German naval base on the Murman and in the White Sea—our sole means of communication with Russia in the north?

Such are the results of the "peace" campaign in Russia. Would Mr. Henderson wish to see them duplicated here or in other Allied countries?

I am, &c.,
YOUR PETROGRAD CORRESPONDENT

1918

◆

WASTE OF HUMAN FOOD

4 January 1918

SIR,—I CANNOT HELP asking myself this question: Are our Ministers in earnest if on the one hand they call upon us all to tighten our belts and eat less, and on the other hand allow up to 15lb. of oats a day per head to 500 chasers for steeplechasing? Who is to benefit by this steeplechasing? No one as far as I can see except the owner of the chaser, certain sections of the Press through increased circulation, shareholders of different racing fixtures, and bookmakers. And who will suffer? Our whole nation, now engaged in a life-and-death struggle. By such means we may be driven to an unsatisfactory ending of this terrible war. The chasers are mainly geldings or mares of little or no value for breeding purposes, so it cannot be said that steeplechasing benefits the breed of horses in any appreciable degree. To maintain the thoroughbred by all means let a few meetings for flat racing be held at Newmarket and let valuable stakes be given to induce owners of good horses to retain them, but let there be no inducement given to maintain common chasers at the expense of the nation. Food to-day is needed for the life of the people and should neither be wasted nor used in such unproductive ways as allowing steeplechasing in these anxious times. Your correspondent who writes under the name of "Farmer" estimates that if the oats now allowed to chasers were given to our underfed cows the result would be some 2,000 extra gallons of milk per day, or if allowed to poultry numbers would be kept up and the supply of eggs increased, whereas now hens are being killed off for want of food to maintain them. On all sides we hear the farmer clamouring for food for his stock and unable to get it. Apart from the consideration of food, these numerous steeplechase fixtures entail a considerable amount of labour, now urgently needed for the prosecution of the war and the production of food.

I remain yours obediently,
J. WOOLSEY SPACKMAN

"THE HUNDRED BEST GAPS"

7 January 1918

SIR,—AS CHAIRMAN FOR this year of the Books, Manuscripts, and Autograph Letters Section of the coming Fourth Annual Red Cross Sale at Christie's may I appeal directly to your readers for help? You, the readers, know what happens. The books and manuscripts are sold by auction, and by the kindness of Messrs. Christie the whole of the proceeds goes to the Red Cross. For these books and manuscripts we come empty-handed to you; we ask for something from your shelves or portfolios that will probably save the life of a man who is risking his life for you. If he himself came to you, pale and bleeding, and stood silently awaiting your decision, how you would run to your shelves! He cannot come, he is occupied in your defence till he falls. You were in his hands till then, afterwards he is in yours. Are you to help those who bring him in and succour him?

The response has always been generous, but the needs are greater than ever. To you who have helped before, who have got into the way of finding that you have still another treasure left, we know that we can come again. You are our standby.

"The hundred best books." How much finer on your shelves to-day the hundred best gaps! Make those gaps and never again let those gaps be filled. Hand them down with their history to your children's children—surely a nobler legacy than though all the places were full and began with the Shakespeare folio.

There is also an army of possible helpers whom we have not yet reached. For our helpers are of two classes—those who have many and much, and those who, having little, may yet have one rare book, manuscript, or autograph. We ask those who have but that one treasure to let us have it in exchange for the man who is lying on the ground. We feel sure that you would rather have him than the book.

For this special purpose only books and manuscripts of special pecuniary value are wanted. They must all be received before the middle of February, and the sooner the better. They should be sent to the offices of the Books and Manuscripts Section of the Red Cross at 20, King-street, St. James's, S.W.1, where they will be gratefully acknowledged by the hon. secretary, E. V. Lucas.

Yours truly,
J. M. BARRIE

RECORDS OF GERMAN CRIME

14 January 1918

SIR,—SIR ARTHUR CONAN Doyle has been lately preaching the gospel of hatred in relation to Germany. But hatred, as distinct from moral reprobation, is, I hope and think, repugnant to the British character. Englishmen generally realize how soon the cultivation of such a feeling of hatred may issue in acts of unjustifiable savagery. They would despise themselves if they were to fortify their courage by writing and singing "hymns of hate."

It is not implacable hatred but invincible resolve that is the spirit essential to victory in the war. May I, then, suggest one measure which it would not be impossible to adopt as a means of strengthening the national will? It has been stated, I think on official authority, that the Government are keeping all through the war, and mean to publish after the war, a complete record of the outrages perpetrated by Germany on land and sea against international law and Christian morality. But will not the publication then be too late? Will it not tend to create difficulties in the way of peace? But the calm, dispassionate recital of Germany's crimes, if it were officially made once or twice perhaps a year during the continuance of the war, would be the most powerful of all influences in stamping upon the mind and soul of Great Britain and the Allied nations the immutable conviction that the war, which they are called to wage at an untold cost of suffering, is a war for all that is high and holy in the civilization of the world.

I remain, Sir, your obedient servant,
J. E. C. WELLDON

THE FUTURE OF EMBASSIES

21 January 1918

SIR,—THE NEWSPAPERS SPEAK of embassies likely to be vacant. Does not this offer a favourable opportunity for doing away with them altogether, in agreement, of course, with those countries with which we now exchange embassies? An ambassador is a pompous and expensive form of envoy. His one exceptional privilege, so far as I know, is the right to demand a personal audience of the Sovereign to whom he is accredited. What this is practically worth we see from Mr. Gerard's narrative of his vain efforts to obtain an audience of the Emperor William during this war. Moreover, the most important Sovereigns with regard to whom this access might be of some slight advantage are the two Emperors with whom we are fighting, and with whom we can never resume ambassadorial relations, which imply something kindly and personal. But an envoy in these days wants to see the Foreign Secretary, not the Sovereign, and indeed the Minister of a great State at a critical juncture would have quite as much weight and right of access as an ambassador. An ambassador requires a very large salary, and yet can rarely live on it, as so much of splendour is expected of him. And he is apt to be punctilious and exacting about his rights and precedence, matters which are sinking into the background. He is, indeed, the survival of a dead past.

Convenience and economy both dictate the abolition of these functionaries, and the relations of countries would not suffer.

OLIM

DISCHARGED SOLDIERS

26 January 1918

SIR,—I AM A DISCHARGED soldier. Although now quite fit to follow ordinary civilian occupation, I am, so far, unable to secure employment. Before enlisting I was employed as general manager to a wholesale house with a salary of five pounds a week. During my absence my place was filled by a single man at a less wage. I possess splendid testimonials as to my character and ability. I have answered innumerable advertisements; made application for employment through the Labour Exchanges and the Association for Discharged Soldiers; interviewed managers of munition factories, &c.; and nowhere have I been able to secure employment. I am now quite destitute. My landlord has given me orders to quit, as I am unable to pay his last quarter's rent. My wife intends getting employment, so that the education of our children shall not suffer. I find there are many discharged soldiers similarly situated. If the Government are unable to help the few of us anxious to secure employment now, what will happen to the lads when they all return?

Yours respectfully,
A DISAPPOINTED TOMMY

———◆———

EXTRAVAGANT DRESS

31 January 1918

SIR,—I HAVE READ WITH great interest, sympathy, and approval in *The Times* of Jan. 26 an appeal from a number of eminent women to their more frivolous sisters, begging them in these days of stress and strain to abstain from wasting money which might help their country on expensive and fashion-changing garments. If I wanted advice as to conduct, philanthropy, politics, literature, or art, I cannot think of any set of women to whom I would rather apply—but dress? The young, who are naturally and rightly those who care most about clothes, are influenced by those but little older than themselves. Actual or possible grandmothers will not convince a young woman, whereas if you would now gather together a band of women, well known in society, to issue a similar appeal, limiting the age to, say, 35, I believe the effect would be much more immediate and satisfactory than that of

A WOMAN OF SIXTY

A REVENUE FROM INTESTACY

4 February 1918

Sir,—The Chancellor of the Exchequer recently stated in the House of Commons that we "ought to raise by taxation every penny that could be safely so raised." There is one way in which an amount—small, no doubt, in comparison with the huge sum required, but not inappreciable—might be raised not only with safety but with positive incidental benefits apart from the money obtained. It is that the State, when a person dies intestate as to any property without leaving any relatives within, say, the fourth degree (first cousins), should take the whole of such property. It might, indeed, be well to extend the rule even to cases where there were no relatives within the third degree (uncles and aunts and nephews and nieces). A windfall from the estate of a cousin who does not care to make a gift in your favour is hardly one of those "reasonable expectations" which it would be cruel to disappoint. This mode of raising revenue would have all the advantages—rarely found together—of a wise tax.

(1) It would cost little or nothing to collect. The executors or administrators would pay over the amount to the Inland Revenue except in cases of doubt. In all such cases the Crown has now to be represented and the change would probably save expense of inquiries in many instances where doubt existed whether distant relatives of a deceased person were living.

(2) It would not hamper or disorganize any trade or industry or discourage thrift. Who would make less effort or save less because if he died intestate the State would take his property rather than a second cousin? If he thought of the matter at all he would make a will.

(3) It would not inflict hardship on any class or disappoint reasonable expectation.

Incidentally it would save expense and delay in the administration of estates. Every one who has any experience of what is called Chancery practice knows the delay and expense of the old inquiries, "who was the heir-at-law of the said A.B., and who by devise, descent, or otherwise," &c., and "who were the next-of-kin living at his death, and which of them has since died," &c.—I quote from memory, not having Seton at my elbow. Again, who has not come across those cases, sad and amusing, where people whose lives might otherwise have been useful, waste them in trying to establish claims—usually hopeless—to the estate of some distant relative?

Are there any arguments against this proposal which will bear statement? A Bill to embody it could be drawn by a competent draftsman accustomed to revenue work in an hour and a half, and the officials at Somerset House could make a rough estimate of the amount likely to be obtained—probably only a guess—but whatever came in would be clear gain.

Since putting down the above points I have by mere chance discovered that a very similar proposal was made by Bentham more than a hundred years ago. His proposals go somewhat further, as he would also have limited the power of making bequests by will in favour of distant relatives. His anticipations as to the revenue to be thus obtained seem excessive, and the tract to which he gives the title "Supply without Burden," adopted above, is far from being a model of clear or brief statement, but his authority on any question of legislation or public policy ought to carry great weight. He specially commends "the proposed resource" first for "its unburdensomeness," secondly for "its tendency to cut off a great source of litigation."

Knowing your power of stimulating the receptivity by Government Departments of useful proposals, I venture to trust that an introduction through your columns may save this little bantling, now traced to such respectable ancestry, from premature consignment, unnoted, to the limbo of the official waste paper basket. Your blessing might secure its permanent adoption, with some benefit to the revenue and considerable collateral advantages.

I am, Sir, yours faithfully,
ALFRED HOPKINSON

New rules on intestacy would be introduced by legislation in 1925.

WAR MEMORIALS

12 February 1918

SIR,—WE ALL WANT to do honour to our heroic dead and keep their glorious deeds fresh for the generations to come. We also want that this cruel war, and all it has entailed, shall never be forgotten. Is not some unanimity in the memorials that will be erected throughout the land a means of attaining both these objects? The reality of the Napoleonic wars was impressed on me as a very small child by seeing the Martello Towers. I would suggest something in the form of the Staffa cross, which could be erected in the market place of small towns and in central spaces of larger ones, and in village churchyards. The cost could be made to suit all localities, and not to interfere with any other scheme for commemorating local heroes.

Yours faithfully,
C. C. WHITE-COOPER

MEAT FROM THE ANTARCTIC

14 February 1918

SIR,—YOUR NOTE IN YOUR recent issue on "Oils from the Antarctic" is not new to some of us who brought home full ships of sea-leopard oil, Weddell seal oil, and crab-eating seal oil to Britain over a quarter of a century ago, which was then sold for purposes now named. Penguin oil was also brought back to Scotland by the Scotia naturalists in 1904.

But there is another most important product for the present day, namely, meat. Has Lord Rhondda taken steps to secure this? Has the National Service sought or accepted the expert advice and help of those who have practical knowledge about this meat? Antarctic seal meat and penguin meat formed our staple diet on the Dundee sailing ships mentioned in 1892-93, as it did also on the Scotia (Scottish National Antarctic Expedition) in 1902-04. We enjoyed it and lived well on this meat. In Spitzbergen I have also eaten and enjoyed seal meat, and I have lived well for months on whale meat and enjoyed it. Mr. W. G. Burn Murdoch, in a recent publication on "Modern Whaling," says, "The best whale meat is better to eat and tastes better than the best beef; it is lighter and more appetizing." Mr. Burn Murdoch is right. Should canning factories and refrigerator vessels not be immediately started in the rich Antarctic whaling grounds, where 15,000 to 20,000 huge whales are killed annually and have their meat merely turned into guano instead of being used for food?

The seals and penguins are an additional supply; besides millions upon millions of "new laid" penguin eggs, larger and better than hens' eggs.

Yours,
WM. S. BRUCE

PIG-BREEDING

19 February 1918

SIR,—I AM A PEDIGREE large black gilt. My master says I am a war pig. Perhaps you may like to know what this is. I was farrowed at the end of last winter in an open shed in a field. My dam was of ancient lineage, and was always telling us what she had to eat when she was being prepared for shows in her youth, and how hurt she was to think that nothing of the kind came our way nowadays. But all nine of us grew strong and healthy by help of the summer herbage in spite of the poor quality of trough food, which we used to call skilley. The clover was particularly good last summer, and we learnt to eat it weeks before we were weaned.

Mother used to say, however, that she could not have done her duty by us unless master had got for her something he called offal, which humans could not eat. I have heard of barley meal and maize meal, but have never seen them. I think they were some sort of forbidden food, which pigs enjoyed when they lived in palaces where Providence used to come round two or three times a day with a bucket. Most war pigs think this a fable. The fine time for us was when the trees round our range dropped beechmast and acorns every night, only the greedy fowls and ducks were so quick at picking up the acorns. Later on we rooted about from dawn till night on our own, which was great fun, till after an unseemly scuffle with some humans something went wrong with our snouts so that now besides rough grass we can only forage for brambles.

My brother Verax, whom I have not seen for many weeks, used to tell me that his great ambition was to become a subsidized sire in war time, and that he hoped to succeed because his breeding enabled him to thrive on very short commons. Anyhow, it is all sound war work, though chopped hay, kohlrabi, and the offallest of rubbish are our trough food. The only thing which makes us inclined to go on strike is the thought that someone in authority says that after all our toil to grow into meat we should be valued only at 18s. per score. We think this insulting to our war-time exertions. But personally I am most anxious about the future. This spring I hope to have some young ones of my own, and mother and aunts all tell me that I shall never be able to do my duty by them unless master can get me some middlings. This anxiety has caused me to write you this letter, which otherwise would be a very forward thing to do.

I remain your trusty war-worker,
MOORLAND VERA, No. 18492

BROTHELS IN FRANCE

21 February 1918

Sir,—In your issue of this morning it is stated by Mr. Macpherson that the question of brothels in France is "one entirely for the French civil authorities, and we cannot therefore take any action." This is not true; it is known at the War Office not to be true. There is much they can do. One thing they can do: they can avoid encouraging the men to visit these places by entries on camp leave-cards which give the hours during which they are "not out of bounds" for British soldiers. They can take a leaf out of American Army custom and not stultify discipline and moral appeals, as has been thus done. The honour and morality of our public policy is being besmirched by this silent consent to the action of men who are in favour of the utterly discredited policy of the C.D. Acts. The chaplains know and hear enough to make one ask, Why do they not threaten to resign in a body? What are the headmasters of England doing whose young boys are going out to temptation in French areas?

Your obedient servant,
T. C. FRY

RATIONS FOR CHILDREN

23 February 1918

Sir,—In view of the ever-increasing importance to the nation of a sound and healthy race, we feel it our duty to draw attention to the following grave defects in the proposed rationing for children: —The diet is lacking in the essentials for normal and complete development at an age when mental and physical growth are specially rapid, and education becomes increasingly difficult to underfed children. The fat and meat rations being insufficient for the needs of rapidly growing children, we would urge the following additions:—

(1) Full meat ration should be given to children over five years, and from then up to 16 years of age should not include suet.

(2) The weekly 4oz. of butter or margarine should be supplemented from 5-16 years by 4oz. suet.

(3) Immediate attention should be given to better control and distribution of milk. (N.B.—Some adult households are known to be getting a pint per head daily, while young children get less than ¼ pint or even none.)

(4) The suggestion made by Sir C. Bathurst at Swansea on February 16 that the sugar ration should be further diminished in order to allow those with gardens to make jam for their own consumption constitutes another great menace to the diet of our children and should not be allowed.

All food legislation should aim at mitigating as far as may be the disastrous consequences of the war for future generations by securing sufficient diet for the children of to-day. Ministries of Health and Reconstruction, &c., are useless unless healthy men and women are available to carry on the world's work.

Yours faithfully,
ELÖISE ANCASTER
LETTICE BEAUCHAMP
A. BUTE
WILL CROOKS, M.P.
MARGARET McMILLAN
ETHEL PERROTT, R.R.C.
EMILY WILBERFORCE, President, Mothers' Union
J. WALTER CARR, M. D., Senior Physician to Victoria Hospital for
  Children, Chelsea
MARION VAUGHAN, Medical Officer, West Islington Infant Welfare Centre

Increasing shortages of food – Britain had just six weeks' supply of wheat at the end of 1917 – had led to panic buying, and so rationing of foods such as sugar and meat was gradually brought in from January 1918.

THE NATION'S YOUNG LIVES

25 February 1918

SIR,—MR. GALSWORTHY, in his article in to-day's *Times* on "The Nation's Young Lives," strongly advocates the adoption of widows' or mothers' pensions, and the proper protection and care of unmarried girl mothers and their illegitimate children. His words are opportune. No amount of Welfare Centres can do anything radical to help the children of widows or those born out of wedlock, until the State has awakened to its grave responsibility for their welfare.

I have, within the last two days, been present at a meeting of a committee of women Poor Law Guardians in one of our great provincial cities. They were engaged, no doubt unconsciously, in a game which, for want of a better name, I must call girl-baiting. I saw a young expectant mother cruelly handled, and tortured with bitter words and threats; an ordeal which she will have had to endure at the hands of four different sets of officials by the time her baby is three weeks old. These guardians told her, in my presence, that they hoped she would suffer severely for her wrong-doing, that they considered that her own mother, who had treated her kindly, had been too lenient, and that her sin was so great that she ought to be ashamed to be a cost to self-respecting ratepayers. They added that the man who was responsible for her condition was very good to have acknowledged his paternity, but expressed the belief, nay, rather the hope, that he would take an early opportunity of getting out of his obligation. Meanwhile, a pale, trembling girl, within a month of her confinement, stood, like a hunted animal, in the presence of such judges.

We pray constantly in our churches for "all women labouring of child, sick persons, and young children, the fatherless, the widows, and all that are desolate and oppressed," and yet we continue this oppression of the desolate.

Yours faithfully,
DOROTHEA IRVING

TREATMENT OF NURSES IN FRANCE

18 March 1918

Sir,—Some few weeks ago a letter appeared in *The Times* asking for recruits for the V.A.D.'s. In case the response to this appeal was not equal to expectations, it would not be difficult to indicate some of the causes of so regrettable an occurrence. In many ways the conditions of service for British nurses in France, both trained and partly trained, are unnecessarily irksome and unpleasant. Patriotism alone induces many who are on terminable contracts to re-engage; and dissatisfaction is widespread and profound among Army nurses of all degrees, though it seldom finds expression otherwise than privately.

Maladministration results not only in a direct loss of *personnel*, both by causing resignations and by hindering recruiting; it leads also to a diminished efficiency of those who remain. The petty sickness rate is far too high, and could be considerably reduced by improved conditions, some of which I take leave to specify.

First, I take the question of privilege leave to England, which is granted nominally every six months. Nursing is arduous at the best of times, but on active service during the campaigning season it is doubly or trebly exacting. It is all the more important that leave should be given as regularly as possible. I can recall but few cases of a nurse under the rank of matron getting her leave (other than sick leave) at the due date. Nine, 10, even 12 months are usual intervals, so much so that they are accepted as the normal expectation. Fourteen or 15 months are not uncommon periods of consecutive service without a break if employment in England is reckoned in; and cases have been known of V.A.D.'s being worked 22 months at a stretch without a holiday. I ought to explain how these exceptionally, and to my mind disgracefully, long periods of service arise. There was, and may still be, a practice of sending V.A.D.'s to France at short notice without any "embarcation leave," to which soldiers are entitled. Thus it may, and does, happen that a nurse is sent to France after many months of work in England, only to find herself at the bottom of a leave list with scores in front of her who are already overdue to go. The usual reply when anomalies such as this are brought to the notice of the authorities is that "privilege leave is not a right, and can only be granted as the exigencies of the situation admit"; an incontrovertible platitude, but a disingenuous excuse.

During the winter months hospital cases have been so light that every nurse in France could have been granted a fortnight's leave without detriment to the patients. Quite recently there has been a slight improvement in the leave rate, I am told, but I know that even now, at the end of the slack season, there are still hundreds of nurses whose leave is two, three, or more months overdue. Medical officers have no difficulty in getting their leave regularly, at least during the winter, and they require it for health reasons far less urgently than do nurses.

My next point is that not enough is done to provide healthy relaxation for nurses. The weekly "half-day off" is abrogated by some matrons on the slightest hint of increased military activity, often quite needlessly. The monthly "day off" is, even at the slackest season, almost unknown. There are sisters who have had during three years' continuous work no more than two or three of these days of rest, and Sunday is just as busy as any other day in a military hospital. Concert parties and entertainments are discouraged, though they are not forbidden; the latest regulation, I understand, is that nurses may not "dress up" for them, but may perform or sing in uniform; the cooperation of medical officers, or other males is tabooed. Dancing is a form of healthy exercise and relaxation from the strain of nursing which is strictly forbidden, even at Christmas. No grievance of the nursing services is so widely and bitterly resented as this Puritanical ordinance. Those who control the Colonial and the United States nursing services permit their nurses to dance, much to the advantage of their health. The invidious spectacle thus arises of a British hospital existing side by side with a Colonial or an American one, with this galling and insulting regulation in force on one side of the boundary fence but not upon the other; and it is actually the case that British nurses in their quarters can hear the dances which the British medical officers with whom they work may attend but they themselves may not.

If any further argument were needed against this regulation it could be found, I think, in the methods of the authorities when it is suspected that the rule has been evaded. It sounds incredible, but it is true, that on occasions when rumours to this effect have reached the administration the plan has been adopted of requiring every nurse in the hospital concerned to sign a paper saying whether or not she has ever broken the rule—not merely on the occasion in question, but ever since her arrival in France; and disciplinary measures have been taken against those who have incriminated themselves in response to this un-English and possibly illegal method of inquisition. I was glad to hear recently that at one hospital where this was tried every sister and V.A.D., whether or not she had actually offended, signed a confession of having done so; this defeated the authorities, who had to let the whole affair drop.

Another matter in which there is room for improvement is in regard to the feeding and messing arrangements. These are very much better in some hospitals than in others. I gather that a trained sister, appointed by the matron, is usually in control, helped by selected nurses, usually V.A.D.'s. When the lady thus put in charge is an expert manager and housekeeper the system may work fairly well; when she is not it works very badly. In either event it is a waste of a highly-trained professional nurse. A better method, to my mind, would be to send out capable women specially for these posts, who need not be either fully or partly trained as nurses. Failing that, the nurses should be allowed to elect a caterer, just as an officers' mess elects a mess secretary, for three or six months at a time, with eligibility for re-election. As things are, no one dares to complain of the messing or to offer suggestions for improvement, because the caterer is a nominee of the matron, and not responsible to the nurses whose money she has to expend.

Another matter, if a small one, is in respect of ward breakages. It is important, admittedly, to discourage carelessness, and sometimes even to penalize it; but is it just that the nursing staff should pay for the cost of every broken clinical thermometer, as is frequently done? Even when a patient breaks a thermometer himself the sister or V.A.D. on duty in the ward is surcharged for it if she is weak enough to submit to the imposition. Whether this is a universal practice or merely the whim of one particular matron I cannot say; I only testify that it prevailed in one hospital of my acquaintance.

This letter has been written at the instigation of no one, and in consultation with no one, but solely to draw attention to various points actually observed in France which appear to be more or less gross abuses in the opinion of

A MERE MAN

SMALL BIRDS AND INSECTS

21 *March 1918*

SIR,—IT HAS BEEN RECENTLY stated in the Press that a plague of caterpillars among the fruit trees is anticipated in the coming year. It seems a little early to prophesy this, but nevertheless there is cause for anxiety—from an agricultural point of view—as regards the probability of a very considerable increase in insect pests in the immediate future. And for this reason, that the winter of 1916-17 was so unusually severe that in many parts of the country the smaller insect-eating birds were almost entirely destroyed by the continuous frost and snow. In this district hardly a tit of any variety was to be seen during last spring and summer, and now they are very scarce. Flycatchers were hardly in evidence at all last summer. Few linnets are to be seen this spring, while last year the various warblers were here in far fewer numbers than usual. It is true that the flycatchers, warblers, and many other species of insect-eating birds are migrants; but even the migrants seem to have greatly diminished in numbers owing to the extraordinary severity of the winter of 1916-17, a severity which extended all over Europe. All the birds I have mentioned are purely insect-eating ones; and this being so, may I venture to hope that the educational and agricultural county authorities, as well as those higher powers who issue orders from Whitehall, will, when they—quite rightly—send out their commands respecting the destruction of grain-eating wild birds, especially during the nesting time, urge strongly the advisability of sparing as far as possible all those species which are of the utmost value to farmers by reason of the millions of destructive grubs, insects, and caterpillars they consume?

Sparrows, pigeons, and rooks deserve little mercy, though the latter bird cleans up wireworm very thoroughly. But what should be carefully avoided is the indiscriminate destruction of small birds and their eggs. Unless care is taken in this direction, the considerable diminution in the number of insect-eating birds will prove not a blessing to the farmer but very much the reverse.

I am, Sir, your obedient servant,
RUTLAND

LEITH HILL

21 *March 1918*

SIR,—REFERRING TO YOUR Correspondent's article in *The Times* of yesterday in connexion with the tree-felling on Leith Hill, may I be allowed to correct an error in giving the name of the builder of the Tower? This was Mr. Richard Hull, a gentleman of Irish family, who became proprietor of Leith Hill Place. Nor is the story of Mr. Hull's having directed that his body should be interred head downwards correct. It is stated in Tallis's "Topographical Dictionary" to relate to "an eccentric farmer" believed to be buried in the neighbourhood.

I am yours faithfully,
E. C. P. HULL

14, COCKSPUR-STREET

21 *March 1918*

SIR,—I UNDERSTAND THAT the First Commissioner of Works is proposing to take over the building at 14, Cockspur-street, which has been used since October, 1914, as the headquarters of the Canadian Red Cross Society. Consternation is felt, I know, by many of those connected with the Society, and endless confusion will be caused if they should be compelled to give up a building the address of which is known to countless Canadian soldiers in France, to their relations in Canada, and to many Canadian prisoners in Germany. Is this site necessary? If so, there are other buildings in the neighbourhood—clubs, for instance—whose members would no doubt be only too willing to sacrifice their convenience in order to save the delay and confusion involved in shifting so large an organization as the Canadian Red Cross.

May I urge the authorities concerned to look elsewhere and not alter the address of an office which is visited by, and receives letters from, thousands of persons?

Yours faithfully,
NANCY ASTOR

NEURASTHENIC PENSIONERS

22 *March* 1918

SIR,—IN *THE TIMES* OF March 18 the Minster of Pensions is reported to have made the following statements with reference to hospitals for "shellshock cases," in a speech delivered at Worcester:— "He thought that a system of hospitals for such cases only was not the best method of treatment. He wanted neurasthenic cases mixed with other cases, so that the cheery chap might shed some of the sunshine of his presence over those suffering from neurasthenia."

I hope that the Minister has been misreported, for it is altogether incredible that one who has the interests and the welfare of the soldiers and pensioners so deeply at heart as Mr. Hodge has should deliberately adopt a policy of reaction and disaster, which the experience of the last four years has shown to be the inevitable result of the course he is now suggesting.

My reason for writing is that I was a member of a deputation of four medical men who discussed this very problem with Mr. Hodge three months ago, and called his attention to the fact that as the outcome of a series of informal conferences at the War Office, it was unanimously agreed that neurasthenic patients should not be mixed with other patients, but should be sent to large hospitals specially set apart for the expert treatment of nervous and mental ailments. Sir Alfred Keogh adopted the recommendations of this informal conference of specialists, representing all parts of the country, and they are now being put into practice. A definite statement of the War Office policy in respect of this important matter has been published by the officer responsible for supervising its practical application—I refer to Colonel Aldren Turner's preface to Roussy and Lhermitte's "The Psychoneuroses of War," published as one of the series of manuals of which Sir Alfred Keogh is the general editor. These measures were deliberately adopted by the War Office because such a policy as Mr. Hodge is now talking of adopting in the case of the pensioners had been proved by three years' experience to be a complete failure.

Nor is it difficult to explain why the policy of mixing "cheery chaps" with neurasthenic patients will not "shed some of the sunshine" on the latter. Irrelevant joviality will not cheer up a man with a serious "fit of the blues"; on the contrary, will be only an aggravation.

It has been proved by widespread experience that when patients suffering from the minor mental effects of war experience are mixed in general hospitals with other patients, the manifestations of the former's symptoms, their eccentricities of conduct and behaviour, make them objects of morbid curiosity to their more normal fellow-patients. The consciousness of this is a serious addition to their troubles and does an incredible amount of harm. In a special hospital, where wise and sympathetic physicians treat neurasthenic patients with skill and insight, there will always be a large proportion of the patients who are in various stages of recovery. Having recently been through the phases of the illness which the newer patients present, they understand their condition and can give them sympathetic help instead of offensive curiosity or misplaced joviality. From the moment of their entry into a special hospital new patients see with their own eyes and learn from their fellows that such troubles as they are suffering from are really curable. And this "curative atmosphere" becomes one of the most valuable therapeutic agents in restoring these men to a normal condition of mind.

If Mr. Hodge has been correctly reported, he now proposes to discard these well-established principles and to revert to a practice which has been proved to be a failure—and a particularly disastrous failure for the victims of such rash experiments. I know that Mr. Hodge is anxious to get the best treatment for the men entrusted to his care. If his advisers cannot give him wiser counsel than the Worcester speech contains, perhaps he might take a leaf out of the War Office's policy and see that the pensioners obtain the efficient and sympathetic treatment which is being provided by the special neurological hospitals of the Army Medical Service.

I am, Sir, &c.,
G. ELLIOT SMITH

———◆———

CONSCIENTIOUS MURDER

23 March 1918

Sir,—There is an outbreak of smallpox near this hospital, and, in a crowded neighbourhood like this, it may become very serious. Once started, it is hard to catch up, especially as so many private and hospital doctors have never seen cases of smallpox.

Yesterday an unvaccinated child of 10 was carried by its mother into the hospital with smallpox clearly out on it. The day before, think of it, this child had been at school in contact with hundreds of other children. What madness it is to allow these objectors to vaccination to murder their fellows with impunity, and how vilely cruel to those who obey the laws of their country!

Yours, &c.,
KNUTSFORD

TWO THINGS NECESSARY

30 March 1918

SIR,—THE COUNTRY IS in grave danger. In 1914 we entered the war for the defence of Belgium. We are now fighting with our backs to the wall for our bare existence. Why cannot the facts be faced and the public told? As you say in your admirable leading article to-day, "The British public of every class will always respond to plain speaking, straight dealing, and the proved necessity of sacrifice."

Two things are necessary—a strong lead by the Government, loyal acceptance by the people. The Government should at once summon Parliament and place before them frankly the situation, not only as it now is, but as it may develop. Whatever happens in the Somme battle, more men and greater effort must be required. Preparation is not pusillanimity. The country is ready for self-sacrifice—all it needs is a lead. Let the Prime Minister, with his great hold on the country, come forward in the spirit of Pitt and say what is required, and all the people will follow him.

Yours, &c.,
W. JOYNSON-HICKS
C. A. MONTAGUE BARLOW

In recent weeks, Germany, having captured Minsk and Kiev, had concluded a peace with Lenin, removing Russia from the war. They had also won a victory on the Somme and their artillery had bombarded Paris.

A MINISTRY OF JUSTICE

4 April 1918

SIR,—ONE CAN FEEL nothing but sympathy with Lord Parmoor's general indisposition to the creation of more Government Departments. But for a Ministry of Justice there are two overruling recommendations. First, the present chaotic state of the work undertaken by officials who are often most inadequately served; and, secondly, the lack of a settled system for dealing with one of the most delicate branches of government—a branch which needs, above all things, to be independent of other departments. Responsible to such a Ministry I trust we shall set up a Public Defender, just as we have a Public Prosecutor. Some acquaintance with the working of the Courts of both this and other countries compels me to believe that grave miscarriages of justice, chiefly affecting the very poor, do occur. This is not from any want of good will or careful labour on the part of magistrates and Judges, but simply because the machinery does not exist for properly collecting and presenting evidence in favour of the accused—while it does exist for the prosecution. In this country the very excellent machinery of the Public Prosecutor's department might very well be duplicated for the proper defence of accused persons who are unable to make suitable provision for themselves.

Yours faithfully,
W. BRAMWELL BOOTH

OUR INDIAN SAILORS

10 April 1918

Sir,—There is one class of the King's loyal subjects whose services in the war seem to have been overlooked. We are all heartily proud of what the mercantile marine have done in helping the gallant work of his Majesty's ships of war, and their services have met with the public recognition they deserve. Few, however, know that all the risks of our own brave sailors are shared by many hundreds of Indian sailors, not conscripts, but volunteers, some of whom, to my knowledge, have continued to serve the common cause after they have been more than once rescued from ships sunk by U-boats. They are Mahomedans of humble station and little education, quite unable to say a word in support of their claim to our gratitude and applause. They are probably quite unaware that they are doing anything out of the way. But all Britons who have sailed in liners manned by lascars will, I am sure, support me in my hope that any recognition which falls to our own merchant seamen will not be denied to their modest, efficient, and, let me add, quietly courageous Indian shipmates.

Yours obediently,
J. D. ANDERSON, late I.C.S.

SOUTH AFRICAN HONOURS

10 April 1918

Sir,—There exists without doubt a feeling of intense disappointment and indignation among South Africans at the failure to do justice to the many men who joined up from August, 1914, and fought both in the Rebellion and the South-West campaign. The red chevron is not permitted to be worn for the Rebellion campaign, and no medal has been issued for German South-West. It must be remembered that the majority of the South Africans who volunteered in 1914 did so with the idea of coming to Europe to fight. But they remained in South Africa at General Botha's urgent request, and stood by him in suppressing the Rebellion, a very distasteful piece of work. Thousands went straight to South-West under General Sir Duncan Mackenzie, and spent the best part of a year in the desert under very trying circumstances; although itching to be sent to Europe they remained steadfast to the immediate call. In addition to those who lost their lives in South Africa, thousands of these men have since died on other fields of battle, and it is for their sakes and their relatives, as well as for those still living, that tardy justice should be done.

FLORENCE PHILLIPS

WOMAN-POWER

12 April 1918

SIR,—IT IS SURPRISING, in view of the gravity of the present crisis, that no reference whatever has been made by the Government to the question of woman-power. Large numbers of men are to be withdrawn from civilian employment. Are any special steps being taken to recruit, select, and allocate women to fill the gaps? Appeals for women for various forms of war work are a matter of almost daily appearance. What measures are in contemplation to meet these demands on a reasoned plan, having regard to the character of the various services, the quality of the material available, and the needs of ordinary industrial employment? Vague and indiscriminate appeals to women to come forward and serve their country are worse than useless. They create a maximum of exasperation with a minimum of effective result. What is wanted is the better organization and distribution of supply. It is incredible that any possible source of strength should be neglected at a time like the present, but measures for dealing with woman-power in this emergency still remain lamentably ineffective.

Your obedient servant,
VIOLET R. MARKHAM

———◆———

POTATOES IN LONDON

15 April 1918

SIR,—THE COUNTRY IS being adjured to grow more potatoes, and in South Kensington there is an unusual amount of open land in the shape of semi-public squares and gardens. Yet in an extended walk through the district I have failed to discover a single instance in which any effort is being made to cultivate this land. Personally, and there are others like me, I should be able and willing to look after a vegetable plot if I could get one close to my residence. This condition would be fulfilled by the gardens attached to my flat, but their custodians refuse to allow their amenities to be disfigured by potatoes and cabbages. Thus not only is this land unproductive, but it is absorbing the labour of a certain number of gardeners who at present might be better occupied than in sweeping gravel paths and trimming the edges of lawns.

Yours truly,
SOUTH KENSINGTON

HELP FROM AMERICA

27 April 1918

Sir,—Those who look for American aid to relieve us from our immediate difficulties should read the accounts of the proceedings in the United States Senate on March 27 and the following days. The Senate's Committee on Military Affairs took evidence from an officer in charge of the aviation programme. This officer testified that only one fighting aeroplane had thus far been sent from the United States to France. Senator New declared that of the 12,000 combatant planes which were to be delivered to General Pershing by July 1 not more than 37 will be deliverable by that time. Senator Lodge stated that only two cargo ships had been completed in the yards under the control of the United States Shipping Board. The same authoritative speaker said that, though the American War Department had spent six months in endeavouring to make an improved model of the French "75," it had failed to produce an adequate weapon, so that every gun in General Pershing's lines has had to be brought from a British or a French factory.

As these statements and reports have been widely circulated in the American Press, I am conveying no information to the enemy by repeating them. But I think it desirable that they should be known and appreciated in this country, as they can be without in the least undervaluing the effort or the spirit of our friends beyond the Atlantic. We rejoice in the moral support and the resolution of the American people; we hope that in the end their immense resources and invincible energy may make our victory decisive. But we should understand that for months to come the burden of checking and defeating the Germans' attack must continue to be borne by France and Great Britain.

In native swords and native ranks

The only hope of courage dwells.

America may eventually "save democracy"; but to save our own liberties and our own existence we must, for the present, rely upon ourselves, our own valiant Armies, our own mobilized industries, and our own man-power exerted to the last ounce of available pressure.

I am yours, &c.,
SIDNEY LOW

SCHOOLS AND MAN-POWER

2 May 1918

SIR,—THE VILLAGE IN which I am living presents at the present time a curious contrast. The village clusters round a famous public school. From the village practically all men of military age have been called up, some of whom are notoriously unfit and with many responsibilities. On the other hand, we see the staff of the school comparatively immune. It is somewhat galling to the wives and mothers of these men to see young and apparently quite fit assistant and house masters, with ample leisure for playing cricket and tennis, or "footer" and fives, while their men have been called up. It is not unnatural that they should regard the matter as lacking in justice.

The position is this. If a headmaster regards any assistant master over 30 years of age as indispensable he has little difficulty in getting the Board of Education to exempt such a man. Headmasters are subject to human frailties, and I contend that there are a surprising number of so-called indispensable men in our public schools, and also in the O.T.C.'s attached to them, sheltering from military service. It is true to say that, as a general rule, the public schools are heavily overstaffed, and are still working on a peace time-table. Assistant masters, apart from private coaching, are seldom teaching more than 22 hours per week, and headmasters about 10. The comb should be rigorously applied. For the lower forms ladies can quite well be substituted for men, and the older and unfit men can be given a war time-table.

Faithfully yours,
ARMIS CEDAT TOGA

FALLEN OFFICERS: A WARNING

7 May 1918

Sir,—May I warn any of my fellow-countrywomen who, like myself, are mourning the loss of brave and gallant sons? My son died of wounds in a French town, after having made a splendid defence of a trench, in the doing of which he was mortally wounded. A few days after I received the news of his death, a man well on in years, well dressed, and of very pleasing, gentlemanly appearance, came to see me and said he had come from France, where he had been with his nephew, who was gassed and in hospital. He came charged with a message of sympathy from the nephew and other officers who had known and admired my son. His nephew, he said, had been on a course at Hythe with my boy. I asked this gentlemen to lunch, and he accepted, and before leaving he told me he had had all his luggage and worldly goods held up and could not get at any money, and would I lend him a few pounds? For the sake of my son, I felt I could not refuse him, and lent him a considerable sum, for which he gave me an I.O.U., promising to repay me in eight days. The time has long ago expired, and I have heard nothing of or from him. No doubt this "gentleman" has gone to try to extract moneys from other mothers as heart-broken as I am. These I would save if possible.

I am, Sir, yours truly,
A SUFFERING MOTHER

UNNECESSARY TRAVEL

11 May 1918

Sir,—I have read with much interest the article on "Railway Travelling" in your paper of to-day's issue. Since the war began I have only left my house for strictly necessary purposes, to take my young son to school, to pay two visits to my mother, who is unable to travel, and once to see my solicitor. I have not been for any summer change—which we considered so necessary before the war—and do not find myself any the worse. When I have been on any train journey since the war I have been struck by the enormous number of people travelling for pleasure or for a "day's shopping in town." The train has been crowded with mothers carrying infants—who would be far better in their own homes—they are nearly all being taken to see "Auntie" or "Granny," on unnecessary visits. I was in a carriage with two children sickening for chicken-pox a few months ago, and travelled down with four little ones who had whooping-cough badly. I send you the list from the Court Circular in *The Times* descriptive of the continual movements of people who really might, now traffic is to be restricted, curtail their continual rushing from one place to another. I was talking to a working-class woman the other day, and she said, "We would be quite content to stay in our homes if the 'rich' people set us a good example and stayed in theirs, but you see by the papers they are always rushing about the country; so why shouldn't we have a change?"

Yours truly,
KATHERINE TIGHE

SMOKING BY CHILDREN

17 May 1918

SIR,—MANY EVILS HAVE been attributed to this ubiquitous war, but surely that of allowing young children to smoke is one which may well have been averted? Many of us have seen boys of the tender age of five with the inevitable "fag," and it seems to be quite the ordinary thing for young boys and growing lads to spend their money in cigarettes. If we are to start the next generation properly, ought we not to prevent ignorant children from stunting their growth, ruining their constitutions, and befouling their own (and other people's) lungs with the noisome weed? Whatever the opinion as to the effect of smoking on the adult, medical experience is unanimous in condemning the habit before puberty.

I am, Sir, your obedient servant,
A. C. D. TELFER

———◆———

AN EMPEROR OF THREE EMPERORS

18 May 1918

SIR,—THE MULTIPLICATION of titles and the swollen airs of magnificence assumed by the Kaiser remind a student of that good old English book, "Purchas his Pilgrimage" (1613), of the presumption of the Emperor of Bisnagar. That Monarch thought no small beer of himself in the days of our Elizabeth. This is "the swelling style" in which, according to Purchas, he proclaimed his own glory far and wide:—

"The husband of good fortune, the God of great Provinces, King of the greatest Kings, and God of Kings, the Lord of horsemen, the Master of them who cannot speak, Emperor of Three Emperors, Conqueror of all he sees, and Keeper of all he conquers, dreadful to the eight coasts of the World, vanquisher of the Mahometans, Lord of the East, West, North and South, and of the Sea."

There is not an attribute here that Wilhelm II. would not arrogate to himself, and it all sounds highly intimidating. But, alas! in the year of our Lord 1567 Bisnagar was sacked by four allied Kings, and became "a habitation for Tygers and wild Beasts." History does not say what became of the Emperor of Three Emperors, nor of his ensign, which was "a gilded mast, with an Ape at the foot thereof."

I am, Sir, your obedient servant,
EDMUND GOSSE

THE OUTRAGE ON THE HOSPITALS

27 May 1918

SIR,—I AM IN FULL agreement with Lord Denbigh that it is our own nerveless policy which exposes us to the outrages of the Huns. They will do what they think they can do with impunity, and they will avoid that which entails punishment. When Miss Cavell was shot we should at once have shot our three leading prisoners. When Captain Fryatt was murdered we should have executed two submarine captains. These are the arguments which the German mentality can understand. Two years ago you allowed me to plead in your columns for the bombing of the Rhine towns, and now, when at last it is partly done, we at once hear the cry for a truce in such warfare—the very result which I had predicted. But alas for the two wasted years! Now we have to deal with the bombing of hospitals. German prisoners should at once be picketed among the tents, and the airman captured should be shot, with a notice that such will be the fate of all airmen who are captured in such attempts. We have law and justice on our side. If they attempt a reprisal, then our own counter-reprisals must be sharp, stern, and relentless. If we are to have war to the knife, then let it at least be equal for both parties.

Yours faithfully,
ARTHUR CONAN DOYLE

COMMON-SENSE AND THE
BILLING TRIAL

5 June 1918

Sir,—The grave public importance and the very serious consequences that may follow are the only excuse I offer as a Labour M.P. and trade union official for entering my protest against the evidence and charges made in the case just decided.

I offer no opinion upon the verdict, which, undoubtedly, people will judge according to their opinion, neither do I, as a layman, presume to judge as to the legal right to introduce matter entirely irrelevant to the issue involved. The learned Judge's great knowledge and experience must, I presume, be the guarantee that such matter, although to the lay mind having no connexion whatever with the charges upon which a verdict was sought, may have been in order. This case involves many important principles that go to the very root of public life and vitally affect those who, regardless of party, recognize that, whilst public men and women must expect criticism, they ought at least to be protected from vile abuse and slander by those who are prepared to act on the policy of throwing as much mud as possible with the certain knowledge that some will stick.

Doubtless, just as the writing of this letter will be sufficient evidence for some minds to include me in the great Black Book, the existence of which can now only be proved by the dead, so in conformity with this new purity campaign would the decision of my executive to call a railway strike, which I may be called upon to conduct, be accepted as the clearest evidence of Unity House being under German influence and the executive and myself being guilty of offences too hideous to mention.

By far the most serious aspect of the case is the effect upon the great mass of our people, whose minds and thoughts at this moment are concerned with the fate of their loved ones at the front, whose lives are being freely offered to save the future of their country and democracy. Surely at this great crisis our people ought to be protected in their grief and anxiety from being told by one who, as a British M.P., should display some sense of responsibility that men entrusted with the great duties of statesmanship are corrupt and traitors. Reckless assertions of this kind, entirely unsupported by evidence, and defaming men and women alive and dead, may well have a disturbing effect upon a public opinion already racked with anxiety and tense with emotion.

What also of the effect of these wholesale charges of corruption on our German enemies? What a justification to their people to purge the world of such danger and give us real *Kultur*! The times are indeed black, our destinies are in the balance. Do not let us further weaken our cause and add to the danger by giving credence to allegations for which the Law Courts supply no precedent and common decency no support.

Yours, &c.,
J. H. THOMAS

The dancer Maud Allan, a lesbian, had sued the MP Noel Pemberton Billing for libel after articles in a magazine he ran accused her of being part of a vast network of well-placed British "perverts" who were being blackmailed for their influence by the Germans. Their names were said to be written in a Black Book. Allan lost her action, though Billing later admitted in effect that there was no such plot.

———◆———

GOING TO BED

11 June 1918

SIR,—THE WRITER OF your picturesque article "Twilight in the Woods" does not seem to realize that late hours for children are fully as harmful in the country as in the town. I speak as a school manager of a rural school, where the head teacher has drawn my attention to the bad effect late hours have on the health of the children who are allowed to run about the fields and lanes till dark. They come to school weary, complaining of headache, and unable to learn. To-day I hear the school doctor has paid a visit and found several children suffering from tired hearts, which he ascribes in great measure to late hours. Nursery children are sent to bed punctually and no questioning is allowed, but the uneducated mothers do not take the trouble to enforce obedience, and surely, now that the health of the children of our nation is recognized as a vital matter, steps should be taken to instruct parents that to starve their children from necessary sleep is hardly less harmful than to starve them in their food.

Yours, &c.,
VIOLET MARTINEAU

CELLULOID IN BOOTS

11 June 1918

SIR,—IN ONE OF OUR 21 departments we are making large quantities of boots and gaiters for soldiers suffering from wounded feet, and are supplying them to hundreds of hospitals at home and abroad. It is perhaps unnecessary for me to tell you that the very greatest care is taken in the selection of the materials of which these are made. Two weeks ago we were about to use some black and brown metal eyelets submitted by a wholesale firm. They seemed suitable in every way until a finished experimental boot was placed before the fire to dry. In a few moments some of the eyelets burst into flames, and we found on examination that what we imagined to be black and brown enamel was in reality celluloid.

We think it is only right that the public should be warned of this deadly danger, so that accidents may be prevented. The samples in question burn furiously and would have been sufficient to set any one's clothing alight, and would be especially dangerous in the case of injured feet.

Yours faithfully,
EDWARD F. SLADE

LICE AND DISEASE

12 June 1918

SIR,—TWO YEARS AGO you warned the public of the danger of flies, and as a result a campaign against these pests was organized throughout the country. To-day an equally serious and immediate danger threatens in the shape of lice, and therefore I venture to hope that once again you will use your influence to arouse the public.

So far as the Army is concerned the matter is clearly very serious indeed. It has recently been stated by high scientific authorities that louse-borne diseases now account for half of the total sickness rate from the Western front. Moreover, apart from sickness, the incessant scratching robs a man of sleep at a moment when sleep is vital. Sir David Bruce's Committee on Trench Fever has recently reported that, thanks to the work of Major Byam, louse excreta have been identified as the carrier agents of trench fever—one of the worst scourges of armies. It is recognized that typhus fever—which wrought such havoc in Serbia—and relapsing fever are both louse-borne. The present lousy state of the trenches would certainly result in a fearful epidemic were typhus to break out in France. Over and above this, skin diseases are set up by scratching.

The evil does not stop here. Men on leave stay at Y.M.C.A. huts, hostels, and other places, travel in trains and public conveyances, and in a variety of ways mingle with the civil population; their clothes and kits are often lousy and almost always contain louse excreta, which, as Major Byam proved (*vide* report in *The Times*), retain their virulence after prolonged exposure to air and sunlight, and even after heating to 55deg. Centigrade. A very few lice will cause the disease, and men who have been very lousy are apt not to notice a few lice. Further, a man not obviously ill with trench fever can infect lice in this country, and these then become actively dangerous.

So much impressed has the Local Government Board become by the danger of a spread of malaria in this country, that specialist inspectors have been appointed and attempts made to segregate infected persons. Yet the louse is thousands of times more plentiful here than the *anopheles* mosquito, and the number of trench fever cases far greater than the number of malaria cases. Moreover, the possible remote effects of trench fever, heart troubles and neurastheia, are much more crippling to a community than those of malaria.

Trench fever is a most difficult disease to recognize, unless doctors have been specially trained to recognize it; in its early febrile stages it is apt to be called "influenza," and in its chronic stage "myalgia" or "rheumatism." Thus, because the doctors of this country are apt to consider that this disease can arise only in the trenches—on account of its unfortunate name—and because there is no specific individual sign by which it may be known, cases go unrecognized.

Happily, the weapons of war against lice have been forged to some extent already. Early in the day the Lister Institute of Preventive Medicine, of which Sir David Bruce is chairman, provided funds to assist the investigation of trench fever and enable the necessary experimental work to be carried out, thus helping to secure the valuable information about the exact method of spread of the disease. Any campaign against lice should therefore, it is suggested, centre round the Lister Institute, and should be informed by the store of scientific knowledge there available. Further funds should be provided for an extended investigation into insecticides, so-called "preventive clothing," and other means of checking the pest. The Local Government Board meantime should take measures to destroy lice in schools and elsewhere, and should provide that experts specially trained to recognize trench fever be appointed as administrators and instructors. Finally, the Royal Army Medical Corps should be given a free hand in the matter of destroying lice both at home and in the war zone. Civil and military administrators should work in close touch with the scientific staff at the Lister Institute. Unless measures of this kind are taken at once, I fear that the louse will bring such havoc upon us as flies and mosquitoes would have brought had not the danger in their case been recognized and dealt with, for louse excreta may be carried anywhere by a breath of air, and are in almost all the clothing of soldiers returning from France to this country.

I am, &c.,
ENTOMOLOGIST

"FLAPPER FINANCE"

17 June 1918

SIR,—THE PRESENT HOUSE of Commons by law expired on January 30, 1916, when the appointed occasion arose for the people of the country to declare themselves upon their own affairs by a General Election. It has several times, with the weak complicity of the Lords and in contempt of the people, prolonged its own existence, and is reputed to intend that once again. It has voted a salary of £400 a year to its members without any condition that any one of them shall attend the service of the House, which, indeed, most of them never do. Of its members 164 were on January 6, 1916, serving in the Army, and drawing among them £60,953 of Army pay; while 86 of them are place-men, hold office under the Crown (Paper 58 of 1918), and draw among them £136,620 of pay for those places. The members' salaries, when first proposed in 1911, were estimated at £252,000. The Army pay, place pay, and salaries amount together to within a few hundred pounds of £500,000, which the House, whose mandate from the people expired two and a half years ago, distributes among its members, of whom nearly one-quarter are absent on service in the Army, and nearly one-eighth are place-men holding offices of profit under the Crown.

Such a House has naturally and inevitably let go all holds on the purse whereof it is the special, and now pretends to be the sole, guardian. It gives to the War Cabinet of six, and to the other "Ministers," now (according to the revised list of June 10, 1918) numbering 88, a succession of advances by Votes of Credit, enabling them to spend thousands of millions without any of the customary limits or safeguards. Already during the war these Votes of Credit have amounted to £7,342,000,000, and now the House is to be asked to add to them another such Vote of £500,000,000. This would bring the total thus advanced to the Ministry up to £7,842,000,000. That almost incredible total is more than *three times as much as the whole cost of the whole of the four great wars* we have fought since 1702, as may be seen by reference to the veracious and accurate Chisholm, Chief Clark of H.M. Exchequer in 1869. It has all been voted blind, without previous discussion of estimates, or any full subsequent account or examination. It is a scandalous monument to a Parliament without a mandate, and urgently suggests as our principal and most pressing need a General Election, and a consequent new, free Parliament of unpaid and unplaced members representing the present mind of the people and ready to attend to their duties.

Yet some side-lights are thrown upon the way in which the money goes by the Controller and Auditor-General's recent report on the appropriation accounts of the Ministry of Munitions for 1916-17. His investigations are necessarily incomplete, but even so his revelations are appalling. Here are a few of them:—

"There had also been failure to keep a complete and accurate record of repayable cash advances made to the firm—for example, an advance of £250,000 had not been charged in the contract ledger, while two other advances, amounting to £750,000, had been posted twice in the same ledger (p. 8).

"Only recently it was observed that a contractor had been paid the sum of £111,362 19s. 11d, which he had previously received in the shape of payments on account, and, notwithstanding that he notified the Department of this error, a further sum of £21,540 was issued to him, which he had also previously been paid (p. 9).

"The contract ledger recorded payments of £1,400,000 only, although payments amounting to some £4,700,000 had been made (p. 9).

"The total sum issued as banking loans to this firm has amounted to £6,900,000. The earlier loans were subject to repayment by monthly instalments, but after £2,100,000 had been recovered the payments ceased (p. 11).

"A limited test examination was carried out by my Department of the records concerned with supplies to one of the Allies, and it was found (*a*) that issues approximating to £2,500,000 had been omitted from the claims (p. 18).

"In Paris . . . at March 31, 1917, cash advances to the amount of £2,500,000 were recorded against the Ministry representative, while the value of the material issued to him reached about £3,000,000, but the Ministry had not found it practicable to keep detailed records of the contents in London, and were therefore unable to clear the accounts or to answer the general inquires which inevitably arose out of the situation (p. 26)."

These items alone represent an aggregate of some £17,000,000 of quite inconceivable error, such as could not be perpetrated by a child with the most rudimentary noting of accounts or even the merest rudiment of a memory. And considering that the Ministry of Munitions expended in the year (see p. 2) no less than £522,400,000, and that it has had for its head since July 20, 1917, Mr. Winston Churchill, recalled in order to take charge of it, better things might have been expected than what, without disrespect to school-girls in pigtails, I cannot help calling Flapper Finance.

If the House of Commons, or ten righteous men therein, have any desire to perform the elementary duties of that House, they will not give the Government another 500 millions to spend without having not only some explanation of the perfectly awful waste and the truly idiotic incapacity to keep the simplest accounts hitherto shown, but also some security that these will not be continued.

We are ready to give freely such money as taxation has left us for the national needs. But we are not ready to see so large a portion of what we give flung away in waste without bringing us nearer to the end of the war.

Our resources are vast. For so long as we keep our Sea Power we keep the ocean in fee and a mortgage over half the land of the world. But no resources, however vast, can survive unrestrained waste. That way destruction lies.

Your faithful servant,
THOS. GIBSON BOWLES

A MINISTRY OF HEALTH

24 June 1918

SIR,—IT IS NOW TWO years since Lord Rhondda urged the immediate establishment of a Ministry of Health as an urgent war measure. It is many months ago that the Prime Minister stated that it was incredible "that people capable of the sort of explosive energy which this country has put forth in the last two or three years—that such a nation should have permitted the existence of the slums and the miserable, wretched squalor which are a stain upon the flag that is the glory of our race. We cannot allow it to go on," and he urged that an agreed measure should be obtained. Dr. Addison, as Minister of Reconstruction, has, at the request of the Prime Minister, met in conference various interested parties, and has publicly announced that he was in the position to place a Bill before the Cabinet and had done so.

A significant announcement was, however, made by Lord Curzon in the House of Lords on Wednesday last. Lord Curzon said, "The postponement of the establishment of a Ministry of Health was not due to any congestion of the work of the Cabinet, but to the fact that the question raised most acute and deep-seated differences between the Departments concerned." Is it not desirable that the nature of these departmental differences should be publicly stated, in order that the country may know who is responsible for this grievous delay and enable it to judge whether they merit a further postponement of a measure which grows more urgent as the war continues?

Your obedient servant,
KINGSLEY WOOD

BOOKS A LUXURY

1 July 1918

Sir,—I HAVE SELDOM wished more earnestly that Matthew Arnold, with his rapier-like pen, were among us than when I learnt from your columns that it was proposed to tax books as a luxury. For seldom have the characteristic defects of this country been more painfully revealed. I had thought that we had recognized that we must fight Germany with our brains as well as with our arms, and now we are proposing to tax the very tools of our crafts. At the beginning of the war the whole of the educated youth of this country flocked from our universities to the Army inspired by a great ideal, and we would tax the poets, the orators, the philosophers, and the theologians that inspired them. We demand the well-trained medical student, the accomplished man of science, the accurate engineer, and we would tax the books in which their lore is recorded. It is as if the rifles and machine-guns of our Army were thought luxuries. Our public offices are filled with men working out the problems of law, of history, of economics, that war raises; we require linguists skilled in all the languages of the world, yet a grammar is a luxury to be taxed, and the production of historical, of political, of economic treatises is to be hampered by the State. We have learnt to endow universities with large sums of money, but the poor student (and I have known many such) who scorns delights and lives laborious days, and deprives himself of food and clothing to purchase books, is to be taxed for luxurious living. The spiritual problems of the day exercise many minds, and war, our greatest military writer tells us to-day, is above all a spiritual matter, but the philosopher and the theologian and the moralist, who, as your own columns testify, help so many, are to find a new hindrance to the publication of their work. We have been emptying our shelves to send books to the wounded and the sick, for whom in their long and weary sufferings works of the imagination may be often the best anæsthetic, but now we would tax the imagination.

ARTHUR C. HEADLAM

POPULAR OPINION AND
ENEMY ALIENS

3 July 1918

SIR,—THE PRIME MINISTER'S Committee to investigate this question may conceivably be of service, though legitimate criticism might be passed upon its composition. My object is, however, not to criticize either the wisdom of the inquiry, or the composition of the committee, but to express my humble opinion that the popular felling on the subject is somewhat misunderstood. At last (thanks to Lord Denbigh and others) the view of Germany as she really is, is dawning on the British people. They are finding her to be a great heathen nation, ruthless, a worshipper of pure force, hacking her way with deeds of devilish cruelty and with a never-ending stream of lies and tricks and chicanery to what she hopes will be European hegemony. They are beginning to think that with a nation so polluted and polluting, whose ideals are so false and whose human feeling is so dead, no people acknowledging the morals of Christianity, or even of civilization, ought, as it values its own soul, to have truck or dealing or even speech. But the British people find no expression, not even an echo, of their growing conviction from the lips of their leaders. To the people the war is becoming a holy war—a war of right against wrong, of Heaven against Hell. The leaders are apparently still thinking of strips of territory, of cash indemnities and the future of raw materials. What wonder that, deprived of all true guidance, the people are turning (to express their feelings) against persons of German origin in our midst, and contract all sorts of foolish and exaggerated notions as to their influence and methods. Let the Prime Minister, Mr. Bonar Law, and Mr. Asquith say not once, but often, making it plain from day to day, why we are fighting, that if we are victorious we will vindicate the laws of right and wrong by exacting full and adequate punishment for this defilement of human nature; and that in any event we will do our utmost in the councils of the Allies to deprive Germany of the benefits of civilization until she has, by repentance and amendment, become worthy of sharing them. Then there will cease to be an alien enemy question of any difficulty.

Your obedient servant,
T. B. NAPIER

A MIRAGE

3 July 1918

SIR,—YESTERDAY, SUNDAY, June 30, about midday, I was speaking to a friend of mine, both of us being in the garden here, about half a mile from the foot of the South Downs. The wind was south-east, sky clear, and bright sun. Suddenly, we both of us saw a great number of aeroplanes, apparently about one mile away south-west, and perhaps 1,500ft. up, going through evolutions of an evidently hostile character to each other. I should say there were anything between 25 and 40 of them, all of them over the top of the Downs, and spreading inland at first. My friend and I settled they must be squadrons practising. We watched them for, I daresay, five minutes, and then, as they drew away over the Downs to sea, we ran about 150 yards south-west from where we were to get a better view. But we never saw another sign of them. We had seen, as we thought, certainly two, and perhaps three, come down out of control from our first stand place. In the afternoon I happened to call at a house which lay exactly inland of where we had seen the aeroplanes, and close to the Downs. The lady of the house casually mentioned that she had spent all the morning on the Downs, exactly at the point where we had seen the aeroplanes. She had seen nothing save a single one passing at some distance. I then told her what we had seen, and she was amazed. I ought to add that neither my friend nor I heard any noise, either of shots or of aeroplane engines, whilst we watched. To-day I met a gentleman living between this place and the house. I went to visit, and he told me that he had watched the whole matter, had seen one full quite distinctly, and went to the Downs to look for it, but had found nothing.

There is, therefore, no doubt about three men, with good eyes, having seen the same thing at the same time. Was it an instance in England of atmospheric mirage reflected from the front? The planes, however, did not appear upside down, though they had a rather unsubstantial appearance, that made my friend observe twice that somehow they looked strange. I have often seen mirage abroad, and so had my friend, but it never struck either of us that this might be an instance of it until after I had heard that some one had been sitting on the Downs right under the apparent battle and had neither seen nor heard anything of it.

Yours faithfully,
ALFRED J. BETHELL

MEDICAL WOMEN IN THE ARMY

4 July 1918

SIR,—I AM SORRY TO see that in the House yesterday, in reply to a question by Sir Robert Newman, Mr. Forster, the Financial Secretary to the War Office, refused in the name of the Government to consider the granting of commissions to medical women serving in the Army. He not only did that, but he even denied the existence of those grievances which every medical woman in the Army knows, by her own bitter experience, do exist.

Mr. Forster speaks as if he were unaware of the growing indignation of medical women that the War Office, while continuing to ask more and more from them, persists in treating them as inferior to the men who are doing the same work, and with whom in civil life they are on a professional equality.

He says (1) that women serving as whole-time doctors in the Army for service at home and abroad receive the same pay, ration, and travelling allowances and gratuity as temporary commissioned officers of the Royal Army Medical Corps; and (2) that those serving for home duty only on temporary engagements are treated in the same way as civilian medical men similarly employed. I dispute the accuracy of both these statements.

Women serving abroad receive the same pay as men and the same gratuity, but they receive neither ration nor billeting allowance, and those two allowances come to over 30s. a week. Women serving at home received neither the ration allowance nor the 260 gratuity which is paid to the men. They are also refused the privilege, given not only to officers, but to Army sisters and nurses, of travelling on leave with half-fare vouchers, and they pay income-tax as civilians. The ground for refusing the gratuity and the reduced rate of income-tax is that the woman is engaged on a monthly contract, while the man joins for a year or until the end of the war. But the woman is given no option. She is not allowed to join for more than a month. Yet, whether she joins for a month or a year, she is giving up her home and her private practice.

I will give one example of the way in which the War Office takes advantage of the anomalous position in which women have been placed. Two full-time medical women were instructed to examine recruits for Q.M.A.A.C. The pay for this work to civilian medical practitioners is £2 per day. The A.D.M.S. told the two women that they were not C.M.P.'s, but temporary officers of the R.A.M.C., and therefore not entitled to be paid at the rate of C.M.P.'s. But the same A.D.M.S. refused a railway voucher to another medical woman serving in the same capacity on the ground that she was not in the Army, but only a C.M.P.!

These grievances are sufficiently serious, but they are not all. Medical women have had over two years' experience now of serving in the Army without rank, and they have found simply that it does not work. They are suffering not only financially, but in their professional position. Above all, they have found that, working without rank among a body of men where the whole discipline depends on badges and rank, they have not the authority necessary for carrying out their duties, the authority which they unquestionably have in civil hospitals.

Although many of the medical women serving in the Army not only have a high professional standing in civil practice, but now have a large experience in military hospitals, they rank below the latest joined R.A.M.C. subaltern, and are obliged to take their orders from him. When they travel, they travel not as officers, but as "soldiers' wives." In numerous ways, in dealing with their patients, with the orderlies, with German prisoners, and with coloured troops, they find that they have not the respect and the prompt obedience to which they are entitled and which rank would give them. I could quote many passages from the scores of letters which the Medical Women's Federation has received from medical women serving in the Army in proof of these two statements. It is only fair to add that recently the War Office gave medical women serving abroad the right to wear uniform, but that right does not touch the grievances of which I have spoken. Many medical women have written to say that uniform without rank means nothing, and that it will only serve to emphasize the position of inferiority in which they are at present placed.

Yours faithfully,
JANE WALKER, President of the Medical Women's Federation

THE PRAYER FOR RAIN

9 July 1918

SIR,—AT THIS MOMENT what at one time promised to be a really good harvest seems likely to be only a very moderate one indeed. No rain to signify has fallen for two months, and on the light lands the corn crops are "going back" daily; in places they are "burning up"; on the heavy lands the crops are better. Roots also are quite "parched up," and unless a steady 48 hours or more of rain comes soon a dangerously poor harvest seems imminent. And this without considering the question of the shortage of labour. In these circumstances might I suggest to the Bishops, who, I understand, issue the orders on these occasions, that they should at once instruct the clergy in their respective dioceses to read the Prayer for Rain in their churches? If the high authorities of the Church consider the use of prayer to be of any avail, I should have thought that if ever there was a moment when it should be resorted to, it is now. For the only crop—with the exception of potatoes—which seems likely to be a good one is the hay crop; and I have yet to learn that that can take the place of corn and green vegetables in the dietary of the people.

It would appear that at this moment the Prayer for Rain is of more immediate necessity to the country than any of the services of humiliation and intercession which I gather are soon to take place, and I trust that it may at once be called into requisition.

I am, Sir, your obedient servant,
RUTLAND

INFLUENZA

15 July 1918

Sir,—I am confident you will benefit humanity again by republishing a letter I sent you some years ago.

Yours faithfully,
HARRY FURNISS

Sir,—Now that the influenza is playing havoc with all sorts and conditions of men, perhaps I may be pardoned if I point out, *pro bono publico*, a preventive of which I was informed by a very clever analytical chemist when the dread fiend first invaded this country, and which has preserved me in immunity from his clutches up to the present, although when touring in Scotland I passed through places in which the epidemic raged more furiously than in London. The specific is simple. It is to *take snuff, which arrests and slays the insidious bacillus with great effect.* I have given the hint to several friends, and by taking it they have passed as yet unscathed, and during the last few days I have had my own capacious snuff-box replenished, although so little attraction has the fascinating, though somewhat objectionable, habit for me that I have never thought of indulging in a pinch except when there has been an epidemic in our midst. I may add that when journeying on the other side of the border I not only took snuff, but had a plate of it always on the table, across which I was thus able to interview victims of *la grippe* with impunity.

Yours faithfully,
HARRY FURNISS, Feb. 28, 1895

THE EX-EMPEROR NICHOLAS II

24 July 1918

SIR,—THE TRAGIC AND underserved fate of the late Emperor (not Tsar) of Russia, following on a reverse of fortune rarely equalled, never surpassed, prompts me to ask if I may mention just one occurrence illustrating the real character of a man misrepresented as a gloomy tyrant of the Tiberian type. Shortly before his accession he came for military manœuvres to the neighbourhood of Siverski, where I was then living in a peasant's cottage learning Russian. The head man and the elders met and decided to put on their best clothes and offer bread and salt. I said, "You will hardly see the Cesarevitch, will you?" "We expect we shall," they replied, and started. Late that night they returned in high spirits, and I asked what had happened. The head man said: "We announced our visit to the Heir (Naslednik), and were told that our names would be sent in to H.I.H. Answer came that he was dining, but would see us. We went to the tent and offered our bread and salt. The Grand Duke (Cesarevitch) said, 'How are you, brothers?' and touched one bread and salt. Then he ordered that we should have a good dinner before we went back to our village." It was obvious they had had a good dinner. I said, "You were fortunate to see the Prince." They replied, "It is always thus with our Royal family." I could say more of the simple, unostentatious life of the late Emperor, who before his accession used to drive about Petersburg—surely, alas! that is its proper name—in a single-horse sleigh, of his friendliness, and of his patriotic Russian disposition. He has gone down to his grave in obloquy and misfortune as the result of a revolution which was hailed in this House as fraught with untold advantage to the cause of the Allies!

Your obedient servant,
J. D. REES

The former Tsar and his family had been executed a week earlier.

THE LATE NICHOLAS II

3 August 1918

SIR,—THE LETTER OF "R.F.P." in your issue of July 31, with its appeal to history, amounts to an indictment of the nation that, with remarkable unanimity, rejected the man whom "R.F.P." believes to have been so excellent a ruler. Perhaps, therefore, you will allow a few words of reply.

I need not deal with the motives that prompted the calling of the first Hague Conference, for Dr. Dillon has treated of them in his last book, but I will recall three incidents in Nicholas's reign which explain why he was held in such general contempt.

On May 18, 1896, the gross mismanagement, by Court favourites, of the coronation festivities at Moscow occasioned the death of over 3,000 people and the injury of several more thousands. No public inquiry was instituted and no one was punished, but while people were crowding the hospitals in agony Nicholas II. attended a splendid ball. Nero fiddled while Rome burnt, and Nicholas danced while the Khodinka victims were dying.

On January 30, 1895, Nicholas emphatically denounced the "insensate imaginings" of those representatives of the Zemstvos who ventured to hope that representatives of the people would be allowed some small voice in public affairs; and he pledged himself to "maintain the principle of autocracy as firmly as his never-to-be-forgotten parent" had done.

Finally, during the last year before the Revolution he refused to listen to the urgent warnings addressed to him by the representatives of all parties in the Duma, and even by the Grand Dukes, pointing out to him that the welfare of the nation, the successful prosecution of the war, and safety of the Allied cause made the immediate concession of constitutional government absolutely necessary, and that a most appalling catastrophe would inevitably result from his continued obstinacy. Nicholas II. preferred to be guided by Rasputin and his associates, and the evils which had been foretold have since been more than realized.

History will, I hope, as "R.F.P." expects, "do her duty" by Nicholas II.; unfortunately, it will be a stern duty.

Your obedient servant,
AYLMER MAUDE

7 August 1918

Sir,—Without entering into the question of the character of Nicholas II., one may be permitted to state that your correspondent "R." is evidently under some misapprehension as to what took place on the Khodinka during the Coronation week in June, 1896. I was present on the field of the tragedy by 10 o'clock on the morning in question, and was a witness of what your own correspondent described to me at the time as "worse than anything I saw at Plevna." The origin of the tragedy had nothing whatever to do with a grand stand or the collapse of one. To commemorate the Coronation a distribution was made to the peasants of a packet, wrapped up in a coloured handkerchief, containing a tin mug, some bread, and dried fruit. These were to be distributed from wooden booths which were unfortunately placed in two long lines enclosing an angle. In anticipation of the distribution at 7 a.m. thousands of peasants spent the preceding night on the Plain, and the tragedy arose as the result of the pressure from the incoming crowds in the early morning driving them into the angle between the lines of booths. The person most directly to blame in connexion with the affair was the Grand Duke Sorge, who as local military commander was warned of the impending catastrophe during the night and took no steps to avert it. On the other hand, my recollections lead me to think that the further statement of your correspondent that the Emperor and Empress "went round all the hospitals to make personal inquiries about the sufferers" is an over-statement. There is no doubt that an impression of indifference on their part produced during this unfortunate week was never subsequently dispelled, however little they may personally have been to blame for its ever having arisen.

Faithfully,
J. Y. SIMPSON

INDIAN REFORMS

31 July 1918

SIR,—THERE HAS BEEN time now to digest the Montagu-Chelmsford Report and to arrive at some general conclusions. A scheme for gradually transferring the responsibility for governing India from the shoulders of the British electorate to the shoulders of an Indian electorate must necessarily be an exceedingly delicate operation. If the weight is transferred too suddenly the Indians may collapse under the burden. If we never accustom them to bearing burdens their muscles become atrophied through disuse—and this is precisely what has been happening up till now. We have established order and made administration immeasurably more efficient than it ever was before. But I am not sure that the net result has not been to sap the virility of the Indians and blunt the keen edge of the verve that is in them. Through doing things ourselves in order that they may be well done, and through letting the Indians lean upon us, as they are wont to do in time of stress, we may have withered the development of their native wit and fibre. At any rate we cannot feel confident of having stimulated that development.

Yet from every point of view it is desirable that the Indians should grow up on their own lines strong, healthy, and erect. The vigorous and able Englishmen—all in the prime of life—who go out to India in the civil and military service of Government are wanted badly in many another part of our vast Empire. The stronger India becomes, the more capable of governing herself she grows and the less dependent on us, the better it will be for the whole Empire. Instead of being a strain and drain India might become a source of strength in Southern Asia and a model for every other Asiatic country.

In the last century the main emphasis of our effort was on the establishment of order. In the present century the emphasis will be on education in the very broadest sense of the word—on gradually leading and leaving the people of India to govern their own lives and direct their own destinies, though all the time letting them know that neither we nor the world at large would tolerate their lapsing into the condition of Persia and Mexico, but would require of them that they should fit themselves to take a worthy place in the society of nations and contribute their own particular quota to the world's welfare.

It is a great adventure on which we are about to embark—the boldest and finest enterprise we have ever undertaken—and no nation without our consummate experience could attempt it. But the Report recognizes the caution and care for detail which are needed to make any adventure successful, and to these points too much attention cannot be given before the scheme is actually launched. The public discussion of them is in itself an education both for the Indians and ourselves. It will also let the world beyond ourselves know of our intentions and something of our difficulties.

Your obedient servant,
FRANCIS YOUNGHUSBAND

———◆———

TELEPHONE GIRLS WANTED

2 August 1918

SIR,—I SEE IN *THE TIMES* of yesterday that the Postmaster-General is advertising for able-bodied young women to be taken on by the Post Office as telephone switchboard operators. Does it not occur to this Government official that he has the means of employing men broken in the present war at work which is eminently suited to ex-soldiers who have lost a limb or limbs, or who have been so wounded internally as to compel sedentary occupation? Any intelligent man with good hearing, normal eyesight, and the use of both hands could learn this trade in a month, and, instead of becoming a drag on the State, would form a useful public servant. Let the Post Office set an example at once to other employers of labour.

Yours truly,
LIEUT.-COLONEL

GUINEA-FOWL

8 August 1918

Sir,—I HAVE BEEN reading with much interest the regulations relating to the rationing of game issued by the Ministry of Food which appear in *The Times* of this date. I have been a keen shooting man for many years past, but have never been fortunate enough to hear of a shooting in the British Isles with "guinea-fowl" included. Possibly the Ministry of Food have been rearing guinea-fowl with a view to increasing the food supply of the country, and are strictly preserving certain areas for the praiseworthy purpose of providing hard-worked officials with healthy recreation. On what date does guinea-fowl shooting commence, and is it legitimate to shoot them on the ground, which seems to be their favourite abiding place? In this case two barrels, judiciously administered, would probably settle the question of coupons for some months. In its native state the guinea-fowl is, I believe, addicted to perching on trees, but this peculiarity would, of course, only render the sport more thrilling.

Yours truly,
GALLINA

LAVENDER FAGGOTS

14 August 1918

SIR,—SOME WEEKS AGO I wrote a letter to *The Times* telling how to make use of lavender stalks as faggots for fumigation in hospital wards. Many people, apparently, did not read this, and took it to mean that I wished to collect such faggots and send them to hospitals myself. I write this to make it clear that I cannot receive any lavender myself, and have no greater facilities for sending them to where they are wanted than anyone else. I have always sent my own quite privately.

I am, Sir, yours faithfully,
CAROLINE A. LYTTELTON

BURIAL WITHOUT COFFINS

20 August 1918

SIR,—WITH REFERENCE to the paragraph in *The Times* of to-day on the above subject, is not this the psychological moment for abolishing the use of coffins altogether? In a paragraph headed "A Testator's Unconventional Burial," which appeared in *The Times* of April 19, 1913, it is stated that Captain Walter Gordon Cumming directed that if he should die in Great Britain (as was the case), "his body should be buried without a coffin on the banks of the Findhorn, near Soldiers' Hole, and a cairn of stones erected over him." There does not appear to be any good reason why this simple method of burial should not be adopted in almost all cases. Animals are not buried in boxes or cremated, why should human beings be? Why should not the body be committed to the ground at once, preferably at midnight, as formerly the custom, and costly coffins or the unnecessary and unsentimental operation of cremation be avoided?

I am, Sir, your obedient servant,
ARTHUR F. G. LEVESON GOWER

EQUAL PAY FOR EQUAL WORK

22 *August* 1918

SIR,—OF LATE WE HAVE seen a number of strikes, or threats of strikes, among women workers, of which the watchword appears to be "Equal pay for equal work." Women have taken the place of men in great numbers; as far as they can see, they have discharged the duties which men discharged before with no less efficiency; and they naturally feel that those who wear the same shoes should have the same shoe money. They translate this natural feeling into the metaphysical language of equality and justice; they pass from metaphysics to strikes; and in the name of metaphysics the streets of London are at present empty of omnibuses.

Does it follow that when a woman steps into the shoes of a man she steps into his shoe money, and are the terms equality and justice of any value in a discussion of wages? Wages, and rewards of all sorts, are by no means proportionate to merit, or to service rendered, in the actual dispensation of society. Men of the same capacity, doing what seems equally responsible work, get different pay in different occupations. Men of the same capacity, doing exactly the same work in the very same occupation, get different pay in different districts. On the one hand, the highly skilled fitter gets less than the inferior music-hall singer; on the other hand, the carpenter in Manchester gets less, or more, than the carpenters of other great towns. It may be said of our wages system as it was once said by one of our statesmen of something else, "There's no d—d merit about it." Wages are fixed by custom, by demand and supply, by the bargaining power of collective organization, by the basic needs of subsistence, by many factors; but they are not determined by justice, and there is little equality—absolute, proportionate, or of any other sort—about their determination. They are fixed by the world's coarse thumb and finger, and they are fixed somewhat coarsely.

So far, then, as women are standing for the principle of equality of pay, so far are they standing for something which is not a rule but an exception—a principle not applied elsewhere; and (if we consider the difficulty of determining what is equal to what) almost impossible of application elsewhere. It may be admitted, and admitted cheerfully (at any rate for purposes of argument), that women do "equal work" and that (as Burns might have written to-day) "a woman's a man for a' that"; but it does not automatically follow that women who do "equal work" should receive "equal pay." Let us apply to the problem one of the tests which the world, in its rough fashion, uses in the determination of wages—the test of the basic needs of subsistance. The male worker is generally married, and generally responsible for the maintenance of a wife and (let us say) three children. It hardly matters that some male workers are unmarried; rules have to be made to suit the big majority, and the small minority of unmarried male workers has to be left with an advantage it does not deserve—at any rate until the days

(days much to be desired) of differential taxation of confirmed bachelors. The female worker is generally unmarried, and generally responsible only for her own maintenance. It hardly matters that some female workers are responsible for the maintenance of a family; once more it is true that rules have to be made to suit the big majority, even at the cost of suffering to the minority. It follows that, so far as wages are determined by the basic needs of subsistence, they will be less for a woman worker than they are for the male worker. One may even say in a paradox that the wages of men and women will only be equal—equal in the sense of being equally adjusted to their different responsibilities—when there is a difference between them. The paradox is one which has been recognized in actual legislation. The Industrial Arbitration Act recently passed in Queensland, which attempted a legal definition of a minimum wage, based that definition on the assumption that the wage of a male worker must be sufficient to maintain himself, a wife, and three children in reasonable comfort according to his class of work, and that of a woman worker sufficient to maintain herself in the same position. Queensland is not an undemocratic State. Nor it is undemocratic to criticize the facile formula of equal pay for equal work. The fruits of that formula are inequality, and not equality. Judged by its fruits it is undemocratic, and not the democratic ideal which it appears at first sight to be.

After all, a fundamental fact in the determination of wages is the existence of the family. We readily talk of individual wages; the thing that matters is the wage of the family. (In some parts of South-East France, it is worth mentioning, a *salaire familiale* exists, and wages vary with the size of the worker's family.) But the family is not, of course, the only factor in the determination of wages. One has to remember that if women receive less than men for the same class of work, employers will employ women at the inferior rate. Men will lose employment; the employer will add to his profits. It looks as if we stood between Scylla and Charybdis—on the one hand the prospect of an unearned increment for the employer, if women are paid at lower rates; on the other, the prospect of a differential advantage for the woman worker, if women, generally free from the family responsibilities of men, are paid at the same rates as men. Of the two prospects many may prefer the latter. But if it is to be accepted, let us be clear about two things. The first is that women workers actually in employment will be in enjoyment of superior advantages, and that male workers will not be on an equality with them. The second is that under normal conditions, when a supply of male workers fills the market once more, there is likely to be very little employment for women unless they prove themselves not only as capable as men, but even (for employers, *ceteris paribus*, may show a preference for men) a little better.

I am not concerned to advocate any policy. I am only anxious to protest against the use of an abstract and misleading formula as if it were the whole of the truth. I can understand an attempt to determine wages according to general considerations of social policy. I cannot understand an attempt to determine them by a single and inapplicable formula. I can understand one who should say:—"Pay women at the same rate as men, because, though it may involve grave social disadvantages, the alternative policy of paying women at lower rates has probably graver social disadvantages." I cannot understand those who say:—"Pay women at the same rate as men on the first principles of justice and equality."

Yours obediently,
ERNEST BARKER

27 August 1918

SIR,—I FEEL CONSTRAINED by Mr. Ernest Barker's letter in *The Times* of Thursday to say a few words in defence of the principle "equal pay for equal work." He says the women who make this claim "translate this natural feeling into the metaphysical language of equality and justice; they pass from metaphysics to strikes, and in the name of metaphysics the streets of London are at present empty of omnibuses."

It seems to me that this language bears no relation to the actual facts of the case. The strength of the women's position lay in the fact that when they took up the work of conducting omnibuses they were promised that they should be paid at the same rates as men. The men of the Vehicle Workers' Union also received the promise that the women should not be used to undercut the men. The women struck and the men supported them, because they both considered that this promise had been broken when the Committee on Production withheld from the women the bonus given to the men. Sir George Askwith's Committee, to which the dispute was referred, has supported this view. The women conductors have won their case, they are to receive the same bonus as the men, and the omnibuses have reappeared in the streets of London. I do not see where metaphysics comes in.

In your admirable little article on August 21 it is stated that the one point where the women were to blame was in striking without notice. I am, however, informed that at the end of July the women conductors held a meeting of protest, and announced their intention of "taking drastic action" on August 16 if their protest received no attention. It did receive no attention, and on August 17 work was stopped sectionally. Late that night a special meeting of the Executive Committee of the union took place, the action was approved, and a general strike was called. (See "Common Cause," August 23.) Therefore no censure was deserved on the ground of having called a strike without notice.

Only one word more. Mr. Ernest Barker more than once uses the expression that wages are determined by "the basic needs of subsistence." This principle has been largely inoperative in the case of women. Before the war the wages of large masses of women had little relation to the basic needs of existence. Millions of women were working for wages below subsistence level. Those metaphysicians for the first time in their lives have tasted the sweets of a living wage. They welcome the cry of equal pay for equal work; it is they who, as the firstfruits of their experience, emptied the streets of London of omnibuses a week ago and replaced them there yesterday.

Yours obediently,
MILLICENT GARRETT FAWCETT

THE PROPOSED WAR SHRINE IN HYDE PARK

4 September 1918

SIR,—I AM JUST AN OLD Londoner—one of the many thousands who have watched, with helpless resentment, the gradual uglifying of their beloved city; the degradation of Trafalgar-square, the devastation of the Mall, the heaping up of stupid new buildings, each of them big enough and bad enough to spoil the look of its surroundings. There is something to be said in defence of these offences—some gain of convenience, or of amusement, or of money. But I have been reading to-day of a design for a "permanent war shrine" in Hyde Park, and it has made me ache all over.

This shrine, it seems, is to be "of plaster." So is the White City; and when it was clean, the White City was beautiful, especially of a summer evening when it was lit up. For the White City was an idle fantastical pleasure place, for open-air music, and for lounging and for side shows. But it soon got shabby. So will this plaster shrine in Hyde Park. Doubtless, it can be repainted.

But I read that it "will be oblong in form, and about 70ft. in length." Surely, that is too much plaster for Hyde Park. I should have thought that 12ft. or 15ft. would be long enough for the longest shrine. Indeed, shrines do not go in for length. The present temporary "shrine" is, I am told, a sort of obelisk, with adjacent slabs laid on the ground; a device so unpleasing that one would not care to go near it. But one could hardly avoid an oblong mass 70ft. long.

At the ends of this oblong there are to be "pylons rising 40ft. from the ground." I take it that the gateway of King's College, Strand, which is one of the very ugliest things in all London, is a "pylon." Two things, if they were at all like that, in Hyde Park would be dreadful, so near the good-looking old colonnade at Hyde Park-corner. "On the top of each pylon will be a large cone, the symbol of eternity." That is the real horror. How are we to know that cones are symbols of eternity? I have heard that a circle is a symbol of eternity; nobody ever mentioned cones to me, till this evening. Indeed, I cannot imagine anything less like than a cone to eternity. For a cone comes to an end. Besides, you can measure it; and you can have a truncated cone. Besides, if a cone were a symbol of eternity, why have two of them? Out of the six millions of us Londoners, are there half a dozen whose thoughts turn toward eternity when they see a cone?

I find that I shall be able, as one of the public, to enter through a door in either pylon, walk round a stone, mount six steps, and lay my flowers on a wide ledge. The sort of thing that a performing horse does in a circus!

I have no sons; but I have lost many friends in the war. Who has not? I can say my bit of a prayer anywhere—I find the inside of a church a good place for it; I can reference any little open-air roll of honour, raise my hat to a crucifix, and so on; but Heaven keep me from plaster pylons and cones symbolical of eternity. Let us clear our minds of cant. Which of us now, when the whole nation is in mourning, cares for stage antics in Hyde Park? Besides, this "permanent structure" will not even look well at a distance.

Your obedient servant,
STEPHEN PAGET

A temporary shrine had been dedicated in Hyde Park in August to mark four years of war. Proposals to replace it with a permanent one drawn up by Sir Edwin Lutyens proved unpopular, although he would later design what became the Cenotaph.

OFFICERS' WIDOWS

9 September 1918

SIR,—HAVING SEEN IN your issue of August 16 that the general level of retail prices of food has increased since July, 1914, from 110 to 118 per cent., it appears to me to be time to bring to the notice of the Government the cause of a class which is suffering greatly and in silence—namely, the widows of officers of the Regular Army. When the rate of pensions of these ladies was fixed, money was worth a great deal more than it was even long before the war, and often they found it almost impossible to make two ends meet. Now it is quite so. Many privates' and non-commissioned officers' widows are better off, for they can get highly paid work in munition and other factories which others have not the strength to undertake, and a great many of these ladies are no longer young. How can a general officer's widow, for instance, live and keep her position on £120 a year under present condition?

Yours faithfully,
ONE OF THE SUFFERERS

ARTIFICIAL LEGS

13 September 1918

SIR,—MY EXPERIENCE MAY be of some interest. My father, then Lieutenant Robert Blake, lost his left leg in the Peninsular War, when his regiment, 3rd Buffs, were fighting near Bayonne. As a young man, he has told me, he had a leg with foot and springs at knee, which was all very well for "Society"; but he much preferred, and after 1830 or so used only, a peg leg with spring at knee, and, with a stick, could walk well, and also rode a good deal, and, laying it aside, frequently used crutches, with which he could go farther and faster. The leg was amputated so as to leave a very short stump, and he used to say this was much better than longer stumps, which chafed a great deal more. He lived and enjoyed good health till 1886, when he died, aged 90. He was very abstemious. A labourer on my farm lost his leg by an accident 30 years ago. He wears only a peg leg, supplied by the Guardians, without any spring. With this he can do every sort of work on the farm, ploughing, riding carthorses, loading carts and then getting on to them, &c. I have never seen him fall, except once when his leg stuck in some mud. An inexperienced team man was ploughing a piece of my park last year, and, not doing it very well, this man went to the heads of the horses, and, walking backwards, led them straight and properly all the length of the furrow. His nerve is wonderful. I think legs should not be made too artificial for use—that, at all events, was my father's opinion.

Yours faithfully,
R. HARVEY MASON

UNACCOMPANIED PLAINSONG

24 September 1918

SIR,—AT PRESENT THERE is a widespread feeling for plainsong among English musicians. Its claims are well recognized; but the subtlety and loveliness which supply the artistic justification of these claims are too often misappreciated through the involuntary obscurantism of the accompanist. It is only when sung unaccompanied that plainsong reveals those qualities by reason of which it demands a purely vocal rendering.

To take the salient points. The extreme delicacy both in rhythm and intonation of the ornaments which are an integral part of melismatic plainsong can only be given properly when the voice is unhampered by any reference to a keyed instrument of arbitrary tuning. Figures such as the *strophicus* and the *quilisma* are bound otherwise, either to be slurred out of recognition, or else insisted upon until what should be an ornament becomes an excrescence. Indeed, the tradition of rendering these figures now lies half-smothered under the hand of the accompanist. Again, it should be evident that the character of the ecclesiastical modes is not due merely to various arrangements of tone and semitone, but to the nature of the movement and inflexion of the melodic curve proper to each of them. Even the accompaniment, which is dictated by a feeling for the modes, obliterates these fine distinctions. Here again a tradition is perishing. A modern musician thinks first of a mode in its secondary and derivative harmonic expression, and it is to this that we can attribute a great deal of the misapprehension existing about the modes, and a too common inability to recognize them until the haven of a cadence has been attained.

It is generally admitted that plainsong should be sung without accompaniment. "The extreme purist," says Dr. Frere, "is theoretically unassailable. When plainsong was at its zenith it was always sung unaccompanied." It is significant that this statement should occur in a paper dealing with the best method of plainsong accompaniment.

For these reasons I wish to direct the attention of all lovers of plainsong to an opportunity of hearing it as it should be heard, and so quickening their appreciation of it. At Westminster Cathedral the men of the choir are away during September, and in their absence the music of the service is plainsong throughout, sung by boys' voices, and this week, by reason of an accident to the organ, which I cannot but think a fortunate one, it is being sung without accompaniment. I do not know how long this ideal state of things will last; but while it does so last I recommend all those who are interested in the theory and practice of plainsong to go and listen, and judge for themselves upon a question which is an important one in the development of Church music.

Believe me, Sir, yours faithfully,
S. TOWNSEND WARNER

The novelist Sylvia Townsend Warner was then working primarily as a musicologist.

KEEPING TROOPS FREE FROM TEMPTATION

26 September 1918

SIR,—I HAVE READ with interest Mr. Edward Bok's statement in your issue for to-day. He does not overstate his case.

I have been in nearly all the big camps, barracks, and naval and flying stations in the United States, and have seen the steps taken by the United States Government to prevent drunkenness and immorality among their soldiers and sailors. They have made it nearly impossible for any man in uniform in the United States to obtain drink or to consort with a prostitute. As a result, their men come here in the condition of trained athletes. There can be no finer body of men in the world.

When they land they find it easy to obtain intoxicants, and almost impossible to avoid solicitation by young women. As a result many, even very many, of their men are infected with contagious diseases before they proceed to France. The matter has caused the liveliest concern among American officers. When known in America there will be, as Mr. Bok says, "an outcry . . . in volume and quality . . . extremely unpleasant to the people of Great Britain."

It frequently happens in war that the standards of life deteriorate under the strain. In this war the strain has been intense for more than four years. Very large numbers of young women, all subject, as we all are, to the strain of the war, have been removed by the events of war from the influences of home; their fathers, brothers, and husbands have gone to the front, and they themselves have been left in easy circumstances with every temptation to take what pleasure they can. This condition of things exists in other belligerent countries in Europe, perhaps in all; for in all there are many young people saying, "Let us eat and drink, for to-morrow we die." In this country it is more open and more easy to see than in others.

As it is a condition of things which will most surely harm our prospects (to put the matter on its lowest side first) in this war, by making countless casualties, and make it difficult, after this war to cooperate, as we all hope, in deep and lasting friendship with the United States for the maintenance of the peace of the world, I hope, with Mr. Bok, that "the evil" may "be stamped out."

Yours sincerely,
JOHN MASEFIELD

STONEHENGE

28 September 1918

Sir,—We can none of us be too grateful to Mr. Chubb for his public-spirited gift of Stonehenge to the nation. It may not be feasible, but the thought constantly recurs, why not make this great meeting-place of an ancient British race who worshipped the sun a national memorial of the immortal dead who have laid down their lives that the Sun of Righteousness might arise with healing in His wings for the whole civilized world?

Salisbury Plain as a military training ground has done much towards winning the war. What could be more fitting than that here, in the midst of Salisbury Plain, there should be at this old meeting-place of pre-historic tribesmen and warriors an assemblage on Midsummer Day of each year, or at stated intervals; and that a solemn service should be held in memory not only of Wiltshire men but of all the men of the British Empire who have died for right against might—for justice, freedom, and peace?

The gates of the great stone pylons stand open wide to all the quarters of the heavens, and seem to invite the going forth of light and liberty to all the world. Nothing would be needed but a huge stone Celtic cross in the neighbourhood of the circle, with a simple dedication thereon to the imperishable memory of the gallant dead.

I feel that such a monument in the solemn propinquity of this great British shrine would be preferable to a Priapic monument of cones and Eastern Wells on a huge bare platform in Hyde Park.

Yours truly,
H. D. RAWNSLEY

Stonehenge had been privately owned until it was given to the nation by Cecil Chubb, chairman of Europe's largest mental hospital.

MARSHAL FOCH

3 October 1918

Sir,—In these crowded, happy moments there is no danger that any Englishman will forget his overwhelming debt to the great French soldier and strategist who, by his wonderful sleight of mind, has worked such a magic reversal of our fortunes. Doubtless the united British Empire will, at a fitting moment, make some enduring and substantial acknowledgment of its gratitude to Marshal Foch. But, meantime, is it too early to offer him some general public expression of the deep thankfulness and boundless admiration that every one of us is feeling for his marvellous achievements?

Your obedient servant,
HENRY ARTHUR JONES

Since August, a series of rapid Allied offensives on the Western Front had finally broken through the German defences and destroyed their morale. A statue of Foch now stands near Victoria Station, London.

HEROIC SERBIA

THE URGENT NEED FOR HELP

9 October 1918

Sir,—If I may renew to-day, and in the most urgent terms, the appeal you allowed me to make through your columns just four years ago for organized help to the sorely-tried people of Serbia, the response of the British public will, I am sure, be no less generous than it was then. For Serbia's need is far greater now than it ever was, and she has an even stronger claim on our admiration and sympathy, and on the help in which alone they can find substantial expression.

Twice by her own unaided efforts at the beginning of the war Serbia victoriously repelled the onslaughts of the Austro-Hungarian Armies. Then in the autumn of 1915, stabbed in the back by King Ferdinand of Bulgaria, betrayed by King Constantine of Greece, she fell wounded, as her enemies believed, unto death. The threefold flood of German, Austrian, and Bulgarian invasion closed over her. But her spirit was not killed. For three years the remnants of her people, left to the tender mercies of the armies of occupation, have withstood with indomitable fortitude the alternate brutality and blandishments of Germans and of Austrians and the persecutions still more systematically practised by the Bulgarians, whilst the shattered fragments of her Armies that had made good their escape were being slowly reorganized on foreign soil to play once more a leading part in the liberation of their country—a part so wonderful as to extort a tribute even from the principal organ of Prussian militarism. The *Kreuz Zeitung*, as quoted by you on October 4, admits that Serbia has shown it "to be possible to re-establish a completely conquered and beaten Army which seemed entirely to have disappeared."

Serbia might well say to-day:—

"I too have come through wintry terrors—yes,
Through tempest and through cataclysm of soul
Have come and am delivered!"

But at what a cost! A third, perhaps, of her whole population has perished. Hunger and misery haunt the streets of her cities. The most fortunate amongst her people are those who fled into the forests and wild mountain fastnesses, where they were at least safe from the enemy. Two courageous Serbian Ladies, Mme. Christitch and her daughter, have recently arrived from Belgrade, having stayed on in Serbia after the catastrophe of 1915 in order to carry on, as far as it was possible for them to do so, and at immense personal risk, the relief work on which they were engaged on behalf of the Serbian Relief Fund. At the meeting of our Committee on Wednesday I was privileged to hear from Mlle. Christitch, in the absence of her mother, who was too unwell to attend, a brief account of these ladies' splendid stewardship and of the untold sufferings of which they had been able to mitigate only the merest fraction. Except for a tiny strip of territory in the south, Serbia had been cut off from all contact with friendly countries, and only rarely, and through devious and often surreptitious channels, could help of any kind be introduced from outside.

Now at last, with the victorious advance of the Allied forces and the surrender of Bulgaria, a daily increasing area of Serbia will be thrown open to the relief work which is so urgently needed. The Serbian Relief Fund has never ceased to find a more than ample field for its activities amongst the large number of Serbians who had escaped during the great exodus and have been waiting patiently during three years of exile for the hour of redemption, of which none ever despaired, but these activities have been a heavy drain upon its resources. It has at its disposal all the machinery required for carrying its practical message of comfort and redress into the liberated territories of Serbia, if the British public will supply the ways and means. Can the deep sense of thankfulness amongst the people of this country for the glorious achievements of the last few weeks in every theatre of war find better expression than in helping the Serbian Relief Fund (5, Cromwell-road, S.W.) to heal the wounds of heroic Serbia? Exhausted, and plundered of everything, Serbia is in need of everything, and with the approach of winter the need is frightfully urgent, especially the need of clothes and footgear for the women and children. And it is only by saving the children that the nation can be built up again.

Yours obediently,
VALENTINE CHIROL

VICTORY THROUGH AIR POWER

10 October 1918

SIR,—I AM WONDERING if the public realize how much of the successful fighting and glorious victories of the last two months are due directly and indirectly to the Air Forces of the Allies, and, in particular to our own R.A.F.

From being a comparatively insignificant influence in war four years ago, air power has now become the necessary prelude to military success in the field. Wherever we look, from Scapa Flow to Peshawar, the value of this new factor has become and is daily becoming more significant. In one sphere the airplane and the smaller airship are the most powerful deterrent to the enemy submarine; they guard convoys and send news of other submarines lurking in wait, thinking they are unnoticed. Airplanes guard our shores and our cities from enemy machines. And when we come to the actual battlefields there are the duties of observing and photographing the enemy's positions, of "spotting" for the artillery, of bombing and using machine-guns on enemy troops, of acting as long-range guns with ranges up to 100 miles from our lines, and lastly—perhaps the most valuable service of all—of fighting and destroying the enemy's aircraft, and keeping the enemy blind, preventing him seeing what we are doing, while we know his movements. There are also pitched battles in the air, in which at times hundreds of airplanes are directly or indirectly engaged.

To give a concrete example, the recent wonderful cavalry advance in Palestine owed much of its success to the enemy knowing nothing of our dispositions, due to our complete air supremacy there. For 10 days before the advance no enemy machine was able to overlook us. When the Turkish retreat began, the effect of machine-gun fire and bombs on the retreating masses choked up six consecutive miles of road with dead men and animals and smashed vehicles. The result was that practically the retreat was so delayed and embarrassed that nearly the whole Turkish forces were captured.

On the Western front, besides the regular work of the R.A.F., the development of the Independent Air Force under Major-General Sir Hugh Trenchard has resulted in, not sporadic, but continuous, bombardment—a much more correct term than bombing—of German towns, railway stations, camps, roads, and points of importance. This is much more effective than the German idea of the very long-range gun, with its fixed position and lack of traverse. And the demoralization effected of troops and civilians, of trains and supplies, has been great, and is increasing week by week. The R.A.F. is carrying on the war on German soil, which no other arm can yet do.

Those of us who have believed long before the war in the power and effect of aircraft, and tried ever since war began to convert others to our views, are justified. I can say this in no arrogant spirit of "We told you so," but because the fierce controversies of two years ago have now been settled by the results we see to-day.

At home, both the civilian and military administration—a most difficult task in an organization which is so huge and has grown so fast—is improving daily under Lord Weir and his advisers, while the War Air Staff has fully justified its creation.

But the need for more aircraft with more powerful engines, with greater speed and weight-carrying power, is to-day just as urgent as ever, and a continuous supply of the most gallant youths of this country must be maintained. They form material which no German ingenuity can rival, though they may copy some months behind our mechanical progress.

I set out, Sir, to show what our and the Allied aircraft have done already. Space will not allow me to show what they will do in the future in war and peace. The value of air power to-day is established, and it will always be in future a necessary and potent prelude to victory, both on sea and land.

Yours faithfully,
MONTAGU OF BEAULIEU

———◆———

VAE VICTIS

14 October 1918

Sir,—The Central Powers are beaten. Austria would obviously surrender but for the peace negotiations. Turkey is ready to do the same. Germany cannot last a month. Why in the name of common sense should we stay our hand at the very moment of victory? The very soul of Germany is stained with guilt, her atrocities cry aloud for the vengeance of humanity; and our victorious Armies are to stand still while she retires unmolested from the lands which she has outraged to her own well-protected frontier. And so the Hohenzollern dynasty will be saved from the revolution with which it is threatened, and future generations of Germans will be able to say that peace was proposed while Germany was in occupation of enemy territory, and that no foe set his foot within the Fatherland. President Wilson's 14 points (including, as they do, the free use of the sea in time of war) may be admirable matter for discussion after German surrender, but the time is not yet. It was not thus that Germany treated France in 1871. *Vae victis!*

Faithfully yours,
ELLIS HUME-WILLIAMS

MEDICAL WOMEN AND INCOME-TAX

15 October 1918

Sir,—The letter in your Saturday's issue from Dr. Louisa Garrett Anderson is indeed a striking illustration of the heartbreaking stupidity with which competent people are confronted when dealing with Government Departments. Here is a body of fully qualified women doctors, running most successfully a great military hospital, graded and paid as officers, from lieutenant-colonel down to lieutenant, and yet by a senseless official ukase deprived of their rank marks, which, as every one at all conversant with Army work knows, are, if not essential, at all events most helpful in the maintenance of necessary discipline.

Even this aberration of the War Office is, however, eclipsed in folly and gross injustice by the action of the Income-Tax Commissioners. These women doctors are refused the privilege of the Service rate of income-tax, which is enjoyed by all men doctors doing the same work, because, forsooth, their work is "not of a military character." This is not a jest, but an actual quotation from a letter received from the Commissioners of Income-Tax. "Not of a military character," although they are paid direct by the War Ofiice and their only patients are wounded soldiers! Could official stupidity further go? Surely it will only be necessary to ventilate these grievances in order to have them remedied.

Yours faithfully,
W. LEONARD THACKRAH

ALCOHOL FROM SEAWEED

16 October 1918

Sɪʀ,—Tʜᴇ Cᴏᴍᴍɪᴛᴛᴇᴇ ᴊᴜsᴛ appointed by Mr. Long to consider the possibility of producing sufficiently cheap industrial alcohol from non-alimentary materials is presumably, from its constitution, especially concerned with the question of the use of alcohol as a fuel, and particularly as motor fuel. This question has, incidentally, been already dealt with by a Departmental Committee, and there is a considerable body of evidence in existence bearing on the subject to be found in Blue-books and other publications. At the time of the last inquiry, and under the conditions then prevailing, the employment of alcohol in this country as a substitute for hydrocarbons in motor fuel was not a business proposition. It was admittedly surrounded with difficulties—economical, fiscal, and mechanical. Some of these difficulties may be, and possibly have been, overcome. As for the fiscal objections, these will have to be met if it is satisfactorily established that alcohol can be economically used for power purposes. Under the changed conditions due to the war and owing to the great increase in knowledge and experience, it is undoubtedly time that the problem should be officially reconsidered. Many projects have been published from time to time for the production of ordinary alcohol from non-alimentary materials, and there is a large amount of patent literature on the subject. The greater number of these suggestions may be roughly classified under two heads. They depend either on the production of fermentable substances capable of forming ethyl alcohol, or on the synthetic formation of compounds which may be made to yield this alcohol by purely chemical means.

In the first class is the production of alcohol from marine algæ. It has been shown that such seaweeds as *Laminaria digitate, L. stenophylla, L. saccharina*, the common wracks or tangle, and the various *fuci*, the black and bladder wracks, all of which are abundant on our shores, and some of which were formerly of importance to us as sources of alkali and iodine, may be made to yield considerable quantities of alcohol by appropriate treatment. Thus it has been stated that 100lb. of red wrack, dried to a moisture content of 10 per cent., when heated for a short time with weak sulphuric acid and the acidity still further reduced after cooling, may be fermented with brewers' yeast and is then capable of yielding about 6 litres of alcohol on distillation. It is alleged that under industrial conditions this amount may be increased.

If these statements can be verified, we have in our seaweeds a ready and cheap source of alcohol and the possibility of employment to a poor population whose means of livelihood were greatly impoverished by the loss to them of the kelp industry. The mode of collection and preliminary treatment of seaweed for use in the chemical arts were largely worked out by the late Mr. E. C. C. Stanford many years ago, and are applicable to the present suggested application. In addition we have the experience of America: the collection and utilization of the giant weeds of the Pacific coast is now an established industry.

I am, Sir, your obedient servant,
T. E. THORPE

———◆———

PEACE CONFERENCES

19 October 1918

SIR,—IN THE TIMES OF this morning the remarkable admission is made that the Allies desire "no Peace Conference of the sort which disgraced diplomacy at Vienna a century ago, or which sowed at Berlin in 1878 the seeds of the present catastrophe."

It is worth recalling that for 200 years, certainly from the Peace of Westphalia to the Congress of Vienna, Peace Conferences were held, on an average, every 10 years. At every one of these conferences deluded peoples were assured that the peace of the world was guaranteed. At every one the "seeds were sown" of subsequent discord. It is surely worth while to break the iron chain of habit, and to employ a new method of garnering the fruits of successful war. The fundamental conception of the American President appears to be an open adoption of certain guiding principles, stereotyped into fixed categories, within which contemporary facts can be shaped by expert commissions meeting where convenience may dictate. This should suit our country, which has rarely been well served by her diplomatists at European conferences, so ineffective are the English mind and temperament when confronted by subtle international agencies. However resolute and clear the general aims of the Allies, that they would be traversed by the enemy in conference would be in accord with every precedent. The obvious conclusion is to avoid giving the enemy a chance.

Yours faithfully,
ESHER

THE "INFLUENZA"

25 October 1918

Sir,—The leading article in *The Times* of October 23 raises some very important questions as to the power of our public health organization in its present form of dealing effectually with serious epidemics in this country and which the war is likely to bring in its train. You have answered some of them. May I suggest, in order to allay the anxiety of the public, that the Government should make a definite statement regarding the nature of the epidemic which is now prevailing in England and Scotland, and which, under the name of Spanish influenza, has attacked so many countries? Has it been established by careful bacteriological and microscopical investigation and by *post-mortem* examination, not in one place, but in different parts of the country, that the epidemic in England is influenza *only*, and that under the name of influenza other diseases are not included? This is important to know, because in all epidemics mistakes in diagnosis are made. There can be no doubt that there is an epidemic of influenza, but is it the only epidemic disease? The general past history of influenza epidemics, though not invariably so, is that it is the precursor of other epidemics, and if not the precursor it is often the companion of some of the most fatal diseases. It is very important from a preventive point of view that these matters should be cleared up, and as soon as possible.

Is it true, as it has been stated in the papers, that some 5,000 persons, of whom 75 per cent. were natives, have died of what is called influenza in less than a fortnight in Cape Town? If not, it should be officially denied and the true state of matters made public. Influenza epidemics have not hitherto shown this mortality, even in the 16th century, when they were most prevalent. The same remark applies to what is stated in the papers regarding the rising mortality and the occurrences in the Sheffield district, where it is reported that at Walkley eight persons have just died in one family, while six are lying dead in another family.

What special precautions in this time of stress and ill-health among the civil population are being taken to prevent the importation and spread of other epidemic diseases?

W. J. SIMPSON, M.D.

What became known as Spanish Influenza – though it probably originated in the United States – would go on to kill as many as 100 million people, 5 per cent of the global population.

CROWDED OUT

2 November 1918

Sir,—The question of quarters for oversea officers is urgent. I wish to suggest that whoever undertakes it should study our system here. It is that of cubicles, each private, with bed and chest of drawers, but with numerous bath-rooms and washing places. Combined with large public rooms, this enables a man to live very cheaply but well. This building, or one like it, could take 300 officers, giving three ample meals of the best materials, bed, and bath at about 3s a day and pay its way. I hope someone will come and see how the soldier fares here; we are unable to take officers, but I am sure the conditions are good enough for anyone.

I am afraid very soon there will by no means be enough beds for oversea soldiers in London. There are first-rate clubs like the Maple Leaf and the Victoria League, but we are all full or nearly so. What is to be done when leave is freely given? I write in the hope that our military authorities will consider the amount of leave given to London in some relation to the accommodation available; I know that many people feel that it is often the sheer absence of decent accommodation which drives the men into bad surroundings. And if an attempt can be made to provide some great central place where at any rate a bed can always be got I hope all Dominions will join in it. The attempt to divide the Forces into clubs, each taking the men of its own Dominion, only causes waste of space—one may be full, another empty. We have mixed them all freely here; we have filled 400,000 beds in three years, and never had a row of any sort or a single fight in the place. We really cannot do too much for these brave men who have come so far; when we have done our best we have done little enough.

Yours faithfully,
HON. TREASURER, King George and Queen Mary's Club for the
Oversea Forces

OUR ARMY IN SALONIKA

A GALLANT FORCE

8 November 1918

SIR,—I HAVE COMPLETED the task entrusted to me and have reached here at Sofia the *ultima Thule* of my expedition. Assisted by glorious weather, and helped at every point by the never-failing kindness of the Commander-in-Chief, I have addressed every fighting unit of the Salonika Army still left in Macedonia or Bulgaria. I have read them the King's message of congratulation, which was cheered with equal enthusiasm in the valleys of Macedonia or the rocky fastnesses of Bulgaria. I have given each brigade a message from home of love and affection, and, as in duty bound, have added to each and all to the best of my power a message from God. St. Paul, who toiled, *not* in a motor-car, along some of the many roads on which I have travelled, would have been ashamed of the 108th Bishop of London if he had not at least attempted the last. From first to last, my threefold message has been received with a touching welcome by the whole Army, from the generals to the youngest private.

But now, before I turn my face homewards, I want to say a word, Sir, through your paper to my fellow-countrymen at home. We have not appreciated at anything like its full value the fortitude, courage, and wonderful success of the Salonika Army, and they have a sore and disappointed feeling that they are neglected and despised. A music-hall song, which ought never to have been allowed to be sung:—"If you don't want to fight, go to Salonika," has been gall and wormwood to those who had almost reached the limits of endurance before. The few who have got home on leave found the opinion common among their friends that they have been spending their time a few miles outside Salonika, with frequent opportunities of visiting on most evenings the cafés in the town.

Now what are the facts of the case? To start with, large numbers have had no leave for three years, and are in many cases greatly distressed as to what may be happening in their homes; so far from spending their time near Salonika, the lines which they have had to hold have been 60 miles from the town, and most of the soldiers have never been able to visit Salonika at all. Malaria and influenza have been so rife and universal that I found on arrival, on October 16, that there were 31,000 sick in the doctors' hands, nursed by 1,600 of our splendid nurses, whose services are beyond praise. I have examined in detail on my way here the positions which were opposed to them, and I have never seen positions of such terrific strength. From the summit of the Grand Couronné, which is 3,000ft. above the plain, a full view could be obtained by the Bulgarian Army of Salonika harbour, and of every road of communication which led from it to the British lines.

In spite of this, and the fact that their numbers, always comparatively small, had been depleted by sickness, they carried out the attack so elaborately planned with consummate courage. No one wishes to depreciate the magnificent dash of the Serbian flank attack on September 9, or the onset of our Greek Allies, but what is not generally known is that this was only made possible by the great bulk of the enemy's forces being gathered opposite our lines by elaborate camouflage and feint attacks from September 1 onwards. In this operation one brigade alone lost very heavily indeed. But it was not until September 18 and 19 that the great attack came which decided the issue. The Grand Couronné and the Pip Ridge, which had frowned down upon our men for three years, were stormed by direct assault to draw away attention from the flanking movement of the Serbs and French. Every man, as he went up, went up humanly speaking to certain death, but not one turned back. One sergeant was found dead 20 yards from the summit, and a very great proportion of those who attacked were killed or wounded. But this sacrifice was not in vain. They had held the main body of the Bulgarian Army long enough for the flank attack to succeed. The retreat began; our flying men swept over and attacked the retreating enemy in the deep gorges through which alone they could attempt to escape, and the fact that I was able to motor through Bulgaria at night, alone with my chaplains, within a month after the battle, and should be writing this as quietly in Sofia to-night as I should be in London, will attest the completeness of their victory. But they have won a moral victory as well. They are leaving Macedonia now for enterprises of which I must not speak, but the Governor-General of Macedonia endorses the opinion of the whole of Macedonia that the best piece of propaganda for the British nation has been the conduct of the Salonika Army. They are leaving with the enthusiastic affection of the whole country. The clean-limbed, clean-living, courteous British soldier who saved them during the fire, and who has never interfered with their women folk or their goods, has won the heart of his Allies at the same time as he has been the first to make his enemy surrender.

May I plead for full justice to be done at home to the work of the Salonika Army?

Yours faithfully,
A. F. LONDON

Allied troops, based at Thessaloniki, Greece, had been fighting the Bulgarians, allies of the Central Powers, since their invasion in 1915 of Serbia.

SEDAN

9 November 1918

Sir,—The remarkable coincidence of our Armies being at Sedan and Bazailles at this moment recalls an historical event of nearly 50 years ago, when Napoleon signed his capitulation in the weaver's cottage there, and directly afterwards surrendered his sword to the Prussian King at the Castle of Bellevue. It is hoped that Marshal Foch may be able to enact the same scene on the same spot with reversed conditions.

Yours obediently,
HERBERT MONCKTON

The German Kaiser abdicated on November 9, and the Austro-Hungarian the next day. On November 11, the Germans signed an armistice aboard Marshal Foch's private train at Compiègne. In 1940, it was Hitler who reversed affairs by enacting the French surrender there.

---◆---

THE MISSING

18 November 1918

Sir,—Permit me to express the hope that his Majesty's War Office will forthwith take all steps possible with a view to relieving, as far as may be achieved, the anxieties of the relatives of these men. It occurs to me that now, when our prisoners of war are being daily released from their incarceration in Germany and other places, an opportunity which has not hitherto been available offers, and it is one which may lead to the friends of some at least of the missing men ascertaining details of such events as caused the disappearance of these brave fellows. Some scheme which would provide for repatriated prisoners having an opportunity of viewing the photographs of missing men and being furnished with such particulars in connexion with them as are available would, I think, be of inestimable service to those near and dear to them.

I have the honour to remain, Sir,
AN ANXIOUS RELATIVE

The number of military and civilian casualties of the war, including those missing in combat, was 40 million.

WAR MEMORIALS

18 November 1918

SIR,—ALMOST EVERY town and village in the Empire has shared and suffered in the Great War, and almost every one will want its own memorial. Surely, however, there will be a general demand for a great central memorial in London representing the whole Empire. What is to be the relation between the two projects? Few people will not wish to subscribe to their own local memorial, but there is a real danger that the central memorial will be supported only by wealthy persons and corporations which can afford to give twice over. It is most desirable that every subscriber, however poor, should feel that he has a share in the public monument which will be evidence of our faith before the whole world, as well as in the intimate commemoration of his own district. This can be done if every subscription is divided between the two schemes. It would be unreasonable to divert any large proportion from local projects, but 5 per cent. of every local subscription all over the Empire would produce a sum of money quite sufficient to represent worthily in the capital the general feeling of us all. Probably one per cent. would be enough, and few local committees would refuse such a quota. A fine engraving of the central memorial might be presented to every locality, to be hung permanently in the Town Hall, Institute, Parish Church, or whatever building is regarded for this purpose as the centre of the district.

There is no time to be lost, for many localities are already forming their schemes. I would suggest that His Majesty the King be respectfully asked to appoint a Committee representing the whole Empire, whose duty should be not only to decide the details of the central memorial but to keep themselves in touch with the separate memorials in all parts.

I do not enter in this letter on the form which the memorials should take, but am anxious to concentrate attention on the vital consideration that every one shall be encouraged to share in the central monument of the British and fellow races, as well as in the more personal monument which will commemorate the sacrifice of each locality.

I am, Sir, your obedient servant,
D. H. S. CRANAGE

INDEX OF LETTER
WRITERS